MEXICO'S ACCION NACIONAL

*A Catholic Alternative
to Revolution*

MEXICO'S ACCION NACIONAL

*A Catholic Alternative
to Revolution*

DONALD J. MABRY

SYRACUSE UNIVERSITY PRESS 1973

Library of Congress Cataloging in Publication Data

Mabry, Donald J   1941–
    Mexico's Accion Nacional.

    Bibliography: p.
    1. Acción Nacional (Mexico)   I. Title.
JL1298.A3M24   329.9'72   73-9975
ISBN 0-8156-0096-8

Manufactured in the United States of America

To Susan

CONTENTS

TABLES   ix

PREFACE   xi

PART I

  I. The Historical Environment   1

  II. Origins of Acción Nacional   16

  III. The Founding Decade, 1939–1949   32

  IV. Catholic Militancy, 1949–1962   50

  V. The Limits of Influence, 1962–1972   71

PART II

  VI. Doctrine, Program, Appeals   99

  VII. Structure: Description and Operation   113

  VIII. Membership and Leadership   132

  IX. The Support System   162

  X. Perspectives   183

NOTES TO CHAPTERS   201

BIBLIOGRAPHICAL ESSAY   243

INDEX   261

TABLES

1. Occupations of the 1939 National Executive Committee and National Council   35
2. PAN Federal Deputy Campaigns, 1943–1970   69
3. Occupations of PAN's 1967 and 1970 Federal Deputy Candidates   137
4. Occupations of PAN's 1970 Senatorial Candidates   138
5. Acción Nacional Presidents, 1939–1972, Biographical Data   146
6. CEN, 1939–1969, Occupational Data   149
7. Regional Presidents, Occupational Data   151
8. 1970–1973 PAN Federal Deputies, Biographical Data   154
9. PAN Candidates to the Mexican Presidency, Biographical Data   155
10. PAN Michoacán Regional Committee Operating Budget (in Pesos) (July 13, 1967–December 31, 1970)   169
11. PAN Michoacán Regional Committee Monthly Dues (in Pesos) (January 1968)   170
12. Federal Entities of Greatest PAN Opposition, 1952, 1958–1970 (10% or More of the Vote)   174
13. PAN Opposition and Mexican Presidential Elections since 1917 (in Percentages of Total Vote)   177
14. Regional Poverty in Mexico and Percentage of PAN Opposition of 10 or More Percent Within Region   178
15. Congressional Voting in Mexico, D.F., 1967, 1970 (in 1,000)   180

PREFACE

Acción Nacional, Mexico's primary opposition political party, has not won a major election in its thirty-three year history, even though its Catholic activist leaders use Catholic reform doctrine in a Catholic country. The explanation of this paradox lies in the successful Mexican Revolution and its aftermath. The secular reformism and virulent anticlericalism of the Revolution reduced the Church to a spiritual institution and removed it from the political scene. Identification with the Church, or Catholicism in general, is counterproductive to political success. Further, since 1928 the Revolutionary government has so controlled the political system that only its political party has any hope of governing the country. In spite of all this, Acción Nacional was created in 1939 to offer what is essentially a Catholic alternative to the Revolution.

Studying such a political party is important for a variety of reasons. Although extensive literature has been produced on the Mexican political system, few studies examine that system from "the other side." Yet, the problems of an opposition party reveal important information about a political system and how it operates. Acción Nacional history suggests the possibilities of electoral opposition to the Revolution as well as indicating some of the strengths and weaknesses of Mexican Revolutionary governments. In Acción Nacional's case, the study of the party suggests what reform-minded Catholics did after the Church lost its conflict with the State in the 1920s and 1930s. Moreover, it shows the limits of Catholic reform politics and Christian Democracy/Socialism in Mexico and perhaps suggests their limits whenever such movements have to face entrenched, successful secular reformers. Acción Nacional's involvement in the major political events since 1940 contributes to our understanding of contemporary Mexican history. Finally, such a study narrows the gap in our knowledge of Latin American political parties.

I first began this study in an attempt to understand why a political party had such a lengthy existence in a country where political parties were a recent phenomenon, and where it had no apparent hope of defeating the popular Revolutionary government. Influenced by the scattered published descriptions of Acción Nacional, I went into the research with the tentative hypothesis that it was a right-wing, Catholic or Church-connected political party financed by millionaires and wealthy bankers who sought to reverse the social gains of the Revolution. Although I made a concerted effort to ascertain if substantive connections existed between the party, its leaders, and its ideas on the one hand, and the Church, business, and wealthy men on the other, my research suggested that I see the party in a context broader than a conservative reaction to the Mexican Revolution. I became aware that what I was reading in Acción Nacional sources was strikingly similar to what I was reading in Christian Democratic/Socialist literature and papal social encyclicals. Although it was not possible to follow this lead as far as one might like, I went far enough to become convinced that the evidence pointed to Acción Nacional being best understood as the Mexican response to the twentieth-century Catholic reform impulse in Latin America. That is, that Acción Nacional was as close to being a Christian Socialist party as one could reasonably expect in Mexico.

The book traces the history of Acción Nacional from its origins in the Church-State conflict during the Revolution to the summer of 1972. It concentrates upon the party's history, but I have tried, wherever possible, to place it into the context of the Mexican Church-State conflict and Latin American Christian Democracy/Socialism. My suggestion that the Mexican party is related to progressive Latin American political Catholicism is a low-level hypothesis which needs to be tested by further research, a task for a different study.

The book is divided into two parts, the first primarily chronological, the second topical. Though not entirely satisfactory, this organization avoids some unnecessary repetition. Summary paragraphs have been included in the chapters. The first chapter seeks to place the party within the context of Mexican history and the current political system. The second chapter represents one of the most complete syntheses of the Church-State conflict (in which many party founders played an active role) and an analysis of the factors which led to the party's founding. Chapters three through five carry the narrative through the summer of 1972, showing the party's evolution, problems, and successes. The second part consists of chapters on doctrine, programs, and appeals; its formal structure and operation; its membership and leadership; and its institutional, electoral, and financial support. Although these are also topics which interest political scientists, I see them as contemporary history and have treated them as such.

In Part II I have used socioeconomic, electoral, and budgetary data to analyze the party in addition to documentary and oral sources. The socioeconomic and budgetary data should be particularly interesting to other researchers, the first because the occupations of hundreds of leaders and members are presented and discussed, the second because the amounts and sources of the party's recent revenue at the national and Michoacán state level is revealed for the first time. The final chapter draws upon the entire work to put the party into perspective. The bibliographic essay following the text hopefully will aid scholars wishing to make similar studies.

Serious difficulties face the student of Mexican political institutions. Much of the information that one seeks does not exist or will not be released to an investigator. Those who investigate opposition parties may well find that they are suspected of being part of the opposition itself. Although Acción Nacional itself was surprisingly open to investigation, at crucial points it became difficult and impossible to find the desired information. Only through introductions by friends of the party or through party leaders was it at all possible to penetrate this barrier. By the careful cultivation of party leaders over a two-and-one-half-year period, I was able to gain special access to party files and to discuss internal conflicts. I made extensive use of informal interviews with party members and people outside the party. I used this information only when I believed it was valid. In order to gain access to some individuals, it was necessary to preserve their identities. I have honored that promise.

The study is based on extensive research into party sources for a three-year period, including field research in Mexico from August 1969–April 1970 and July–August, 1971. In addition to party documents, I used the numerous private writings of party leaders. These categories of sources have been so thoroughly exploited that additional research in these materials would be of dubious value. I read more than 70,000 pages of party material alone. In addition, files at national and Michoacán state headquarters were examined. The condition of the national files made it more rewarding to extract information from the private files of party leaders. The Michoacán files for recent years yielded precise data on membership, finances, and daily activity. More than 120 interviews were conducted at three national conventions, at national, Federal District, and Michoacán headquarters, and at offices of some party leaders. These party sources were supplemented by a survey of the Mexican periodical press for a thirty-three-year period, numerous studies, and commentaries by nonparty members (including ex-party members, government officials, politicians, political commentators, and persons employed by Mexican private enterprise).

I am indebted to many people for the aid they rendered during the course of the study. Without the willingness of Acción Nacional leaders to give me access to party files and documents and to be interviewed, this study could not have been made. A special word of thanks is due Luis Calderón Vega for the many hours he gave me in Mexico City and Morelia. The following are only some of the party leaders who gave time and aid: the late Manuel Gómez Morín, Enrique Creel Luján, Clicerio Cardoso Eguiluz, Manuel González Hinojosa, Eugenio Ortiz Walls, José G. Minondo, Miguel Estrada Iturbide and his sons, Manuel Ulloa Ortiz, and the Michoacán regional committee. I would also like to thank Sr. Ernesto Ayala Echávarri of Nacional Financiera. My debt to Sr. Ayala is of such magnitude that it is impossible to acknowledge it properly. A former party member who remains a trusted friend of many founders, he not only provided the important introductions to party leaders, crucial for the success of this study, but he also extended courtesies to the author and his family that went beyond the normal requirements of hospitality. The persons who aided the author in data collection, particularly by allowing themselves to be interviewed, but who wished to remain anonymous, are also thanked. The author also wishes to thank the history department of Syracuse University for a Maxwell Fellowship which enabled him to conduct this study in Mexico in 1969–70; the Mississippi State University Development Foundation and the American Philosophical Society for grants which allowed him to return to Mexico in July–August 1971 for a study of the Michoacán and Federal District organizations; Mississippi State University for grants for the preparation of this material; Dr. Robert J. Shafer who provided valuable aid and encouragement; and the many other scholars who have discussed this subject while the study was being undertaken and written. Without the patience, understanding, and aid of my sons, Scott and Mark, and of my wife, Susan, it could not have been done.

All errors of fact and interpretation are my sole responsibility.

Mississippi State University   DONALD J. MABRY
September 1972

MEXICO'S
ACCION NACIONAL

*A Catholic Alternative
to Revolution*

PART I

CHAPTER I

The Historical Environment

The sophisticated Mexican political system, of which Acción Nacional[1] is both an integral part and ardent opponent, has produced political stability, social mobility, a climate favorable to the free exercise of civil liberties, and sustained economic growth following the earliest and one of the bloodiest social revolutions of the twentieth century. The revolution which began in 1910 with the revolt of Francisco Madero against the continuance of the long dictatorship of Porfirio Díaz (1876–1910) produced a political system which represents compromises among important national interests and a means to avoid retrogression to revolutionary strife. It is, therefore, to the Revolution[2] and its causes that one should first turn before directing attention to the political system and, finally, to Acción Nacional itself.

The long rule of Porfirio Díaz, the *Porfiriato,* ended the civil disorders and slow economic growth which had characterized Mexico after she obtained her independence from Spain in 1822. Díaz emphasized order and progress and reconciled proponents of both to his regime. The principal advocates of progress, the Liberals led by Benito Juárez, had sought to abolish special privileges, great estates, and ecclesiastical influence inherited from the colonial period, believing that such institutions and practices blocked the creation of a society in which talent could thrive and rule. On the positive side, they tried to create juridical equality, honest elections, a strong republican, federal form of government, public education, and laissez faire governmental economic policies. In short, they resembled fellow nineteenth-century liberals in Western Europe and the United States. Their opponents, the Conservatives, rejected the Liberal plan for Mexico for they believed that its implementation would fail to bring progress (the definition of which was a source of disagreement) but would bring disorder and tyranny. Moreover, the core of Conservative leadership emanated from those groups which enjoyed the special privileges—the *hacendados* (great estate owner), the army, the Roman Catholic Church, and the country's leading families.[3]

1

The Liberal-Conservative struggle was marked by armed conflict in which the Liberals finally won only after defeating domestic and foreign enemies. By 1855 Liberal victories gave them control of the national government in Mexico City, allowing them to pass legislation implementing some of their proposals. The resulting decrees, the *Ley Lerdo* and the *Ley Juárez,* ended the special courts which allowed the Church and the army to act as states within a state and forbade corporations to own large blocks of real property. The latter provision was aimed primarily at the Church because the anticlerical Liberals, children of the Enlightenment, saw in the Church, especially in its control of education, a primary source of fanaticism and obscurantism in Mexico. The Church, which owned perhaps one-third of Mexican land, was restricted to owning property used for religious purposes. The Constitution of 1857, the outstanding Liberal legal achievement, incorporated the *Ley Lerdo* and the *Ley Juárez* and created a republican-federal government based upon equality before the law and laissez faire economics; *La Reforma,* the Mexican Reformation, had arrived.

Opponents of *La Reforma* regrouped and resorted to armed combat to overturn this undesirable state of affairs. From 1857 until 1860, for the duration of the War of *La Reforma,* Juárez and his colleagues successfully fought the Conservative coalition. Defeated in the domestic conflict, the Conservatives then turned to European powers for aid. As a result, a joint Spanish-French-British expedition arrived in Veracruz in late 1861 and early 1862 to seize the customs houses as collateral for Mexican payment of foreign debt claims. France's Napoleon III had more in mind than just debt collection, however, for his troops soon began marching on Mexico City where they were anxiously awaited by the Conservatives who believed that the world would soon be turned right side up. The British and Spanish withdrew, leaving the Liberals to face the Conservative-French coalition alone. Juárez withdrew his government to the provinces when it was clear that the French would capture the capital.

Until 1867 Mexico had two governments, the Juárez government operating in the interior and the Maximilian government controlling the Mexico City–Puebla-Veracruz axis and a few other points. Juárez had the most popular support; the Conservatives had compromised their position by introducing foreigners into the conflict. Maximilian, an Austrian Hapsburg archduke who was initially the client of both Napoleon III and the Conservatives, managed to alienate his supporters without negotiating a compromise with the Juárez group. The Conservatives found him too liberal and the Mexicans found him too foreign. Not only did his Conservative support atrophy, but Napoleon III, faced with European problems, withdrew his troops in 1866. Maximilian chose to stay in Mexico, apparently believing that he was loved by the people. By 1867, the Juárez group had captured and executed him. Few tears were shed, even by Conservatives.

The long struggle for power apparently sobered the Liberals, for the last years of Liberal rule (1867–76) saw the passage of few reforms. The bulk of the changes had been introduced by the 1857 Constitution; the main concern after the final Liberal victory was implementation. Juárez had himself reelected to two more presidential terms, angering many Liberal supporters, including Porifirio Díaz. Juárez died in 1872, shortly after beginning his fourth presidential term. His successor was overthrown in 1876 by Díaz, using the rallying cry "Effective Suffrage, No Reelection."

Porfirio Díaz gave Mexico political stability, public order, and the start of an industrial plant, but neither peaceful nor regular changes of presidential leadership. Except for the 1880–84 term, when he ruled through a puppet, Díaz had himself reelected president of Mexico each four years. Only revolution or death seemed capable of removing him.

Díaz differed from his predecessors because he understood that Mexico had to change if she were to have a significant role in the modern world. Díaz sought foreign capital for economic development, so he made Mexico safe for foreign investors. The army, the urban police, and the *rurales,* the rural police, soon were able to discourage any attacks against the persons or property of the wealthy. Moreover, foreigners received preferential treatment from the government. Whiteness became a supreme value, and Indians, the bulk of Mexicans, were relegated to menial jobs as domestic servants or as workers for haciendas, factories, or mines. Bolstering both economic development and degradation of Indians were the *científicos,* men who used the positivism of Auguste Comte and social Darwinism as the sources of their intellectual authority. *Científicos* sought economic progress and considered the Indian population a major obstacle, one that would have to be removed by encouraging the immigration of white foreigners. These foreigners, combined with "white" Mexicans, would form an elite to run the country for its benefit. Everyone would receive his share, but the share of Indian and mestizo brutes would "naturally" be much less than that of the superior white classes. As a result of this policy, the Indians began losing their village lands at a more rapid rate than before; the Díaz government encouraged, tacitly at least, the alienation of the land from the natives, for the new owners would contribute more to Mexico than the lower classes ever could and the natural aristocracy would have the power it deserved.

With this encouragement, foreign capital swarmed into Mexico, built railroads and factories, dug mines, and created large agricultural and pastoral estates, all with the help of ambitious Mexicans who grasped at opportunities for pelf. The foreigners' disdain for the Mexicans created resentments which would flare as virulent xenophobia during the Revolution. The new middle classes created by this economic activity as well as some of the former prominent Mexicans who had no piece of the action especially resented the favoritism shown to outsiders, making the former eager recruits for revolutionary activity.

Immediate threats to the continuance of the *Porfiriato* came, however, from local strongmen, known as *caciques,* and not from foreigners or the masses. Throughout the nineteenth century, various men had been able to dominate their home areas by force of will and arms. They resented direction from Mexico City or from state governors, and obeyed commands only when it was expedient to do so. Upon taking power, Díaz recognized the threat inherent in this situation and moved to diminish it by granting *caciques* virtual autonomy and support in their local areas as long as they cooperated with the national government on the most important matters. In addition, they were given some access to the national spoils of rule. Because the economic exploitation of the country substantially increased these spoils, they became increasingly tied to the national government. By 1900, at least, Díaz was strong enough to remove most *caciques* who were unable to see the advantages of the system.

Díaz also brought reconciliation with the Church. His posture vis-à-vis the Church was primarily one of neutrality; he neither encouraged it to expand its influence and power nor did he discourage it. Under Díaz, the institution began to regain the ground it had lost during *La Reforma.* It acquired some land, erected new buildings, and participated actively in Mexican life. It preached obedience to authority and that rewards would come in the afterlife, that one should be content with the lot God had cast for him. Although the positivists, including the *científicos,* were basically hostile to the Church, they recognized its functional value in maintaining public order. The ecclesiastical support of the Díaz regime, which had begun to wane in the last decade of the *Porfiriato,* would be a principal cause of Revolutionary anticlericalism.

The Díaz regime was not without tensions, especially in the later years when the dictator was older and weaker and the question of succession began to stir political leaders. The economic transformation which had been going on had brought new groups into the society: urban middle classes, a small proletariat, small industrialists, and commercial farmers. These groups began demanding a share of power. Regionalists continued to be unhappy with rule from Mexico City, a rule which increased with the building of railroads. Nationalists resented the foreign domination of the country and foreign condescension towards Mexicans. Liberals sought to depose the man who had used Liberalism to create a conservative state. Peasants brooded over their exploitation. Even the Church had begun to question the morality of the Díaz regime. Even though there were small indices that the *Porfiriato* was in trouble, Mexico approached the centennial celebration of independence in 1910 with confidence. No one suspected that Díaz would be in exile by 1911 and a great socioeconomic revolution would be under way.

The Revolution began as a move seeking to force open governmental positions to younger members of the bourgeoisie. Its leader, Francisco I. Madero, son of a wealthy *hacendado* family in the northern state of Coahuila, saw little need for immediate socioeconomic reforms and limited his appeals to a change in political leadership. The demands of indigenous communities, of the nascent proletariat, or of regionalists chafing under centralized government were virtually ignored in Madero's Plan of San Luis Potosí. Victor in the 1911 presidential election, Madero adopted a moderate gradualist policy towards the problems which had caused Díaz's downfall.

The felling blow against the Madero regime came from the right of the political spectrum, but the exigencies of defeating the rightist coup forced a leftward shift in Mexican politics as combatants sought the aid of dissident groups. Victoriano Huerta, encouraged by groups which had enjoyed privileges during the *Porfiriato,* overthrew the Madero government. His complicity in the assassination of Madero cost him needed support while, simultaneously, it raised Madero to martyrdom among the left-wing revolutionaries. Venustiano Carranza, himself a former *Porfirian* senator, led the anti-Huerta forces as First Chief of the Constitutionalist Armies. By 1917 Carranza had beaten Huerta and rival claimants to national leadership. In that year Mexico produced another Constitution, still in force today, which reflected the disagreement among the revolutionary forces. Long and often contradictory, the Constitution of 1917 closely resembles the 1857 document, but, indicating the changes which had occurred since the Madero phase of the Revolution, included important social reform measures and assertions of national sovereignty. In particular, these constitutional articles changed the role of the Mexican state from one of passivity to activity in favor of the masses.

Though most of the fighting ended by 1917, the struggle for ideological control of Mexico continued until 1940. Alvaro Obregón and Plutarco Calles, erstwhile Carranza generals from Sonora, found the

Carranza government too conservative and overthrew it in 1920. The Sonora Dynasty, as the Calles-Obregón coalition often was called, ruled Mexico until 1928 with Obregón serving as Mexican President from 1920 to 1924 and Calles serving from 1924 until 1928. Although basically conservative themselves, Obregón and Calles in order to broaden their political base, began to support organized labor, redistribute land to the peasantry, and support public education. Their social reform efforts were limited, however, for their primary goal was to create a modern national bourgeois capitalist state. Calles grew more conservative as the 1920s progressed, enough so that some observers compare his presidency with that of Calvin Coolidge in the United States.[4] The one issue on which he was not conservative, however, was that of the relationship between Church and State.

The Constitution of 1917 had gone farther than its 1857 predecessor in asserting the primacy of the secular state over the Church. Under Article 130 of the document, the Church was forbidden to own any real property, nor could individual clergymen inherit real property from anyone other than close relatives. The Church was forbidden to participate in politics, and the use of religious names or symbols was forbidden to political parties. Clergymen were denied suffrage. Public religious ceremonies were prohibited as well as the wearing of clerical garb. States were given the right to determine the number of clergy operating under their jurisdiction. Most threatening to the Church, however, were the educational prohibitions. Article 3 of the Constitution forbade parochial schools at the elementary level, a provision which the Church believed would block its primary means of access to young Mexicans.

In 1926 Calles began enforcing the anticlerical provisions both because he was anticlerical and because he believed the Church to be reactionary and, therefore, a threat to Revolutionary rule. Mexican Catholicism responded on two levels. The ecclesiastical hierarchy in 1926 gave orders to suspend all sacraments until the State ceased "persecuting" the Church, placing Mexico under an interdict, as it were.[5] Lay Catholics, with some ecclesiastical support, resorted to arms, engaging in guerilla action against the government from 1926 to 1929. Called the *cristero* rebellion, the civil war was limited principally to the western and north-central states. The government won the war but, faced with other domestic problems and foreign pressures arising from disputes over oil rights, it compromised its anticlericalism. The Church withdrew the interdict and promised not to intervene in politics; the government tacitly agreed to ignore the most stringent anticlerical requirements, an act which allowed Church schools to exist.[6]

The primary domestic crisis, the assassination of president-elect

Obregón in 1928 by a Catholic fanatic, was resolved by the creation of an "official" Revolutionary political party which has supplied almost all elected governmental officials since 1928. Obregón and Calles had had the constitutional provision prohibiting absolute no reelection amended to no immediate reelection only, thus allowing Obregón to serve another presidential term. With Obregón's death, Calles faced a dilemma; he wanted to retain control of Mexico but would surely face a potentially successful rebellion if he tried to impose himself on the Mexican people. The resourceful leader solved the problem by getting rival political leaders to form the *Partido Nacional Revolucionario* (National Revolutionary Party; PNR), organized on a geographical basis. Disputes among the major Revolutionary leaders would be settled within the confines of the party, not on the battlefield. Ambitious politicians would have to run as PNR candidates to be victorious.[7]

The first national election in which the PNR participated set the basic pattern of Mexican politics from that time onward. The Calles-selected interim president, Emilio Portes Gil, called presidential elections for 1929 to choose a man to complete the unexpired term for which Obregón had been elected. Pascual Ortiz Rubio, the relatively unknown PNR candidate overwhelmed his principal opponent José Vasconcelos, famous educator and philosopher with 93.6 percent of the vote.[8] Vasconcelos, although popular and supported by Catholics, was unable to withstand the PNR juggernaught. The point was clear: official party backing was a virtual guarantee of victory and its rewards.

Even though Mexico now had a popularly elected president, Calles managed to control Mexican politics covertly until 1934. The 1928–34 period had three presidents—Portes Gil, Ortiz Rubio, and Abelardo Rodríquez—and the country remained politically stable, for it was Calles who directed affairs from his home in the nearby resort town Cuernavaca. Through the PNR mechanism politics was institutionalized. Calles became increasingly conservative and leftists within PNR began to chafe.

The selection of Lázaro Cárdenas as PNR presidential candidate for the 1934–40 term resulted in a shift in Revolutionary emphasis. Cárdenas had been a Revolutionary general and an honest and progressive governor of his home state, Michoacán. Although a member of the establishment, he had a considerable following among leftists, making him an ideal compromise candidate.

Cárdenas's presidency did not disappoint the social reformers. From the first, during his campaign, he showed that he was not going to be another front man. He campaigned strenuously throughout the country for months, meeting the citizenry and listening to their problems. Having garnered enough support by 1935 to eject Calles from Mexico, he consolidated his position by formalizing his popular support. Thus he encouraged Marxist intellectual Vicente Lombardo Toledano to organize *Confederación de Trabajadores Mexicanos* (Mexican Labor Confederation; CTM) to supplant the more conservative Calles labor union, the *Confederación Regional de Obreros Mexicanos* (Regional Confederation of Mexican Workers; CROM). CTM and other labor unions were given government support in labor-capital conflicts, drastically increasing the number of strikes. The peasants, especially *ejidatarios* (members of communal or collective farms), were organized into the *Confederación Nacional Campesina* (National Peasants' or Farmers' Confederation; CNC). Land was massively redistributed to the peasantry, not only in the form of small property (favored by the Sonora Dynasty), but also as *ejidos* (communal or collective farms). The Cárdenas land redistribution program was spectacular on two counts: more land was redistributed than by all other Revolutionary presidents combined, and massive collective farms were created from the henequen plantations of Yucatán, which produced cordage fiber, and from the cotton farms of La Laguna in northern Mexico.

On other fronts Cárdenas completed nationalization of railroads, turning their management over to labor. Foreign oil properties were nationalized and placed under the management of a governmental corporation, *Petróleos Mexicanos* (PEMEX). Nationalists rejoiced that Cárdenas was asserting Mexican sovereignty. Less spectacularly, but probably more importantly, Cárdenas daily showed his concern for the welfare of the average Mexican. The government had taken a stand in favor of the masses.

Cárdenas's strength rested on his institutional changes as well as his dramatic acts. Borrowing ideas from Italian fascism and Marxism, the PNR was reorganized in 1938 into the *Partido de la Revolución Mexicana* (Mexican Revolutionary Party; PRM). In place of PNR's geographically organizational structure, PRM used a functional basis composed of four sectors—Labor, Agrarian, Military, and Popular. The Labor Sector included most labor unions but was dominated by the CTM. Heading the Agrarian Sector was the CNC. The inclusion of a Military Sector was an apparent recognition of the continued importance of the military in Mexican politics. The outcry against the formal institutionalization of the military in politics along with Cárdenas's efforts to professionalize the military enabled his successor, Manuel Avila Camacho, to delete the Military Sector in 1940. The Popular Sector remained amorphous until 1943 when it was reorganized and strengthened.

Even large-scale private enterprise and the Roman Catholic Church, the only major interest groups not included within the new Revolutionary party, were not neglected by Cárdenas's restructuring of Mexican politics. The anticlerical and socialist thrust of the Revolution precluded the inclusion of these two groups. The Church, of course, already had its own structure. The Cárdenas regime began to reconcile the conflicts between Church and State, and the Church supported the oil expropriation measure, although tension between the two continued. Cárdenas, however, did take steps to strengthen the organization of private enterprise into formal interest groups. Merchants whose businesses were capitalized at forty dollars or more were required to join the National Confederation of Chambers of Commerce (CONCANACO). Industrialists had to join the Confederation of Chambers of Mexican Industry (CONCAMIN). In the 1940s a new industrialists' organization was created, the National Confederation of Industries of Transformation (CNIT). Employers had already begun to create and join the Mexican Employers' Confederation (COPARMEX) in the 1930s. Groups such as bankers and cattlemen also joined formal interest groups.

The Cárdenas presidency represents, therefore, a major turning point in the Revolution, for he not only effected more social change than his predecessors, but he also created the institutional basis through which future conflicting claims of different interest groups could be reconciled. Traditionally weak economic groups—peasants, small farmers, and labor—had been insured a voice in national decisions. Subsequent governments could not ignore the demands of these sectors, though they might selectively determine which promises to fulfill. Even though the Cárdenas program had emphasized the importance of the masses, the private sector had been guaranteed informal access to the government. Moreover, the publicity surrounding the Cárdenas social reform program obscured the aid to industry and commerce that his regime actually delivered. The private sector prospered during his six-year term and the prosperity would increase, building on the foundation that Cárdenas had laid. In retrospect, the Cárdenas regime was not so much socialist as New Deal in character.[9]

The basic goals of the Revolution also received definition during the 1930s. By 1940, if not earlier, it was possible to speak of a discrete body of Revolutionary beliefs. The Revolution had been pragmatic in nature and had failed to develop a concrete ideology. Instead, it is perhaps best to follow Brandenburg's lead and speak of a "Revolutionary Creed."[10] The Creed has been the basic justification for all governmental actions since Cárdenas. All public acts are realized in its name. Opponents of the Creed are political heretics, either as Communists or anti-Revolutionaries.

The Revolution, as opposed to the actual fighting, means that Mexicans are trying to create a democratic state with a balanced, modern economy and equitable income distribution. Brandenburg best summarizes the Creed: (1) Mexicanism; (2) constitutionalism; (3) social justice; (4) political liberalism; (5) racial tolerance; (6) religious tolerance; (7) intellectual freedom and public education; (8) integrated economic growth; (9) mixed economy; (10) financial stability; and (11) a share in world leadership and prestige. These broad categories need further explanation for they are important in understanding post-Cárdenas governments and the behavior of Acción Nacional.

Mexicanism, or Mexican Nationalism, is founded on the belief that Mexico enjoys a unique, intrinsically valuable culture unsurpassed by any other. Part of this nationalism stems from the exaltation of indigenous cultures, particularly those of pre-Columbian days, and from pride in the Revolution. Manifestations of Mexicanism include such diverse activities as studies of the national character, assertions of national sovereignty over natural resources, laws requiring Mexican control of the economy, and insistence that Mexico develop its own solutions to national problems. In particular, Mexicanism rejects foreign imperialism in any form.

Constitutionalism is an inclusive point, for it includes many of the ideas debated between 1910 and 1940. The Constitution of 1917 is long and often contradictory. It does include, however, demands for a federal republican, presidential form of government; free, universal, and secular education; freedom of religion with circumscriptions aimed primarily at the Roman Catholic Church; national ownership of subsoil rights; public, private, communal, and cooperative ownership and initiative for economic development; limitation of agricultural ownership to small private farms, cooperatives, and communal farms; right of political asylum; equality before the law; Mexican birth as a requisite for high political office; and state responsibility for the defense of labor rights.

The ubiquitous term social justice defies precise definition because everyone invokes it. Stripped to its essentials, it means that the society, generally, and the government, specifically, have the duty to maximize socioeconomic opportunities while improving the quality of Mexican life. This concept is translated into practice by the construction of libraries, schools, hospitals, parks, and public housing; by the establishment and extension of a comprehensive social security system; by land redistribution; by the construction of sanitary facilities; by the marketing of food and clothing to the poor at reduced prices; and by the redistribution of national income.

Political liberalism is the point on which the Revolutionary elite receives the most criticism. In theory, it means republicanism, federalism, separation of powers, effective universal suffrage, no immediate reelection to public office, an independent judiciary, autonomous state and local governments, an independent national congress, civilian supremacy, political stability, career civil service, anticlericalism, and freedom of speech, press, assembly, and religion. In practice, it means tolerant rule guided by the wisdom of the Revolutionary Creed. As Mexican political scientist González Casanova notes, important decisions are made at the presidential level and passed down to lower levels for execution; the national government monopolizes public revenues, leaving state and local governments as its weak dependents; and the national congress is a willing servant of the executive branch. The only branch of government with any independence is the federal judiciary, but it does not consider political matters.[11] Other scholars agree that the realization of effective suffrage, local autonomy, a stronger judiciary and legislature, effective political opposition, and real freedom of press, speech, and assembly are far in the future.[12]

Racial and religious tolerance are realities, however. The ordinary citizen is conscious only of being Mexican, whereas the relatively few Indians, in a cultural sense, are being integrated into the all-pervasive Mexican culture. All religious beliefs or lack of beliefs are tolerated, but prohibitions exist against parochial schools or public manifestations of religiosity by institutions.

The greatest problem in intellectual freedom stems from governmental inability to expand the educational system fast enough. Restrictions on intellectual freedom are almost nonexistent. However, since there are not enough public schools, the mass of the population struggles to upgrade its educational level. While the government has worked assiduously to eliminate educational deficiencies, its success has been impeded by limited resources and population increases.[13]

Integrated economic growth, mixed economy, and financial stability are interrelated. Mexico seeks simultaneously to expand its agricultural production both for domestic consumption and exportation while replacing industrial imports with domestic manufactures. Since the mid-1950s, she has been particularly concerned with producing balanced growth. To accomplish this formidable task, she has encouraged all forms of initiative and ownership, using the public sector to create and operate what the private sector cannot or will not do. Moreover, she has sought to maintain monetary stability and a balance of payments.

Finally, Mexico seeks to become a leader of the Third World, particularly in Latin America. Mexican refusal to break diplomatic relations with Castro and her hosting the 1968 Olympic Games are two different examples of this activity.

Governments since Cárdenas have given different degrees of emphasis to this Creed, but a noticeable shift to the right is evident. Economic development has received priority over social justice. Private property and initiative have been favored over communal, cooperative, and public efforts. Manuel Avila Camacho (1940–46) sought to create a national unity government to heal the wounds opened by Cárdenas while exploiting the opportunities presented by the Second World War. Miguel Alemán (1946–52) led the postwar industrial expansion of Mexico and so favored private enterprise that Cárdenas apparently had to intervene to insure the selection of a more leftist president for the 1952–58 term. The Alemán regime represented the high point of probusiness government, but private enterprise has clearly had a major role in economic decision-making since. During the Alemán regime, important bankers and captains of business and industry began backing government party candidates. The decline of revolutionary zeal is indicated by the renaming of the official party as the *Partido Revolucionario Institucional* (Institutional Revolutionary Party; PRI). Presidents since Alemán— Adolfo Ruiz Cortines (1952–58); Adolfo López Mateos (1958–64); and Gustavo Díaz Ordaz (1964–70)—administrators who have risen through governmental and PRI ranks—have sought balanced economic growth as the best solution to Mexican problems. For the most part, dramatic acts in the name of Revolutionary goals have been replaced by administration of existing programs. Increases in the well-being of the masses have come from the trickling down effect of economic growth.[14]

Although many observers and critics of the Mexican Revolution argue that the Revolution ended with the moderate government of Avila Camacho, the fulfillment of Revolutionary goals continues. Surprisingly, perhaps, it was during the Alemán presidency that the masses' share of national wealth increased, not during the Cárdenas presidency when, in fact, real wages declined. Most Mexicans have benefited from the economic changes occurring since 1940.[15] Post-Cárdenas governments have tried to sustain this economic betterment by continuing land redistribution, opening new areas to agricultural settlement, constructing irrigation works, expanding the educational system, and introducing profit-sharing, for example. Whether such measures reduced the gap between the rich and the poor remains a political issue, however.

The commitment to both economic development and to the Revolutionary Creed has generated tensions throughout Mexican society. Each economic interest group seeks a larger share of national wealth. PRI itself contains at least three wings, with the left stressing the need for income redistribution through governmental action while the right argues for economic development led by the private sector. Organized private enterprise resists increased state economic intervention. The increasingly important middle class, which has gained a disproportionate share of elected offices, has demanded and received economic benefits and access to decision-making at the expense of other social strata.[16] In noneconomic terms, the degree of democracy in Mexico is an issue. Some Mexicans are beginning to chafe under "functional" or "guided" democracy. Partisans of the Roman Catholic Church have continued to fight against government anticlericalism and secularism in Mexico.[17]

The ruling elite remains in a strong position, however, for it has created a political system which insures political stability and periodic changes in leadership. The political system may be the most important effect of the Revolution, for the ability to accomplish any of the Revolutionary goals is dependent upon the legitimate, orderly maintenance and transfer of power.

Students of contemporary Mexican society agree upon the basic elements of the political system.[18] Functionally, decisions are made in the national capital by the president and his advisers and orders are sent down to hand-picked lower-level office holders and administrators. Federalism is fiction, for the president can remove recalcitrant governors, state legislators, and municipal officials and control their sources of revenue. Popular participation in decision-making through PRI is negligible or nonexistent.[19] PRI candidates are picked by PRI leaders and the national executive as rewards for loyalty or as a means of co-opting dissidents. Leaders of the PRI sectors are expected to serve the ruling elite, not their obstensible constituencies. The Revolution and patriotism are consistently and publicly identified with PRI and the incumbent government. Opposition parties and opinion are allowed to exist, even encouraged at times, as long as they do not seriously threaten the continuance of rule. Through the PRI sector organization, the government maintains a monopoly of access to the masses and the sector organization can be used to prevent or to repress dissidence or to show massive support for governmental policies.

This is not to say, however, that Mexico is a totalitarian state or that Mexican political leadership can ignore popular opinion. One aspect of the genius of the Mexican system is that it has allowed wide latitude for disagreement not only by oppositionists but also within PRI. Some of the liveliest political debate can be found in *Polémica,* a PRI magazine. Oppositionists have the opportunity to influence decisions by presenting better ideas and exerting pressure. On another level, the government responds to public physical acts against the regime. Riots and demonstrations against an unpopular official can quickly bring about his dismissal, as it did in the case of the Durango governor in 1966, who mishandled university student protests of governmental policy of exporting Durango iron ore to Monterrey steel mills instead of building a steel mill in Durango.[20] Leaders who cannot maintain public order and support are expendable. On the positive side, loyalty is rewarded. Labor supported the government against the students in 1968 when the students demonstrated for educational reforms, reorientation of national priorities towards social reform, and for student power. The 1969 Labor Law was apparently partial payment for that support.

The ruling elite will not voluntarily yield power. Perhaps one explanation for the almost total official party monopoly of public positions lies in manipulation of electoral returns. Ex-President of Mexico Emilio Portes Gil recently stated that election returns are manipulated for the benefit of the ruling elite, confirming a suspicion long held by observers of Mexican politics.[21] A different example of the determination of the ruling elite to stay in power is found in the case of Carlos Madrazo, president of PRI from 1964 to 1965. Madrazo tried to institute a direct primary system to select PRI candidates, hoping to increase popular participation and democracy within the party. Two strong state governors bucked him. He failed to get the support of President Díaz Ordaz, who had appointed him, and was dismissed shortly thereafter. The lesson is clear: that kind of popular participation is unwanted.[22]

Opposition parties apparently assume that they will never be allowed to hold significant elective posts, so they seek to maximize their influence with the decision-makers. Their techniques vary but include leading public demonstrations, trying to recruit members in order to claim broad popular support for their proposals, participation in elections both to gain access to public forums and to demonstrate their loyalty to the system in hope of obtaining rewards, and propagandizing the citizenry.[23]

The acceptance of the political system by the opposition parties points up one basic fact about contemporary Mexican politics. The Revolution is a sacred symbol which demands homage, even from those politicians who wish that it had never occurred. Popular support for the Revolutionary Creed is deep and widespread: only the Revolution is legitimate. Yet, the Revolutionary Creed provides a set of behavioral norms. Regardless of the intensity of belief that public officeholders may have, they must identify with the Revolution. So too must opposition groups.

This is the environment within which Acción Nacional, the leading opposition party, has had to operate since its founding in 1939. That a nongovernmental party has survived for over three decades is a novel event in Mexican history, but that an independent opposition party has survived that long is intriguing, for it represents a major break with the Mexican political past and raises questions about the potentialities of political party activity in what is essentially a one-party political system. Why a group of men came together in the late summer of 1939 to found a permanent political party when there was little hope of its survival beyond a few months is the subject of the next chapter.

CHAPTER II

Origins of Acción Nacional

The approximately one thousand delegates who created Acción Nacional in Mexico City on September 14–15, 1939, were a coalition united by common distaste for the Cárdenas reorganization of Mexican life and fear that the 1940 presidential election would result in the selection of a man equally radical. On many other points, especially the nature of the government which they preferred, they disagreed substantially. They had come by different routes to this convention and the differences were not dissolved by their common fear of socialism and radical change.[1]

The most important group in the constituent assembly was the young Catholic university activists, who maintained control of the party long after others left. These Catholics represented neither the Church's political position nor all Catholics. The government and its party, PRM, contained larger numbers of practicing Catholics and probably most Mexican Catholics were completely uninvolved and unaware of the actions of the Catholics who had chosen this political action. Certainly the Catholics in the *Unión Nacional Sinarquista* (UNS)[2] had not chosen to join. The Acción Nacional Catholic founders had been recruited primarily from participants in the Church-State conflict of the twentieth century and particularly the conflict over socialist education. Most were from the middle and upper strata of Mexican society: intellectuals and professionals, university students, and a scattering of owners and managers of large private enterprises who were motivated in part by their religiosity or concern for the survival of Catholic values in an increasingly secular world.[3] Therefore, the complicated Church-State conflict of the twentieth century needs to be examined briefly.

Tension between Church and State in Mexico was no new phenomenon. As noted earlier, Church-State conflict had been a basic pattern of nineteenth-century Mexican politics. Under Díaz, this conflict had abated, for Díaz saw in the Church a bulwark for order and an unnecessary enemy. Relations between Díaz and the Church were not idyllic,

16

however, and towards the end of the *Porfiriato,* the Church began to concern itself with social issues.

Church concern for social change emanated from the papal social encyclical *Rerum Novarum* (1891) and the influence of priests who had studied in Europe and who had been involved in contemporaneous Catholic reform movements.[4] Catholic Social Congresses, meeting first in Puebla in 1903, were called to discuss means of implementing the goals of the encyclical. Other Congresses met in Morelia (1904), Guadalajara (1906), and Oaxaca (1909). From the Congresses and the workers' Diet of Zamora (1913) came proposals to improve the living conditions of the working classes, to create savings banks, workers' mutualist associations, cooperatives of the Reiffeisen type; to redistribute land as family farms; to establish minimum wages; to protect child and female labor; to assist in housing; to create social security and profit-sharing systems; to prevent the concentration of wealth; to extend technical and financial assistance to agriculture; and to use compulsory arbitration in wage disputes. The Congresses did not argue for the forceful implementation of these reforms but sought to convince governmental and wealthy leaders to make the changes voluntarily. The weakness of this position can be seen in the call for large landowners to subdivide their estates to sell the land to the peasants and to aid the peasants in starting viable farms. Reform Catholics sought not independent labor unions but mutual aid societies and corporative structures of both labor and capital through which issues such as wages and working conditions could be amicably resolved.[5]

The Church hierarchy gave little support to the reform movement, even though such proposals were a common phenomenon in European countries, so Mexican reform Catholics were only able to start a few organizations before the outbreak of the Mexican Revolution. Initially, a Union of Workers of Our Lady of Guadalupe appeared in 1905 but disappeared shortly thereafter. By 1908, Churchmen had created the Mutual Workmen's Society with 7,213 members and a Working Women's Mutual Society with 9,275 members. The hierarchy prevented further attempts to implement the proposals of the Social Congresses, apparently content with the status quo. A Catholic youth group, the Catholic Association of Mexican Youth (*Asociación Católica de la Juventud Mexicana;* ACJM) was created in 1911 to work for the social justice doctrine of the Church, but it, too, was not allowed to do much.[6] The ACJM was modeled on the Catholic Association of French Youth, reflecting the influence of European Catholicism upon the Mexican Church. Important for the future of the Church in Mexico and for the founding of PAN (as Acción Nacional is commonly called), ACJM recruited from the brightest, wealthiest, and most prestigious class of Catholic Mexican young men.[7]

The outbreak of the Revolution in 1910 quickly ended Catholic attempts at moderate social reform through persuasion because the Revolution, by destroying the old order, changed the political equation in Mexican society. New bases for legitimacy had to be discovered and found; the Church had to find a new role in society. Its highly placed friends were ejected with the collapse of the Díaz government. Madero's spiritualism offended the Church and it gave only lukewarm support to Madero's short government. Madero was not interested in representing the Church's interests, so the latter encouraged the formation of a National Catholic Party which ran candidates for deputy and senatorial seats in the 1911 elections. The deputies elected sought to reverse some of the anticlerical provisions of the 1857 constitution still in force, but without much success. The Church soon committed suicide as a political force for it supported the Huerta government after Huerta overthrew Madero in 1913.[8] Anti-Huerta revolutionaries, many of whom were already anticlerical, saw the Church as an enemy, as an ally of the forces of reaction. The Constitution of 1917, written during the Carranza regime, was virulently anticlerical and the Church was systematically excluded from politics.[9]

Denied political participation and believing itself threatened by the anticlerical provisions of the constitution, the Church responded by creating and expanding its network of lay associations. In 1917, it created the National Parents' Union (*Unión Nacional de Padres de Familia*) to combat the anticlerical education provisions.[10] Led by Father Méndez Medina, a reformist priest, the bishops created the Social Secretariat in 1919 to promote Catholic reform ideology; the radicalism of some revolutionary leaders had now made the social reform ideology of Catholic progressives palatable to conservative bishops. In the next year the Church created the Confederation of Catholic Associations of Mexico to coordinate the efforts of all groups interested in the social reform program. The Social Secretariat, in turn, established a network of social reform organizations: Catholic Workers' Unions, Women's Social Union, labor unions, rural workers' unions, a Federation of Reiffesen Credit in the states of Michoacán and Jalisco, and Federations of Trade Unions in various states. By 1922, the Catholic labor unions were joined into the Catholic National Federation of Labor during a labor congress held in Guadalajara. Attending were 1,374 delegates representing approximately 80,000 workers.[11]

These activities were not just the result of the hostility of Mexican revolutionaries to the Catholic Church which they saw as a reactionary force, but part of an international trend in Catholicism. The Mexican activities represented part of the thrust of what has since become known as Catholic Action.[12] The work of the Social Secretariat, in fact, was the start of extending Catholic Action to Mexico. Catholic Action in the international church was a move to use laymen to spread Church doctrine and the ideas of social reform, as represented by *Rerum Novarum*. Catholic Action sought to recoup from the losses created by the growing secularization of society, the rise of anticlericalism, and the sparsity of ordained clergy. Pope Benedict XV unified Italian lay activity in 1915 under the name Catholic Action, whereas Pius XI confirmed it as a lay apostolate. In Argentina, Catholic Action ideas were spread by Miguel de Andrea, titular bishop of Temnos, and it was formally established there in 1928. In Spain, it was called Popular Action. In the United States it became the National Catholic Welfare Conference. Mexican Catholic Action was not formally established until after the Church lost its conflict with the state from 1926 to 1929. In short, the Catholic Church had begun to move away from its traditional opposition to social change and towards a position where it could lead the change in directions consistent with Catholic doctrine. The inroads made among working classes by secular forces, particularly socialists, and the threats to Catholic influence represented by the 1917 Bolshevik victory in Russia catalyzed Catholic involvement in social questions affecting the common man.[13]

In the Mexican case, however, the threat came not from socialists or Communists, though many Catholics thought so, but from domestic revolutionaries who were determined to break the power of the Church. This determination had been demonstrated in the 1917 Constitution and the public attacks upon the Church by politicians. Although unpopular among many governmental officials, the Church managed to weather all storms until 1926 because the government did not systematically implement anticlericalism.

Amicable relations between Church and State finally collapsed in 1926 when both institutions fought for supremacy in Mexico. In 1923 the Church had antagonized revolutionary leaders by crowning Christ as King of Mexico during a ceremony in Guanajuato state near the geographical center of Mexico. Whether the Church meant this literally or not, secular politicians interpreted the action as an attempt to assert the supremacy of the Church over the State. The final break came in 1926 when a daily newspaper in Mexico City published a letter written by Archbishop José Mora y del Río condemning the Revolution and demanding that Catholics not support the Revolution or any government emanating from it. The letter was old and not Church policy, a fact not fully known until later, but the anticlerical Calles took the opportunity to eject the Archbishop from the country, order the expulsion of foreign priests, close Catholic schools, and begin the enforcement of other anticlerical provisions of the Constitution. Moreover, Calles encouraged the foundation of a schismatic Orthodox Catholic Apostolic Church. Faced with another *Kulturkampf,* the Church responded by withdrawing all sacraments from Mexico until the government ceased its anticlericalism.[14]

Churchmen, both ecclesiastics and laymen, took other important courses of action to win the struggle. In Jalisco, the secret Society of the U was formed; in Guanajuato, the Association of the Vassals of Christ. Previously, in 1925, the *Liga Nacional Defensora de la Libertad Religiosa* (National Defense League of Religious Liberty) had been formed as a reactionary counterpart to the Social Secretariat. The League, in particular, became the chief instrument of Church policy.[15] As the coordinator of lay activity during a period when the hierarchy found it difficult to obtain a hearing, the League became a focal point of Catholic activity. It was the League which led the Church's boycott against nonessential commercial transactions, a boycott which the Church hoped would force the government to yield to ecclesiastical demands. Later in 1926, when the boycott appeared to be failing, the League organized armed bands of lay Catholics (*cristeros*) to fight government troops and to resist anticlericalism by attacks upon public schools and their teachers.[16] Most of the activity was concentrated in the strong conservative Catholic areas of the country—western and north-central Mexico. The Church never acknowledged sponsorship of the League, especially its guerrilla activities, both because the Church was forbidden to participate in politics and because the Church hierarchy was split on the question of armed force as a tactic. A majority of the hierarchy apparently supported the *cristeros,* for Durango Archbishop José María González Valencia, president of the Bishops' Committee, issued a statement in November, 1926, sanctifying the use of force on such occasions. Significantly, the bishops had just held a meeting to decide what course of action should be taken if the boycott failed.[17]

The ACJM led the League coalition. René Capistrán Garza, ACJM president and League vice-president, coordinated the *cristero* rebellion. When some Catholics created a government in exile, Capistrán Garza was named its head. The other lay groups within the League coalition provided men, money, and material for the rebellion and the important pacific pressure exerted upon the population. Even a brief list suggests the extent of the organization of the laity which existed by the mid 1920s: the National Parents' Union, the Knights of Columbus, Catholic

Women, Catholic Labor Union, National Catholic Party, and the Popular Union. The National Parents' Union specialized in prostelytizing against governmental closure of Catholic schools and in keeping these schools open. The Popular Union, founded by Anacleto González Flores in Jalisco state, contributed guerillas. The other groups aided by such actions as raising money, rolling bandages, and hiding refugees.[18]

The Church also moved to gain control of secondary and preparatory students in 1926 by creating the *Confederación Nacional de Estudiantes Católicos de Mexico* (National Confederation of Catholic Students of Mexico; CNECM) under the spiritual leadership of Jesuits. The idea for such an organization had originated in the National Preparatory School for the purpose of combating government anticlericalism, inculcating Christian ideas, and defending student professional interests. Technically, CNECM was part of ACJM, but CNECM members refused to be a specialized branch of the larger organization. They were, however, enrolled in the ranks of the League. Numerous future PAN founders were also founders of CNECM: Manuel Ulloa Ortiz, Luis Calderón Vega, Luis Islas García, Luis de Garay, Armando Chávez Camacho, Carlos Septién García, Carlos Ramírez Zetina, Daniel Kuri Breña, Jesús Hernández Díaz, Miguel Estrada Iturbide, and Luis Hinojosa.[19]

By the end of 1926, Catholic leaders were operating on three fronts in their efforts to assert the prerogatives of the Church. The bishops, some of whom were operating from exile in the United States, sought to pressure the government by rallying foreign, especially United States, Catholic support and, through them, support from foreign governments. Both the Vatican and the United States Church hierarchy were sympathetic to the Mexican Church cause and it was representatives of these two who later acted as negotiators. Inside Mexico, lay Catholics led the fight. The League fought guerilla actions while CNECM tried to hold secondary and preparatory students within the Catholic fold. Some Church schools remained open and masses were clandestinely said in private homes. It was, however, the middle and upper class Catholics who were able to maintain close contact with organized Catholicism, for they were the ones who had the resources to send their children to schools, public or private, and to have masses said in homes.[20]

That the Church could not successfully marshal the force of the Mexican people to stop government anticlericalism revealed both the weaknesses of Mexican Catholicism and the strength of progovernment sentiment. Perhaps equally important in explaining the Church's loss was the tenacity of its chief opponent, President Calles; a weaker man might have yielded in the face of the pressure the Church was able to mount.

Probably the most important factor explaining the Church's failure was its misunderstanding of the nature of Mexican Catholicism and, therefore, of its hold over the people. The hierarchy as well as many priests were European in outlook, if not in origin. Their ideas appealed to the middle and upper classes, who also looked to Europe for guidance, but these ideas were alien to most Mexicans. Mexican Catholicism, instead, was deeply imbued with the remnants of ancient religious practices predating the Spanish conquest. The Mexican commoner found it easy to continue his religious practices during the absence of priests. He did not need the Church so much as the Church needed him. Moreover, such past governmental programs as expansion of the public educational system, land redistribution, support of organized labor—in short, the Revolutionary program—had won the loyalty of the population. The worst fears of the Church had come true. It had failed to indoctrinate its clientele properly but the secular state had succeeded.[21]

After months of secret negotiating, Church and State arranged a truce in 1929. By 1928, it had become clear to most Churchmen that the rebellion was hopeless. The armed tactics were no real threat to the government and the absence of priests in the churches was more threatening to the Church than the people. Through the good offices of United States Ambassador Dwight Morrow, conversations were opened between President Calles and Father John Burke of the National Catholic Welfare Conference. The assassination of President-elect Obregón by a Catholic fanatic in July 1928 temporarily halted the talks, but by June 30, 1929, Catholic services were resumed. The moderate bishops, who had gained control of affairs, agreed that the Church's integrity would not be destroyed, but that it must remain a spiritual institution. They had adopted the Constitutional formula of Church-State relations.[22]

The League's unhappiness with this turn of events forced the Church to take special measures to discipline League members. Some League members and other *cristeros* continued to fight government troops. Others were outspoken in their belief that the cause had been betrayed, that the moderate prelates, with the prodding of the Protestant Dwight Morrow, had sold out the Church. The hierarchy responded by reorganizing the lay associations. The ACJM, the core of the League, was brought into Mexican Catholic Action along with the Catholic Mexican Union of Women, the Union of Mexican Catholics (for men), and Mexican Catholic Young Ladies. Catholic Action was put under strict ecclesiastical control by the new, more moderate Archbishop of Mexico, Pascual Díaz. Catholic Action was to concentrate upon teaching catechism, not armed revolution.[23]

The Vasconcelos presidential election campaign of 1929, however, gave Catholic and other dissenters from governmental policy a chance to vent their anger. With the death of Obregón, new presidential elections had to be held and Emilio Portes Gil, interim President, had called them for 1929. The government candidate Pascual Ortiz Rubio, running with PNR backing, was a sure winner. José Vasconcelos made a palatable alternative to those who sought an end to domination by the Sonora Dynasty. Vasconcelos had been a Revolutionary, having served as Minister of Education under Obregón. In this post he had actively sought to extend public education throughout Mexico and had encouraged the execution of murals on public buildings. As an intellectual and university leader, he was well known and respected by the literate population. Most important, perhaps, he had both charisma and the backing of wealthy conservatives. Young people in particular flocked to his campaign, giving it the appearance of more strength than it actually had. His party, the National Anti-Reelectionist Party, actually had had difficulty in choosing a candidate. Vasconcelos had tried to create a National Labor Party incorporating the disparate elements backing him but had finally had to use the Anti-Reelectionist vehicle.[24]

Vasconcelistas hoped that their man would reach the Mexican presidency either through electoral victory or a coup d'état but the candidate failed in both instances. The PNR machine crushed the Vasconcelos band, registering an overwhelming 93.6 percent of the vote in favor of Ortiz Rubio. *Vasconcelistas* cried fraud and called for the candidate to lead an armed rebellion against the government. Vasconcelos and his advisers surveyed the situation from the United States, where they had fled to when the election results had become apparent. Several advisers, including Manuel Gómez Morín, unofficial treasurer of the campaign, argued against leading a coup. Gómez Morín encouraged Vasconcelos to start a permanent opposition party in hope of attaining power in the future. Vasconcelos declined. The Vasconcelos movement, for the candidate was the glue of the coalition, quietly died away. Members began to seek other ways in which to influence public policy.[25]

Catholic leaders began planning for the future with the reorganization of CNECM into a university student movement called the *Unión Nacional de Estudiantes Católicos* (National Union of Catholic Students; UNEC). The CNECM members had been graduating from their schools and moving into the universities. CNECM leaders such as Manuel Ulloa Ortiz, Luis de Garay, Jesús Pérez Sandí and Jesús Toral Moreno worked with the Church hierarchy in Mexico City to create UNEC in February, 1931.[26] That UNEC was part of a Latin American movement within Catholicism was shown when UNEC became the principal organizer of the *Confederación Iberoamericana de Estudiantes Católicos,* hosting the latter's first Ibero-American Congress of University Catholic Action in Mexico City on December 12, 1931.[27] The Latin American hierarchy was trying to counteract the rising impact of Marxist thought in universities. Moreover, some UNEC leaders were chosen to attend the Latin American Student Congress in Rome in 1934 which was the seminal meeting of the Latin American Christian Democratic movement.[28] UNEC believed that the leading Mexican university student organization, the National Students' Confederation, was Marxist-dominated. Therefore, it created secret cells to infiltrate and conquer the National Students' Confederation.[29] Blocking the path was Vicente Lombardo Toledano, brilliant Marxist intellectual, labor leader, and director of the National Preparatory School, a subsidiary of the national university. In 1933 and 1934, a full-scale philosophical debate raged through the national university and literate Mexican society. Lombardo Toledano supported Marxian theory whereas Antonio Caso, his former professor, Manuel Gómez Morín, university rector, UNEC, and conservative forces supported an antiscientific, Bergsonian school of thought. Lombardo Toledano was expelled from the University and later created what became the Workers' University.[30] UNEC countered with its first victory, believing that it had been instrumental in saving the university from Marxism. This victory combined with its successful infiltration efforts made it the dominant university student organization.

The thrust of UNEC also included an interest in social reform. The movement was part of Catholic Action, but UNEC found its particular parent organization within Catholic Action, ACJM, too conservative and reticent.[31] In its 1931 national convention, UNEC declared itself for Catholicism and Revolution.[32] It started retreats for students and night schools for workingmen.[33] When Cárdenas expropriated the oil industry in 1938, the UNEC national convention applauded the move.[34] Such activity had brought it into conflict with the ACJM in 1933, but UNEC retained its independence.[35] By the late thirties, however, the Church hierarchy decided that UNEC had to be brought under the discipline of Catholic Action. UNEC resisted.[36] Students from another Catholic organization infiltrated UNEC and vitiated it. This conflict between the loyal Jesuit-sponsored UNEC members and the Christian Brothers' *conejos* (rabbits) continued until 1944 when UNEC disbanded itself rather than accept full incorporation into Catholic Action.[37] In the meantime, the politically minded UNEC members joined Acción Nacional when it was created in 1939.[38]

The 1929 agreements had been only a truce. Proclerical and anticlerical charges continued from that date, since politicians found anticlericalism to be an effective tool to gain support. From 1931 to 1936 anticlericalism raged again, most of it confined to the state level where state after state reduced the number of priests allowed, some to the point of not allowing any. At the national level, anticlericalism took the form of amending Article 3 of the Constitution in 1934 to require that all education be "socialist" in character. A second but minor *cristero* rebellion was quickly squelched.[39]

The reaction of the conservative hierarchy and the League to the revival of anticlericalism was to see it as a vindication of their uncompromising attitude in 1929, and the moderate hierarchy, still in charge, had to move quickly to prevent the conservatives from regaining control of the Church.[40] The various Catholic social and civic action groups were incorporated into a National Action Council (*Consejo de Acción Nacional*) in December 1931.[41] In late 1932, the Church created the Legion, a secret, elite, lay organization which was to drain off Catholic discontent through non-League tactics. The Legion was composed of selected, devout Catholics, usually from Marian Congregations trained in the Jesuit *Spiritual Exercises* who took vows of loyalty to the Church and the Legion. Organized into cells, the members did not know members of other cells. Directions were supplied by a Supreme Council which in turn, took orders from the hierarchy. Ideological direction was given by the publication of Pius XI's encyclical *Quadragesimo Anno* (1931), a document which affected UNEC and other Catholic groups as well. Because it was closely identified with the Church, Catholic Action was to be kept aloof from the Legion which was to lead the lay counterattack against anticlericalism. The militant League and the Legion found cooperation almost impossible. They could agree on priorities—to fight anticlericalism first, then work for social reform, and finally for political reform—but they could not coordinate their efforts.[42]

By 1934, the Church decided that the Legion was ineffective and it was necessary to reorganize it along corporate lines, drawing from the corporatist thought in *Quadragesimo Anno*. The new organization, the Base, was organized into occupational sectors. Emissaries from the secret Base would reach out into every sector of national life, recruiting Mexicans to Catholicism and Catholic social philosophy. Borrowing techniques from the Sodalities of Our Lady, from which some Base members had come, the Base organized Workers' Sodalities to teach the catechism and social thought and to infiltrate unions bringing them into Catholic control. The Base set up a boarding school (the Home of the Proletarian Student in Tacubaya, a suburb of Mexico City) with the support of Lombardo Toledano who did not realize Catholics were backing it.[43]

One of the primary functions of the Base was to keep conservative militants from leading the Church into another pointless combat with the government. With the increase in government anticlericalism between 1931 and 1936, many Catholics wanted to start another major rebellion against the government. It was the Base's job to contain this anger by dissipating it through peaceful activities such as public demonstrations and working at the local level for gradual change.[44]

The secrecy surrounding the Base has prevented serious scholars from understanding the full implications of its organization, activities, and relationship to other Catholic organizations. A non-Mexican priest, Joseph Ledit, who had close connections with the putative leader of the Base, has seen the Base as the creator of the UNS in 1937 and as an anticommunist reform group particularly concerned with labor problems.[45] One scholar, using Ledit, argues that the Base was the instrument of the relatively enlightened post-1929 Church hierarchy.[46] Fuentes Díaz, an anticlerical socialist and PRI politician, has seen the Base as the fount of both the UNS and Acción Nacional, the peasant sector of the Base having organized the former in 1937 and the employers' sector having organized the latter in 1939.[47] Acción Nacional leaders deny any connection between the party and UNS.[48] According to Fuentes Díaz and other anticlericalists, both UNS and Acción Nacional were reactionary while the former was sympathetic to fascism in the 1930s and 1940s.[49]

Although the secrecy surrounding the Base and UNS makes scholarly research difficult, there are grounds for believing that printed assertions on the relationship among the Base, UNS, Acción Nacional, and fascism are overdrawn. In my interviews with Luis Calderón Vega, a participant in UNEC, the Base, and Acción Nacional, Calderón Vega has been very frank in talking about his experiences in Catholic movements of the 1920s–1940s period. Other interviews with participants, which were much more guarded, corroborate the story Calderón Vega tells. Calderón Vega asserts that the Base supplied personnel to both UNS and Acción Nacional, but that the Base's politicized progressives joined Acción Nacional while the conservatives went into UNS. Miguel Estrada Iturbide and Salvador Abascal were Base leaders in Morelia, Michoacán, Calderón Vega's home. Both were local aristocrats, but Estrada Iturbide, as a Catholic intellectual, was oriented by world-wide Catholic movements and read such progressive Catholic theologians as Jacques Maritain. Estrada Iturbide became the founder of PAN in Michoacán while Abascal became a founder of UNS. They remained politically opposed. This split was apparently common in Catholic elite circles in the 1930s and explains why UNS and Acción Nacional have some doctrinal similarities but oppose each other.

Furthermore, Calderón Vega disclosed that the Base was not the innocent organization that it pretended to be. The Base was planning a coup d'état against the government to take place after the population had been indoctrinated. Since the Base and *sinarquismo* were virtually the same after PAN was founded in 1939, this perhaps explains why the UNS did not engage in political party activity. During the 1930s, Base members also physically assaulted their opponents, particularly public school teachers whom they believed to be Communists, that is, those who were secular-minded. Since the Base still exists, the truth will not be known for some time.[50] It is possible that the Base and Opus Dei in Mexico, a covert coalition of paternalistic wealthy men who seek to extend Church influence by using their occupations and aiding one another, are synonymous.

The Church hierarchy has been very careful to disown any connnection between itself and Acción Nacional, the Base, and UNS, especially the latter which operated on the fringes of acceptable public behavior. Because it is a secret organization, scholars have been slow to study the UNS and one can only suggest its scope.[51] Apparently it was organized in 1937 with an extremely rigid hierarchical command structure. Most of its recruits came from the peasantry, especially in the states in which the *cristero* rebellion had been strongest and benefits from the Revolution least.[52] Ideologically, it exalted medieval corporatism, Spanish culture, order, discipline, Franco's Spain, paternalistic Catholicism, and private property while opposing the Mexican Revolution. Both Marxism and liberal democracy were enemies. Sinarchist activities were marked by secret handshakes, salutes, codewords, and military discipline —hallmarks of European fascist movements. Unlike the European organizations, however, sinarchists contented themselves with peaceful marches and demonstrations against the Revolutionary government, particularly in opposition to socialist education.

Government anticlericalism was the concrete issue which catalyzed Catholics to oppose the Mexican government in the 1930s, but the fear that Cárdenas was trying to create a socialist state was more important. The most threatening act of the 1931–36 revival of anticlericalism had been the 1934 amendment of Article 3 of the Constitution to require socialist education. President Cárdenas had also allowed Communists to infiltrate the education ministry to implement socialist education.[53] Catholics interpreted these actions as a state attempt to exclude not only the Church from teaching young Mexicans but also as the prelude to restructuring society into a Marxist mold.[54] The antipathy of the Church towards the Cárdenas regime continued even after the 1936 détente between Cárdenas and the Church, a détente which had produced overt ecclesiastical support for the social reform measures of the Revolution and the termination of Cárdenas's support for anticlerical activities.[55]

A series of actions by the Cárdenas government after 1936, however, gave evidence to the Church that Cárdenas was preparing to convert Mexico into a socialist state in which the Church would have a minimal role at best. Cotton plantations in the La Laguna region of northern Mexico and henequen plantations in Yucatán were collectivized. The land redistribution program was changed to favor the creation of communal farms, the *ejido,* and peasants were organized into a national confederation closely linked to official circles. Lombardo Toledano, a Church enemy, was encouraged by the Cárdenas government to set up a massive labor union, the CTM, which became closely tied to the government as a member of the official party. Though the Church applauded the nationalization of the railroads and the oil industry, the Cárdenas decision to turn over the management of these institutions to the workers frightened most Catholics, as well as many other Mexicans. The creation of the PRM in late 1937 on a popular front model along with Cárdenas's support of the Loyalist forces in the Spanish Civil War seemed to indicate that Cárdenas was preparing a drastic alteration in Mexican life. Finally, in 1939, the Church saw mounting evidence that Cárdenas was planning to support legislation to implement the socialist education requirements.[56]

Mexican Catholic anxieties about the course of events in their own country were exacerbated by their assessment of the contemporary world. In their view the increasing secularization of Western society was encouraged by two forces incompatible with Catholic social doctrine: Marxism and liberal capitalism. Communism was the greater threat because it was totalitarian, materialist, and collectivist in its thrust and had the announced goal of converting the world to its position. The Bolshevik revolution had frightened traditionalists in the Western world and many Catholics saw a direct relationship between Bolshevism and the increase in anticlericalism in many countries during the interwar years. Moreover, the Spanish Civil War appeared to be proof that Communists were attempting to destroy Spanish Catholicism, a Catholicism which was the heritage of Mexican Catholics. The Franco-Falange forces seemed, therefore, to be defending Catholicism against Communist atheists.[57]

But the liberal democracies offered only slightly better promise. The leading liberal capitalist powers, the United States and the United Kingdom, were Protestant, and, consequently, not interested in preserving Catholicism. Moreover, their forms of capitalism emphasized individualism, materialism, and profit seeking, which were inconsistent with Catholic corporate theory. To Catholics influenced by *Rerum Novarum, Quadragesimo Anno,* and the neo-Thomistic revival, liberal capitalism produced exploitation and social injustice. Mexican Catholics tended to internalize this perception of the international scene by viewing the Revolutionary governments as containing both elements. The Cárdenas faction represented the communist elements while the Calles faction represented the liberal or bourgeois capitalist elements.

Catholics were attracted to those movements on the international scene which valued Catholicism, tradition, and order while opposing communism and liberal capitalism. The first of these had been Italian fascism, especially after the Lateran Treaty of 1929. Italian fascism was based on a corporate model similar to Catholic corporate thought and the Catholic church and the Italian government cooperated in the key issues of education and morals. Post-1929 Vatican criticisms of Mussolini diminished their enthusiasm but did not extinguish it. Such governments as that of Getulio Vargas in Brazil, Antonio Salazar in Portugal, and Francisco Franco in Spain equally attracted Mexican Catholic support. All three protected and fostered the Catholic church while fighting communism and carrying out social reforms (at least on paper). The authoritarian aspects of such regimes troubled progressive Catholics, but they could agree with their conservative brethren that the central values of Catholic civilization were being preserved.

By 1939, then, many Mexican Catholics had reached the conclusion that something decisive had to be done in Mexico to stem the tide that threatened to inundate Mexican Catholicism. The National Sinarchist Union provided one outlet for these anxieties and frustrations but did not promise to bring about substantial change. What was needed was an organization and leadership which would offer a real alternative to the Cárdenas government.

The events and policies which had been troubling Catholics during the Mexican Revolution also had been troubling men of a secular bent. Opposition to Revolutionary governments fluctuated in content and intensity in direct proportion to changes in Revolutionary leadership and emphasis. Each change in government produced a new opposition, for those excluded from the new government, either for personalistic or ideological reasons, were angered by their loss of power or influence. By the time Cárdenas had solidified his power, the opposition groups were numerous and diverse. There were, for example: (1) remnants of the Porfirian upper classes, (2) *maderistas,* (3) *huertistas,* (4) *carrancistas,* (5) *delahuertistas,* (6) *obregonistas,* and (7) *callistas.* Besides these politicians there were: (1) former *hacendados,* (2) small proprietors threatened by encroachment from *ejidos,* (3) businessmen and industrialists threatened by the rise of organized labor, (4) middle-class elements who resented the Cárdenas emphasis on labor and the peasantry to the exclusion of their interests, (5) traditionalists who thought they saw Mexican culture being destroyed, and (6) those who believed that Mexico was not democratic under Cárdenas but should be.

In spite of the successes of Cárdenas, or perhaps because of them, the last years of *Cardenismo* were a period of crisis.[58] Cárdenas had realized that his restructuring of Mexican society produced tensions; the détente with the Church in 1936 had been adopted to reduce tension emanating from anticlericalism. After the oil expropriation in 1938, the Cárdenas government became more moderate. It had become necessary to concentrate his efforts upon preserving his accomplishments, a consideration which led to his favoring the moderate Avila Camacho as his successor. Workers' real wages had declined during the Cárdenas administration. Capital was hiding or fleeing the country. The business community was anxious. The administration of the national railroads was a complete disaster. Dislocations and production decreases accompanied the substitution of Mexican for foreign management of the petroleum industry. Inflation was rampant by 1939–40. Landless peasants were demanding land; landed peasants were demanding the means to work the land, including credit and irrigation. The collective *ejidos* in La Laguna and Yucatán were in great trouble. Agricultural production as a whole had declined and Mexico had to import basic foodstuffs. Organized labor was going beyond Cárdenas's intentions, calling too many strikes. Cárdenas had to appeal to their patriotism to step up production. Corruption existed in official circles. The middle classes were rapidly becoming disillusioned.

The disillusionment of the middle classes was important because of their increasing numbers and their tendency to supply leadership in society. In the decade of the 1930s there had been a significant increase in the rural and urban middle classes. Small agricultural proprietors increased 10 percent to 78,000. In the cities, especially Mexico City, the middle classes had increased with industrial expansion and emigration from the countryside fostered by land redistribution. The difficulty was that the bureaucracy and the educated middle class had grown too rapidly to be absorbed by the economy. All these middle groups were hurt by the economic crisis of the late 1930s.

Possible extinction frightened them as much as their economic distress. The collectivization of agriculture, the expenditure of government funds for *ejidos* instead of industrialization, the granting of asylum to Trotsky, the turning of railroad and petroleum management to labor, the granting of exile to Spanish Republicans, the unionization of government bureaucrats, and indications of the renewal of anticlerical legislation (which did occur in 1940) seemed to be the prelude to the extension of Godless socialism to Mexico.

Anticipation of the 1940 presidential election spurred Mexican politicians into action as each sought to determine or influence the outcome of the election. Within the Revolutionary coalition, leftists rallied behind General Francisco Múgica and rightists behind General Juan Andreu Almazán. When General Avila Camacho was selected as the official candidate, the leftists reluctantly supported him. Almazán, however, created the *Partido Revolucionario de Unificación Nacional* (Revolutionary Party of National Unification; PRUN) and became the principal opposition candidate in the election.[59]

The origins of the Almazán candidacy are one measure of the extent of discontent in Mexico. Almazán was a wealthy general who had been military zone commander in northern Mexico. During his tour of duty he had been winning support from the industrial complex at Monterrey and from dissidents within the labor movement. However, his support was national in scope. He promised to reverse the more radical policies of the Cárdenas regime, socialist education, governmental anticlericalism, and to return Mexico to procapitalist policies. Ideologically his appeal ranged from moderates to reactionaries.

Various other groups had been formed to influence the selection of a moderate presidential candidate or to support Almazán once he decided to run on his own platform.[60] A few examples are indicative of this political shuffling. Anticommunist groups proliferated as did groups in favor of the middle classes.[61] In February, 1939, a group calling itself the Revolutionary Committee of National Reconstruction announced its existence in an *Excélsior* advertisement, calling for the end of the *ejido,* socialist education, and encouragement of the class struggle. The next month, the National Front of Professionals and Intellectuals announced its existence and goals similar to the above.[62]

By late 1938, then, conditions were ripe for the creation of a new political party. What was necessary was a leader who could bring together Catholic dissidents, middle class groups, and captains of enterprise and finance for the common purpose of destroying "socialist" policies.

CHAPTER III

The Founding Decade, 1939–1949

From the midst of the turmoil and anxiety of the final years of *Cardenismo* emerged a civilian politician-lawyer-financier who welded a loose coalition of anti-Cardenistas into Mexico's first permanent opposition party and who guided it through a momentous decade to the point where it could survive without him. Acción Nacional written and oral history abounds with accounts of the prodigious energy expended by Manuel Gómez Morín during the founding years of 1938–39 and his subsequent ten years as party president. The challenges facing an opposition politician in this initial period were enormous. First, he had to canvass the country, convincing cynical citizens that it was necessary to risk their futures to enter the political fray to end *Cardenismo* and to capture control of the Revolution. Concurrently, he had to organize cadres; to solicit funds; to debate ideology, organization, strategy, and tactics; and to minimize the differences of opinion among the men who responded to his call. During a decade when Mexico redefined the Revolution, participated in the Second World War and its ideological debates, began rapid industrialization, and experienced four federal elections, Gómez Morín had to teach his fragile coalition how to be a loyal, democratic political party and, through it, to teach that a loyal opposition party was possible and desirable. The first decade of Acción Nacional, the subject of this chapter, is indelibly stamped with the personality of Gómez Morín.

He had the credentials to satisfy the various people who sought his aid in altering the course of Mexican history. Born in Batopilas, Chihuahua, in 1897 of a Mexican mother and a Spanish father, he had been educated in Chihuahua state, Guanajuato state, and Mexico City, and received his law degree from the national university in 1918. As a university student he had been one of the "Seven Sages of Greece," an intellectually gifted group which included his Marxist rival Vicente Lombardo Toledano. In his early twenties he served as a legal adviser to the Soviet Embassy, an act which reflected his short flirtation with radicalism. A few years later he was undersecretary of finance in the Obregón government and acted as financial adviser to the subsequent Calles government, during which time he had a material role in writing some of the most important economic laws of the period: the organic law of the Bank of Mexico (1925), the agricultural credit law of 1926, and the first Mexican income tax law. Shortly after graduating from the university he had joined its law faculty. By the late 1920s he was a member of the university governing board. In 1933–34 he served as university rector and as one of the leaders of the fight to remove Marxist influence and Lombardo Toledano from that institution and its subsidiaries. His prestige and financial expertise won him a place in 1937 as a technical advisor on a United States technical commission to advise Ecuador on monetary problems. In his private career he specialized in corporate law and banking and was especially adept at organizing mixed domestic-foreign capital enterprises such as the Euzkadi (Goodrich) rubber company. Normally, he sat on the board of directors of any enterprise he organized. As an officer of the private Banco de Londres y México, he had extensive capitalist connections. In short, he had the prestige, financial backing, and expertise necessary to organize a political party from the assorted dissidents in the late 1930s.[1]

Gómez Morín was politically ambitious; he wanted to influence Mexican affairs. Because his father was Spanish, he would never be allowed to run for president of Mexico.[2] Since he would never be Mexican president and because he had developed close ties to capitalists during a leftist period, his political influence had waned. He believed, however, that his generation was destined to build a new Mexico and that he should be the leader of a new era.[3] Handsome, self-confident, talented, and smooth, he attracted followers. He admired Salazar of Portugal, another economist who had acquired the power Gómez Morín sought.[4] Initial attempts to organize his own party had failed in 1929 when Vasconcelos had refused to participate.[5] The Cárdenas era gave the necessary impetus.

In late 1938, he began contacting friends to discuss their willingness to aid him in founding a new political party, one which would seek to influence not just the 1940 presidential election but Mexican affairs for the foreseeable future. These friends and their contacts began traversing Mexico, talking to trusted associates and other potential members. By January 1939, they had reached fundamental agreement in such matters as organization, doctrine, strategy, and tactics. In February, they formally constituted themselves in Mexico City as an organizing committee and set up a central office. From February until September, the committee continued membership recruitment and prepared organizational and doctrinal proposals.[6]

Essentially three groups were drawn into the new party. The most important group consisted of Catholic activists, who, in 1933–34, had fought anticlericals in the national university with Gómez Morín; most of UNEC joined the party.[7] Next in importance were professionals and intellectuals who knew the founder from their university days. (Many of the lawyers had been his students.) Finally, leaders of business and industry joined in the hope that Gómez Morín could protect their financial interests without leading them to commit financial or political suicide.[8] The bulk of the founders, however, were young men with university connections. Their idealism combined with respect for an eminent teacher had been their essential motivation.[9] The men who entered for protection of their capital were the smallest number and the least loyal to the party, most of them leaving within the first decade.[10]

An analysis of the National Executive Committee and the National Council suggests the socioeconomic and religious background of the new party. Table 1 shows the occupational distribution of both organizations. Lawyers constituted 31% of the Committee while constituting 37.2% of the Council. Classifying lawyers, engineers, physicians, architects, journalists, teachers, chemists, generals, and university professors as professionals sets the number of professionals on the Committee at 54.8% and 73% on the Council. The significant difference between the two is in the number of bankers, for 24.2% of the more important Committee members were engaged in some form of banking. On the Committee, over one-third were UNEC members while a smaller percentage of UNEC people were on the Council. Over half of all Committee members had been or were Catholic activists, either in UNEC, Catholic Action, or some other lay association.

The significance of the new political grouping lay not only in its middle class and Catholic activist background but also in the experience, prestige, and intellectual capacity of its leadership. On the Council and the Committee were such ex-rectors of the national university as Valentín Gama (also a noted philosopher), Ezequiel A. Chávez, and Dr. Fernando Ocaranza; such ex-directors of university faculties as Mauricio Campos and Trinidad García; and such intellectuals as Agustín Aragón (leading positivist philosopher), Dr. Bernardo Gastelum, Jesús Guiza y Acevedo, and Nemesio García Naranjo, Minister of Public Education and Fine Arts (1913–14) and a leader of the National Museum of Archeology. Many were former government officials. Manuel Bonilla had been Minister of Communication in Madero's cabinet. Toribio Ezquivel Obregón had been a leader in Madero's Anti-Reelectionist

TABLE 1

Occupations of the 1939 National Executive Committee
and National Council

Occupation	Committee		Council	
	Number	%	Number	%
Lawyers	9	31.0	30	37.2
Bankers	7	24.2	5	6.5
Generals	—	——	1	1.3
Physicians	2	6.9	11	14.1
Engineers	—	——	7	9.1
Journalists	4	13.8	3	3.9
Artists	—	——	—	——
Teachers	—	——	6	7.8
Rentiers	1	3.4	—	——
Architects	1	3.4	2	2.6
Cattlemen-Farmers	—	——	2	2.6
Businessmen	4	13.8	3	3.9
Workers	1	3.4	—	——
Employees	—	——	2	2.6
Chemists	—	——	1	1.3
Unknown	—	——	5	6.4
TOTAL	29	99.9	78	99.3

SOURCE: Calderón Vega, *Memorias,* 37–39 lists the members; see Donald J. Mabry, "Acción Nacional: The Institutionalization of an Opposition Party," unpublished Ph.D. dissertation in history (Syracuse University, 1970) p. 45 for a note on biographical sources.

Party until he resigned in 1909, and later served in Huerta's cabinet. Aquiles Elorduy had been a founder of the Anti-Reelectionist Party, had been a Maderist federal deputy, had represented Mexico at the 1928 Pan American Conference in Havana, and had been a government lawyer in oil disputes. Miguel Alessio Robles, one of Obregón's close friends, had served in the Obregón cabinet as Minister of Industry and Commerce, then as ambassador to Spain. By 1939 he was part of the Banco de Londres y México. Dr. Gastelum had been head of the public health department, subsecretary of education, and a diplomat to Italy and Uruguay. Private enterprise was represented on these directive bodies by Juan B. Amezcua, a financier, Emilio Cerví of the Banco Mexicano, Manuel F. Escandón of the Banco de Comercio, Miguel Estrada Iturbide of General Hipotecaria, and Carlos Novoa of the Banco Industrial. Novoa was also general manager of the Mexican Bankers'

Association from 1937 to 1941. Bernardo Elosúa, wealthy owner of a Monterrey brick factory, Ernesto Robles León, later director of Bacardí, Antonio L. Rodríguez, Monterrey financier and industrialist, Joaquín Casasús, founder of many banks and credit societies, and Roberto Cossío y Cosío, lawyer for chambers of commerce, completed the list of notable entrepreneurs.[11]

Catholicism was more important than property interests for recruitment and party activity. Monterrey industrialists and Mexican Employers' Confederation members were interested in a paternalistic Catholic welfare doctrine and their religious beliefs were probably as important as their fear of radicalism.[12] Moreover, only some capitalists entered PAN; more supported Almazán. It was possible to be both an ardent defender of Church causes and a capitalist. Efraín González Luna, the other principal founder of PAN is an example.

Efraín González Luna was almost as important as Gómez Morín as a PAN founder for he not only recruited members from his native Jalisco, a traditionally Catholic state with a large industrial base, but also became the party's principal ideologist. Born in 1898 in Jalisco to a very devout family, he had been educated in Catholic schools but received his law degree from a public law school. In 1916, Anacleto González Flores, later a principal *cristero* leader, took González Luna to a meeting of the Leo XIII Circle where he learned the teachings of *Rerum Novarum* and converted to a Christian-socialist viewpoint. The Circle became the Jalisco chapter of the ACJM and González Luna served as its diocesan president. He refused to join the *cristero* rebellion when invited by González Flores because he disagreed with violence as a tactic, but he remained a supporter of his friend. He had too much to lose by going into rebellion against the government for he had married into an important Guadalajara family and had become a prominent lawyer. In addition to law, he founded the employers' center in Guadalajara and was one of the stockholders of that city's Banco Capitalizador. Religion was his primary interest, however. His leadership in Mexican Catholic circles enabled him to serve Acción Nacional for he remained a force in Catholic Action. Recognition of his activities came in 1942 when he cochaired a panel with his friend Jacques Maritain as a meeting of the National Catholic Welfare Conference.[13]

Militant Catholics such as González Luna clearly controlled the new party. The principal authors of the neo-Thomistic *Principles of Doctrine* were the Catholic intellectuals González Luna, Miguel Estrada Iturbide, and Rafael Preciado Hernández, as well as Gómez Morín who was sympathetic to Catholic doctrine.[14] Moreover, although the official version asserts that the party name was meant to convey the idea of political action on a national scale instead of localized debate among intellectuals, the name probably had a Catholic origin.[15] The similarity between *Acción Católica* and Acción Nacional was too coincidental in light of the high percentage of Catholic activists. Another possibility suggested by a semiofficial source is that the name, but not the doctrine, was borrowed from *Action Française*.[16] Of the names considered, at least half reflected Catholic thought: National Corporatist Union, Social Democracy, Christian Democratic Front, Syndicalism, and Mexican Falange (in the sense of the Chilean Falange, a forerunner to that country's Christian Democratic party).[17]

PAN could not identify itself as a Catholic party for several reasons. Mexican law forbade the use of religious symbols or names in politics. Identification of the party with the Church would bring attacks from anticlericalists. Besides some devout members did not want ecclesiastical political involvement. Other coalition members, uninterested in pursuing clerical ends, would defect. Acción Nacional could ill afford to lose any of its small membership. The crisis seemed too great for PAN leaders to allow the party to be identified with particularist ends while trying to present it as a reasonable alternative to the Revolutionary group.

The divergent goals of the initial PAN membership manifested themselves immediately. After the first assembly had formally ratified the decisions of the organizing committee, it became a political convention to discuss PAN's posture vis-à-vis the upcoming federal elections. Gómez Morín, speaking for the committee, stated the basic choice—participation which would include supporting a presidential candidate and proselytizing or abstention with efforts directed towards membership recruitment and citizen education with PAN principles.[18] The only candidate that the convention would seriously consider supporting was Almazán, for he was the only nongovernment candidate who had any chance.[19] Gómez Morín, accompanied by other party founders, had interviewed Almazán before the convention but had left the interview unfavorably impressed.[20] The majority of the organizing committee, including Gómez Morín, preferred not to support a candidate rather than back Almazán, but the decision was thrown open to floor debate.[21] Because he wanted an open convention and realized that any attempts to impose a decision would split the party, Gómez Morín hid his personal feelings. The antiparticipation forces were led, however, by González Luna, a clear sign that the principal founders were opposed to political participation so soon.[22] When it became apparent that convention opinion favored supporting Almazán, Gómez Morín suggested running González Luna as a token candidate, but, after further debate, the convention voted eighty-nine to forty to participate.[23] Almazán would not be the PAN candidate, but

PAN would support him as long as he accepted Acción Nacional principles. If he deserted the people to seek only his own interests, PAN would desert him. He was being supported because the convention was anxious for political participation and he was the only serious opposition candidate.[24]

During the 1940 campaign itself, PAN did withdraw most of its support for Almazán except in northern Mexico. Instead, party leaders used the campaign to recruit members and spread ideas.[25] Years later, Almazán complained that PAN had betrayed him, asserting that its leaders were in collusion with Cárdenas, with the Archbishop of Mexico, and with Josephus Daniels, United States ambassador to Mexico, to prevent the candidate's election.[26]

Tying the infant party to the Almazán candidacy was a mistake for which PAN would pay for years. PAN was claiming that it was a democratic party interested in social reform within a capitalist framework and that it was fighting against personalism and violence in politics by peaceful political participation and citizen education. Almazán, however, was a reactionary adventurer whose followers threatened a coup d'état if their candidate lost. Some of PAN's initial membership shared Almazán's views, and had joined PAN in the hope of placing their man in the Mexican presidency. Other early members became disillusioned with the rapidity with which PAN had swung behind such a candidate. When the election was over and it was clear that Avila Camacho was the next Mexican president, PAN membership rapidly declined.[27] Lost were not only members but some of PAN's financial backing.[28] Although PAN's gains from participation included a few new members, more public notice, and some bitter experience, the acquisition of a negative public image outweighed these meager gains.

The Almazán episode was illustrative of the problems faced by Acción Nacional in its first decade. Its leaders were political novices; more sophisticated politicians would have realized the dangers of such a campaign and avoided it. The desire and perhaps expectation to change Mexico immediately had been met with violence, death, and disillusionment. PAN was not even the largest group backing Almazán—it could not present itself as a real threat to the government. In fact, PAN's resources were youth, intellectuality, and zeal, not numbers or money. Gómez Morín had recognized reality and had been trying to lead the party into a long-range plan for the conquest of power,[29] but the Almazán partisans and political idealists had opted for participation. After that experience PAN concentrated upon using its intellectual resources to present polemics and position papers to the Mexican public, choosing to participate in elections only where it had some hope of winning. The

Almazán affair had shown the party how weak it really was and where its strength lay.

PAN had also chosen other forms of political activity. Candidates were presented in a few municipal elections in 1940 and thereafter; the party was too weak to offer federal deputy or senatorial candidates.[30] In April, 1940, the second national convention met in Mexico City to adopt the *Minimum Program of Political Action,* a more specific document than the *Principles.*[31] Beginning in 1940, the party began the long series of seminars, study groups, interregional conventions to prepare specific positions on such issues as the *municipio,* small property, agricultural development, political reform, religious persecution, and the national railway system.[32] In the first half of the decade, PAN members were also active in demonstrations against constitutional Article 3, usually in alliance with the UNS or the National Parents' Union.[33]

Party leaders recognized that PAN could neither win electoral majorities nor attain power by violence, so they sought to influence Mexican decision-makers. The basic strategy was simple: PAN would use its intellectual resources to educate Mexico to the PAN viewpoint while arguing that popular participation in decision-making was the only salvation of the country. In the long run, PAN hoped to create enough popular support to reach positions of power while in the short run it hoped to offer alternative policies to the ruling elite.[34] Tactically, PAN put pressure on the government with publications, demonstrations, selective electoral participation, and specific alliances with other groups, such as the anti-Article 3 campaigns or with citizen groups in municipal elections.[35] Acquisition of power was the PAN goal, not intellectual debate, but Mexicans first had to believe that PAN was a loyal opposition party interested in their welfare.[36]

PAN's loyalty was impugned not only by its early association with Almazán but also by its attitudes towards the Second World War, Franco, fascism, and communism.[37] PAN leadership was vehemently anticommunist, tending to see more communist influence in Mexico than in fact existed.[38] Moreover, PAN leaders initially supported the Franco take-over in Spain as the salvation of Spanish Catholicism and culture while a few leading *panistas* were outspoken profascist or procorporate state.[39] Both PAN and the authoritarian regimes of Salazar, Franco, Vargas, and Perón (after 1943) showed a common corporate ideology. All condemned the United States capitalistic penetration of Latin America. In the first three and one-half years of its history, PAN had advocated Mexican neutrality, a posture which favored European rightist powers.[40] Moreover, PAN's rejection of what it considered to be the exaggerated Indianism of the Revolution could be tied to German racism.[41] Leftists saw this combination as ample reason to tag the party as reactionary, fascist, and counterrevolutionary.[42]

In fact, Acción Nacional was trying to steer Mexico onto an independent nationalist course, one which adamantly rejected the major competing ideologies of the war years. It saw Mexico as a mestizo, Catholic nation that should use democratic procedures and capitalism mitigated by welfare measures.[43] The Mexican nationality, in its view, had developed gradually from the process of *mestizaje* and Catholic culture. For most of Mexico's history the greatest threat to this nationality had been United States armed intervention, cultural penetration, and economic expansion. Many Mexicans, therefore, feared the United States, an attitude on which the Axis unsuccessfully had tried to capitalize. PAN argued that Mexico should reverse the spread of American influence in Mexico and avoid being a satellite. Hence, Franco's attempts to counter Pan-Americanism with *Hispanidad,* the emphasis upon Spanish culture, appealed to *panistas.* PAN made a distinction between valuing Mexico's Spanish cultural heritage and Franco's attempts to regain Spain's former colonies, asserting that Mexico was both Indian and Spanish, each being of equal value, a position unacceptable to Franco. Equally important, PAN condemned both rightwing authoritarianism and Pan-Americanism, the latter for being an attempt to extend bourgeois capitalism and American influence throughout the hemisphere. On the left, PAN condemned communism as an alien, atheistic, and materialistic doctrine which sought to destroy tradition, religion, and individual rights and to dominate the world. Faced with threats from a hostile world, Mexico should adopt a course of action which would preserve Mexican uniqueness and independence. With regard to the current war, Mexico should remain aloof to avoid combat with belligerent powers and to exploit economically a neutralist's advantages.[44]

Once Mexico entered the war on the Allied side, however, PAN dropped its neutrality in favor of public support for the war effort.[45] This was not a reversal of policy, for as early as 1939, PAN had argued that if the United States entered the war, Mexico should enter on her side.[46] In fact, even before Pearl Harbor changed the political climate, *La Nación* had stated that any other position would be suicidal, criminal, and unpatriotic. PAN had not wanted the defeat of the United States but an end to its dominance of Mexico.[47]

Support for the war was never fervent because PAN believed that the Mexican government was too willing to allow the country to be exploited by the United States. One reason for PAN support of the Mexican declaration of war had been fear that the United States would intervene militarily, a fear purportedly encouraged by President Avila Camacho.[48] Mexican governmental actions seemed to favor the United States more than Mexico. The *bracero* program (the exportation of Mexican agricultural laborers to the United States) was an especially sore point, for it pointed up Mexican weaknesses. PAN saw the program as proof that Mexico had failed to solve its agricultural and employment problems. PAN preferred that the Mexican government pressure the United States to expand agricultural development in Mexico. PAN also saw evidence that Mexican *braceros* were being exploited by the racist United States with the connivance of the Mexican government. United States abuses in treaty arrangements on housing, wages, and protection were publicized, accompanied by attacks on the Mexican government for failing to protect its citizens. PAN had also fought enlargement of the Mexican army by conscription, fearing in part that the army would be used against domestic opposition. When the Mexican government agreed to send armed forces abroad and to allow Mexican nationals to enlist or be drafted into the United States armed forces, PAN was furious. Additional proof that Mexico had become the lackey of the United States, according to PAN, was Mexico's failure to press settlement of the *El Chamizal* controversy, the boundary dispute created by the meanderings of the Rio Grande river between El Paso, Texas, and Ciudad Juárez. In short, PAN believed that Mexico was failing to reap the maximum harvest from Mexican aid to the United States.[49]

PAN-Mexican governmental relations were much better, however, than such attacks suggest. It was customary for opposition groups to attack the government as corrupt and antidemocratic. Relations between the party and President Avila Camacho were good, for the moderate, self-professed Catholic sought national unity. During his term the socialist education requirements of constitutional Article 3 were removed and the leftist Minister of Education was replaced by a moderate conservative. Supreme Court appointees, including PAN founder Olea y Leyva, were more conservative.[50] According to PAN sources, Avila Camacho, in the interest of national unity, had offered a cabinet post to several PAN founders.[51] Most important, he gave tacit recognition to PAN, guaranteeing its right to participate even though its registration could be canceled at will.

In spite of PAN's assertions about the authoritarian character of Mexico, the party did participate, albeit unsuccessfully, in the 1943 federal deputy elections during the height of the war. Meeting in May 1943, the third national convention voted forty-nine to thirty-one to participate. González Luna led the antiparticipation forces, probably indicating that the leadership did not want to participate, but equally prominent leaders spoke in favor of participation. The arguments advanced in the debate typify the basic tactical split which has existed throughout PAN history: whether PAN should legitimize what it considered a corrupt political system by participation or whether it should abstain as a sign of contempt for fraud. Partisans of participation argued that the party would be inconsistent to urge citizen participation while it would not participate itself and that the campaign would facilitate citizen education. In 1943, they also stressed participation as a patriotic duty that might bring recognition of triumphs as Mexico tried to export a democratic image. Antiparticipation forces countered that PAN would be playing the government's game, allowing it to assert that Mexico was democratic when it was not. Once the decision was made, however, the party closed ranks.[52]

The election was an almost complete failure. The leadership could find only twenty-one candidates and ran a poorly organized campaign, garnering only 21,000 votes.[53] PAN claimed that fraud had deprived the party of the few seats it had won, but it is unlikely that any of its candidates had won.[54]

The Avila Camacho period of PAN history served as training for the young party. Although the 1940 and 1943 elections were disastrous in terms of electoral victory, the party had begun to learn how to operate in elections, its members were gaining experience and public exposure, and the party had proved that it was neither disloyal nor transient.[55]

The 1946 federal elections became a turning point in PAN history. With the selection of the pro-private enterprise Miguel Alemán as the government party candidate, capitalists began leaving PAN in even greater numbers, freeing the Catholic militants to assert their brand of social reform more strongly.[56] The Alemán candidacy and the end of the war softened the procapitalist, profascist charges often leveled against PAN. The party broadened its scope by adopting the national unity tactic, trying to run a moderate Revolutionary as its presidential candidate and establishing an alliance with a branch of the UNS. Finally, four PAN candidates took office as federal deputies.

When PAN met in February, 1946, in its fourth national convention to consider participation, the main presidential contenders had already been chosen. Alemán, the government candidate, was to face Ezequiel Padilla, erstwhile PRI member and, until the election campaign, Minister of Foreign Relations.[57] PAN's choices were limited to supporting one of the two, abstaining, or running its own candidate. Neither candidate was acceptable: Alemán because he was part of the ruling clique and Padilla because he was part of the clique and too pro-American.[58]

The convention chose to offer its own candidate, a man who it believed could unify the country and lend prestige to PAN's activity. Many members were anxious to join the political fray, believing that the party was too intellectual in its approach.[59] The political commission recommended participation with a national unity candidate, even though it believed that the election would be fraudulent, because:

> Acción Nacional ought to carry its barricades against the conservatism and demagoguery of the Regime . . . We have already proclaimed . . . the civic duty, and this is being fulfilled; now we should make a call so that the people of Mexico will comply with their duties of Social Justice.[60]

Before accepting the commission report, the convention deliberated as to who might be such a candidate. PAN leaders Preciado Hernández, Aquiles Elorduy, and González Luna were quickly suggested. González Luna temporarily stopped the convention by nominating Luis Cabrera as the best possible candidate. Cabrera, although conservative by 1946 standards, had been an adviser to Carranza and subsequent Revolutionary governments. González Luna argued that Cabrera could end the divisiveness which was disrupting Mexico. Neither PAN nor Cabrera were in complete agreement, he said, but PAN should nominate him as an example that national interest should supersede partisan interest. After a two-hour recess delegates then suggested three more PAN leaders as well as Padilla, Octavio Véjar Vásquez, Minister of Education, and Miguel Henríquez Guzmán, a PRI dissident. The issue had already been decided before the necessary three votes were taken; 155–13 to participate, 162–6 to participate with a national unity candidate, and 153–2 for Cabrera, with two abstentions.[61]

Cabrera foiled the tactic by refusing the nomination. Appearing before the convention on February 5, he announced that it was the highest honor ever bestowed upon him, but that he was too old and had too many enemies to do the job. PAN could accomplish its purpose by nominating one of its own, even an unknown. Undaunted, the convention refused to nominate another candidate, resolving to pressure Cabrera to accept. Until his final refusal in May, Cabrera was besieged by pleas from state and district nominating conventions.[62]

The national unity tactic also adopted for senatorial and federal deputy elections met with more success. By allying with Popular Force, the UNS political party, as well as with prominent PAN sympathizers,[63] the party was able to elect four federal deputies. The addition of non-PAN votes appears to have made the difference between the 1943 election and the 1946 election. Three of the victorious candidates were from central Mexico, the principal area of collaboration.[64] The selection of Antonio L. Rodríquez of Monterrey as a federal deputy probably represented both PAN strength and a concession to the industrialists there. Aquiles Elorduy, representing Aguascalientes city, was a popular Revolutionary. Miguel Ramírez Munguía from Tacambaro, Michoacán, and Juan Gutiérrez Lascuráin, from the Federal District, were Catholic militants.[65] Popular Force also gained a seat in the chamber.[66]

Acción Nacional–Popular Force cooperation did not represent a religiously based alliance but was rather a common recognition of weakness. Popular Force was a splinter movement of UNS, only recently organized, and anxious about government reaction to its participation. PAN was stronger, but it was still a minority party with limited membership. They shared the common ground of agreeing that religious persecution, as they saw it, should end and that Mexico should be ruled by Catholic social doctrine. PAN was basically secular in its approach, however, whereas Popular Force was religious. In the preelectoral national convention, Miguel Estrada Iturbide had beaten down an attempt to attack constitutional Article 130, the heart of anticlericalism in the Constitution, because PAN was not a clerical party.[67] In fact, PAN campaign appeals, based on its *Minimum Program,* called for political democracy, social reform, and the end of governmental policies producing such evils as inflation and labor corruption.[68]

PAN's legislative program in the 1946–49 sessions of the Chamber of Deputies was political and economic; no bills were presented to end anticlericalism nor to serve clerical interests. Instead, PAN sought to democratize Mexico politically and to resolve immediate and long-standing economic problems. All the bills had been foreshadowed by party propaganda since 1939 and represented the basic thrust of PAN's discontent with Mexican conditions.

Politically, PAN deputies unsuccessfully proposed to grant suffrage to women in municipal elections, to institutionalize party politics, to insure impartial elections, and to strengthen municipal government. The December 1946 PAN female suffrage bill was sent to committee while the Mexican presidential proposal was passed.[69] Legislation requiring political parties to be three years old before they could participate in elections, to be financially independent of the government, and to have voluntary, individual membership instead of compulsory, group members such as PRI had was introduced in the Chamber of Deputies.[70] Impartiality in elections would be guaranteed by an independent federal election tribune and the intervention of the Supreme Court in electoral disputes. The Supreme Court would select two of its own members, two of five names from a list proportioned among political parties, and one from a list of notaries public. Members would have the rank and privileges of Supreme Court justices. While members of the tribune, Court justices would leave the bench. Other members could not have held governmental posts higher than the municipal level for the prior five years. Party members would be thirty-five to sixty-five years old and of recognized integrity. The tribune would convene fifteen to thirty days before an election, have access to police powers, publicly announce the electoral results which it had compiled, and dissolve after completing its functions. The entire Supreme Court would be given clear constitutional authority to adjudicate electoral disputes.[71] Finally, municipal government would be strengthened by: (1) giving it control of its finances and a share of state and federal tax revenue it generated; (2) removing governmental agencies between it and state government; (3) instituting permanent voter registration, referendum, recall, initiative, and adjudication of electoral disputes; (4) requiring public accountability; (5) prohibiting municipal governmental participation in state or federal electoral processes; and (6) expanding popular participation in decision-making. The last reform would convert *municipios* with less than 2,000 inhabitants into open councils; larger *municipios* would have a council elected by direct popular election with minority party representation. All of these proposals died in committee.[72] For PRI to have passed any of them would have been politically unwise since Acción Nacional would have been encouraged and PRI could always pass the more valuable proposals under its own label whenever it wished.

A somewhat different proposal was its effort to institute a law of responsibilities for government employees. Upon entering and leaving office, such employees would have to divulge their personal finances. Moreover, these officials would be liable to criminal prosecution if audits revealed peculation.[73] The PAN bill was rejected but a similar law was passed by PRI in 1952 in the face of public disgust with widespread financial corruption in the Alemán government.

The economic bills were designed to solve immediate and future problems in the realms of transportation, monetary policy, governmental enterprises, agriculture, labor, and social security by fixing responsibility, broadening participation in decision-making, instituting selected planning, and fomenting development. In all cases the state was to be active but not unilateral in its actions. PAN proposals represented neither laissez faire nor statism.

Since 1939, PAN had been arguing that the problem of rural areas was the most serious and pressing; the 1948 program of action sought to effect a permanent remedy. The key proposal was a national planning commission for the countryside, recruited from all concerned sectors, which would inventory national resources and institute action to end deficiencies. Specifically, production would be increased by granting legal title instead of usufruct rights to *ejidatarios*, granting the writ of *amparo* (an injunction to block government action) to all agriculturalists, and by extending technical assistance, cheap, easy credit (both public and private), and small irrigation works. The Rockefeller Foundation's successful seed improvement in Mexico would be copied by a proposed national seed service. Monopolies in trucking, especially in the transportation of agricultural products, would be forbidden. To raise rural living conditions further, the broad social security system would be extended into rural areas.[74]

PAN had proposed universal social security in 1939, had supported the 1943 law instituting a partial system, and had criticized the system since then as being too narrow and politically operated. Now, the party proposed that the system be converted into a decentralized agency operated by technicians for all Mexico.[75]

Decentralized agencies and state-participation enterprises were to be brought under public scrutiny. A list of these institutions would be published semiannually so that the public could know which ones existed. Further, each one had to render public accounts annually. Existing institutions would be investigated to determine their soundness and integrity.[76]

The monetary system would come under greater governmental regulation to curtail inflation and prevent harmful manipulation. The government's Banco de Mexico would be restricted to regulating currency and emitting soundly backed money to public enterprises. The stock market and credit institutions would be watched to prevent fraud and damage to the economy.[77]

On the other hand, government-labor control of railroads would be decreased with the institution of a nine–man mixed national railway commission. The Mexican president would appoint five men for five-year terms. CONCANACO and CONCAMIN would each appoint a man for an indefinite term. Labor would appoint two representatives for an indefinite term. All members would also have alternates. Since the balance of power would always be with the government appointees, neither labor nor capital was assured control. The commission would have full authority and responsibility to rebuild the system, extend it, and increase its efficiency. PAN believed that this could be done without rate increases because the existing problems resulted from bad management, lack of planning, and labor-management conflicts resulting in part from labor union control of the railways since Cárdenas.[78]

Although the party had an antilabor reputation, its labor bills were designed to increase labor's power by making it more effective as an economic interest group. Internally, unions would be required to be democratic and leaders would be made responsible to the membership. Unions would be forbidden to join political parties, but individual members could affiliate. The unions, however, were to be forbidden to discriminate among members on the basis of political activity. Strikes in essential public services were to be prohibited.[79]

The 1946–49 PAN legislative program was neither clerical, reactionary, nor conservative. Although CONCANACO and CONCAMIN had proposed similar railway legislation,[80] the PAN proposal insured that the government, which might be prolabor, would have the decisive votes. The party's other proposals would decrease the economic and political power of conservative sectors. The absence of proclerical legislative proposals indicated that PAN had not been organized to fight for ecclesiastical interests.

Nevertheless, the party retained its clerical image. Aquiles Elorduy, an atheist, withdrew from PAN because some *panistas* criticized his outspoken anticlericalism.[81] In addition, some *panistas* participated in anti-Article 3 municipal campaigns in Michoacán and Guanajuato in alliance with Popular Force.[82] *La Nación,* PAN's organ, continually blasted the Article as communist-inspired.[83] Prominent party leaders such as José González Torres served as Catholic lay leaders.[84] In 1946, Rafael Caldera, Venezuelan Christian Democratic leader, visited PAN to exchange ideas.[85] In fact, the two parties supported each other in their respective magazines.[86] When leftists attacked PAN's Catholic ideology as a new fascism because of its Catholic leanings, the clerical image was buttressed.[87]

The important result of PAN's entry into the Chamber of Deputies and its subsequent legislative program was that the party gained public recognition of its legitimacy, thereby encouraging it to continue and to participate in the 1949 federal deputy elections. After a short debate, the February 1949 convention unanimously approved participation.[88] The campaign platform was essentially the same as that of 1946 with the addition of a call for the end of PRI as an "official" party and the enfranchisement of women at the federal level. Campaign appeals were based upon the platform and the legislative program.[89] Popular Force, having lost its registration, supported PAN candidates, especially in Jalisco and Michoacán.[90] For a short time PAN was optimistic that the lean years were over, but, before the election was concluded, it declared them fraudulent and appealed for Supreme Court intervention.[91]

Irrespective of any possible fraud, PAN benefited from the election. The government recognized 600,000 votes for PAN. In the Federal District PAN won 31 percent of the votes.[92] Four PAN candidates entered the Chamber of Deputies: Eduardo Facha Gutiérrez of the Federal District, Jaime Robles y Martín del Campo of Jalisco, Gonzalo Chapela y B. of Michoacán, and Juan José Hinojosa of Nuevo León.[93] Even though four victories out of sixty-nine candidates in twenty-three districts represented a smaller percentage of victory than in 1946, PAN had managed to keep representation, even in a nonpresidential election year.[94] Gómez Morín praised the membership for what he considered a successful campaign.[95]

The second half of the 1940s also brought the first municipal and state legislature victories. In 1947, PAN won its first municipal council seat in Acámbaro, Guanajuato. In the same year, it also won the *municipio* of Huajuapan del León, Oaxaca; captured a seat in the Michoacán state legislature; and prevented the PRI candidate from occupying the municipal presidency of Quiroga, Michoacán, when he declared the election a fraud and then joined PAN.[96]

By February 1949, Gómez Morín had enough confidence in the party's future that he could announce his retirement as its president so that a younger man could take over. Because party leaders feared that a preelection resignation by the founder would be misinterpreted, he delayed his retirement until September when he relinguished the office to his successor, Juan Gutiérrez Lascuráin.[97]

In his last speech as PAN president, Gómez Morín assessed the role of Acción Nacional in its first ten years of life and suggested its future course. He admitted that not many electoral positions had been gained, the party's primary goal, but he believed that it had proven that a loyal, democratic party could exist. It had encouraged and obtained greater popular political participation and shown that politics was a legitimate concern for honorable men, that they could participate without being corrupted.[98] The task of the party in the future was the same as it had been in 1939: "it had to move the souls" to make a better Mexico.[99]

In summary, by 1949 Acción Nacional had accomplished the two tasks essential to its continued existence: self-definition and governmental acceptance. Originally an anti-Cardenist coalition of business–industrial leaders, of members of the liberal professions, and of young, university-trained Catholic activists, party leaders through their actions defined PAN as a secular, independent, loyal, and Mexican political alternative to the Revolution. As a party, the members were more interested in influencing Mexico to follow paths consistent with Catholic reform philosophy than in defending the privileges of Catholicism or capitalism. The thrust of PAN's first legislative program combined with the absence of proclerical activity on the part of the party support this interpretation. Governmental acceptance of the party in its early years was related to the composition of the coalition. Since it was led by Gómez Morín, who circulated among the higher echelons of Mexican elites, and since many of its leaders were or had been prominent intellectuals, capitalists, and politicians, its importance and influence were greater than the party's sheer numbers might suggest. Ultimately, however, its continued existence was dependent upon the government's deciding that PAN served a useful function. Not only governmental acceptance but encouragement came in 1946 when PAN was awarded four federal deputy seats. By this action, the government publicly acknowledged PAN as a legitimate and respectable political organization. The party was further encouraged by recognition of victories at the state and local levels and by winning four more seats in Congress in 1949. PAN had proven to be a loyal but nonthreatening opposition during a time when Mexico was interested in exporting a democratic image. Once definition and acceptance had been achieved, Gómez Morín could relinguish the party presidency to a young man and argue, as he later told this author, that PAN had demonstrated that Mexican political parties could be based on ideas and not personalism.

CHAPTER IV

Catholic Militancy, 1949–1962

By recruiting prestigious and influential members as well as by carefully avoiding disloyal actions during the war years, Gómez Morín left the PAN presidency satisfied that his party had gained access to the Chamber of Deputies and a few other minor public offices and was the only legally recognized permanent opposition party, but his first three successors were lesser men; they changed the character of the coalition and adopted new tactics which eventually rent PAN with profound factionalism and possible cancellation of its registration. Gómez Morín was a politician who had been an active participant in politics for over thirty years, during which time he had come to know Revolutionary leaders well. He was a secular man though sympathetic to Catholicism. His successors, on the other hand, had no political experience outside of their PAN activity or Catholic lay associations, and this proved to be a severe handicap in their quest for a dynamic and productive tactical combination to advance PAN's welfare. As a result, Acción Nacional increasingly became identified as a militant Catholic party instead of as a national, secular party as Gómez Morín had intended.

The character of the three presidents partially explains this shift. Juan Gutiérrez Lascuráin (1949–56), an engineer, was born in 1911 and joined PAN only six years before becoming its president. A federal deputy for the 1946–49 congressional term, his only other political experience had been in the ACJM and the Union of Mexican Catholics. *Panistas* respected his intellectual ability and dedication but criticized his lack of charisma and drive.[1] Anyone would have appeared grey in contrast to Gómez Morín, but Gutiérrez Lascuráin's inadequacy was more fundamental. He was a follower, a trait which made him acceptable to Gómez Morín but which would allow him to lose important financial support, to tie PAN to the Church and UNS, and, finally, to be replaced by a more dynamic successor.

Alfonso Ituarte Servín (1956–59) encouraged the development of uncompromising political Catholicism which the party's important youth sector was pressing upon it. His training as an accountant and his prosperous wine business were secondary to his long-standing partisanship in favor of the Catholic Church. His career as an ardent proponent of Church rights and privileges began in 1926 when as a twelve-year-old student he saw his parochial school closed by Calle's anticlericalism. As he matured, he increased his efforts on behalf of the Church, founding two Catholic Action groups in the Tacubaya suburb of Mexico City, fighting in the League in the 1930s, and joining the Pro-Liberty of Teaching Association in its fight against sexual education. When he reached thirty-five, he moved from the ACJM to the Union of Mexican Catholics, serving as diocesan secretary and then as president (1953–55). As with the young Gutiérrez Lascuráin, his political experience consisted of PAN politics and a term as a federal deputy (1952–55), but, unlike his predecessor, the greying Ituarte Servín was aggressive and committed. But, when his leadership created a PAN–governmental crisis and heated intraparty debate, he failed to control the situation, yielding power to his secretary-general.

The ascetic, deeply religious ex-Jesuit seminarian José González Torres (1959–62) tried to save Mexico with Christian Democracy. As the son of a prosperous Michoacán ranching family, he was educated by Marist Brothers and Jesuits until he left the seminary to take a law degree from the national university in 1945, graduating at the age of twenty-six. Rafael Preciado Hernández and Manuel Ulloa Ortiz, two of his law professors, recruited him into PAN in 1943, but he devoted most of his energies to Catholic lay activities. He had entered ACJM in 1934 and served as president of its central committee from 1944 to 1949. From 1947 to 1949 he was president of *Pax Romana,* international university Catholic Action. Next, he served as president of Mexican Catholic Action from 1949 to 1952. In recognition of his services, Pope Pius XII made him a Knight of the Order of St. Gregory and of the Order of the Holy Sepulcher. Listing such extensive involvement with Catholicism fails to capture the man's religious intensity. Tall, strong, with an eloquent booming voice, González Torres exudes authority and commands respect, traits augmented by his serious personality and somber dress with his customary use of black clothes, reminding one more of a cleric than a politician.

The trend towards closer identification of PAN with political Catholicism brought a concurrent shift in the composition of the coalition. Each president recruited members who supported his position to the point that the religiosity of the González Torres presidency alienated secularly oriented *panistas,* causing some to curtail or cease party activity. Related to this phenomenon was the departure of almost all of the major capitalists within the party. Some had left in the 1940s when it became clear that the Revolutionary government would preserve capitalism. The probusiness policies of Miguel Alemán (1946–52) stimulated a general desertion. The high point of capitalist influence in PAN was 1949. As a favor to Gómez Morín and González Luna, important capitalists supported the latter's bid for the Mexican presidency in 1952, but PAN had ceased to represent their interests much earlier, and, as PAN altered its image, these capitalists feared being embroiled in a potential Church-State conflict. So, as the result of external and internal factors, PAN lost the financial support necessary for significant electoral success.[2]

Inspired by the Church's concern for social justice and their mutual fear of communism in the Cold War era, PAN stepped up its anti-laissez-faire capitalist campaign, a move facilitated by the loss of capitalist support. In PAN's 1950 national convention the party called for the institution of profit-sharing for workers in Mexican industry, a demand reiterated in the 1953 convention and thereafter. According to these conventions, labor was to be aided further by family salaries and protections against government, capitalists, and corrupt labor leaders. Gutiérrez Lascuráin clarified PAN's decreasing dependence upon important entrepreneurs by lashing out at the rich and at governmental favoritism towards them.[3] Not surprisingly, the Church's public pronouncements were identical. Both institutions saw the world's future as either Catholic social justice or communism.[4]

Acción Nacional leaders normally cooperated with ecclesiastical programs as private individuals, but the party went a step further in 1951. Unlike joint anti–Article 3 campaigns with the National Parents' Union, technically a voluntary secular association, or having PAN leader Juan Landerreche Obregón's *Anticonstitucionalidad del Artículo Tercero* used as a basic text by a Jesuit in an article for the mass-circulation *Mañana, panista* involvement in the Guadalajara Diocesan Peasant Convention of April 1951 was so extensive as to warrant calling it a jointly sponsored meeting.[5] This may only reflect the initiative of the diocesan clergy and *panistas* in Jalisco, but it was certainly indicative of the new trend within PAN, since it was a reversal of party policy.

If any doubt still remained as to PAN's shift towards clericalism, its expanded cooperation with the fanatically religious UNS dispelled it. Such an alliance had occurred in 1946 and UNS had supported PAN candidates in 1949. Beginning in 1951, however, the two organizations moved towards formal alliance. Both groups needed each other: UNS because it had lost its registration as the Popular Force political party in 1949 and PAN because it needed to augment its numbers, especially to extend its activities into the countryside where UNS had influence. The problem of their divergent goals was suppressed in favor of their common commitment to Catholicism. UNS sent observers to the November 1951 PAN national convention and agreed in January 1952 to support the González Luna presidential bid. By July 1952 numerous *sinarquistas* were running for office under the PAN label. Even though none of the *sinarquistas* were elected, the religious propensities of the new PAN deputies were sufficient as a reward. Cooperation between the two continued in the 1953 Baja California state gubernatorial campaign, the 1952 Jalisco state campaign, and in PAN lawyers securing the release from jail of Juan Ignacio Padilla, UNS president. In 1955, UNS reversed an earlier announcement and agreed in late April to support PAN candidates in that year's federal deputy elections. The success of this joint venture, a success which aided PAN more than UNS, led to the signing of a formal alliance in 1956 to work together for the common good of Mexico while each retained its autonomy. The UNS was tiring of this one-sided arrangement, however, and soon withdrew.[6]

The abrupt end of formal UNS support for PAN is one hallmark of the latter's growing strength and respectability. The UNS had originally been the stronger and larger of the two, but the 1944–45 split had considerably weakened it. PAN's involvement with UNS had primarily been with Popular Force, the political activists who were the more progressive *sinarquistas*. *Sinarquistas* had been defecting to Acción Nacional since it was founded, a movement stepped up by the great UNS split and the cancellation of Popular Force registration. *Sinarquismo* was a dying movement and the attempt at political alliance had only aided its rival, PAN.

However, it was the 1952 federal election campaign, a strictly secular effort on PAN's part, that solidified PAN's popular image as a Catholic party. In its November 1951 national convention the party had overwhelmingly selected Efraín González Luna, Catholic lay leader and intellectual, as its presidential candidate over the more secular Roberto Cossío y Cosío, PAN secretary-general under Gómez Morín, and Antonio L. Rodríguez, Monterrey financier.[7] González Luna had suggested to the National Council in September 1951 that the convention date be changed from its customary January meeting to November so that a presidential candidate could be nominated.[8] The platform adopted in this convention, a call for political democracy and social justice based on contemporary progressive Catholic thought but without using religious symbolism or nomenclature, was sufficiently secular for the leading Mexico City daily, *Excélsior,* to commend it to PRI.[9] The combination of González Luna's fame as a Catholic leader and UNS support convinced many Mexicans that PAN was a stalking horse for the Church. In addition, several instances during the campaign strengthened this belief. José González Torres, speaking as a Catholic Action leader, called for all Catholics to vote for candidates who would help Catholicism, a thinly veiled plea to vote for PAN. When a "Catholic Front of the Federal District" attacked González Luna in June as a betrayer of the Church and Anacleto González Flores, martyred *cristero* leader, during the *cristero* rebellion of the 1920s, Catholic Action rose to the candidate's defense, although the Church claimed that it supported no one in the campaign. PAN's principal support from organized labor during the campaign came from the National Front of Workers, a Catholic labor union led by *panista* Jacinto Guadalupe Silva, who was also ex-president of the diocesan council of Catholic Action Workers and ex-national subchief of the workers' section of ACJM.[10] Finally, three of the five new PAN federal deputies were known for their Catholic militancy.[11]

Ironically, during the Gutiérrez Lascuráin presidency the party was actually secular in its activities and neither took direction from ecclesiastical authorities nor desired to do so. Since the Church-State détente of the 1940s, the Church remained apolitical and discreetly supported the government.[12] Since its doctrine taught that Catholics as individuals could and should participate in politics, the Church could not prevent some of its lay leaders from joining political parties. Such men who were also PAN leaders never publicly connected the two but the public could make the connection. In fact, they had joined PAN because they believed that secular men should offer an alternative to the materialistic, bourgeois Mexican Revolution, an alternative which was progressive and secular but of Catholic origin. In short, *panistas* who were also Catholic militants were often at odds with the ecclesiastical hierarchy.

Of PAN's major electoral campaigns under Gutiérrez Lascuráin, only the 1952 campaign had religious overtones. In the 1953 Baja California gubernatorial and legislative campaigns, its first as a state, PAN ran joint candidates with UNS, but also with the Federation of Mexican Peoples' Parties, a completely secular party.[13] PAN quickly built an organization in the state not through religious appeals but through exploiting regionalistic resentment of control from Mexico City, a resentment exacerbated by United States economic and cultural influence. In the 1955 federal deputy campaign the party had the support of the UNS but it had come too late to give a significant religious cast to PAN's campaign.[14] The party was certainly aided by religious votes but not very much since four of the six newly elected deputies came from areas with strong secular influence—Federal District and Ciudad Juárez, Chihuahua. The following year PAN gave spirited opposition to the unpopular PRI gubernatorial candidate in Chihuahua by exploiting discontent with PRI and regionalists' animosity towards Mexico City. Luis H. Alvarez, the PAN gubernatorial candidate, was a product of an El Paso, Texas, high school, the University of Texas, and Massachusetts Institute of Technology. The young engineer was a small-scale textile industrialist. He had been a founder of Boys' Town, a Catholic charity in Ciudad Juárez, but he was not known as a clericalist.[15]

Nevertheless, political Catholicism was one major reason for the overthrow of Gutiérrez Lascuráin as PAN president. The other was the president's failure to improve PAN's electoral fortunes. Dissatisfaction with his leadership had erupted in 1953 but he had maintained control.[16] When complaints burst into the open again in the National Council meeting in October 1956, he resigned. The outburst came during Council debate on tactics. The dissidents attacked the leadership for failing to increase the party's electoral successes, to defend party candidates vigorously before electoral organs, and to capitalize on the Chihuahua gubernatorial election, which was the closest PAN had come to winning. Leading the dissidents was ex-federal deputy Francisco Chávez González who had been pressing PAN since 1954 to fight for Christian Democracy. He did not represent majority opinion at the time and shortly thereafter left the party, but his attitude was indicative of the current within the party. The Council elected Ituarte Servín as its new president; his credentials as a militant, uncompromising Catholic were impeccable.[17]

Aided by young *panistas,* the new president immediately adopted a more aggressive posture. The flaccid and vague youth sector which had existed since 1943 was organized into the dynamic Youth Organization under the leadership of Javier Blanco Sánchez and given extensive responsibility for electoral campaigns.[18] Young *panistas* had been a primary source of the dissatisfaction with what they considered to be the dilatory tactics of Gutiérrez Lascuráin, and they were anxious to give combat for Christian Democracy. Ituarte Servín, the Youth Organization, and the PAN federal deputies condemned the 1956 Russian intervention in Hungary and the British-French-Israeli attack on Egypt. They demanded that Mexico expel Russian diplomats, lead an international boycott against Russia, and end governmental subsidizing of "Moscow agents."[19]

The Youth Organization got its first chance to use its muscle in the 1957 Coahuila gubernatorial campaign, one which served as practice for the 1958 federal campaign. Coahuila was important to PAN because, as a northern state, it was a potential PAN stronghold; it was the home of Francisco I. Madero; and the PRI candidate was Madero's brother Raul. PAN considered itself the true heir of the Revolutionary Madero. The Madero family had given Acción Nacional his portrait as the true heir of the leader, and many former *maderistas* had helped organize PAN. Now, another family member was the PRI candidate, an affront to PAN sensitivity. Acción Nacional unsuccessfully charged that Raul Madero was ineligible because he was a Federal District resident. PAN made its most extensive effort to date to elect its candidate, even in the face of harassment, but lost anyway.[20]

While the Coahuila campaign progressed, preparations were in progress for the 1958 federal elections. Twenty-six regional presidents met in May 1957 to plot the course of the campaign. As a result of this meeting, regional organizations met, discussed problems, voted to participate, and suggested candidates.[21] By the time of the November national convention, regional and district conventions had proposed ten candidates, only seven of whom would actually be nominated in the national convention. Three more persons were nominated from the floor.[22]

The selection of a candidate was quickly simplified in the convention. The nomination of Ernesto Uruchurtu, the presidentially appointed regent of Mexico City and a PRI member, as a possible PAN candidate was quickly disallowed because he was not a *panista*. His candidacy had been suggested by the Querétaro delegation but he was never a serious possibility. Four other candidates for the nomination withdrew for personal reasons. One of these, Antonio L. Rodríguez, had been the front runner but PAN leaders decided that running a prominent financier as the party's candidate was inadvisable in light of the charges that PAN was reactionary and of the poverty of the average Mexican. Luis H. Alvarez received 178 of the needed 262 votes on the first ballot, followed by González Torres with 100; the other four candidates received a total of 47 votes. After González Torres withdrew, Alvarez was unanimously nominated on the third ballot.[23]

That PAN selected a relatively inexperienced political unknown as its presidential candidate deserves comment. The party does not expect its presidential candidate to win; in private, party leaders have admitted to this author that PAN is too weak to win the presidency. They do assert, however, that PAN's presidential candidate actually receives 35 to 45 percent of the vote, but that the government will not admit it so as to discourage support for PAN. Running a presidential candidate serves other purposes: (1) it legitimizes PAN's claim to national party status, (2) it has a coattail effect on federal deputy campaigns, (3) it gives PAN the opportunity to propagandize nationally, and (4) it serves as a rebuff to personalism since voters are urged to vote for the party, not the man. Alvarez was selected to fulfill this role because he: (1) was a party hero as a result of the Chihuahua campaign, especially to the Youth Organization, (2) was young and energetic, and (3) had the personal financial resources to conduct the campaign.

Alvarez's platform and appeals were virtually identical to those of González Luna with several notable exceptions. The 1958 platform condemned Article 130 (a sign of increased clericalism within PAN) and clearly stated that the government should intervene in the economy to aid the masses. In press interviews Alvarez attacked the government for favoring the rich and for not doing more to end poverty and sickness. Alvarez castigated the Revolution for failing to deliver on its promises while claiming that PAN would create a revolution in freedom.[24] The new clarity of PAN's position had brought ex-Mexican President Emilio Portes Gil, an old enemy of PAN, to assert in 1957 that the party advanced positions that sustained much of the thesis of the Mexican Revolution.[25]

Alvarez and his campaign team were astute enough to pitch their appeals to pro-Revolution and antigovernment sentiment, but their inexperience and zeal led them into unpleasant incidents and violence in the campaign. They thought they could change Mexico overnight. They were aggressive in their confrontations with PRI and, at times, reckless; they taunted PRI members, fought police when the latter tried to disperse PAN rallies, and interfered with free carnivals and music staged by PRI during PAN rallies. Such actions escalated to sporadic outbreaks of violence on both sides. Young *panistas* were shot at in Michoacán and a PAN district chief was assassinated in Ciudad Juárez. Alvarez himself was thrown in jail temporarily in one incident, and, in another, he, his wife, and the wife of Gómez Morín had to take refuge in the city hall of Tlanepantla, a suburb of Mexico City. Both sides blamed the other, and PAN appealed to its members not to engage in violence.[26]

The PRI electoral machine swamped PAN, but the latter showed a slight gain over 1952. Alvarez was credited with 9.5 percent of the vote compared to González Luna's 8.1 percent. PAN was eventually awarded six federal deputy seats after it withdrew from the counting process amid cries of fraud and its refusal to recognize the legitimacy of the new government.

The combination of high expectations for significant electoral gains and the violence of the campaign produced a major tactical debate within PAN, a debate which has been the subject of some confusion to outsiders since. *Panistas* believed that Alvarez and the party had fared much better against Adolfo López Mateos and PRI than the government admitted. They argued that millions of false votes had been cast to produce López Mateos's 90.5 percent majority. When the preliminary results in the federal deputy races showed a PAN victory only in Mérida, Yucatán, party leaders were convinced that the government was going to end PAN access to public positions. To deal with what they considered to be an incredible fraud in the face of PAN's energetic electoral effort, a meeting of the National Council was called for July 12–13, 1958.[27]

In the Council meeting, the debate centered on two questions: PAN's attitude toward the counting process and its future tactics. Each debate will be considered separately.[28]

The question of the immediate tactic was debated within the political commission chosen to present a position paper and then by the entire Council. In the first debate, Gómez Morín, González Luna, and Salvador Rosas Magallón, Baja California leader, argued that PAN should withdraw from the counting process because it should not cooperate with a corrupt regime nor allow itself to be used to give the semblance of democracy in Mexico. Opposing withdrawal were Felipe Gómez Mont, ex-federal deputy who would be given another term in this election, and Jesús Sanz Cerrada, also an ex-federal deputy, who argued that PAN had an obligation to defend the vote. The commission followed the lead of the founders and voted for withdrawal.

The debate became even more virulent when read to the entire Council. Two sessions of debate were necessary to accommodate all the speakers. Leading the prowithdrawal forces were Rosas Magallón, Adolfo Christlieb Ibarrola, González Luna, Hugo Gutiérrez Vega, Youth Organization president, and Mauricio Gómez Morín, son of the founder— all prominent members. They argued that the party should not condone such fraud by participating and should seek a road other than mere discussion to rectify Mexican problems. Gómez Mont, Sanz Cerrada, and Javier Blanco Sánchez led the group opposing withdrawal. The Council voted to declare the election fraudulent, to withdraw from the counting process, and not to recognize the government issuing from the election.[29]

The report on future tactics also produced division because it recommended the continuation of past tactics. Youth leaders and Rosas Magallón blasted the report for being theoretical while the house was burning. Gómez Morín intervened to bring about a compromise, effected after another commission was appointed. PAN would plan permanent action along the line of past activity while immediately organizing protest meetings and other legal forms of pressure.[30]

Complicating the postelectoral maneuvering was the outbreak of numerous strikes, particularly among teachers and railway workers. One reason for the selection of López Mateos as PRI's presidential candidate had been his ability to produce labor peace, but many segments of labor believed that they had paid too high a price in not receiving acceptable wage increases. Now that the government was weak because of the coming succession of a new president, one supposedly prolabor, unions exploited the opportunity. One leader of the railroad workers was Demetrio Vallejo, a Communist. Claiming that the strikes were instigated by Communists for political purposes, the government broke them with force. PAN, suffering from governmental attempts to disperse the party's protest meetings, supported the strikers, asserting that the communist issue was a red herring to draw attention away from the exploitation of labor by corrupt labor leaders, the government, and capitalists.[31]

Confusing the scene still further was the emergency meeting of the Federal District regional organization in August 1958, because it appeared to be speaking for the entire party. Many Acción Nacional leaders lived in the district and attended the convention, a natural source of confusion. The convention called for more extensive organization, recruitment drives, financing of operations solely from dues, and continuance of the defense of citizens' rights. An attempt to create a workers' sector in PAN was defeated on the grounds that PAN made distinctions based on age and sex, but the party was clearly attempting to capitalize on the labor disputes.[32]

As a result of such pressure, the Electoral College began to recognize more PAN federal deputy victories. On August 27, Eduardo Molina Castillo was declared a victor in Mérida, Yucatán. August 28 brought recognition of the victory of Antonio López y López in Puebla state. Germán Brambila (Baja California state), Humberto Zebadua (Chiapas), and Jaime Haro (Zacatecas) were recognized on August 29. On October 14, Felipe Gómez Mont was named for the third district of the capital, one he had represented before.[33]

The pattern of selection suggests that further splits within PAN were being encouraged. The party had said that none of its deputies would take their seats, but all of the new PAN deputies, except Gómez Mont, came from districts which had never had PAN representation, tearing them between party loyalty and the desire to be deputies. Gómez Mont may have been selected as a reward for having led the fight for PAN participation in the counting process. In fact, all except Gómez Mont and Jaime Haro yielded to the pressures being exerted and took their seats. PAN expelled them from the party.

Whether Acción Nacional had any justification for its actions cannot be known, but that it believed itself justified is important in understanding subsequent events. PAN was a small, weak party, and López Mateos was a handsome, popular candidate with backing of PRI and private enterprise. There is no question that he won the election. The only question might be whether or not he won by the announced margin. At the congressional level, PRI undoubtedly won a substantial majority but may not have won as much as it claimed. The Mexican left claimed that the election was a fraud; an American political scientist reported seeing fraud; and a Mexican journalist pointed out fraud in this and prior elections.[34] PAN leaders believed that the party had been cheated of its rightful victories and recognition of its strength and were convinced that it had to arouse public opinion against such events if they were ever going to be stopped.

PAN would not have to marshal all its resources to preserve a handful of Congressional seats if Mexico used a proportional representation system, as do most Latin American countries. In Mexico, as in the United States, a congressional candidate must win a clear-cut victory, either by plurality or majority, to obtain a federal deputy seat because Mexico uses a single-member, majority type representation system. Such a winner-take-all system denies minority representation and discourages the growth of opposition parties. For example, PAN can poll 30 percent of the vote in the Federal District yet not place a man in the Chamber of Deputies. PAN's pleas for a proportional representation system go unheeded because the government wants to preserve PRI's ascendancy. PAN is forced to adopt the tactics used in this 1958–59 episode to maintain any representation in government.

By March 1959, PAN had a list of persecutory acts which it claimed the government and PRI had instituted against the party when PAN sought to defend its rights. In the December 1958 Yucatán elections, PAN leaders claimed that the government had stolen the elections, that the Motul offices had been burned, and that the Motul PAN municipal chief had been assassinated. When PAN held a protest meeting in Mérida, three were killed, three hundred jailed, and others injured. In Campeche state, PAN was not allowed to hold meetings or to participate in elections. Meetings were also forbidden in Veracruz state and propagandists were arrested there. The PAN convention in Zacatecas had been broken up and members arrested. In Chihuahua state, members had been attacked and jailed. One party leader counted twenty dead *panistas* in the first four months of the Lopez Mateos presidency.[35]

When the party met in March 1959 for a combination national convention-general assembly, the atmosphere was charged with excitement and tension. That the meeting was also an extraordinary general assembly portended statutory changes. The National Council was also meeting to replace Ituarte Servín, who had ceased directing the party, allowing González Torres, the secretary-general, to assume control. The Youth Organization was also meeting to insure that its wishes were heard.

Debates over the control of the organization and its future tactics rocked the convention as Acción Nacional sought means to increase its effectiveness in light of the disastrous 1958 election and its aftermath. No one was satisfied with the meager rewards of PAN's participation in the election as the only legal opposition to PRI's presidential candidate. Six federal deputy victories had been recognized only after the party strenuously objected to the counting. Subsequent conflicts between PAN and governmental and/or PRI forces had damaged PAN. Some members now sought to answer PAN's problems by selecting new leadership and modifying the statutes. Others wanted to increase pressure on the government in the belief that it would respond in PAN's favor. Both debates were interrelated because members desiring more militancy wanted to preserve presidential power for a dynamic president.

The National Council's election of González Torres as PAN's president was an early victory for the militants and an indication of the course to be taken by the convention. Because he was virtually acting president, he had the advantage, but the seven other candidates, most of whom had been active party founders, also had substantial support. It was Youth Organization support which provided the margin of victory, creating a debt that would be paid.

The statutes were amended to tighten the party's organization and to increase the influence of the Youth and Women's Organizations. Both were juridically and organically incorporated into the party. General assemblies, the final authority on party affairs, were freed of the five-year meeting cycle so they could be called when necessary. The National Council was increased from 250 to 324 members (two for each federal electoral district) to provide broader national representation.[36]

Attempts to reduce presidential powers were defeated after protracted debate. First, dissidents tried to change the National Council into a decision-making body instead of an advisory body. González Luna led the defense of the structure, asserting that such a change would cause collisions between the Council and the Committee and incapacitate the party at critical times. Reformers then tried to put the presidential decision-making powers in the hands of the Council but Gómez Morín and González Luna had it defeated as well. Finally, reformers proposed to put the selection of regional presidents completely in the hands of regional organizations. Again, González Luna led the opposition forces. Because the vote was close, Gómez Morín had three more votes taken, but the party stood by the first decision.[37]

The origin of the debate was twofold: dissatisfaction with the president's ability to act unilaterally and regionalist resentment of Mexico City domination of the party. Not everyone was happy with PAN's reaction to the 1958 election because it was pointless and embarrassing. The decision had been made by Mexico City despite the wishes of important regional organizations because the president controlled the National Committee and the Federal District committee, the two largest blocks of votes, and the votes of weak regional committees. That the opinion of the Federal District emergency assembly of August 1958 had been interpreted as official PAN national opinion was a blow to the pride of regional organizations such as Jalisco, San Luis Potosí, Guerrero, Yucatán, Baja California, and Chihuahua. Moreover, four of the expelled federal deputies came from the provinces, two from states proposing the reforms.

The tactical debate which followed was an old one in PAN history, but it had intensified with the aggressiveness of the Youth Organization. The commission report, read by Manuel González Hinojosa and Manuel Sierra Macedo of the old guard, was a rehash of past tactics with a proposal to support the labor movement in its current strikes. As one Mexico City daily observed, it was a moderate document.[38] Older members argued that more violence should not be risked, that one act of heroism was not as important as daily realization of the program, that illuminating Mexican conditions was a slow process, and that this was a debate on action in general, not on specific measures to be taken. With Gómez Morín and González Luna supporting this position, it was virtually unbeatable. Young *panistas,* led by Hugo Gutiérrez Vega and Manuel Rodríguez Lapuente, Youth Organization leaders, and supported by Gómez Mont, lashed out at the commission's recommendations claiming that the report offered no solution to existing problems. For them, the time for talk had ended; PAN had to take concrete action to take power. Gómez Mont went a step farther by calling for the use of force.

The final decision of the convention was a compromise. The report was approved in general terms and then in specific terms, but the convention then adopted some of the proposals of the militant faction. PAN would: (1) make public protests by all adequate and legal means whenever the government violated civil liberties; (2) publicize the Mexican situation among compatriots in other countries; (3) use the National Committee to defend members in the federal entities; and (4) turn discussion of concrete plans over to regional chiefs. The report did not approve violence as a tactic.[39]

PAN's new aggressiveness was quickly demonstrated in the border states of Baja California and Chihuahua. The latter had been the site of the assassination of a PAN leader the year before. It was also the birthplace of Gómez Morín and Luis H. Alvarez, the latter a dynamic PAN state leader. Both states differed from central Mexico because of their proximity to the United States and greater prosperity. In Ciudad Juárez, Chihuahua, and throughout Baja California, the dollar, not the peso, was the medium of exchange. Hence, these states were more independent of the central government than most states and resented Mexico City control. PAN had been exploiting these factors in Chihuahua since 1939 and in Baja California since its organization as a state in 1953. In the Chihuahua elections of 1959, young *panistas* fought battles with PRI and exchanged harassment of each other's rallies.[40] The Baja California situation was more complicated.

Braulio Maldonado, PRI state governor, and his henchmen had been using government power to enrich themselves and their friends since 1953. Tijuana and Mexicala were important gates of entry to the rich United States as well as important tourist centers. Prostitution, drugs, liquor, and gambling had provided ample sources of illicit income. Such activities had not been unusual, but Maldonado had created a zone assertedly containing 8,000 prostitutes in Tijuana. Resentment against the regime increased even more when his friends, organized as Muebles y Maquinaria, S. A. and aided by the government, laid claim to two million square meters of occupied land, forcing thousands of inhabitants to vacate. Only one lawyer was willing to defend the residents against eviction—Salvador Rosas Magallón, PAN state leader. Rosas Magallón was unsuccessful in his legal maneuvering but residents still hoped to get some relief from the new governor to be elected in 1959. Maldonado, however, chose a crony, Eligio Esquivel, as his successor. Thousands of Baja Californians rushed to PAN as their only hope, backing Rosas Magallón as PAN's gubernatorial candidate.[41]

Maldonado was ideal for PAN's purposes. As a widely known corrupt, arbitrary, personalistic, leftist politician, he could be used as a symbol of all that PAN believed to be wrong with Mexico. The rise of Fidel Castro to power in Cuba in January of that year and the subsequent increasing radicalization of Cuba unnerved many Baja Californians oriented towards the United States. PAN had been an old antagonist of communism and quickly exploited these anxieties.[42]

Maldonado had thrown a windfall PAN's way, but now unleashed his forces to prevent the opposition from capitalizing on it. Masses of citizens flocked to PAN rallies, campaigned for its candidates, and joined the party. They were using PAN as a protest vehicle against PRI and Mexico City. In response, meetings were teargassed; party equipment destroyed; the Tijuana office looted; *panistas,* including the candidate, arrested; signs ripped down; and meetings dispersed by force. The Maldonado government justified these actions on the grounds that PAN was subversive and threatening to overthrow the government, a charge which PAN ridiculed.[43]

The conflict continued past the August 2, 1959, elections. PRI claimed total victory, a claim PAN contested. PAN appealed to the Supreme Court and the Minister of Government to intervene, citing federal constitutional Article 9 which guaranteed the right of peaceful assembly, a right which PAN said had been upheld even during the Mexican-American war. The plea was unsuccessful and demonstrations continued into October.[44]

There are ample grounds to believe that PAN won the election. The animosity towards Maldonado was widespread because thousands of citizens had suffered. Several newspapers, both Mexican and American, reported numerous cases of vote manipulation and ballot box robbery as well as photographs of the acts in progress. A recent study has presented massive evidence indicating that PAN won. Finally, Maldonando was arrested the following January, after he had vacated the governor's chair, for stealing vast quantities of money during his term of office.[45]

Frustration with its inability to capture Baja California combined with a fear of the consequence of a nearby Communist government encouraged the continuation of PAN's demagogic anticommunist tactic. The creation of the leftist *Movimiento de Liberación Nacional* in 1961 under Cárdenas's titular leadership also influenced latent PAN fears of communism in Mexico. *La Nación* articles traced anticlericalism from the French Revolution through communism. The government free textbook program, instituted in 1959, was attacked as an attempt to impose a mildly procommunist official line. PAN favored free textbooks but opposed the lack of choice, especially since the history books were anticlerical. It feared that the current books were only a prelude to a more overt communist line as Mexican Communists would increase their influence in government circles with the aid of their Cuban counterparts. PAN demanded that Mexico break relations with Cuba and strongly condemn its efforts to subvert the hemisphere.[46]

PAN's 1961 federal deputy campaign was keyed on the communist issue. González Torres warned the February 1961 national convention that Mexico was threatened by communist inroads. Campaign appeals argued that Mexico's choice was communism or the adoption of the

Christian principles of social justice.[47] Mexicans ignored these appeals, and, although PAN won five federal deputy seats, it had run its weakest slate of candidates to date.[48]

Presenting Christian social justice as the alternative to communism was actually part of PAN's long-term shift toward a Christian Democratic posture. Latin American Christian Democrats, at least, had long seen communism as their major enemy. González Torres's abortive efforts to make communism an issue in Mexico was related to the general anticommunist upsurge among Christian Democrats which had been provoked by Castro's success.

The connections between Acción Nacional and the Latin American Christian Democratic movement predated the founding of the former. UNEC members of PAN had led the creation of the Latin American University Catholic Action movement (CIDEC) in 1931.[49] Future *panistas* attended the 1934 International Congress of Catholic Youth in Rome where the modern Latin American Christian Democratic movement was born. Through these contacts, *panistas* such as Luis Calderón Vega and Miguel Estrada Iturbide knew such Christian Democratic leaders as Rafael Caldera of Venezuela and Eduardo Frei of Chile. PAN, the Chilean Christian Democratic party, and the Venezuelan Christian Democratic party had similar origins—young professionals, intellectuals, and university students breaking away from more conservative parties to create moderate to progressive parties based on Catholic social justice principles. This core group for PAN had been UNEC and was augmented by other Catholic Action members.[50]

PAN could not declare itself a Christian Democratic party both because of Mexican constitutional prohibitions and objections from secular-oriented members of the coalition, but it did maintain ties with other Christian Democrats. Calderón Vega, as CIDEC president, observed the 1944 Chilean elections as a guest of the Chilean Falange, the forerunner of that country's present Christian Democratic party. Caldera came to Mexico in 1946 in temporary exile during which time he exchanged ideas with prominent *panistas* and attended PAN's annual Christmas supper. PAN and COPEI (the Venezuelan Christian Democratic party) supported each other in their respective presses in the late 1940s and again in the early 1960s. *Panistas* attended the 1961 Caracas and 1962 Santiago Christian Democratic conventions as invited observers. Informal relations were established after the November 1962 PAN national convention.[51]

Although there are numerous parallels between the history and ideology of PAN and its Chilean and Venezuelan counterparts, those between PAN and COPEI are the most striking. COPEI had begun as an electoral committee which sought power by awakening citizen consciousness, the PAN strategy. COPEI began calling itself Acción Nacional two years after the Mexican party of the same name was founded. Both allied with more conservative groups early in their histories, but then, after the Second World War, adopted more progressive positions.[52]

All three parties share a common ideology, distinguishable primarily by the problems peculiar to each country. They are against anticlericalism, but assert that they are nonconfessional and receive their inspiration from the Church's teachings not ecclesiastical authorities. They see themselves as the only viable alternative to communism and liberal or laissez-faire capitalism, both of which they consider to be inherently undemocratic and exploitive. Instead, they believe societies should be operated for the common good as determined by Catholic doctrinal norms. Political democracy is indispensable to the well-being of society, in their view, and this democracy must be based not only upon individual rights but also on societies' rights. Profit-sharing, strong independent unions, worker participation in management, and, since the 1960s, labor's coownership of enterprises are devices to be used in redistributing income equitably. In international affairs, they seek an end to nuclear weaponry and want a system based on international cooperation and arbitration. Faced with the choice between capitalist and Communist powers, however, they favor the former.[53]

The source of PAN's movement towards open advocacy of Christian Democracy in 1960–61 came from the Youth Organization, not from long-time party members. Cries to fight for Christian Democracy in Mexico had been ignored in PAN conventions until 1956. In that year, Ituarte Servín became president of PAN and encouraged the reorganized youth group to fight for Christian Democracy. Since its first national convention in 1956, the Youth Organization had repeatedly announced that PAN was a Christian Democratic party and tried to recruit members on that basis. Gutiérrez Vega and Rodríguez Lapuente, aided by some older members, toured the country trying to drum up support. González Torres announced that he was a Christian Democrat, a tendency he had had for years, and he further encouraged the youth.[54]

Encouragement also came from non-Mexican quarters. Caldera wrote in 1960 that PAN was an ideological brother and in 1962 that he expected to see PAN heading hemispheric social Christian movements soon. Messages of encouragement from leading Christian Democrats were sent to PAN Youth Organization meetings in 1960. The Italian and German Christian Democratic parties offered scholarships to young *panistas* and economic aid to the party.[55]

In response, PAN took more steps to align itself with Christian Democratic thought. The 1961 platform called for Mexico to adopt a "third world" foreign policy, to encourage the prohibition of nuclear weapons, and to institute profit-sharing in Mexican business and industry. PAN bills to implement these planks were rejected by the Chamber of Deputies but were later passed by PRI under its own label. The government instituted a profit-sharing plan in 1962 which PAN considered unsatisfactory because it favored capitalists at the expense of labor. The tripartite board (capital, labor, and government) would decide if profits warranted being shared and how much would be distributed. To PAN, this meant that the procapitalist government would cheat labor by casting its votes with capital. Adolfo Christlieb Ibarrola, future PAN president, berated capitalists for their greed and resistance to the profit-sharing system in a speech to the Social Union of Mexican Empresarios (USEM), a Catholic paternalistic businessmen's club related to Opus Dei. In another speech, this time to the Sowers of Friendship, Mexican variety of Rotary International, Christlieb condemned capitalists not only for resisting profit-sharing for forty years (the Constitution of 1917 calls for it), but also for not preparing for the next step—the co-ownership and management of enterprises by workers. According to Christlieb, capitalists not only had to cease thinking only of their own wealth, of absolute property rights, and of workers as cogs of machinery, but had to understand that society must be operated for the common good of all. To cap off PAN's maneuver, Rafael Caldera came as a special guest to address the November 1962 PAN national convention.[56]

This shift towards Christian Democracy, although it might have surprised capitalists and casual observers who considered the party to be a bulwark for private enterprise, was understandable to the thoughtful observer. PAN had always contained Catholic militants with social reform ideas. Gradually, these men had increased their power within the party until they completely dominated it. As educated men, they responded to the ferment in the Catholic world. It was no coincidence that the party as a whole began its rapid shift while the Catholic Church was moving towards Vatican II and the *Mater Et Magistra* and *Pacem En Terris* encyclicals of John XXIII; PAN was moving in conjunction with developments in Christian Socialist thought. The election of Ituarte Servín and González Torres meant increases in the Catholic content of PAN politics. The Christian Democratic idea appealed to the new generation of *panistas* who became influential in the mid-1950s. After the futility of 1958, becoming Christian Democrats seemed the answer. They could attach themselves to an international movement with power in Germany and Italy and rising strength in Chile and Venezuela. By using the anticommunist tactic, so usefully exploited by Chile's Frei in 1958, they hoped to duplicate his success in 1961.

As attractive as this serious flirtation with the Latin American Christian Democratic movement might have been, Acción Nacional leaders had to recognize the fundamental dissimilarities between PAN's place in the Mexican political system and that of Christian Democratic parties in such countries as Chile and Venezuela. The terms Christian Democracy, Christian Socialism, or Christian social reform have appeal in Chile and Venezuela but are the kiss of death in Mexican politics. Further, Mexican nationalistic sentiment rejects ties to international movements. On a more significant level, the profound differences in political systems precluded PAN's becoming a full Christian Democratic party. COPEI and Chilean Christian Democrats compete in a multiparty system with proportional representation whereas PAN competes in the aforementioned single-member, majority-type system. Supporters of COPEI and the Chilean Christian Democrats know that they will have representation and that their parties might be the key to a coalition government. In other words, they can reasonably expect dividends from their vote investment; PAN supporters cannot. Such a system forces these parties to appeal to a cross-section of the population by offering the broadest possible positive appeals consistent with their ideology. Because of their potential power and broad appeal, they can and do garner support from people who ignore the term Christian in party ideology. PAN's identification with anything labeled Christian would immediately create serious defections as well as provoke reprisals. Finally, whereas COPEI and the Christian Democrats of Chile enjoy substantial support from labor and agriculturalists, the Mexican government and PRI maintain this as their private preserve, thereby maintaining control and encouraging the idea that PAN is only an elitist, clerical party.

Even given the gross differences between Acción Nacional and the two leading Latin American Christian Democratic parties, the comparison, superficial though it may be, has to be drawn. The leadership of PAN has been responding to the same stimuli that had produced reform Catholic parties in Latin America. Too many important *panistas* since 1956 had been asserting that the party was Christian Democratic and PAN was clearly courted by the Christian Democratic movement in 1960–62 and came very close to joining the movement in 1962. Moreover, as will be seen in later chapters, Acción Nacional continued to have relations with Christian Democratic parties and to take similar, if not identical, ideological positions. Finally, cross-references between PAN and its Chilean

TABLE 2

PAN Federal Deputy Campaigns, 1943–1970[a]

Year	Total Districts	No. of PAN Candidates	No. of Entities with PAN Candidates	No. of Victors	Percentage of National Vote
1943	147	21	12	0	n.a.
1946	147	64	23	4	n.a.
1949	147	69	23	4	8.9
1952	161	143	27	5	7.8
1955	161	88	21	6	n.a.
1958	161	139	30	6[b]	9.5
1961	178	95	19	5	7.6
1964	178	174	30	2 (18)[c]	11.5
1967	178	176	30	1 (19)[c]	12.4
1970	178	171	30	0 (20)[c]	14.1

SOURCES: James W. Wilkie, "New Hypotheses for Statistical Research in Recent Mexican History," *Latin American Research Review,* VI:2 (Summer 1971), 5; Luis Calderón Vega, *Reportaje Sobre el PAN* (Mexico: Ediciones de Acción Nacional, 1970), 64–70; Cline, *United States and Mexico,* 311; and various periodicals.

[a] Figures are for proprietary candidates only.

[b] Four took their seats against party orders and were expelled from PAN.

[c] Initial figures represent victories by majority vote. Figures in parentheses represent seats received from the party deputy system introduced in 1963; see Chapter V for an explanation of this system.

and Venezuelan counterparts will serve to suggest PAN's position within the context of political Catholicism in Latin America and to point up PAN's social reformism in Mexico. In short, PAN was born of the social reform impulse affecting many Latin American intellectuals and professionals in the 1930s and continued in this tradition until, in this period of Catholic militancy, party leadership brought the party to the brink of Christian Democracy but dared not take the final plunge.

Actually, PAN leaders were grasping at straws as they sought some tactic to save the party from the morass into which it had fallen. Its efforts to gain power at the state level had failed completely. Even in the few instances where the party might have won or did win gubernatorial contests, it was unable to take office. Entry into state legislatures had come once, in the late 1940s. Occupying a few municipal posts was not very gratifying. Access to federal deputy seats had leveled off. Table 2 shows

PAN's federal deputy election record. Only ninety-five candidates could be found to run in nineteen states and PAN's percentage of the vote had declined.[57] González Torres had hurt the party. The demagoguery of his presidency had given the party a negative image; the Christian Democratic gambit caused membership losses; and the party was running the risk of having its registration canceled.

Acción Nacional saved itself. Caldera spoke to the convention and was wildly applauded. Formal relations with Christian Democratic parties were established. But, instead of declaring itself a Christian Democratic party, Acción Nacional elected Adolfo Christlieb Ibarrola as its president and gave him the power to name his own national committee. Within three years, he would lead the most drastic change in PAN history while terminating overt identification with Christian Democracy.

CHAPTER V

The Limits of Influence, 1962–1972

The presidencies of Adolfo Christlieb Ibarrola (1962–68) and Manuel González Hinojosa (1969–72) best represent Acción Nacional's dilemma as an independent party in opposition to the successful Mexican Revolution. Regardless of PAN's shifts in tactics, ideology, programs, and membership, PAN's success has been ultimately determined by the government, to the extent of warranting the assertion that the party is an unwilling instrument of its rival, the Revolutionary coalition. As Acción Nacional has sought to develop a more influential role for itself, its members have engaged in heated debate, accepted the Revolution while castigating its management, and re-examined the value of continued existence as a political party in the face of such meager returns. Solutions to PAN problems have not been discovered. Yet, frustration, bitterness, and alienation from the government mix with the hope that new members and new techniques may save the party and with it what *panistas* consider to be one of the few hopes for democracy and social justice in Mexico.

This period of PAN's history had a rhythm of its own. First, Christlieb quickly discarded traditional tactics and modernized party thought. Second, the government responded by giving PAN more access to the decision-making apparatus, resulting in significant PAN victories and near-victories. Third, governmental difficulties with students tipped the balance in favor of hard-line PRI politicos who feared further PAN successes and PAN's progress was abruptly halted by the government. Finally, once governmental intentions became clear, thoroughgoing debate and reevaluation within PAN began. At the time of this writing, no definitive conclusions have been reached.

Nothing in the curriculum vita of Christlieb would have suggested that he would revolutionize PAN. Born in the Federal District in 1919, he received his law degree from the national university in 1945. As a preparatory and university student he did not join his UNEC friends in their fight against anticlericalism even though he was an equally devout Catholic. Both he and González Torres were recruited into PAN in 1943

71

by law professors who were also party founders, but Christlieb adjured political and religious activism in favor of his legal career. The 1958 postelectoral crisis forced him to speak out in party councils. Later, he joined the Federal Electoral Commission as PAN representative, an experience which would make him a popular selection as PAN's president and which would establish his contacts with future Mexican president Gustavo Díaz Ordaz, then Minister of Government.[1]

Within his short, stocky frame, the politically realistic Christlieb possessed a keen, trained, and ironical mind. A formidable opponent and a valuable ally, he commanded respect from friend and foe alike not only for his political acumen but also for his ability to disassociate his personal religious intensity from his public role as a secular politician. Acción Nacional elected him to rescue the party from its collision course with the government. He took full control immediately, impressing his ideas upon the membership with argument, cajolery, and, when necessary, presidential power.

As he evaluated PAN's past from his newly acquired vantage point, he realized that drastic changes had to be instituted rapidly. Party influence had peaked in 1958. Contrary to hopes and expectations, the addition of millions of women voters in the 1958 federal election had not been the key to increased PAN influence. Since that time González Torres had led the organization down the dangerous road of intransigence towards the government and open position of Christian Democracy, an avowal which caused secularly minded *panistas* to defect from the party and identified PAN as a clerical party, illegal in Mexico. As a result, PAN had been unable to field as many candidates in the 1961 election as it had in prior years. Moreover, González Torres, a supercilious and demagogic anticommunist crusader, discredited PAN in many eyes, including some of its own membership. Although Christlieb himself was a firm anticommunist, a Christian Democrat, and a skeptic toward the government's esoteric democracy,[2] he dropped the anticommunism campaign, expelled *panistas* who insisted on calling PAN a Christian Democratic party, reframed its *Principles of Doctrine* into a clear Christian Democratic document, and instituted a policy of dialogue with the government.

Acción Nacional had always been a coalition of secular men and religious activists. Usually the latter curbed their religious zeal to mollify the seculars, but the Christian Democratic episode meant that they were willing to lose most of the secular support in favor of the international ties and financial aid from the Italian and German Christian Democratic parties. By late 1962, four major groups had developed within the party. Their agreement on most issues and their common opposition to the government enabled them to cooperate on most issues but the key difference was on their conception of the role of private property. The left-wing Christian Democrats, or Christian socialists, demanded massive redistribution of income and socialization of property through democratic communitarian ownership of the means of production and distribution. Young *panistas* and party intellectuals formed the bulk of this group. Most of the UNEC and older Catholic Action participants argued in favor of Christian or social welfare capitalism. Secular *panistas* rejected religious inspiration for their ideas. The secular capitalists were paternalistic defenders of property rights but would accept some welfare measures, whereas the secular socialists were moderate social democrats. All four groups rejected Marxian socialism, laissez-faire capitalism, and state capitalism.[3]

Each group was led by important men. The bulk of the secular capitalists came from northern Mexico and accepted the leadership of Gómez Morín and Antonio L. Rodríguez. Most of the UNEC group as well as González Torres and Ituarte Servín formed the leadership of the Christian capitalists. Twenty years before, their position had represented progressive capitalism. These two groups had built and financed PAN since 1939. By the 1960s, however, PAN had not only broadened its membership to become a middle- to lower-middle-class party but a new generation, including many founders' sons, was also contesting for power. With these changes, old-time Christian socialists, such as Luis Calderón Vega, were finally able to escape their isolation and influence the direction of the party. Christlieb himself was a leader of this group. The leading light among younger *panistas* was Efraín González Luna Morfín, son of the founder, an intellectual who returned to Mexico in 1959 following a ten-year university stint in the United States, France, and Austria under Jesuit direction. Perhaps because of the son's influence and/or because papal encyclicals were demanding more social concern, Efraín González Luna was migrating from the Christian capitalist camp to its socialist counterpart, acting as a bridge between the two in the process. The secular socialists had no clearly identifiable leader although Mauricio Gómez Morín, son of the founder, and Rosas Magallón sometimes performed this task. Open splits between the two major groups usually had been avoided because they needed each other—the capitalists supplied the money, the socialists the ideas. Christlieb's task was to restore this cooperation while molding the party in his own image. He had to avoid the González Torres mistake of alienating the seculars with religiosity and the socialists by a too ardent defense of capitalism.[4]

Within a few months of taking office, Christlieb, supported by the socialist defectors from the capitalists, expelled those Christian Democrats who could not accept the new direction and explained his and PAN's conception of the relationship between religion and politics. Lost were Alejandro Aviles, one of PAN's best writers, and youth leaders Hugo Gutiérrez Vega and Manuel Rodríguez Lapuente along with an indeterminate number of others.[5] Aviles continued to support PAN through his *Excélsior* articles, but the two youth leaders loudly denounced both PAN and PRI as capitalistic and reactionary and set up their own Christian Democratic movement with membership in the Christian Democratic "International" in hopes of creating a legitimate Christian Democratic party in Mexico.[6] Although PAN also quietly maintained relations with Christian Democratic parties, particularly in Latin America, Christlieb repudiated the Christian Democratic label because Mexicans would always believe that such a party was really an instrument of ecclesiastical power. To him, religious parties led to totalitarianism, and the Church should stay out of politics, contenting itself with spiritual and social concerns. Although secular politicians might be inspired by the Church's teachings, they should not turn theology into another social reform ideology. Politics and religion were and should be separate spheres; the old Church-State conflict should be avoided.[7]

In spite of PAN's overt maneuvering away from labeling itself a Christian Democratic party, the party moved even closer to a doctrinal position compatible with Latin American Christian Democracy. In the same interviews wherein Christlieb tried to separate PAN from the Church, he admitted that there were many similarities between PAN and Christian Democratic parties. Although he did not mention them by name, he did admit that PAN had informal cultural relations with other democratic parties; in fact these relations were principally with Latin American Christian Democratic parties.[8] The 1964 platform, the 1965 Principles of Doctrine, and the 1967 platform were consistent with the doctrine of the Christian Democratic wing of Latin American political Catholicism, again an indication that PAN ideologues were as responsive to trends in Latin American Catholicism as they were to purely Mexican events.

The 1964 platform was the most conservative of the three, resembling the 1961 document, but without mentioning Article 3, vigorously attacking the *ejidal* system, state economic intervention, and threats to private property. Instead, PAN argued for the creation of a National Planning Commission composed of government, private enterprise, labor and consumer representatives to solve Mexican economic problems.[9] During the campaign itself, Christlieb and other leaders indicated PAN's new direction, which would appear more clearly in later documents. He launched an attack upon white unions as well as government paternalism, calling for a labor movement which could and would defend itself against capital.[10] In the *Principles,* labor was declared preeminent over property. Female workers were to receive equal treatment. Protection of working mothers and the introduction of family salaries as well as wages were demanded. Most important, PAN demanded that labor be integrated into the functioning, property, profits, and decision-making of enterprises. In the agrarian sector, PAN still preferred family farmers organized into democratic cooperatives but now only demanded the democratization of *ejidos* instead of their demise.[11] The 1967 platform went even further by demanding governmental credit for small- and medium-sized industries, betterment of living conditions and production in the countryside, the creation of jobs, the training of the labor force, and the augmentation of individual and family capacity to save and invest as priorities in natural planning. Foreign investment was to be rechanneled from manufacture of luxury items into Mexican-controlled transformation industries. Social security would be made universal for all Mexicans and students would be included from age sixteen until they completed their studies.[12]

Demands were also made in the 1965 and 1967 documents to democratize Mexico further as well as to attend to urban problems. Proportional representation in all elected bodies in order to insure minority representation was the key political demand. Urban areas were to be cleared of environmental pollution. Large cities were to be subdivided into zones or wards which would correspond to administrative and utility districts, each headed by an elected councilman. Urban planning to insure the rational use of resources and to stem the flow of migrants from the countryside was seen as critical for the future. The Federal District was to be placed under a popularly elected mayor and council instead of the presidentially appointed government. The urban planks reflected PAN's desire to expand its urban strength by capitalizing on the increasing urbanization of Mexico.

PAN's new position appeared to be Revolutionary "me-tooism," but actually Christlieb was leading the party beyond traditional PRI rhetoric. Popes John XXIII and Paul VI had signaled the new direction with their encyclicals: *Mater Et Magistra* (1961), *Pacem En Terris* (1962), and *Populorum Progressio* (1967). The Latin American Bishops' Conference had gone even further in calling for the institution of Christian socialism or democratic communitarianism. Christlieb, friend of the Cuernavaca, Mexico, bishop Sergio Méndez Arceo, a progressive Catholic leader, and other *panistas* responded to these leads. Participatory democracy in political, social, and economic spheres was to be the wave of the future.[13]

Simultaneously with secularizing PAN's image and leading it into more modern doctrinal positions, Christlieb began his policy of dialogue with the government. Instead of just criticizing the government, PAN began to praise some governmental actions.[14] When Díaz Ordaz was elected Mexican president in 1964 over PAN's González Torres, PAN broke all precedent by publicly conceding defeat.[15] After he entered the Chamber of Deputies in 1964, Christlieb and PRI leaders would often consult each other concerning debates and proposed legislation. *Panistas* began to receive key committee assignments and to serve as Chamber vice-presidents. Christlieb also obtained direct access to the Mexico City regent and President Díaz Ordaz.

The government responded favorably to this redefinition by PAN. Mexican President López Mateos supported the adoption of the party deputy system in 1963 which had the foreseeable effect of guaranteeing twenty seats to PAN.[16] Both PAN sources and a leading PRI source credit Christlieb with an important role in its adoption. PAN sources assert that the very idea emanated from Christlieb and that he planted it in Díaz Ordaz's mind when both served on the Federal Electoral Commission. The PRI source attributes the creation of the system to Christlieb without specifying in what manner.[17] Even if it originated within the Revolutionary coalition, which has turned the system to its advantage, it is clear that the timing was the result of the new direction given to PAN by Christlieb. The 1964–67 Mexican Congress also modified the Federal Electoral Law along lines suggested by PAN: (1) measures to prevent multiple voting, (2) tax exemptions for political parties, (3) use of national totals in allocating party deputy seats, and (4) prescribed announcement dates for the composition of the Chamber of Deputies.[18] The PRI-dominated Congress also passed several former PAN measures as its own: (1) closer regulation of decentralized and state-participation enterprises, (2) denuclearization of Latin America, (3) restrictions on foreign investments, and (4) reforms of the Federal Labor Law, including obligatory reinstatement of workers dismissed without cause.[19] PAN even managed to pass a few of its own proposals: (1) creation of a new circuit court in Guadalajara, (2) penal code reforms for the Federal District and territories, (3) a stronger antipornography law, and (4) changes to facilitate credit to workers buying homes.[20]

PAN also began to meet electoral success. When the UNS made a deal with the dying Mexican Nationalist Party (a right-wing party of Catholic orientation) to use its registration to run candidates in the 1964 election, an act which threatened to put twenty *sinarquistas* into the Chamber of Deputies and cut into PAN's expected twenty deputies, the government yielded to PAN pressure and canceled the Mexican Nationalist Party registration.[21] In both the 1964 and 1967 federal deputy elections, PAN received twenty seats—eighteen party deputies in 1964 and nineteen in 1967.[22] Since the party deputy system aided PAN by giving it more patronage and allowing it to guarantee seats to worthy members, this was governmental encouragement of PAN. In addition, when the 1967 PRI federal deputy candidate for the ninth capital district seat was forced to withdraw as a result of an embarrassing altercation with the police, PRI allowed PAN's Javier Blanco Sánchez to run unopposed.[23] At the municipal level, PAN won control of Garza García, a Monterrey suburb, for two terms beginning in 1965; Mérida, Yucatán, the state capital; Hermosillo, Sonora, the state capital, and thirteen other municipalities in 1967. PAN now had rewards to offer its members.

These successes saved Christlieb from conservative *panistas* in the 1967 National Council meeting. Dr. Francisco Quiroga Fernández, National Parents' Union leader, and Federico Estrada Valera attacked Christlieb for recognizing the victory of Díaz Ordaz in 1964, claiming that he acted unilaterally, and for praising Mexico's strong presidential system in the Chamber of Deputies. Neither González Torres nor González Hinojosa accepted their nomination as president to replace Christlieb. The Council rallied behind the incumbent because he had increased PAN's influence.[24] Undaunted, the conservatives bided their time until the debate on the 1967 platform, assured that they would have more support from the general membership. Throughout the debate, the dissidents hinted that Christlieb's policy of dialogue was actually a sell-out to the government. Particularly agitating the conservatives was the omission of an anti–Article 3 plank in the 1964 and the proposed 1967 platforms. To them Christlieb was yielding to external pressure in adopting a "pink" plank. They had been consoled in 1964 with the presidential candidacy of González Torres; in 1967, they were allowed to amend the platform to include the anti-Article 3 plank.[25]

Beginning in 1967, however, the doors were slammed on PAN. Its apparent victories in the 1967 Sonora and 1969 Yucatán gubernatorial elections and the 1968 Baja California municipal and state legislative elections were converted into PRI successes under suspicious circumstances. PAN also believed that the party deputy system had been corrupted. Although 2.5 percent of the vote was necessary to receive any party deputies, PPS had been awarded ten deputies seats in 1964 with 1.37 percent of the vote and ten in 1967 with 2.37. PARM got five seats in both years with only 0.71 percent and 1.39 percent of the vote in 1964 and 1967, respectively. PAN did not accept the government's argument that it was obeying the spirit instead of the letter of the law. Instead, it believed that the Díaz Ordaz regime was using the sincere López Mateos reform to guarantee deputy seats to the opposition while rewarding all PRI candidates.[26]

PAN had decided to stay out of the 1967 Sonora gubernatorial election until it spotted the fight within the state PRI organization over the boss-directed nomination of the unpopular Faustino Félix Serna. A month after the nomination, several PRI renegades, aided by various other dissidents, went to PRI headquarters in Hermosillo demanding that Serna's candidacy be rescinded. Violence and bloodshed erupted. Students attacked Serna's campaign entourage in April and gave battle to police; several deaths occurred. Mexico City ordered federal troops to the state, but they now faced an outraged citizenry. More violence ensued. The use of tear gas quickly purchased or borrowed from Arizona raised a xenophobic outcry. By late June, fifteen had died. PAN watched the events and looked for a candidate until May, for it had a negligible organization in the state. Finally, it persuaded Gilberto Suárez Arvizu to run as its gubernatorial candidate.[27]

Suárez Arvizu was a wise choice for he had been a prominent PRI politician until he switched to PAN in May. He was a fifty-nine-year-old lawyer with extensive governmental experience. In Sonora, he had been general director of education, president of the Supreme Tribunal of Justice, state secretary-general, and interim governor. In Mexico City, he had been a penal judge, a high functionary of the Ministry of Government, and, until he accepted the PAN nomination, the chief of the alcohol department of the Federal District Treasury. Other PRI dissidents followed him into PAN, seeking municipal and state legislative posts.[28]

After the July 2 voting, PRI claimed victory in the gubernatorial election, in most municipal contests, and in all but one state legislative race, conceding victory to PAN in eight municipalities, including the state capital, Hermosillo, and in one state legislative race. PAN protested that it had won the governorship and more municipalities, and a majority of the state legislature but that PRI had resorted to massive fraud to reverse the results. PRI-government election statistics claimed that PAN had carried Hermosillo in the mayoralty race but had lost the city in the gubernatorial and legislative races by substantial margins. To no avail, PAN displayed acts of scrutiny from Hermosillo signed by pollwatchers showing PAN victories in all races. The election was a net gain for PAN since the party gained offices and national attention as a serious force, but it had been denied its first real opportunity to claim that it was an effective opposition to PRI.[29]

The Baja California municipal and state legislative elections the following year were an even more bitter experience for PAN. Baja California was a principal area of PAN strength; its organization extended down to the city block level and the state organization had issued a detailed study of the state's problems in 1964.[30] PAN believed that

PAN's Rosas Magallón had beaten PRI's Esquivel in the 1959 gubernatorial election. Since then, PAN asserted, party members had been persecuted by the state government.[31] Exacerbating tensions in 1967–68 were the maneuvers of ICSA (Inmuebles Californianos, S. A.) an organization which laid claim to the entire city of Tijuana except for its public facilities. Tied to the ICSA entrepreneurs was ex-Mexican President Miguel Alemán, which meant that ICSA had support from some of the richest and most powerful men in the government and the private sector. The complicated story of how ICSA had managed to inherit legal title to Tijuana has been related elsewhere,[32] but three key facts relating to the 1968 election stand out: (1) ICSA's legal title had been recognized by a federal court in 1967, (2) ICSA and its backers would make millions, and (3) outraged property owners organized as the Committee for the Defense of the Community of Tijuana under the leadership of such outraged PRI members as Luis Encisco Clark. PRI was also facing repudiation in the state capital, Mexicali, as citizens sought to end the reign of corruption, prostitution, and narcotics. PAN jumped into the election using ex-PRI leader Encisco Clark as its Tijuana mayorality candidate and ex-PRI leader Norberto Corella in Mexicali, backed by numerous PRI defectors.

Charges and countercharges flew in the campaign. PRI accused PAN of being bankrolled by rich men, of using priests in the campaign, of using wealthy men as candidates, of being in league with a land company to reclaim some of the property of Tijuana, and of using a candidate in Mexicali (Corella) who was not Mexican. PAN countered that the land company was owned by PRI members, that PRI was pressuring private enterprise to support PRI (which did occur), and that PRI was trying to discourage people from voting.[33]

The July 2 election results were confusing. PAN claimed that it had won the Tijuana and Mexicali municipalities and six of the nine state legislative seats (in Tijuana and Mexicali). PRI also immediately laid claim to victory, asserting that it had swept every race. They even disagreed as to the number of polling places. PRI claimed that there were 162 in Mexicali and 179 in Tijuana; PAN claimed that there were 270 and 267. Moreover, on June 20, 1968, Minister of Government Echeverría declared that "irregularities" had occurred and that the state legislature had been ordered by the national government to annul the results and to hold new elections. The irregularities boiled down to two key charges: in Tijuana, ballot boxes had been stolen and in Mexicali the citizenship of Norberto Corella was challenged. Neither charge was given much credence since Mexican and United States periodicals had shown pictures of government and police officials stealing ballot boxes, verifying accounts of eyewitnesses, and since Corella had a better claim to Mexican citizenship than his opponent. The United States–born Corella had become a Mexican citizen at age 18 and had served as a citizen in the Mexican armed forces.[34]

Several additional bits of evidence indicated that PAN actually won the races it claimed. Writers in *Excélsior,* a usually progovernment newspaper, took the unusual step of asserting that PAN had won.[35] PAN's traditionally strong state organization had been augmented by PRI defectors. Both Encisco Clark and Corella were handsome men who appealed to women voters. Since 1968, several nonpartisan political observers have asserted that PAN won. Besides, new elections were never held. Instead, the PRI-dominated state legislature performed gymnastics to conserve PRI control. The Tijuana and Mexicali municipal elections were annulled and joint PRI-PAN civic governing boards installed, but the legislature did not invalidate the state legislative elections which occurred at the same time, in the same polls, and in the same manner as the municipal elections.[36]

PAN continued to protest the Baja California machinations. National headquarters appealed to the press, the Chamber of Deputies, and the Supreme Court to no avail. In Baja California, PAN students demonstrated and instituted hunger strikes.[37] PRI and the government refused to budge.

The reasons for the government's adamancy are not difficult to discern. If PAN gained a foothold in Baja California, the party would extend the Baja California tactics throughout the country. Concurrently with the threat from PAN in northwestern Mexico were threats to government power and legitimacy by students in Mexico City throughout the summer and early fall of 1968.

Although the student difficulties had started as a not-uncommon fight between private high school and vocational school students, governmental handling of this and subsequent incidents catalyzed student opinion against the government and led to a crisis of major proportions. The initial confrontations quickly escalated, changed in nature, and became more violent. The government was nervous because of the Baja California elections and anxious that its frantic preparations for the 1968 Olympic Games in Mexico City, to be a showcase for modern Mexico, might be disrupted. As a result, it overreacted. By October 1, 1968, the government, through mismanagement and the use of repressive force, found itself confronting a coalition of the National Federation of Technical Students (a PRI dependency), the National Confederation of Democratic Students (a Mexican Communist Party youth group), the Mexican Communist Party, a National Strike Committee composed of usually mutually antagonistic national university and national polytechnical students, the national university's rector, faculty, and most of its students, the National Polytechnic Institute, PAN, parents, and much of the government's own bureaucracy. The government had used police, troops, cajolery, and assertions that the trouble was being instigated by Communists and the CIA to no avail. It also made it perfectly clear that it would use whatever force necessary to maintain control and to hold the Olympics. As a final effort to regroup and mobilize public support, radical students called for a giant rally on October 2 in the Plaza of the Three Cultures in the Tlatelolco housing project. The rally turned into a massacre as the army and police appeared on the scene in armored vehicles and shooting began. An unknown number of people were killed, including many innocent victims, and new prisoners were added to the already large numbers arrested since June.[38]

PAN saw all this as more evidence of what it had been saying for years: the corrupt Mexican government would maintain itself in power at all costs. PAN did not believe that the students were completely innocent, but it did believe that the government had been unable to make distinctions and to act accordingly. Instead, it had blamed foreign and communist involvement and met legitimate dissent with violent repression. The iron hands of Díaz Ordaz and Echeverría were felt by non-*panistas*.

Before discussing the 1969 Yucatán election, the last of the trilogy of elections which caused an internal crisis in Acción Nacional, it is necessary to discuss interim events, for Christlieb suddenly resigned PAN's presidency in September 1968. Christlieb stated at the time that he was retiring because of poor health. PRI claimed that the conservative faction, unhappy with the changes Christlieb had wrought in PAN, had forced him out, that PAN was now reverting to its former "reactionary" role. Fourteen months later Christlieb died of intestinal cancer. Secretary-general Ignacio Maurer Limón acted as caretaker until Manuel González Hinojosa was elected president in February 1969.[39]

Speculation continued within and without PAN as to whether the Christlieb spirit ended with the selection of the more conservative González Hinojosa since he was not Christlieb's candidate and his national committee included an increased number of old-line *panistas*.[40] The fifty-seven-year-old native of San Luis Potosí was one of the many lawyers who had founded PAN in 1939. He had been a PAN leader in his native state until the mid-1950s when, PAN claims, he was driven out by the state political boss. He still jokes that his antigovernment fights in San Luis Potosí, first as a Catholic Action militant and later as a *panista,* gave him prematurely grey hair while he was still in his twenties. The

move to the Federal District was a good one. He headed a large successful law firm, taught agricultural and sociological law in the national university, and agricultural law in the Jesuits' Iberoamerican University. He
had long been active in PAN politics and had earned the confidence of
conservative *panistas*. Moreover, he had selected Juan Manuel Gómez
Morín, eldest son of the founder, as his secretary-general. The younger
Gómez Morín is a very serious man who lives in his father's shadow.
The father, however, is more liberal than his son; his position in society
is more secure. Thus, the new leadership appeared to represent a repudiation of the open-minded progressivism of the last six years.[41]

González Hinojosa was more progressive than observers realized. One
cause of the confusion was that, whereas Christlieb was dynamic, decisive, and domineering, the thin, narrow-faced González Hinojosa was
soft-spoken, cautious, and self-effacing. Lacking the political acumen of
his predecessor, he had been unable to catalyze the party or to exploit
opportunities fully. Christlieb's intellectual heir, Efraín González Luna
Morfín, and other progressives sat on the National Committee prodding
González Hinojosa. The president had supported the Christian socialist
Democratic Change of the Structures position promulgated in the February 1969 convention. His conservative image in some quarters resulted,
then, more from personality traits than from his ideological tendencies.
He had not been able to give PAN the leadership it needed, however.

Perhaps even the best leadership could not have resolved the problems of the Yucatán crisis which exploded in November 1969.[42] Relations between Yucatán and Mexico City have been strained since colonial
times as the independent-minded, separatist Mayas have resisted control
by the central government. In the 1840s this tension had exploded into
the Caste War and *yucatecan* requests to be annexed to the United States
to escape Mexico City control. Yucatan was a gigantic henequen plantation, the principal source of sisal fiber. By the time of the Revolution, a
small, affluent elite, the "Divine Caste," ruled the land and the people
with strict controls and low wages. Cárdenas made a special case of
Yucatán, turning it into a gigantic collective farm. In a very real sense,
yucatetcos worked as peons on a government plantation. Synthetic fibers
slashed the demand for sisal and, consequently, Yucatán was thrown
into almost permanent economic crisis. To bolster prices, the government created CORDEMEX to manufacture and market sisal products.

Political problems plagued Yucatán as well. Official party monopoly
of public office was traditionally strong. The PRI state organization was
weak not only because decisions were made in Mexico City but also because it seldom faced competition. No opposition gubernatorial candidate had been offered for seventy years. One result had been administra-

tive and moral laxness. Popular discontent had risen in the 1960s as numerous scandals swept the state, including waste of an Inter-American Development Bank loan earmarked for a public water system which was never built. Corruption also rocked the principal *ejidal* agency, the Department of Agrarian Affairs and Colonization. As a result, labor began to desert PRI for PAN and *ejidatarios* were dropping their traditional support of PRI.

PAN's *yucatecan* organization, led by Victor Manuel Correa Rachó, reaped the benefits. The PAN state organization had existed since 1939 but had only been able to win a federal deputy seat in 1958. In 1967, however, the corrupt incumbent municipal government of Mérida provided the proverbial back-breaking straw, and Correa Rachó and PAN rode the tide to success by sweeping Mérida municipal offices and obtaining state legislative seats. Correa Rachó then rewarded his supporters with honest, efficient government. Governor Luis Torres Mesías retaliated by harassing PAN. Correa Rachó was publicly denounced; a PAN state legislator was removed; prominent *panistas* were cajoled into defecting; state aid to Mérida was withheld; and strikes by taxi and bus drivers were encouraged. On June 9, 1969, armed soldiers and the head of the state police took control of the Mérida police force. *Yucatecos* applauded Correa Rachó when he stood fast in true *yucatecan* tradition.

PAN had unquestionably found the right combination for its first gubernatorial victory. Its efficient, extensive organization headed by the charismatic, smooth, and politically sophisticated Correa Rachó faced Carlos Loret de Mola, a newsman and former PRI senator who had not lived in the state for years, and a divided, unpopular PRI Yucatan state machine. As a former *panista* who had since been friendly towards PAN through his news organization, Loret de Mola was somewhat manacled. PRI's disarray was phenomenal. Neither Loret de Mola nor PRI national president Alfonso Martínez Domínguez could heal the split. Worse still, PRI defections to PAN meant that PAN had so thoroughly penetrated PRI that it knew PRI's plans intimately. While Correa Rachó played upon *yucatecan* regionalism and resentment of PRI and the government without promising more than honesty, hard work, and popular participation in decision-making, PRI committed one error after another. Correa Rachó supporters and PAN offices were physically attacked. Martínez Domínguez made two serious blunders further alienating the state. In a secret meeting, he insulted the Mérida archbishop by demanding that the priest prevent clerical support of PAN, an allegation which the archbishop denied. He demanded of private enterprise that the men withhold financial support of PAN and prevent their wives and daughters from aiding it. They replied that they were supporting PRI, as they had always done. News of the two meetings leaked out. Support for PAN swelled.

Unable to win legitimately, PRI stole the election. This harsh judgment is supported by abundant evidence. Throughout the campaign, the Correa Rachó rallies had been large and enthusiastic, unlike Loret de Mola's meetings.[43] The PAN candidate had begun visiting state leaders in the summer, listening to their problems and establishing personal contacts which he used effectively in the fall campaign. Loret de Mola, on the other hand, made brief campaign stops by helicopter, never staying long enough in one place.[44] The state government never printed and posted official lists of polling places and disqualified numerous PAN pollwatchers.[45] The *Diario de Yucatán,* which supported PAN, published the list of polls on the morning before the November 27 election, but almost all of the copies were immediately bought and burned.[46] On election day, many polls were undiscoverable and a few others were in neighboring Quintana Roo. PAN claims that peasants were trucked in from neighboring Chiapas state to vote for PRI. Mexican and foreign newsmen reported seeing armed robbery of ballot boxes and numerous other instances of fraud.[47] Half an hour after the polls closed, Loret de Mola announced his victory by a 90 percent margin, which coincided with later government figures, even though voting was by paper ballot and communications within the state were difficult.[48] Martial law was declared within a few hours after the election. Belief that PAN won was widespread in Mexico. Finally, important governmental officials have privately told the present author that PAN did win but that the government cannot allow the inexperienced PAN to run a state nor gain significant strength.

Further analysis of this election and the ones in Baja California and Sonora offer a clearer picture of PAN's role in the political system in the 1960s and of the government's willingness to allow PAN more than a token opposition role. These elections were unusual and the reader should not conclude that the government was in trouble all over Mexico. They do form a pattern, however. Each state is on the Mexican periphery and regionalistic antagonism played an important part. Each state is atypical in its wealth—Baja California and Sonora because they are on the high end of the income scale, Yucatán because it is on the low end. The two northern states could afford to act independently whereas *yucatecos* resented their continuing poverty. In each election, it was dissatisfaction with the government rather than PAN's appeal that created the possibility of an opposition victory. PAN was the vehicle of protest voting. The clumsy and heavy-handed governmental handling of the nomination process and the subsequent violence drove PRI leaders and ordinary citizens into PAN. Although state government officials played the key role in creating these conditions, the ultimate responsibility lies with Díaz Ordaz, who also used blunt, coercive tactics to destroy the student movement in 1968. The use of such violence seems to be tied more to the personality of Díaz Ordaz than to the political system as a whole. Díaz Ordaz apparently underestimated the effects of his early encouragement of PAN and then found it necessary to use decisive measures to prevent the party from becoming a serious threat.

PAN played an active role in creating the possibilities of these serious challenges. The Sonora situation was serendipitous, but the rapidity with which PAN responded and the willingness of prominent PRI leaders to join PAN were the result of the Christlieb changes in PAN. Christlieb had nurtured a positive party image while preparing the party for just such an eventuality. These changes were important in Baja California and Yucatán as well, even though PAN had long been operating in those states. Christlieb has realized that PAN had to have allies if it was going to break PRI's monopoly.

To continue its monopoly the government had to demonstrate that it would not allow any opposition to use these tactics. If they paid off, the defection of PRI dissidents might become more general, thereby threatening to split PRI. Once the repressive measures started, the government had to use them in all three elections because the public martyrdom of PAN in each election helped the party in each subsequent election by bolstering its argument that only it opposed government tyranny. For PAN to capture control of a state either through the governorship or state legislative and municipal elections would have encouraged opposition groups across Mexico to attack governmental control of states.

PAN benefited from the experience. It increased its credibility as an independent opposition party committed to political democracy. It spread its propaganda into previously unreceptive quarters while recruiting new members from diverse social sectors. Finally, it learned its most effective tactic for competing with the government, that of exploiting bona fide dissatisfaction. Since then, the party has been ready to spring at similar opportunities thus forcing the government to stay more alert to undercurrents of discontent.

Even though PAN had come to expect fraud in the Yucatán election, the extent and nature of it when it came rocked the party to its foundations. Its public forewarnings of fraud had been intensifying since September, but the government made no efforts to rectify the situation. In desperation, the Yucatán delegation to the November 1969 national convention, supported by others, pleaded with the convention to suspend decision on participation in the 1970 federal elections until after their electoral battle, hoping to pressure the government into holding honest elections. National leaders had difficulty convincing the *yucatecos* to return to the convention after they stormed out in disgust with the convention's refusal to agree to their demand. But, after the Yucatán debacle and the Mexico (state) and Nuevo León municipal elections the following month (in which PAN also claimed fraud had denied it victory), the *yucatecos* supported by the state committees of Baja California, Sonora, Sinaloa, Chihuahua, Durango, Nuevo León, Jalisco, Michoacán, and Colima, forced PAN to hold another national convention in January 1970 to reconsider participation in the upcoming federal elections.

The seriousness of the step of holding a second convention should be seen in the light of the November convention. From my observations and conversations at that convention, it was clear that PAN was enthusiastically in favor of participation. The convention hall, a large skating arena, reverberated with the shouts of 4,000 delegates as they chanted the names of the two leading candidates for the nomination: Efraín González Morfín and Salvador Rosas Magallón. After heated debate, the delegates shouted their votes for participation. With equal enthusiasm, the delegates turned to the long process of choosing a presidential candidate, electing González Morfín on the third ballot when Rosas Magallón withdrew. The victor had failed to capture the required 80 percent of the votes on the first ballot but had led all the way—210.5–144.5 and 224–131, respectively. He was supported by the progressives, the Federal District, and most of the national leadership. The delegates were jubilant.[49]

In contrast, the January 17, 1970, extraordinary national convention was somber and racked by dissension. The slightly more than one thousand delegates realized that PAN faced its greatest crisis, its very existence, an attitude very evident as the present author milled around the floor conversing with delegates.

Three courses of action were proposed in the convention. González Hinojosa, Rafael Preciado Hernández, and Rosas Magallón argued for full participation as the only hope for PAN influence and the only posture consistent with PAN ideology. Partial abstentionists such as Correa Rachó and Juan Landerreche Obregón wanted to use the presidential candidate to spread PAN ideas and to attack the government's legitimacy. Luis H. Alvarez, José González Torres, and Gerardo Medina Valdés, *La Nación* editor, spoke for total abstention because PAN should not legitimize the election, which would surely be fraudulent, but should force the issue of dictatorship in Mexico. PRI-government actions since the 1968 Baja California elections were cited as proof of governmental intentions.

When the vote was taken, full participation won by a thin six-vote majority. Out of 355 votes, full participation received 183.5, partial 30, and abstention 141.5. More serious, however, six of the twenty-nine national committeemen who had voted for total abstention were important national leaders: Enrique Creel Luján, PAN treasurer, Medina Valdés, González Torres, Abel Vincencio Tovar, Astolfo Vincencio Tovar, and González Morfín. They wanted PAN to become a resistance movement once the government canceled the party's registration. Finally, Baja California, Chihuahua, and other states distant from Mexico City had voted for total abstention as an attack on the dominance of PAN's Mexico City leadership. Correa Rachó tried to introduce regionalism into the debate but had been cut off.[50]

In the first quarter of 1970, PAN was in a state of crisis. Important national and regional leaders did not want to participate. By late March, only the Federal District organization had begun nominating congressional candidates. By the July election, PAN had found only 171 candidates for 178 federal deputy posts and 54 senatorial candidates out of a possible 60, fewer than three years before, a nonpresidential year. Efraín González Morfín, or Efraín as he was called during the campaign, began his campaign in compliance with party discipline although he had voted against participation. Because of the delay, PRI's candidate, former Minister of Government Luis Echeverría Alvarez had gotten a two-month head start. PAN's usual prospects looked even bleaker.

The selection of Echeverría actually benefited PAN in the long run. As Minister of Government since 1964, he had been Díaz Ordaz's chief political officer and, thus, had presided over the Sonora, Baja California, and Yucatán elections as well as the 1968 student conflict, when his authority was second only to that of Díaz Ordaz. As a result many Mexicans, especially students, disliked him. Throughout Mexico his campaign posters were often defaced by the word "assassin" written on them. His "Upward and Onward" campaign slogan promised more of the same. Ironically, perhaps, many of his proposed reforms, such as extension of social security to the countryside, were PAN positions of the early 1940s. Not surprisingly, important bankers and entrepreneurs, including some former *panistas,* toured Mexico with him;[51] PRI was tacitly admitting that it was the bulwark of private enterprise.

Efraín, on the other hand made concerted appeals to the disgruntled and the alienated. He carefully defined PAN's position as leftist, meaning "disquietude with the present and the desire to better conditions." He sought to identify PAN with progressivism while castigating the government as bourgeois, conservative, and repressive. Throughout the campaign, PAN used his first name, the blue and white PAN symbol with the word Peace (*PAZ*) interchangeably with PAN, and United Nations symbolism. His platform was an amplification of the *Democratic Change of the Structures* document which he had co-authored with Christlieb. As he traveled 31,000 miles through every state and territory, meeting with voters and holding rallies, he pushed PAN's position even further leftward. By June, his speeches resembled warmed-over Marxism as much as progressive Catholic thought.[52] Large numbers of students, workers, and peasants began joining PAN, an institution which a few years before they had usually considered to be conservative and/or a tool of the regime.[53] With his 14 percent of the vote, the largest ever recognized for a PAN presidential candidate, he swept twenty party deputies into office.[54] More significantly for PAN's future, he had captured control of the party.

Although Efraín was an intellectual and not a politician, he was an ideal presidential candidate and party leader for the 1970s. Prior to the campaign, his political experience had been limited to a term in the Chamber of Deputies (1967–70) and a short stint as PAN regional president in the Federal District. The presidential campaign, however, gave him the experience and contacts necessary to lead a political party. Out of respect for his father, conservative *panistas* supported him, as had the UNS, but he was neither obligated nor influenced by them.

A native of Jalisco, Efraín had left Mexico in 1949 at the age of twenty-one, after having been educated in Church schools and the national university. His ten years abroad were spent studying economics, philosophy, political science, theology, and languages in the United States, France, and Austria. He acquired thorough knowledge of contemporary European social thought outside the influence of Mexican culture, allowing him more detachment as he viewed the problems of his native land. After he left a Jesuit seminary, he also acquired a French wife. His Jesuit ties are significant, for these priests have been leading radical and progressive Catholic movements. The Jesuits have been instrumental in founding Christian Democratic parties in Latin America.

When Efraín returned to Mexico in 1959, he joined Acción Nacional, the only political alternative to a son of a PAN founder. He obtained a job as an economist with the Banco de Londres y México, which employed many *panistas,* and supplemented his income as a translator. His presidential campaign forced him to change his career. The Banco de Londres y México, by then owned by a Monterrey consortium, fired him to prove its loyalty to the government. He recently took a law degree from the Jesuit's Iberoamerican University where he had been lecturing. His personal qualities also aid him. He is young, attractive, well-educated, and intelligent. Throughout all the attention focused upon him, he has remained personable and modest but mentally tough.

González Hinojosa and not Efraín led the February 1971 meeting of party chieftains which created the Centers of Municipal, Legislative, and Leadership Training and started a program of systematic reevaluation of PAN's and Mexico's future. As a result of this meeting, regional organizations began writing position papers on program, tactics, and internal operation of the party to be presented in an August national meeting.[55] Efraín, however, had been playing a decisive role in these changes.

Between the February party chieftains' meeting and the August 1971 national meeting, Acción Nacional's leftists maneuvered to gain complete control of the party. As a first step, they authored the new internal leadership training documents and led the subsequent training sessions.[56] Next, they supported structural reforms to decrease national control of regional organizations, to reduce national presidential powers, and to increase the power of the youth and women's organizations. These reforms were adopted in the August national meeting.[57] Finally, they pushed for thorough study of past tactics and ideas to give themselves time to remold the party in their likeness.

As the present author observed the reactions to these events and the concurrent maneuvering within PAN, it appeared that the Efraín group would ultimately win. The leftward shift threatened to curtail or terminate financial support from rich but conservative members and supporters, but PAN's ongoing conversion into a party of the masses should overcome whatever deficits occurred. Also, PAN would probably continue to receive support from many of its traditional sources because party founders were not likely to adandon their creation nor will small and medium-sized enterprises be likely to favor PRI, which supports large enterprises. So, the leftists no longer believed that they had to placate the conservatives. In addition, the leftists had the majority of the young and new members on their side, for it was Efraín who recruited them. The leftists were led by talented men: Efraín, Eugenio Ortiz Walls (*oficial mayor* or party manager), Luis Calderón Vega, Enrique Creel Luján, Rosas Magallón, and Fernando Estrada Sámano.

In the midst of the jockeying for position within PAN, governmental reaction to new student demonstrations and another Baja California state election in the summer of 1971 gave *panistas* (and perhaps other Mexicans) a *déjà vu* experience and aided PAN leftists by driving more frustrated Mexicans into PAN's ranks. Even though only incomplete data are available because of the recentness of the events and their controversial nature, tentative comments are warranted because of their effect on PAN.

No one was expecting violence on June 10, 1971, for student-governmental relations had been basically pacific since the Tlatelolco tragedy in October 1968. Many student leaders of the former struggle were in jail or in exile. Lacking leadership and fearing governmental reaction, students had launched no new mass demonstrations. In Monterrey, however, University of Nuevo León students had started demonstrating for educational reform in the spring of 1971, and these actions had met active resistance by the state government. Nothing occurred on the 1968 scale however. Feeling confident, Mexico City leftist student leaders from the National Polytechnical Institute, aided by students from other schools, planned a gigantic march on June 10 from the Polytechnic to the Monument to the Revolution to demand support for their Monterrey counterparts, the end of repressive governmental tactics, and the freeing of political prisoners. Police and troops arrived on the scene, ostensibly to maintain order. While the parade was still in progress, recently painted grey trucks, buses and jeeps rolled up and disgorged hundreds of young men armed with high-powered rifles and other weapons. Shouting military commands, using radio transmission facilities, and using military tactics, the Falcons, as they were called, attacked the demonstrators. The police and troops did not stop them; in fact, some sources assert that they aided the Falcons by providing radio communications. After killing eleven and injuring hundreds more, including journalists covering the event, the Falcons reloaded and drove away without being arrested. The number of dead and injured is not known, for the Falcons followed their victims to hospitals and kidnapped some, many of whom have not been seen since. The paramilitary nature of the Falcons and the apparent collusion of the peacekeeping forces as well as comments overheard on the scene by eyewitnesses led many Mexicans, including PAN, to charge that the Falcons were a secret instrument of the Mexico City government. Further, according to some sources, many, if not all of the Falcons, were part-time policemen and their vehicles were thinly disguised city vehicles.[58]

Governmental handling of the aftermath also suggested official backing of the Falcons and the June 10 incident. Mexican President Echeverría expressed disgust, promised to launch a full investigation, and promised to punish the culpable.[59] On June 15, the Mexico City regent, ex-PRI president Martínez Domínguez, and the city police chief "voluntarily" resigned.[60] No disclosures of the investigation results nor arrests had been made by September 1971. Journalists, television cameramen, bystanders, students, and *panistas* (the incident occurred near PAN headquarters) had offered to testify. The pressure on the national attorney-general became so intense by mid-August that he too resigned. Some observers believed that these resignations were dismissals.

In contrast, the August Baja California elections were pacific, but PAN declared that once again it had been denied victory in Mexicali and Tijuana by fraud. It conceded victory to PRI in the state's other two *municipios,* Tecate and Ensenada, registering pride that PAN had increased its share of the vote, but the party asserted that the ballot boxes had been stuffed and their contents intentionally miscounted in three Mexicali districts and in all Tijuana districts. From the published charges it was not clear that PAN was only claiming victory in the Mexicali and Tijuana municipal elections and not also in Rosas Magallón's gubernatorial bid, but several PAN leaders have privately admitted to me that Rosas Magallón did lose.[61]

PAN decided to interpret the Baja California electoral event as another indication that Echeverría would be as close-minded as Díaz Ordaz even though the party admitted that it had less popular support there than in 1968. In its view, the abnormally low voter turnout (less than 50 percent) hurt PAN because the reduced numbers facilitated vote manipulation. Baja California apathy was induced by cynicism towards the integrity of the electoral process and by an extremely hot election day which drove thousands of citizens to the beaches in search of relief.[62] In confidential conversations with me, several *panistas* in Michoacán and Mexico City expressed doubt that PAN had won any of these contests because the party had not been able to find an issue with which to excite the voters. From these and other conversations as well as perusal of newspaper accounts, the present author believes that PRI swept Baja California.

Acción Nacional believed that the June 10 incident and the Baja California election were only part of a more general approaching crisis in Mexican politics. Party leaders believed that the Mexican citizenry was becoming increasingly disenchanted with the failure of the government to resolve the problems which plagued the country. One sign of this growing alienation, in their view, was the increase of guerrilla and terrorist activity in the country, which, they believed, the government was tacitly recognizing when it arrested North Korean-trained Mexican guerrillas in the first months of 1971. Another sign was what they believed to be the low urban voter turnouts in the 1970 federal elections.

Acción Nacional's analysis of Mexico's socioeconomic problems was contained in the *Problemático Nacional* paper adopted by the August 1971 national convention. Significantly, this paper was authored by two of the leading Christian socialists in PAN, Efraín González Morfín and

Fernando Estrada Sámano.[63] In education, 50% of Mexico is illiterate; the six-year and older population has completed an average of 2.6 grades; almost four million school age children have no schools; only 33% of students who enter primary school finish; only 50% of the education budget is spent; whereas half of urban students finish primary school only 10% of rural students do; 70% of the rural schools do not have six grades; in Guerrero, Oaxaca, and Chiapas only 60% of the students ever enter school; and, nationally, only 1.91% of those who begin primary school ever obtain a university degree. In general, Acción Nacional argued, the highest socioeconomic strata have been favored in spite of Revolutionary declarations to the contrary. Educational reforms instituted through popular participation in decision-making in formulating educational policy and planning was imperative to solve these problems.

Educational deficits were intimately related to income distribution and marginality. In 1963, the poorest 68% of the population received 30.3% of national income while the richest 6% received 30.9%. PAN believed that income distribution was even worse than these figures suggested. The share of the poorest 19% of the population fell from 3% in 1950 to 2% in 1957 to 1% in 1963 while the richest 1% of the population received 42% of national income in 1963. Seven percent of the population, according to PAN, lived at the marginal level. According to PAN, Mexico continued to be a dual society because the rulers have betrayed the Revolution. The party believes that priorities must be redirected to aid the poor, who, because they have been carrying an inhuman burden for the benefit of the rest of the country, are the "true heroes of Mexican development."

Acción Nacional believed that the rural areas suffered the greatest social injustices because the government decided to stress industrialization at the expense of the 40% of the labor force who live in the countryside. According to PAN statistics, almost 59% of the farms yield only 4.2% of total agricultural production and produce an average of only 750 pesos of annual income. Eighty percent of all farms did not produce subsistence-level family incomes. Two-thirds of Mexico's unemployed were rural. Between two and three million persons had no land even though they had a legal right to it through the government's land reform program. The bitter irony was that the village of the Revolution's legendary peasant leader Emiliano Zapata had an average income ranging between thirty-six and forty-two dollars. Lack of appropriate credit, insecurity of land title, strangulation of internal markets, and political exploitation were the causes. The party demanded that Mexico redirect investment to rural areas and terminate the political manipulation of the rural population.

To Acción Nacional, Mexican socioeconomic problems resulted directly from the illegitimacy of its autocratic, paternalistic, elitist, and overly centralized government. Power is concentrated in a few hands, often invisible to the public, instead of being shared by the citizenry through democratic decision-making. As a result, the government maintains itself in power by chicanery, mythology, fraud, and violence. Because there are few legitimate means of representation, this institutionalized violence is met by radicalization, and consequently, counterviolence. The government in 1971, in the PAN view, was facing a dilemma: either a democratic opening and a more human society, which would reduce the power of the Revolutionary coalition, or increased repression of popular demands, which would lead to the government's overthrow.[64]

The party saw its immediate task as being the search for viable courses of political action to establish a responsive, legitimate government. Such courses of action would have to be nonviolent and nondemagogic. The party had to act as a vehicle of protest and pressure, but also had to educate and mobilize the citizenry. National, regional, and local PAN meetings were to be called immediately to identify specific problems and to offer coordinated programs of action.

To lead this search the party dropped the relatively ineffective González Hinojosa as president and elected José Angel Conchello Dávila in February 1972 in hope that he could find solutions to PAN's problems. Conchello's election was a victory for the Christian Socialist wing for he was the candidate of González Morfín. Like Efraín, Conchello was multilingual, a lawyer specialized in economics, a former federal deputy, a native of a provincial capital (Monterrey), a late entrant into PAN's ranks (1955), and experienced in foreign study, having had a United Nations fellowship to study industrial promotion in Canada. The forty-nine-year-old CONCAMIN employee had lived in Mexico City since 1952. His experience and connections meant that he would be acceptable to both the "socialist" and the capitalist wings of the party.

To Acción Nacional in 1971–72, the election of such a man seemed particularly important because the party believed then that whatever delusions Mexicans may have had that the new Echeverría regime (1970–76) would bring an opening to the left should have been shattered by the June 10 incident and the Baja California election. They believed at that point that the Echeverría government was promising more of the same: betrayed progressive promises with the benefits actually accruing to the privileged and favored. Unless national action (*acción nacional*) of the citizenry could be aroused to force needed changes, the prognosis for Mexico would be escalation of polarization, violence, and repression.

PAN was interpreting the prevailing conditions and predicting future events more on the basis of what party members hoped would happen than on the realities of the Mexican political situation. The party was correct in asserting that the Revolutionary government under Díaz Ordaz was losing popular support because of its repression of the popular will in the three major disputed elections, because of its overuse of force in suppressing the student movement, and because it had done little to reverse the trend towards worsening socioeconomic conditions for many Mexicans. Opposition groups were benefiting from this growing popular disgust. Nevertheless, PAN was believing its own propaganda too readily and was subscribing to a devil theory of politics. It was refusing to recognize that, whatever else they might be, Revolutionary leaders are committed to social reform and capable of altering governmental policies to deal with problems as they arise. They had interpreted the mailed-fist policy of Díaz Ordaz as being one to which future governments were unalterably committed. In the context of the events of the summer of 1972, they believed that Echeverría would be another Díaz Ordaz and that PAN would benefit.

At the time of this writing, Echeverría has begun to teach all Mexican politicians the fundamental fact of Mexican politics for the past forty-odd years: that the Revolutionary governments are the masters of events. They create the conditions which lead to massive protest but they also learn from their mistakes and reap the benefits. Echeverría and his government have publicly acknowledged the conditions about which PAN and other Mexicans have been complaining. But, unlike PAN, Echeverría can actually do something about them. In his first eleven months of office, he traveled over 27,000 miles throughout Mexico pushing reforms which he believes must be made. In answer to charges of corruption and lackadaisical bureaucrats, he has launched a campaign against corruption, raised customs officials' salaries, and forced bureaucrats to work late at night. To reduce inflation (which rose to 10% in 1970) he cut governmental expenditures by 10% and raised taxes. To force the redistribution of national income and of the country's resources, he has reworked the tax laws to increase revenues from corporations, has added a 10% luxury tax, has been taxing all capital gains, has reduced depreciation write-offs, has put more teeth into income tax laws, has given economic incentives for industries to locate in economically-depressed areas, and has stressed public investment in agriculture and the rural sector. He has recognized China and traveled to Japan and the United States seeking to expand and diversify markets. He is encouraging foreign investors into export and development-oriented industries in Mexico. He has been pushing for new concessions to labor, democratic labor unions, better wage policies, new social security measures, special programs for marginal groups, more vocational training, and the extension of public health services, rural development, and low-cost housing.

His political measures have been equally reform-minded. He has promised greater press freedom and an expanded role for opposition parties. He has announced that he will seek the reduction of registration requirements for political parties and to give them free postage and communication rights. The minimum age for federal deputies has been reduced to twenty-five and for senators to thirty. The possible number of party deputies has been increased to twenty-five, while the minimum percentage of the vote to receive five party deputies has been dropped to 1.5%. To lead this effort, Echeverría appointed his own man, Jesús Reyes Heroles, as PRI head. To convince cyncial and apathetic critics of his sincerity, he made a pilgrimage to Chile, where the Marxist Salvador Allende is president, and to the United States, which he lambasted during a joint session of Congress. Finally, the guerrilla-terrorist activity has been slowed down by a combination of this reform effort, a governmental crackdown on known leaders, and increased protection for various politicians.

Whether Echeverría is successful in accomplishing all these measures remains to be seen, for he has to overcome opposition within the government coalition, but the effort and the publicity surrounding it removed PAN's potentiality of capitalizing on national discontent. For the time being, PAN can only oppose the techniques of the reforms rather than the reforms themselves.

PAN's long-range hope has to be that the government will become trapped in a situation from which it cannot extricate itself, either because the unresolved internal conflicts within the coalition immobilizes it or because some strong Mexican president can and will force the creation of a truly competitive political system. Nothing in Mexican history, even the current reform effort, suggests that either is likely to occur. Acción Nacional has reached the limits of influence.

MEXICO'S
ACCION NACIONAL

*A Catholic Alternative
to Revolution*

PART II

CHAPTER VI

Doctrine, Program, Appeals

PAN ideology has slowly evolved from its early, vague, and conservative tone to a precise, progressive Christian Democratic line. The core of the party's views of man and society has remained the same; the shift has been one of emphasis not content. Both the 1939 *Principles of Doctrine* and the *Principles of Doctrine—Their Projection in 1965* share the same philosophical roots: (1) Catholic social doctrine as stated in the papal encyclicals *Rerum Novarum* (1891) and *Quadregesimo Anno* (1931), (2) the Mexican social Congresses, and (3) the neo-Thomist writings of Jacques Maritain and others, but the 1965 *Principles* reflect the changes in Catholic social doctrine which became clear with Vatican II. Thus, the newer ideology is also based on *Mater Et Magistra* (1961), *Pacem In Terris* (1963), and *Populorum Progressio* (1967). Within Latin American Catholicism, an even more progressive social doctrine has been outlined by the Latin American Bishops' Conference, a doctrine to which the Mexican hierarchy officially subscribes. These sources have also been the sources of Latin American Christian Democratic parties.[1]

DOCTRINE

Significantly, Acción Nacional calls its ideology "Political Humanism." Other Latin American Christian Democratic parties use the terms Christian Humanism and integral humanism. All are trying to focus their ideas upon the human person, the object of all societal action.[2] The terms "human person" and "humanism" are important, for these parties are rejecting the liberal conception of the atomistic individual. They deny that man is a mere biological organism.[3]

Instead, the person or human is a complex creature who has both material and spiritual qualities. As a material being, he lives in the temporal world and has rights and duties within it. Above this level, however, as a

99

being created in God's image, he has a spiritual nature which ties him to the Eternal. As the image of God, each person has intrinsic worth, more important than his temporal status. Because of this intrinsic worth, the human person has inviolable and inalienable rights. He has the right to dignity, to live above the subsistence level and to save, the right to control his own destiny, the right to enjoy civil liberties and civil rights, and the right to contribute to the general well-being of mankind. He also has the duty of living the Christian life, of respecting the rights of fellow humans, and of aiding them in the enjoyment of their rights.

The multifaceted human person always lives in societies; he is never the isolated individual of liberalism (a unit in the whole) nor part of an undifferentiated mass as in Marxism or fascism. Instead, he lives in a symbiotic relationship with natural communities. He is born into the primary society or community, the family. Throughout his life he will participate in other societies—governments, work associations, cultural groups, religious groups, and recreational groups. Each has the function of aiding the individual to fulfill his destiny, his maximum potentiality. Therefore, the societies also have rights which must be protected.

Political Humanism posits, therefore, the idea of constructing and operating politics so that man-in-society can enjoy justice, meaning each receives his due, and liberty. The just society promotes the common good—the existence of conditions which permit liberty and promote human responsibility. By the 1960s Acción Nacional was using the Christian Democratic terms solidarity and communitarianism to denote this interdependence inherent in human affairs, but the concept that "no man is an island" was fundamental to the earliest PAN writings. Human dignity could be protected and human happiness furthered only by persons working as individuals and within intermediate societies to create the perfect society, one in which the common good reigned.

Human potentiality can only be reached with dignity through democratic subsidiarity. Between the individual who determines his own destiny and the State which insures the existence of the common good exists a multitude of natural intermediate societies to serve the needs and desires of the persons composing them. The most important intermediate society, the cellular social unit, is the family. A properly run family supports its members economically, socializes them, and transmits the cultural values as part of its task of providing the common good for its members. If it does its job well, there is little else for other societies to do. When a single family reaches the level of its competence, it seeks the help of other families: the *municipio*. When this political body reaches its level of competence, it seeks the aid of the next highest government, a process that culminates at the national level. Man also has economic, social, cultural, religious, and recreational interests. Therefore, the person is simultaneously a member of various societies. Each of these societies makes its own contribution to individual and common good and is the arbiter of the common good within its level of competence. The common good can be determined, however, only by democratic decision-making for only that technique allows the person to protect his perceived self-interest.

Under the rule of democratic subsidiarity, no single society can control either the individual or another society. The common good results when each constituent member of society performs its function. Unlike fascist corporatism to which the ideology bears some resemblance, the national state cannot dictate the common good. *Panistas* distinguish between the governmental apparatus and the nation. The latter is the total collectivity which has its own traditions and life and is composed of the people and societies within it. The function of the national governmental apparatus is to execute the decisions of the nation. Whenever the governmental apparatus does not base its decisions on the common good it is oppressive. Fascist, Marxist, and liberal capitalist states are condemned because none seek the general common good but seek the common good of only part of the nation—a ruling elite, the proletariat, or the atomistic individual.

In such a context, property becomes an instrumental not an absolute right. Because the human person must control his own affairs, he needs the means to accomplish the task: the right to acquire and use property. The necessity of respecting the rights of others as well as the demands of intermediate societies upon property limit the property right to a social function. *Panistas* agree with the Marxists that capitalism concentrates wealth in the hands of the few, leaving the masses in varying states of misery, but agree with capitalists that individual initiative is the best motor for economic development. Acción Nacional tries to avoid the evils of the two systems by asserting that individuals have the right to property insofar as private property serves a useful social function and economic misery does not exist. For those persons unable to provide themselves with a decent living, the collectivity must step in and provide comprehensive social security (medical care, recreational facilities, unemployment and accident compensation, and cash income). The family, however, has the primary responsibility for its members and therefore must have its own patrimony. In rural areas, this patrimony would be family farms capable of providing the entire family with a decent living and allowing it to save for future needs and desires. In urban areas, businesses and industries would pay family salaries (subsidies) as well as individual wages. Other social groups also have the right to property necessary to fulfill their functions. For example, each governmental unit should have sufficient tax revenue to fulfill its functions.

A competitive political and economic system which guarantees liberty and order is the means of determining the common good of the various constituent parts of the nation. Acción Nacional rejects the romantic view of the Mexican social congresses that voluntary cooperation would produce human well-being. For example, strong, independent labor unions must be created to defend the economic interests of their workers as well as to provide for their social needs. On the other side, employers should also organize to defend their interests. The State would referee. Other groups would similarly organize to promote their interests. Since men have many and often conflicting interests, the democratic play of political parties, each representing a variety of interests, would select the leadership of governmental bodies. Minorities, however, would be guaranteed a voice through proportional representation.

For this system to work, individuals have the moral duty of political participation and of guaranteeing, through the appropriate public institutions, that the popular vote is respected. Society must be governed by law not by personalism. As a consequence of its Political Humanism doctrine, PAN has devoted its activities to citizen education as the means of creating this idealized society. In the final analysis, citizen education is more important than PAN's conquest of power.[4]

The 1965 principles of doctrine clarified the earlier principles. Labor was declared preeminent over property as the ordering principle of political economy. Female workers were to receive equal treatment with male workers. Most important, labor-capital divisions would be ended by creating communitarian enterprises in which workers would be integrated into their functioning, profits, management, and property. In the countryside, the democratized *ejido* would coexist with family farms organized into voluntary cooperatives, supplied with cheap, easy credit and technical aid from the government (which PAN had preferred earlier).

The new principles dropped the 1939 stress upon the community of Hispanic nations in favor of international cooperation among democratic, progressive nations. The earlier document has emphasized the special heritage of Mexico that distinguished it from other countries. The only transnational movement which held PAN's interest was Hispanicism, for the party feared cultural envelopment by the United States, Russia, and some fascist European power.[5] The result of the statement had been to identify the party with Franco's *Hispanidad* program.[6] González Luna, in speeches and articles, denied that PAN wanted Mexico to reenter the Spanish orbit. To him, Mexico was a mestizo nation and its *mestizaje* was a source of great pride. What had happened was that the Revolution brought the rise of anti-Spanish sentiment which denied half of Mexico's national heritage and, therefore, its special identity. He condemned fascism and Franco's Spain as unjust societies.[7] By the late 1950s Acción Nacional was arguing for the realization of the international common good along humanist lines with each nation preserving its special identity.[8]

By 1969, Acción Nacional ideology had evolved still further, calling for a total, peaceful revolution in the political, economic, and social structures led by the masses in order to create a completely democratic pluralist society based upon the principle of solidarity and the goal of social justice. According to the *Democratic Change of the Structures* document:

> the only reasonable response to the demand and promotion of substantial changes, in a people which faces the national menace of chaos and violence, which does not agree to a "political stability" converted into stationary status, is to open the doors to personal participation in the collective decisions that affect the destiny of Mexicans.[9]

Perhaps the most important point about the document is that its ideology could serve not only any Latin American Christian Democratic party but also the left wing of these parties.[10] The authors, Adolfo Christlieb Ibarrola and Efraín González Morfín, had finally brought PAN into the mainstream of progressive, even radical, Catholic thought and made PAN ideology equally or more progressive than PRI ideology.

A recent study confirms PAN's dependency upon Catholic social doctrine as the source of its ideas. PAN had started at the forefront of progressive Mexican Catholic thought of the 1930s. Moreover, as militant Catholics gained control of PAN in the 1940s the dependency upon Catholic doctrine increased. In 1939, 62.1% of the ideas emanated from Catholic thought; by the 1965 document, this had risen to 72%.[11] The ideological content of the *Democratic Changes of the Structures* document has almost perfect positive correlation with Paul VI's *Populorum Progressio* (1967), the Pastoral Letter of the Mexican Hierarchy on the Development and Integration of the Country (1968), and the Second Latin American Bishops' General Conference (1968).[12]

PROGRAMMATIC STATEMENTS

Acción Nacional's criticisms of the existing government and the party's proposals to alter Mexican law flow logically from its ideologically influenced perceptions of Mexican reality. The Revolutionary governments have never met the requirements of Political Humanism. PAN believes

that Mexico is run by and for an oligarchy which makes only the necessary concessions to maintain itself in power, and that this oligarchy uses
deceit and coercion when public demands threaten its monopoly. Because
of traditional public apathy and political inexperience, the oligarchy (at
times called the Revolutionary Family or a mafia) has seldom faced
serious threats except from its own membership—Almazán in 1940, Padilla in 1946, and Henríquez Guzmán in 1952—or by the great labor
strikes of 1958–59 and the student revolt of 1968. The oligarchy has
hidden its true nature by calling itself the only repository of Mexican
nationalism and by wrapping itself in the Revolutionary mystique it has
developed.

As *panistas* have surveyed the Mexican scene since 1939, they have
seen institutionalized violence, the continuance of poverty, poor health,
insufficient and inadequate educational facilities, inadequate food supplies and distribution systems, child labor, alcoholism resulting from de-
spair, labor abuses, wide gaps between the opulent few and the impover-
ished many, high unemployment, corrupt labor unions, and fraudulent
elections, among other evils. In their view, the Revolution has been a
fraud and the government emanating from it illegitimate because it has
not been based upon the true popular will. What the necessary upheaval
of 1910–40 produced was a new and more vicious *Porfiriato,* a paternalistic technocracy which has been deluding the populace into believing
that the government represents the citizenry and not the plutocracy to
which it is really allied.

The Acción Nacional mission has operated from the assumption that
only the people themselves can actually overturn this system and create
the necessary democratic, pluralist, solidarist society. PAN has tried to
arouse the population from its apathy, to educate the citizenry with
PAN ideology, to politicize, and to maintain pressure on the oligarchy
by electoral participation and propaganda barrages.[13] PAN does not
claim to have the monopoly on the truth—that has to be determined
by the process outlined in PAN ideology—but it does believe it has the
moral duty of political participation.[14]

Within this context, the contents and direction of PAN's programmatic statements have meaning. Criticisms of the government abound in
the political platforms, speeches, handbills, pamphlets, and *La Nación*
articles, giving a negative cast to PAN's image. Half of PAN's platforms, which one would normally expect to be programmatic, contain
basic ideological statements.[15] PAN's programmatic statements have
varied little over the years; the *Minimum Program of Political Action*
(1940) formed the basis for the subsequent campaign platforms, legislative proposals, and the programmatic statements.

Because of the great similarity of PAN's programmatic statements, regardless of their date, they have been categorized with examples for each. The categories are: (1) *campo,* (2) *municipio,* (3) *education,* (4) *labor,* (5) *family,* (6) *economy,* (7) *legal,* and (8) *political.*

Campo

Since 1939, Acción Nacional has considered the problems of the country-side to be the most pressing ones in the nation because, until the 1960s, the majority of Mexico lived there in poverty, unable to produce enough to feed themselves properly or supply the needs of Mexico's industrial plant. PAN's proposed solutions have been essentially technical. Both living conditions and production would be improved by converting *ejidos* into family property and giving families and other small proprietors the security of full legal title to their lands.[16] A 1946 legislative proposal would have given the right of *amparo* (an injunction against governmental action) to *ejidatarios,* small proprietors, and communal agriculturalists.[17] The government would extend cheap and easy credit, technical assistance, and small irrigation works to farmers; would train farmers; build houses; and facilitate access of agricultural products to markets. PAN also argued that the government should allow private financial institutions to extend credit and aid to farmers while making certain that this did not result in abuses. Because collective arrangements are advantageous, voluntary producers' and consumers' marketing cooperatives would be encouraged. Social security would be extended to the *campo* to elevate living conditions. Political controls over farm organizations, especially their forced membership in PRI, would be abolished.[18] A National Planning Commission, composed of all concerned sectors, would be established to coordinate agricultural development.[19]

PAN tried to implement this program through proposals in the Chamber of Deputies in the 1946–49 session. Because Chapter III gives the details of these proposals, they will not be repeated at this point. Although the party has continued to argue for these changes, the only other attempt to implement part of the package was the October 22, 1956, legislative bill to convert *ejidos* into family patrimony.[20]

Municipio

The *municipio,* to PAN the most important governmental unit, should be autonomous, free, and financially viable. Its tax base should be broadened, and it should be allowed to retain the bulk of the revenue collected within its boundaries. Small municipal governments should be run as town meetings while large municipal governments should have city councils elected from wards. Proportional representation should be instituted to guarantee a voice to the minority. Governments should render regular, verifiable accounts publicly. Recall, referendum, and initiative procedures should be adopted.[21] In 1967, PAN platforms began to include planks on urban problems, especially the need for democratic urban planning.[22] The 1970 platform attacked urban *latifundios,* the concentration of urban property in a few hands.[23]

As with the *campo,* the bulk of PAN's legislative proposals came in the 1946–49 session of the Chamber of Deputies. In 1965, the party introduced legislation to make the Federal District mayor and city council posts elective.[24]

Education

Acción Nacional has promised that it would guarantee academic freedom, give parents the right to choose the education of their children, build more schools (especially in rural areas), provide more grade levels of instruction, provide more technical-vocational education, pay teachers better, allow private sources to provide educational facilities, depoliticize the schools and teachers' unions, and allow choices in the selection of free textbooks.[25]

Because education has been the major source of Church-State tension in recent years and because parochial schools actually exist, the party has not introduced much legislation on the subject. In 1963, it presented a bill to promote and amplify rural education.[26] To aid poor students to attend school, it proposed a National Commission of Student Credit in 1968.[27] In December 1968, PAN tried to raise Federal District teachers' salaries.[28] PAN's attacks on Article 3 and official textbooks, which seem to indicate clericalism, are deceptive. The party's federal deputies do not introduce bills to alter them. The author's impressionistic content analysis of PAN publications reveals that those publications aimed at the general public—platforms, handbills, programs, and position papers—rarely mention either Article 3 or the official textbooks. The platforms, except in 1964, make some reference to Article 3 or the necessity of freedom of education, or the right of parents to choose their childrens' education, meaning legal operation of parochial schools. One long pamphlet has been devoted to criticism of the official textbook program because, PAN asserts, the books contain an "official" version of Mexican history. Part of PAN's complaint is the criticism of the Church contained within those books. Probably 90 percent of PAN's attacks on Article 3 or the textbooks are contained within *La Nación*, which is essentially an internal organ. The height of *panista* participation in public anti–Article 3 demonstrations occurred in the first half of the 1940s. In short, attacks on anticlericalism in education are important for party discipline and as one part of the general ideology, but not as a political issue.

Labor

Most of PAN's labor program has been presented as bills in the Chamber of Deputies. Its October 1948 bill sought to prevent union leaders from abusing their powers and ignoring the wishes of the membership while guaranteeing that workers could not be expelled or excluded from unions because of their political views or activities. This proposal also sought to prohibit union affiliation to political parties while allowing unions to participate in politics.[29] Similar proposals were also introduced in 1951 and 1966.[30] PAN has advocated democratic unions and sought to guarantee their existence through legislation requiring the use of secret ballots in union elections, forbidding the reelection of union officials, and mandating that union leaders give regular accounting of union budgets.[31] PAN bills to aid workers include the 1946 bill to create a Social Security Study Commission to expand the coverage and put the system on a sound actuarial basis.[32] The 1956 bill to increase pension benefits to federal bureaucrats,[33] the 1968 proposal for a national employment service,[34] and the successful 1968 reform of constitutional Article 21 to limit administrative fines to one and one-half days' wages for *ejidatarios, minfundistas,* communal farmers, wage workers, and women and minors less than eighteen years old who depend upon another person for their livelihood[35] indicate PAN's positive interest in labor. PAN also gave vigorous support to the 1969 Federal Labor Law, the most prolabor law in Mexican history.[36]

Family

Since the party considers the family to be the fundamental social unit, it has given special attention to the need of protecting families. Some of the already mentioned proposals were justified, in part, as being means of family protection. The creation of family patrimonies is one important example. In addition, PAN has introduced other legislation to protect families. In 1965, it introduced antipornography legislation.[37] A year later, it sought to protect abandoned families by providing stiffer penalties for abandonment and continued family access to rights derived from the father's employment.[38] To save marriages, a 1969 bill for the Federal District sought to create personal separation as a legal marital status to reduce divorces.[39] Financial aid to families would have come from the introduction of a family salary system (1966)[40] and from granting social security benefits to students until they reached twenty-one years of age.[41]

Economy

Acción Nacional economic programs have stressed that private enterprise is the best source of increases in wealth and that the private sector should be allowed to perform this function under close government regulation. PAN opposed economic statism but agreed that the government had to intervene in the economy by regulation, monetary policy, planning, building the economic infrastructure, taxation, income redistribution, investment policy, trust-busting, and building economic facilities which private enterprise cannot or will not do. The party is against wholesale interventionism, which it believes is dangerous to civil liberties, governmental monopolies of enterprises which could be in private hands, and unilateral planning.[42] Plans should be drawn through public debate and executed by joint government-labor-capital commissions.[43] Interestingly, PAN had been arguing for planning while CONCANACO had been opposing it.[44]

Proposed economic legislation has actually been concentrated upon a few items in the program. Chapter III gives the detailed 1948 PAN economic program which sought to stabilize the monetary system, increase controls over enterprises in which the government had a fiduciary interest, abolish trucking monopolies, and introduce multisectoral national planning. Since that time, the party has again tried to obtain more governmental regulation of decentralized and state-participation enterprises and to force them to render public accounts (1953 and 1968).[45] On the positive side, PAN fought a 1962 1 percent tax for education because it would hurt the poor more than the rich;[46] tried to create a Regional Economic Development Fund (1968);[47] obtain greater regulation of foreign investments;[48] and protect Mexican subsoil rights, particularly petroleum sources near the United States border and on the continental shelf (1969).[49]

Legal

Most of the proposals in this category have been to extend or define civil liberties and civil rights. A 1953 proposed amendment to constitutional Article 107 was an attempt to expedite trials and to protect the right of *amparo*.[50] In 1966 and 1968, PAN sought to widen the coverage of the *amparo* writ.[51] A 1966 proposal would have allowed liberty to persons accused of crimes until their trials.[52] Along these same lines, a 1968 petition, following the student revolt and the Baja California elections of that year, was to guarantee the right to petition.[53] Since PAN argued that individual rights are violated in electoral fraud, it has tried to get the Supreme Court to intervene in electoral disputes.[54] The Court had rejected such appeals by claiming that it has no jurisdiction. A 1947 PAN proposed reform of the federal Constitution would have granted that right to the court.[55] The 1965 antiabortion proposal was an attempt to protect individual liberty.[56]

Other proposed changes in Mexican law included a 1965 bill to claim the Gulf of California for Mexico, and a 1966 bill to extend the territorial limits to twelve miles.[57] In 1961, PAN requested a congressional resolution asking the Mexican government to negotiate treaties with other countries to stop nuclear testing. Later, the party also proposed the ban of nuclear weaponry and testing in Latin America. Similar PRI proposals were passed within a few years after the Acción Nacional proposals were defeated.[58]

Political

Acción Nacional believes that the solution to Mexican problems is essentially political, that the Mexican people are capable of solving their own and national problems if they are given an effective voice in public affairs. Democratization of political life not only would tap the currently unused resources of the population but also would build national unity, essential if the country is to be strong and progressive. In order to democratize the country, PAN has argued for universal adult suffrage, nonpartisan vote-counting boards, a competitive party system, proportional representation in all elected governments, permanent voter credentials, and the end of governmental support of political parties.[59]

Because of the importance of politics to Acción Nacional, this category contains the most numerous legislative proposals. Within days after the first PAN federal deputies took their seats in September 1946, the party proposed the extension of the suffrage to women in municipal elections.[60] Twenty-five months later, PAN proposed granting female suffrage in federal elections (five years before the PRI proposal).[61] In 1969, PAN supported the eighteen-and-over suffrage movement.[62] To insure honest elections, PAN has proposed a national electoral register (1947, 1966), a Federal Tribune of Elections (1947, 1948), and most of the reforms mentioned above in reference to the Federal Electoral Law (1968).[63] Several proposals would have increased regulation of political parties. The most comprehensive was the 1948 political parties law described in Chapter III. Since PRI was aided in its implicit claim to be the true Mexican Party by virtue of the fact that illiterates often vote not for a party but for the national colors, PAN tried to stop PRI's exclusive use of the national colors with a 1957 bill to prevent all parties from using them.[64] In the same year, another bill would have forbidden the use of public monies to support political parties or partisan ends, which PAN had been accusing the government of doing in behalf of PRI.[65] PAN had long argued for proportional representation and the 1963 introduction of the party deputy system initially appeared to be a step in that direction.[66] In 1966, PAN tried to extend the new system to the Senate and down to state legislatures.[67]

Attempts were also made to strengthen existing governmental institutions: bills in 1947 to force the Mexican president to send budgetary and revenue proposals to the Chamber of Deputies in time for their full study, a 1968 proposal to require the president to send territorial budgets to Congress for approval, a 1967 proposal to require more complete accounting and efficient use of public funds, a 1965 rule to require senators and deputies to work in committees when Congress was not in session, a 1966 proposal to restore and protect congressional archives, and a 1964 proposal to define the jurisdictional boundaries between the federal and the state governments more closely.[68]

Acción Nacional's programmatic statements contradict the common assertions that the party serves or tries to serve the interests of private enterprise or the Church.[69] Although it may be argued that the party would be foolish to propose laws which would clearly aid the Church because Mexicans would then dismiss the party as only a special interest group, the present author, judging from the thousands of pages of PAN documents he has read as well as from the numerous interviews with *panistas* and non-*panistas* over a two-year period, does not accept this argument. Similarly, those few proposals which private enterprise and PAN both support—control over state participation and decentralized enterprises, a greater role for private enterprise in decision-making, and emphasis upon private initiative as the source of economic progress, among others—are not positions which PAN supports because private enterprise favors them, but because they are part of PAN's Catholic doctrine and appeal to middle-class urban supporters. Moreover, most of PAN's proposals have been technical rather than ideological in nature, reflecting both the socioeconomic composition of the party and technical orientation of Christian Democratic parties in general.

Although it is sometimes difficult to separate Acción Nacional's ideological statements from its programmatic statements, this survey of approximately 80 of slightly more than 150 PAN legislative proposals is the best indicator of PAN's program for Mexico. Not all of the legislative proposals were mentioned, because many are repetitious or concerned with procedural matters in Congress. It is significant that the basic PAN program was introduced in the 1946–49 congressional session. PAN believes that if these technical solutions had been adopted it would control Mexico, it would have convinced the voters that PAN offered the best ideology and leadership, and Mexicans would have responded to PAN's demands that they participate in decision-making. The party believes that, as long as they are systematically excluded from power, the party's chief difficulty will continue to be the failure of the Mexican voter to take the party seriously, to see Acción Nacional as a real alternative. PAN also argues that the vagueness of its programs is the direct result of its systematic exclusion from power, a policy which prevents *panistas* from gaining the practical experience necessary for making more specific proposals. Because of this situation, party leaders assert that they can only run against the government, promising to give better government if PAN is elected.[70]

APPEALS

A survey of available speeches, pamphlets, and handbills corroborates these findings. Most of the handbills are reprints of campaign platform planks and speeches of presidential candidates, Gómez Morín, and González Luna. The appeals call upon the voters to use the suffrage and to create a democratic Mexico by voting for PAN: they blame the government and PRI for all Mexican evils and demand free *municipios* and the end of labor corruption. In short, they call upon Mexicans to vote for PAN if they want a progressive, noncommunist, honest government which will obey the Constitution.

Four significant generalizations can be made about PAN ideology, programs, and appeals. First, although the party's ideas emanate from Catholic social doctrine and are part of the mainstream of Christian Democratic thought, the party does not seek to reestablish ecclesiastical privilege, nor does it overtly court a potential Catholic vote. It is, as members constantly assert, a secular political party which seeks to apply a Catholic-derived social reform model to Mexican society and not a clerical or confessional party. Second, the party's documents reflect its social composition inasmuch as technical and pedantic approaches reflect the work of intellectuals, academicians, professionals, and such private enterprise types as bankers. Third, these dry and overly sophisticated approaches elicit no emotional response from the average Mexican, who finds it difficult to identify with PAN. The party itself has thus significantly reduced its possibilities of mass membership and, with this failure, its potential political impact. Finally, these documents have enabled PAN to identify itself as independent of the Revolution and to adjust its ideas to changing Mexican and world conditions while maintaining internal discipline. Commitment to PAN doctrine and programs rather than electoral rewards has kept the party in existence for more than thirty years.

CHAPTER VII

Structure: Description and Operation

For any political party to operate successfully in a country as large and complex as Mexico, effective political organization is needed. This is even more important for a small opposition party such as PAN, which needs organization to augment its small membership. Moreover, PAN leaders believe that organization is important and considerable party energy has been expended on organizational matters. Finally, political parties as they are known in Western Europe and the United States are relatively recent in Mexican history. If one interprets PRI as something other than a political party then PAN is the first political party to emerge from the Revolution.

Party organization or structure can be examined in two ways: politico-geographical and functional. For the sake of clarity this chapter is divided into a description of the politico-geographical organization of the party as stipulated in party statutes and regulations and an examination of how the structure actually functions, including the importance of factional differences.

DESCRIPTION

Some aspects of political party organization in Mexico are mandated by federal electoral laws. These laws have changed as the government has sought to create a more efficient political system. The 1938 law under which PAN was organized had broad and minimal requirements for a political party to achieve legal recognition.[1] The 1946 Federal Electoral Law, which PAN supported but believed inadequate, tightened the requirements for government recognition. To obtain a position on the ballot, a political party must have a minimum number of members (the number has been consistently increased to the point where it is now 75,000) and it must have a minimum number of members in at least two-thirds of the federal entities. The purpose and effect are to discourage regional parties; transient, personalistic parties; and other organized political opposition. The parties must issue principles of doctrine and a monthly party publication. Before they can participate in elections, all must be registered with the Ministry of Government which thus controls their very existence. Changes in the structural requirements of parties since 1945 have been primarily to raise membership requirements.[2] Federal Electoral Law structural requirements force all parties to model themselves after PRI: all have to have a national assembly, a national executive committee, a directive committee in each federal entity where the party meets the minimum recognition requirements, and a monthly party organization.[3] Political parties compete on the government's terms or not at all.

PAN structure will be examined at two levels: (1) national, and (2) regional and local. Greater attention will be given to the national level of organization because it was organized first, is more visible, and its activities and organization are more thorough than the lower level. Since PAN structure is essentially pyramidal, analysis of the national level will yield more clarity.

The statutes of PAN have been altered since founding for two reasons: (1) requirements of the federal electoral laws, and (2) attempts to make the structure more effective, including the necessity of appeasing internal factions. The following description is based on the 1968 edition of the General Statutes and the 1959 edition of the *Regulations*. The 1971 statutory reforms are included. Note is made in footnotes and in text on prior requirements.[4]

National Organization

At the national level six organs are specified: The General Assembly, the National Convention, the National Council, the National Executive Committee (CEN in Spanish), the President, and the General Board of Vigilance. Statutorily, the order of importance is: General Assembly, National Council, CEN, and the President; functionally the importance is different.

The General Assembly is the supreme power of the party; all other organs are bound by its decisions. Doctrine, programs, and activity are approved or disapproved at this level. The Assembly not only can control the decisions and personnel of the party, it can override any decisions made by the leadership or by prior Assemblies.

Safeguards have been built into the Statutes to insure control of the General Assembly by the membership. The Assembly must meet each three years but can meet more frequently. Normally, the CEN calls the meeting but the Council, at the solicitation of twenty of its members, or five regional organisms, or by 5 percent of the active party members, can also convoke an Assembly. Regardless of who calls the Assembly, the call must be expedited twenty days before the actual meeting and must be distributed to all party members or to all municipal, district, or state committees and through PAN publications. The agenda must be published. In the Assembly itself, which is a public session unless it votes to close itself, all members may voice their opinions. Voting is restricted to those delegates accredited by the regional committee and the CEN, without which the Assembly cannot be held. Changes in the party statutes, dissolution of the party, and fusion with other groups can only be done by an Extraordinary General Assembly, called in the same means as the General Assembly but with only ten days' anticipation.

Delegates, except for the CEN, are selected by the regional organs. Although all party members are allowed to attend and speak, the voting is done by the regional organs. Each regional delegation has twenty votes plus one more for each federal electoral district within the entity. The Federal District has twenty-four federal electoral districts, giving the regional delegation there forty-four votes; Quintana Roo only has one federal electoral district, giving that regional delegation twenty-one votes. The CEN vote is the average of all the regional committee votes.[5] Regional delegations can split their vote, but when there is 80 percent agreement the delegation votes as a unit. Voice votes are used unless three delegations ask for a secret ballot. The Assembly operates by a simple majority.

The National Convention is essentially the General Assembly called for purely political purposes. The Convention meets at least every three years, but can be called more frequently. It uses the General Assembly rules. The Convention decides on political participation, the forms of political participation, a party platform, and a presidential candidate if it is a presidential election year. Presidential candidates need 80 percent of the convention vote for nomination.[6] General Assemblies and National Conventions can be held simultaneously.

One of the most important decisions of the General Assembly is to choose the National Council, its surrogate between sessions. National councilors hold office for five years or until the next General Assembly. The Council functions as the Assembly does—approving budgets, lines of action, tactics and strategy. It can call both Assemblies and Conventions and is designed to resolve conflicts within the party quickly or when they do not warrant the Assembly's attention.

The Council chooses both the National Executive Committee (CEN), which operates the party on a day-to-day basis, and the party president. In addition, it names a thirty-man Permanent Commission from within itself to watch the daily party operations. The Permanent Commission itself contains commissions for the study of such matters as finances, organizations, politics, and propaganda. Five members of the Council form the General Board of Vigilance whose special duty is to audit party finances.

Both the frequency of its meetings and the number of its members have fluctuated since the party was created. Originally, the Council had to meet during the first ten days of February and August of each year. Currently, the Council has to meet once a year. It can be called into session by twenty of its members, by the CEN, or by three regional committees. Membership on the Council was originally set at 30 to 120 active members, changed in 1949 to a range of 10 to 250, changed in 1959 to from 100 to 324, in 1962 to from 100 to 200, and in 1971 to the number of federal electoral districts (178). The Council usually has operated with less than the maximum allowable number. Although the Assembly chooses the Council initially, vacancies and vacant slots can be filled by the Council itself. The most important change in the composition of the membership came in 1959 when regional representation was introduced. The 1959 change guaranteed two representatives from each regional organization. The 1962 changes stipulated that the regional presidents would automatically be included on the Council. The councilors selected by the Assembly are nominated by the regional committees after consulting their respective district and municipal committees.

The Council's procedures are structured to prevent regional factions from controlling it. Its meetings are valid when it has a simple majority of its members as long as two-thirds of the federal entities in which regional committees function are present. Decisions are taken by the majority present.

The National Executive Committee is the executive collegiate body in PAN.[7] Its powers, numerous and important, are to:

1. act as consulting organ to its president (who is also the party president) and approve the internal party regulations;

2. fulfill the functions given it by the Assembly and Convention;

3. approve the programs of activity of the party;

4. agree to PAN collaboration with other national political organizations;

5. designate commissions to aid the president;

6. approve entry or resignation from the party;

7. act as legal representative of the party, usually through the president;

8. form the budget and approve expenditures;

9. approve presidential reports to the Council;

10. convoke the General Assembly, National Convention, and the National Council;

11. veto the decisions of the municipal, district, and regional committees or councils and their respective assemblies, and, if requested by the Organ, carry the appeal to the National Council;

12. exercise any other powers given by the Statutes and Regulations;

13. create regional organizations when there are not enough members in the entity to do it;

14. vote in strength equal to the largest delegation; and

15. select a secretary-general who is also secretary-general of the party.

Part of the importance of the CEN is not just in its delegated powers but also in the size of its membership and the frequency of its meetings. The CEN is composed of seven to forty members selected by the Council but drawn from both active and adherent members. Originally CEN members served at the pleasure of the Council. Since 1949 they serve one-year terms.

This small membership allows concerted and rapid action whenever necessary, giving it an advantage over any other party collegiate body. Moreover, it usually meets weekly. Since 1959 special efforts have been made to include women and young men on the Committee. From 1959 to 1971 these normally included the presidents of the then existing Women's and Youth Organizations.

The composition of the CEN is regulated by statute. The numerical composition has already been discussed. The party president, selected by the Council, is automatically a member of the CEN and its executive officer. Aiding him is a secretary-general, selected by the CEN president. Using the broad powers granted by Article 45, the CEN and the president appoint commissions from its membership, a treasurer, and an adjunct secretary. The current commissions are: political, organization, propaganda, studies, treasury, national, and press.[8]

President

The president is the most powerful member of the CEN; in his hands are most of the powers and means of execution of the party. Selected by the National Council, he holds a three-year term at its pleasure. His charge is to:

1. serve as president of the CEN, the Council, the General Assembly and the National Convention;

2. formulate the party Regulations, subject to CEN approval;

3. propose to the CEN party programs of activity;

4. represent the party in official terms;

5. be an ex-officio member of all regional, district, and municipal directive committees as well as of all commissions named by the Council or CEN;

6. coordinate activities of all party organs;

7. designate departments for the better organization of active and adherent members;

8. maintain and create proper relations with civic or social organisms that have similar principles or activities with PAN;

9. control functionaries and employees of PAN;

10. designate the various delegates and commissions necessary; and

11. do all those things necessary to further party aims.

With regard to regional, district, and municipal committees, the president has the power to:

1. nominate and remove the regional chiefs, councils, and committees; (The council is to be selected from leading members of the party in the region taking in consideration nominations by regional, district, and municipal committees. The regional chief and committee are selected with advice from the regional council.)

2. call regional council meetings; and

3. attend or send representatives to regional meetings. In short, the president is the chief decision-maker of the party.

Periodicals

The Federal Electoral Law, not the PAN statutes, requires a monthly party publication, a role which *La Nación* fulfills. Statutory authority derives from Article 2 allowing the party to create organs necessary for party functions. *La Nación* was created in 1941 as an independent weekly magazine unidentified with the party PAN. Financed by bankers and edited originally by a Catholic Action journalist, *La Nación* sought to enlist Mexicans in PAN causes. By the late 1940s it identified itself as the party organ. Beginning in 1965 it began publishing twice monthly as an economy measure. Preceding *La Nación* were *Voz Nacional* (1939–40), an "independent" general-interest magazine used for recruitment, and the *Boletín de Acción Nacional,* organ first of the Federal District regional committee and then of the CEN. The *Boletín* lasted from 1939 to 1942, having been forbidden to use the mails in 1940.[9]

Amendments and Dissolution

Special articles regulate the amendment process and dissolution of the party. In the former case, amendments must be approved by two-thirds of the delegates voting in an extraordinary General Assembly. An extraordinary General Assembly is also required for party dissolution; the dissolution vote has to be 80 percent. The patrimony must be given to an organization that has similar principles to PAN, to the national university, or to a charitable institution.

Tremendous power is concentrated in the national level reflecting the hydrocephalic structure of Mexican politics, but regional organs are also important and powerful.

Regional and Local Organs

Mexico is a large, diverse country having many political subdivisions. There are 29 states, a federal district, two territories, and approximately 2,400 *municipios,* units similar in size to counties in the United States. Each state has two federal senators, a governor, and a unicameral legislature. There are 178 federal deputy districts. All *municipios* have elected mayors and city councils except for the Federal District which is ruled by a presidentially appointed regent and advisory board.

The PAN regional organs perform the key roles of this level, roles similar to those of the national level. As the national organs exercise considerable power and influence over the lesser organs, the regional organs are the key organizing and controlling units for the district, municipal, and precinct levels. Regional organs are based on state boundaries and the terms regional and state can be used interchangeably even though the statutes allow regional organs to encompass larger areas.

The basic article concerning regional organs states that they are autonomous in affairs peculiarly concerning them but that they are subject to the discipline of national organs for matters of general interest to the party.

Each federal entity (state, territory, and Federal District) has a complex of PAN organizations headed by the regional organs: president, council, and committee. The region also holds conventions. Below the statewide level are federal deputy districts and state legislature districts.

The former is important only for the triennial elections. Both have a district council and committee as well as a district chief. At the base are the municipal committees headed by a chief. These may also be divided into subcommittees where the urban entity is large enough to warrant it.

Regional Council

The regional council resembles its national counterpart; its primary function is to act as a watchdog on the regional committee and president. It is a consultive organ which also initiates programs, approves the budgets of the regional, district, and municipal committees, reviews (at the request of the regional committee) the agreements of the district and municipal committees, and proposes the members of the regional committee to the CEN.

The regional council is a relatively small organ with explicit organizational requirements. Its nine to sixty active party members, selected for two-year terms, are named by the national president from names submitted by party organs within the region. These members elect a president, secretary, and at least three permanent commissions—program, organization, and treasury—each having three members. Ex-officio members of the council are the regional chief, treasurer, and secretary of organization. Commission meetings are monthly, but the entire council only is required to meet semiannually. Extraordinary sessions can be called by the national president, the regional chief, or by five regional councilors. Decisions are made by majority vote; procedure is standard parliamentary procedure.

Regional Committee

The regional committee is the chief collegiate institution. The national president selects five to forty members from regional council nominations. Committeemen serve two-year terms. The committee is a consultive organ; controls membership recruitment; agrees to collaboration with other groups in its region; raises money for its own operations; conducts statewide campaigns; names its own secretary-general and commissions; and ratifies the nominations of the district and municipal chiefs. It meets twice a month or when called into extraordinary session.[10]

The key decision-making organs at the state level are the regional committees for the same reasons that give the national committee power. They are located in the state capital and meet weekly. Regional councils have an advisory role at best, for the regional committee usually convokes a regional convention when it does not want to act unilaterally. Regional committees are similar in their socioeconomic composition. The Michoacán and Federal District committees are representative. The Michoacán committee has thirteen members; three of whom are wives of committeemen. Committee members average forty years in age. President Quiroz is in the first half of his forties whereas Secretary-General Juan José Mejía Guerrero, accountant for General Hipotecaria, is twenty-six. One physician, two small industrialists (ice cream bars and gelatin), two lawyers, two house contractors, and an insurance agent constitute the other eight men on the committee. The three women are housewives. Three committeemen are ex-presidents. The Federal District committee, on the other hand, has twenty-three members, only two of whom are women. Thirteen are lawyers. There is one architect, one engineer, and one physician. The rest are employees and workers. Their average age is in the middle forties. Both of these committees have representatives of the former youth and women's organizations.[11]

Just as the national executive committee guides the work of the regional committees so do the latter guide the work of the district and municipal committees. The similarity in the decision-making pattern is too close to warrant further comment.

Judging from the Michoacán and Federal District regional organizations, the state PAN organizations share common problems with the national level organization. All PAN leaders assert that the party's greatest problem is the lack of adequate income, followed by governmental intimidation of the citizenry. The Federal District organization fares better than other regional organizations on both counts because it has the aid of the national committee and operates in a large metropolitan area. Its main offices are housed in two rooms of national headquarters. One room is a reception area, the other a large, virtually empty room used by the regional president. In addition, it maintains an office in each of the twenty-four federal deputy districts, usually one room with a secretary and telephone. Each district committee pays its own costs and contributes to the regional committee budget. Michoacán, on the other hand, has its power centered in the regional office in Morelia, an old house in the midtown area which contains meeting rooms, archives, lounges, secretarial work area, and an informal dispensary. In 1971, the state was divided into sixteen state legislative electoral districts. PAN planned to have a president and committee for each district but had not completed the reorganization by late summer, 1971. Each of these districts chooses its own candidates. For federal deputy elections and state elections, the decision to participate is made by a state convention, and, for the former, candidates are recruited by the regional committee. In the Federal District, the decision to participate is made by the regional convention but the candidates are selected by district conventions.

Both regional committees operate as the Statutes require. When they are not engaged in elections, most of their time is devoted to membership recruitment and fund-raising. The regional committee leads the party but is closely tied to the decisions of the regional assembly or convention because they can be convoked easily. The regional council rarely, if ever, interferes with the regional president and his committee. The general membership can and does influence PAN decision-making at this level whereas it usually ratifies decisions in national assemblies and conventions. These regional organizations operate primarily in urban areas and find it extremely difficult, if not impossible, to organize in rural areas.

Regional President

The regional president has duties similar to those of his national counterpart. He is designated by the national president at the suggestion of the regional council. He is responsible not only to the regional committee but also to the regional council and the national president. He supervises the work of all organs below the national level; is the liason man between these organs and the national president; maintains relations with other regional chiefs; supervises the municipal committees and appoints the district and municipal chiefs as well as other functionaries needed by the regional committee.

District Organizations

The district level organizations exist primarily for state legislative and triennial federal deputy elections. Although a district council is allowed, a committee headed by a chief is the common practice. Both are dependencies of the regional committee. They nominate candidates and conduct electoral campaigns.

Municipal Committees

The base of the party structure is the municipal committee. Municipal committees have rights over membership recruitment and discipline, nominate municipal candidates, and conduct electoral campaigns. In addition, these committees submit status reports to the regional chief every three months, thus serving an important role in the party's communication net. Large *municipios,* either geographically or based on population, often have municipal subcommittees. Each committee is headed by a chief, appointed at the municipal level by the regional chief, at the subcommittee level by the municipal chief—both subject to the ratification of higher organs.

OPERATION

Operationally, Acción Nacional's structure differs from its formal Statutes in terms of extension, accrued organization, and decision-making.

Extension

PAN does not and cannot have effective organizations in every political entity. The extent of PAN organization in the 1969–71 period can be briefly summarized—there were regional committees in every state and territory and in the Federal District. Of the 178 federal deputy election districts, PAN had 123 permanent district committees. Of the over 2,400 *municipios,* approximately 834 had PAN municipal committees.[12] Municipal subcommittees, group organizations, and block organizations existed only in a few towns, principally in highly politicized areas such as Baja California, or in large urban clusters such as greater Mexico City and Guadalajara.[13] Most of the *municipios* are rural, and PAN has been unable to organize successfully within them, thereby giving the municipal level of the party an urban cast. The existence and strength of municipal organizations depends upon sympathetic local leaders. Hence, a fair statement about PAN municipal organization is that the number of such organizations fluctuates yearly but are more permanent in urban areas than elsewhere. The geographical distribution of PAN municipal committees is relatively even throughout the country once the two territories are excluded. Baja California state, with four urban clusters, is the best-organized state and the Federal District is probably the best-organized city.

District organizations are important primarily for federal deputy elections. The organization of these committees is not as important to the party as municipal and regional committees are. During the election period, there are district committees throughout the country, but during off years the number drops back to 123. States that do not have any or their full complement of deputy district organizations include the two territories, Chiapas, Tabasco, Nayarit, Campeche, Sinaloa, and Durango. The Federal District is an exception. Although the federal deputy district organizations wax and wane with elections they do exist in permanent form with an office, a telephone, and a secretary.[14]

Regional organizations currently exist in all states, territories, and the Federal District but their number has fluctuated with historical circumstances. The weakest have always been in the two territories. The original regional organizations were created by friends of Gómez Morín. Hence, states such as Chiapas, Campeche, Tabasco, Colima, Nayarit, and Sinaloa were organized late in PAN history because PAN founders knew very few people there. Some states, such as Sonora, were poorly organized until a critical event beyond PAN's control created an environment conducive to organizing opposition sentiment. Sonora was organized effectively in 1967 during a crisis over the imposition of an unpopular governor; some PRI leaders left PRI and organized a strong PAN unit. In the 1940s, PAN had regional committees in over 83 percent of the federal entities but it was not until 1951, in anticipation of federal elections the following year, that regional organs functioned everywhere.[15] The quality of these organizations varies. The best-organized regional committees exist in the Federal District, Jalisco, Baja California state, Yucatán, Chihuahua, Michoacán, and Mexico state.[16]

The state of the extension of PAN organization in Mexico means that the party cannot hope to influence all of the citizenry directly and consistently. Permanent organizations are obviously advantageous for the operation of a political party but the ability to create them is simply beyond the scope of PAN resources. Reliance upon temporary committees at election time is necessary but prevents the party from gaining the experience necessary to the conquest of significant posts of power. Moreover, it aids the claims of rivals that the PAN would be incapable of ruling the country if the party were ever to win a presidential election.

The regulations attempting to create vertical structure down to the city block or country zone level are another aspect of PAN organization necessitating comment. This would be an ideal base for political organization insuring continuous and meaningful access to the citizenry on the part of the PAN. To operate such a system a party needs a well-trained leadership that can dispense rewards and favors to its constituents. PAN has no such leadership nor extensive means of rewards. In Baja California such an organization is possible, but this is an exceptional case. Data on the number and location of *municipios* where such intensive organization exists is not available. Possibly such organization exists in Yucatán in recent years and scattered *municipios* in Michoacán, Guanajuato, Jalisco, Chihuahua, Nuevo León, and Mexico state. Even in the Federal District, the most important area of PAN activity, it has been impossible to extend the organization to such a level.[17]

PAN's rejection of a functional or corporate structure merits comment. PRI adopted this form of organization in 1938 when it was called by another name. PAN, organized in 1939, immediately and emphatically rejected such a structure, even before its effectiveness was known. This is particularly noteworthy since there is evidence to indicate that many PAN leaders, including Gómez Morín, were interested in Italian fascism and the movements of Salazar in Portugal, Franco in Spain, Vargas in Brazil, and, later, Perón in Argentina.[18] Although a plan to organize the membership horizontally according to occupations (using the broad categories or professionals, rural and urban workers, employees and others) was written, this project was neither incorporated into the Statutes or Regulations nor used extensively even on an ad hoc basis.[19] PAN could not accept such an organizational scheme because it represented the institutionalization of class conflict while PAN was denying that class conflict was inevitable.[20] Moreover, it had a pragmatic basis as well—PAN would be overwhelmed if Mexican politics were organized functionally since PAN was composed of only a fraction of the middle and upper classes with little peasant-worker support. More important than the pragmatic reason was the ideological reason. PAN leadership did not want a fascist state but a democratic state. The corporations in which it was interested were the natural corporations long posited in Catholic social thought—the family, work associations, governments, religious institutions, and cultural institutions. PAN's corporation was designed to promote these through democratic procedures with each individual participating, not through the government forcing their creation or operating them.

Accrued Organizations

In addition to the mandated institutions Acción Nacional also has had a number of institutions created from the broad statutory grants of power to the president. Such institutions included the Youth Organization, Women's Organization, Institute of Social and Political Studies, Bureaucracy, special election teams, interregional conventions, social service projects, and PAN federal deputies as a group. These institutions were created as the party grew.

Although abolished in 1971 as part of PAN's democratization, the Youth and the Women's Organizations warrant discussion because they existed throughout most of the period covered by this study. Neither had explicit roles. Both had structural similarities with the national party, but the points at which they entered into the decision-making process and the justifications for their existence were not stated in party statutes. Both had the usual complement of officials, headed by a president, and both extended down to the municipal level. Conventions at the national and regional levels were held but their importance in the total operation of the party appears to have been negligible. One variable affecting their importance was the dynamism and quality of their leadership. Under energetic, ambitious leaders, such as that of Hugo Gutiérrez Vega in 1957–62 in the Youth Organization, these organizations were able to influence party behavior.

Women's Organization

The existence of the organization reflects historical circumstances. Women were immediately recruited into the party and worked for party goals. Female suffrage in Mexico came in 1947 at the municipal level and in 1952 at the federal level. In prior years PAN women were allowed to participate and vote in party affairs but they were marginal to the national political process since they lacked the vote. The existence of separate organizations allowed the party to (1) use it as a recruiting device, (2) capitalize on feminine energy and enthusiasm, and (3) pander to masculine egos which might object to female equality. With the extension of the suffrage to women, their political importance grew. The feminine organization was institutionalized in 1959 and, in 1962, women were guaranteed seats on the CEN.

As a separate entity, the feminine section of the party performed distinct functions. Much of the drudgery of party operations has been assumed by women. Food concessions at conventions, a source of party income, have been operated by them. Most important have been the female sector social service activities. Data on such activities are scarce. Currently two social service works operated by the feminine sector are worth noting. In Michoacán, PAN women collect used clothing for repairs and cleaning and then sell them at low prices to the poor.[21] In Puebla, the women operate a school of nursing.[22] A recent addition has been the Monica M. de González Morfín literacy school in Villa Nicolás Romero, Mexico state, operated in conjunction with the Mexico state regional committee.[23]

Youth Organization

The Youth Organization was more important. Reserved for men under thirty-five, the organization was a training ground for future party leaders. It was originally organized on an informal basis in 1943 by Jesús Hernández Díaz at the suggestion of Gómez Morín. By 1956 it had become a more formalized institution and was exerting influence on party decisions. It was the Youth Organization that gave the party a reputation for aggressiveness and irresponsibility in the events surrounding the 1958 presidential election and which made the overt flirtations with Christian Democracy. Because of this influence and in order to control it, young men have automatically been guaranteed CEN seats since 1959.

Federal Deputies

Incumbent PAN federal deputies have no special statutory role in the party but they have become increasingly important in party deliberations. Since 1964 when the first deputies of party were created, PAN has had at least twenty people holding public office who live at least part of the year in the Federal District. Some of these men are members of the CEN or the Council, giving them a voice in the affairs of the party. It has become customary, however, to consult all of them on major issues. Many important public actions are taken by the federal deputies. Party proposals and criticisms of governmental legislative bills made by the federal deputies must be integrated into the party's activities. The deputy delegation has its own chief (the national president if he is a federal deputy). The Chamber of Deputies provides office and office help for federal deputies which gives the PAN deputies an office in the Chamber building and some patronage. Because they help finance the party from their earnings as federal deputies, their wishes cannot be ignored.

Interregional Conventions

An effective device developed by PAN for educating its members and for studying Mexican problems has been the interregional convention, where the members in specified areas of Mexico are called together to study particular problems such as agriculture or the *municipio*. These meetings began in 1940 and have been used extensively.[24] Members from various states prepare position papers on various aspects of the problem under consideration. These are read and debated. Usually the outcomes of the convention are published and become part of the party literature and doctrine.[25] Whereas the *Principles of Doctrine, Minimum Program of Political Action,* and party platforms tend to be vague, befitting their genre, these studies are detailed.

Interregional conventions of party heads have also been used to coordinate the party's position vis-à-vis elections. In 1969, regional chiefs met in Puebla to discuss participation in the 1970 federal election, possible candidates, and the platform that PAN would present.[26] Such meetings prevent public airing of divisions. This function is less well known, and I do not know how extensively these conventions/meetings have been held.

Institute of Social and Political Studies

The Institute of Social and Political Studies was a direct result of the attempts of the Youth Organization to manage the party and to push it into a Christian Democratic alliance. Christlieb, party president at the time, found it necessary to discipline youth leaders, causing a small split when the more vocal ones left the party, publicly condemning it. Christlieb issued an appeal to both PAN and Mexican youth to follow PAN as the only party responsive to youthful dissatisfactions.[27] To cap off this recruitment appeal, the Institute of Social and Political Studies was created to teach party doctrine, political science, and tactics. Basic texts include party doctrine, platforms, and speeches; studies of Mexican and foreign politics; and theoretical works on communism and democracy.[28]

Special Election Terms

The bulk of campaigning is done by youth leaders since they have energy, enthusiasm, and time, but the party also creates a special election team for the presidential candidate. Young men in the party affix the posters and banners, distribute propaganda sheets, and operate the loudspeaker systems. The tasks of arranging interviews and rallies, of transporting the candidate throughout the country, of maintaining data for candidate speeches, and of typing speeches are performed by this team, which exists only for the campaign. The teams vary in size but usually have five members. The candidate selects these helpers.

Bureaucracy

As PAN has increased in size a small bureaucracy has been built. Originally the party operated from an office but now national headquarters are located in three floors of an old rented building in Mexico City within walking distance of PRI headquarters. The first two floors of the five-story building are occupied by a furniture company. The third floor has the offices of *La Nación;* the fourth floor has the Federal District regional organization offices and an auditorium; and the fifth floor has the CEN and National Council offices. The fifth floor has four rooms, one encompassing most of the floor. It is partitioned off into offices for the *official mayor,* the secretary-general, the president, the head of the studies commission, a meeting room for the CEN and a library. The party has sixteen full-time employees. There are also an unknown number of part-time employees. Volunteer labor often outnumbers paid labor.

The national offices are used continuously. On a typical day workers begin arriving at nine o'clock. The offices seldom close before ten o'clock at night, and *La Nación* offices commonly remain open longer. Visitors constantly enter, including *campesinos* and workers. Meetings are held there daily.

Decision-Making

Acción Nacional likes to assert that decisions are made as the Statutes stipulate: that the general membership, through a general assembly or convention, dictates policy by voting after open debate; this is not true. Assemblies and conventions have rarely thwarted the wishes of the national leadership. The decision to participate in the 1940 elections and the inclusion of an anti–Article 3 plank in the 1967 platform are two unusual examples of the exercise of this power. The national and regional presidents occupy the strategic positions through their broad powers and constant attention to party affairs, followed in importance by the national and regional committees. Since the presidents usually choose their own committees as well as influence heavily the selection of their respective councils, PAN's elite is self-perpetuating.

This self-perpetuation has been a source of intraparty conflict, shown most recently by the August 1971 unsuccessful attempts to limit the reelection of presidents and to create councils which change half their membership every three years.

The power of the national president has been particularly great since he can veto every decision of regional and lower organizations. He also can control the CEN which has its own large block of votes. The CEN, until 1971, had as many votes as the Federal District, the largest regional committee. The national president selects the Federal District regional president.

Moreover, the most important party decisions are often made by the party leadership behind closed doors. Party chieftains gather before assemblies and conventions to decide which issues will be encouraged in public debates and to determine the scope of the debates. Convention and assembly votes usually ratify these decisions.

The general membership has more power and influence than these comments might suggest. First, party leaders have to maintain as much harmony as possible among their generally highly educated, sophisticated constituents and have to be very responsive to their wishes. Second, regional leaders come to national meetings with mandates from regional conventions or assemblies which have become increasingly independent. Attempts to ignore their constituents would result in the repudiation of the leadership, which PAN can ill afford. Finally, convention and assembly votes are not predetermined, for regional delegations, influenced by debates, can and do switch their votes from what the regional presidents had been anticipating. The close vote in the 1970 convention on electoral participation surprised national leaders, especially since many delegations had switched sides by the following morning.

The debates on tactics are more important for minority political parties in Mexico than they are in the United States. In the latter's political system, the basic tactics focus on vote aggregation in anticipation of reasonably fair elections. Major United States parties can assume that they will hold public posts sufficient to satisfy some of the interests they represent. Mexican parties, except PRI, make opposite assumptions. Perceiving the political system as detrimental to their success, Mexican political parties face a different dilemma. The basic question is not how to articulate interests or couch appeals to win votes but whether they should cooperate with the system. The decision taken is important because participation legitimizes the political system and nonparticipation risks cancellation of party registration. Because Mexican minority parties are primarily motivated by ideology, as has been the case with socialist parties in the United States, tactical questions are also questions of party unity. Each debate on tactics threatens party dismemberment. Dissension may lead to dismemberment. Debates have to be allowed in Acción Nacional not only because the party claims that it is democratic but also for therapeutic value. Debaters can: (1) vent their frustration over their inability to obtain power in Mexico, (2) exercise influence within the narrow confines of the party, and (3) purge themselves of bitterness that would make them dangerous as electoral campaigners.

Platform debates are equally important. Unlike the United States where platforms are debated, approved, and then forgotten, political platforms in Mexico are critical for minority parties, which are sustained by ideology, not political spoils. National party unity is at stake but also survival since extreme deviations from the norms acceptable to the Revolutionary coalition may mean governmental persecution and reduced effectiveness, as in the case of UNS. Although minor parties such as PAN have gained support for nonideological reasons, offering ideological alternatives is a main raison d'étre of Acción Nacional's existence.

The actual operation of the party is indicative of the party's ideological consistency and, for lack of better evidence, suggestive of how it might run Mexico if it could reach power. Since most of the statutory structure is mandated by external forces, it is not particularly useful for this purpose. PAN is a paternalistic democracy which follows popular sentiment as well as trying to direct it. In this respect it differs little from Mexican (as well as most Latin American) practice. Nevertheless, PAN is more democratic than PRI or the government because serious, open debate which can and has determined party action has taken place, because the party is relatively open in its operation, and because the leadership is forced to satisfy the rank and file. While the president and the CEN have what appears to be almost absolute power, conditions have never allowed them to exercise it on that level. What they can do is to give strong leadership. PAN is not as democratic as its leaders assert nor is it ever likely to be.

CHAPTER VIII

Membership and Leadership

PAN has sought the widest possible membership since its founding and membership recruitment has been one of its primary concerns. The development of party leadership has been of equal concern to the party. Of the two, leadership is easier to identify and study, allowing its more complete analysis. The chapter is divided into these two major sections with summary generalizations at the end of each section.

MEMBERSHIP

The Statutes require that PAN members meet the following conditions, that they: (1) be Mexican citizens, (2) have an honest means of livelihood, (3) fully accept PAN principles, and (4) pledge to work in permanent and disciplined form for the party. Entrance into the party is technically through sponsorship by two existing members, but the party actually accepts almost anyone. Membership applications are processed at the municipal, district, regional, and national levels, but the most common level of entry is at the municipal level. The General Assembly has final control over membership entry but this has not been exercised.[1]

Membership is divided into three categories—founders, actives, and adherents—but only the last two have any functional significance. Founders are those members who signed the founding acts of the party in 1939. They are not given special privileges within the party; the distinction is simply bestowal of prestige. Actives are regular members of the party and have full rights. Adherent members cannot vote in party affairs nor can they serve on decision-making bodies. Prior to the 1949 change in the Statutes, adherent members could sit and vote in the National Executive Committee. By that year, the importance of persons who did not want to be identified with PAN but who aided it had declined. Now they can participate in party debates and receive information about party activities. Adherents are those persons who support the party by such

132

means as contributions, votes, and propaganda but never acquire the character of actives. They are signed into the party by answering affirmatively the question: will you be an adherent member of PAN?[2]

The existence of an adherent status is the result of the anxiety felt by many prominent Mexicans in the early years of PAN organization. Persons who did not want to be identified as members of the government's opposition—such as employees, businessmen seeking or holding government contracts, or other persons who thought themselves vulnerable but were willing to support PAN—were given adherent status. As conditions changed to reduce or eliminate this anxiety the number of adherent members declined. Early plans to organize adherents into occupational groups were quickly discarded. At present, the adherent status is virtually nonfunctional.[3]

The origins of the idea of adherent status is difficult to determine. PAN is the only Mexican political party using adherent status but it was not PAN's original idea. The Spanish Falange, which interested many *panistas,* used the active-adherent dichotomy,[4] but Venezuela's Acción Democratica, which has no contacts with PAN or *Falangismo,* uses a similar system, dividing its membership into actives and sympathizers.[5]

Party Statutes spell out the rights of all party members, actives and adherents. All members have equal rights (with the exclusion from suffrage and membership on directive bodies of adherents). Members can participate in all decision-making bodies, debate in assemblies and conventions, expect equality of treatment within the party, and be guaranteed appeal rights from party disciplinary actions. Party doctrine stipulates that the party recognizes no essential differences among Mexicans and rejects class divisions.

Obligations of members are specified. Members agree to (1) work for the party in all its undertakings, (2) attend party meetings or send a representative, (3) contribute a portion of their income to the party treasury (on a sliding scale based upon income level), (4) participate in decision-making at appropriate levels, (5) accept decisions reached by the proper party authorities, (6) not criticize or air party differences outside of party meetings, and (7) participate in Mexican civic life.

Failure to fulfill these obligations or to cease to meet membership requirements can result in suspension or cancellation of party membership. The directive committees of the party can suspend or expel any member who they believe has not met these requisites. The member can appeal the decision to the National Council. In practice there have been few cases of party expulsion of members; the most notable were the departure of Aquiles Elorduy in 1947[6] and the expulsion of the PAN federal deputies who took their seats in the Chamber of Deputies in 1958 against party directives.[7] Elorduy, an atheist, was expelled for making antireligious statements in Aguascalientes. *Panistas* told this author that he left because he was independent-minded. Years later he ran for public office on the PRI ticket.

The membership is organized both vertically and horizontally. The vertical system of organization from the national level down to the block or zone level has already been noted. The Statutes also require further organization within the local party levels so that there are groups of blocks and zones. Zones are used when the membership is too widely dispersed to use the block system. Functionally, this system does not operate except in a few places, such as Baja California. Horizontally, the two most important membership organizations have been based on age and sex: the youth and feminine organizations of the party. They obtain a fuller sense of participation through these organizations than they could through the party as a whole which is run primarily by older men.[8]

Data on membership is difficult to gather. Early recruitment was done through personal contact. Gómez Morín contacted those men whom he thought would be interested in joining such a movement and they, in turn, contacted their friends. This formed one basic nucleus of the party.[9] Another important source of recruits has come through Catholic lay groups. Originally the UNEC moved en masse into PAN. Other Catholics, especially those involved in Catholic Action or the *cristero* movement joined the party. Catholic Action, Catholic labor unions, and other Catholic lay associations still provide many PAN recruits.[10] The percentage of recruits from these sources is not known nor does the author suggest that most members of Catholic lay organizations join the PAN. Since some PAN leaders also serve as Catholic lay leaders the probability that these organizations are a source of members is obvious. PAN wanted members from all economic sections but was unable to recruit them because of the aforestated PRI monopoly of the masses and because party organizers had little contact with the common man.

Recruitment is institutionalized in the organization committees of the party. Each level is obligated to recruit members but the bulk of the recruitment takes place at the local level, a main task of municipal committees. The organization commission of the municipal committee or subcommittee works closely with municipal and district chiefs to bring people into the party. In addition, all members are understood to have the obligation of recruiting other members. When there are no municipal committees another vertical committee assumes the job. Most recruitment apparently is done through personal contact rather than by systematized recruitment campaigns. Rewards of party membership are few but can be decisive. For those persons interested in being public figures PAN offers easy access to its internal decision-making levels. Prominent individuals can move into important party positions within a year after joining. The party deputy system allows PAN to reward party workers. For lesser persons, party membership can aid in acquiring jobs or promotions with party backers or leaders, many of whom are engaged in private enterprise. The extent of this motivation in membership recruitment is unknown and probably unknowable. Miguel Estrada Iturbide, founder of General Hipotecaria, a private mortgage bank, and of Acción Nacional in Michoacán, told me that many of his employees are party members, some probably with the expectation that it will incur favor with him, but he asserted that it would not.

Upon entering the party, recruits complete a simple membership form which is placed in the permanent files. The form asks for such standard information as name, home and business addresses, telephone numbers, place and date of birth, marital status, literacy, education, and occupation. In addition, recruits are queried as to the work they can offer the party inside and outside electoral campaigns, the type of vehicle owned, to which rural poll they are willing to go, place and people with whom they have contacts and influence, financial quota they are willing to accept, membership in other organizations, and relatives.[11]

Socioeconomic Characteristics

Available data on the socioeconomic composition of the membership offers some hypotheses as to who is recruited, as well as aiding in the explanation of why PAN continues to exist. Information on how many people have joined PAN or who they were is not available. The earliest years of the party, 1939–41, were the period when the greatest number of capitalists and other rich men were involved in the party.[12] One author asserts that 80% of PAN in the early years were bankers, industrialists, employers, secretaries, employees and families.[13] PAN sources basically agree with this description, complaining of the high number of capitalists who were in the party to protect their property interests, but assert that the number of professionals, intellectuals, and students was higher.[14] The 80% figure is too high, but there were large numbers of capitalists in the party. Gómez Morín as a prominent corporation lawyer and banker knew these people and he would logically turn to them. They were frightened by the course of the Revolution under Cárdenas and believed that Gómez Morín could help them without leading them to disaster.

The importance and number of men of enterprise and of financiers in PAN has steadily declined since 1940. The moderation and national unity policy of the Avila Camacho regime assuaged the anxieties of private enterprise in Mexico creating defections from PAN. The pro-private enterprise administration of Miguel Alemán made membership in PAN as a means to protect property interests not only unnecessary but counterproductive at that point since both the power and will to do such things was in the hands of PRI. Most had left by 1949. Many of these private enterprise types who stayed within the PAN probably did so because of their relations with Gómez Morín, either as his friends or clients. A Mexico City daily reported that the 1951 PAN national convention was composed of 50% farmers (primarily from Guerrero, Michoacán, San Luis Potosí, and Oaxaca), 15% workers (primarily from the Federal District, Nuevo León, Chihuahua, and Tamaulipas), 10% students (Federal District, Durango, Aguascalientes, and Zacatecas), and 25% professionals, industrialists, businessmen, and employees.[15] The figures for farmers, judging from later conventions, is probably too high even though there are grounds for believing that PAN had some peasant support in 1951. The UNS decided to support PAN in the 1952 presidential election and probably brought some of their peasant members to the convention. The PAN leader in Guerrero, Filogono Mora, was a lawyer for peasants there and may have brought many to the convention. The figures for workers is probably accurate since miners in Chihuahua had affiliated with PAN in reaction against PRI labor politics, because Nuevo León industrialists, who run white unions, probably brought some laborers with them, and because the Federal District was a center for Catholic labor activity.

More recent data affirms this trend away from membership based upon leaders of private enterprise towards recruitment among the middle sectors of the population, with an increasing ability to recruit workers and agriculturalists. Table 3 shows a comparison between the 1967 and 1970 PAN federal deputy candidates including their alternates. The occupational definitions were provided by the source and their precision is unknown. This list should be representative of the general membership because it is the basic office to which PAN seeks election and one for which PAN has to draw upon all its resources to complete a slate. Those areas where PAN has large membership and leaders available to run as candidates are counterbalanced by other areas where PAN is weak and has to draw upon every member to field a slate of candidates. The inclusion of primary and alternate candidates makes this data even more valuable since the alternate candidates can be persons to whom the party is trying to give experience or recently recruited members.

TABLE 3

Occupations of PAN's 1967 and 1970 Federal Deputy Candidates

Occupation	1967	1970	Occupation	1967	1970
Agriculturalists	28	36	Industrialists	18	11
Cattlemen	2	1	Administrative (private		
Peasants	0	1	enterprise)	3	2
Agricultural machine			Functionaries (private		
operators	0	1	enterprise)	1	0
Aviculturalists	1	0	Pattern makers	0	1
Students	1	9	Merchants	64	43
Teachers	12	27	Jewelers	5	3
Professors	0	2	Watchmakers	0	2
Publicists	0	1	Brokers (comision-		
Photographers	0	2	istas)	4	7
Printers	2	2	Barbers	0	1
Journalists-writers	6	2	Housewives	10	11
Announcers	2	0	Engineers	6	19
Physicians	8	5	Accountants	16	16
Optometrists	0	1	Bank functionaries	1	0
Dentists	4	1	Pilots	0	1
Pharmacists	2	0	Transporters	0	1
Lawyers	26	35	Architects	0	2
Technicians	4	6	Artisans	10	4
Workers	13	14	Contractors	3	1
Railroad workers	2	0	Construction foremen	5	2
Mechanics	0	11	Builders	1	0
Electricians	4	0	Economists	0	1
Employees	44	46	Chemists	3	1
Salesmen	13	4	Social workers	2	0
Federal government			Seismologists	1	0
employees	0	1	Various professions	10	0
Sculptor	1	1	Nonspecified	13	1
Fashion designer	0	1	TOTALS	352	337

SOURCES: *La Nación* XXVI (May 7, 1967), p. 27; *La Nación* Supplement, XXIX (June 14, 1970), 4–16.

The sources of membership indicated by Table 3 are relatively clear; most of the members come from within middle sector occupations with a predominance of professionals and businessmen. Most of these candidates would qualify for the Popular sector of PRI. Most interesting is that PAN has increased its membership from the urban working classes while it is still unable to attract much farmer support. The number of persons in the agriculturalist category might belie this, but they certainly represent small proprietors, some of whom could be engaged in commercial agriculture. The use of the peasant category precludes their being included in this group.

Table 4 provides similar data for the 1970 PAN senatorial candidates and can be used for the same purpose. Although the Senate has higher status than does the Chamber of Deputies, one cannot conclude that these candidates are significantly different from the deputy candidates. PAN's best men enter both races. They go into deputy races in those

TABLE 4

Occupations of PAN's 1970 Senatorial Candidates

Occupation	Number	Occupation	Number
Agriculturalists	8	Administrators (private	
Coffee growers	1	enterprise)	2
Teachers	3	Functionaries (private	
Journalists	2	enterprise)	1
Physicians	6	Merchants	21
Optometrists	1	Watchmakers	1
Dentists	2	Brokers (comisionistas)	5
Lawyers	4	Housewives	5
Technicians	2	Engineers	8
Workers	3	Accountants	3
Railroad workers	2	Bank functionaries	1
Mechanics	2	Artisans	2
Employees	13	Carpenters	1
Travel agents	1	Army captains	1
Industrialists	7		
		TOTAL	108

SOURCE: *La Nación,* XXIX (June 14, 1970), pp. 4–16.

districts where PAN is likely to garner enough votes to have a party deputy, insuring seats for party leaders in the Chamber but they also go into senatorial races where PAN has some hope of winning. Recently PAN has turned increased attention to the possibility of electing a senator in order to strengthen party claims to national leadership. As a result, the quality of senatorial candidates has risen.

The data provided shows rather conclusively that PAN's membership is recruited from men in liberal professions and from businessmen. The percentage of professionals as PAN federal deputy candidates in 1967 and 1970, respectively, was 26.4% and 33.2%. For businessmen, it was 43.8% and 35.3%. In other words, of the 1967 PAN federal deputy candidates in 1967, 70.2% were businessmen and professionals; in 1970, the figure was 68.5%. The difference may indicate a shift towards more professionals as candidates but the shift is not great. Approximately 70% of PAN membership probably comes from professionals and businessmen in this proportion. Data on the senate candidates is consistent with the trend observed. Professionals accounted for 28.7% of the candidates whereas businessmen composed 44.4%. Combined, this is 73.1% of the total candidates.

The observation that businessmen and professionals constitute approximately 70% of PAN's membership is supported by additional, though fragmentary, evidence. Studies of Ensenada, Baja California, and Ciudad Juárez, Chihuahua, found that the majority of PAN members in those two entities had been recruited from these sources.[16] The Ensenada study also found that one-third of the municipal committee was composed of workers, indicating that PAN has been able to recruit from lower socioeconomic classes.[17] The Michoacán regional organization includes workers and peasants but professionals and small businessmen predominate.[18] Since 1970, the Federal District organization has been able to recruit larger numbers of average Mexicans. Several Mexican political observers as well as some PAN leaders have asserted that most *panistas* are middle class, particularly from urban areas.[19] Efraín González Morfín, 1970 PAN presidential candidate, identified the PAN as a middle and lower-middle class party.[20] Other PAN leaders agree but quickly stress that PAN wants to recruit from labor and farmers but has been blocked by PRI monopoly of these social sectors, and, significantly, that PAN's ideology and programmatic statements are difficult to articulate to the common Mexican. My observations of delegates to the November 1969 and the January 1970 PAN national conventions were consistent with these findings.

The socioeconomic characteristics of the membership varies with locale. Michoacán and the Federal District are good examples. Michoacán is a traditionally Catholic rural state wherein the bulk of the population are *campesinos*. Almost no industry exists. The state capital, Morelia, is a prosperous and beautiful colonial city of some 200,000 inhabitants which has been declared a national monument in order to preserve the integrity of its colonial architecture. Uruapan and Zamora are the next largest cities. The remainder of the state is composed of small towns and villages. PAN membership strength is in these three cities. A crude survey of PAN's Michoacán membership files produced the data that most members were part of the provincial middle classes: small businessmen, employees, clerks, teachers, technicians, salesmen, insurance agents, and small-time lawyers. In addition, at least 30% were laborers and farmers. A few members were from the traditional aristocracy but not wealthy. Impressionistically, the Michoacán party appeared to be the bulwark of the relatively prosperous, traditionalist, provincial middle class. Although this observation cannot be supported by hard data and is not subject to social science techniques, it is supported by lengthy interviews, by extensive contact, and observation of the Michoacán party. In addition, it more nearly captures the spirit of the party than hard data can. One labor leader in Morelia with whom I had lengthy interviews agreed with this assessment but, surprisingly, pointed out that PAN has a larger labor-peasant membership than the above comments suggest. This leader asserted that the rich in Michoacán support PRI, not PAN. This agreed with the assertions of *panistas*. In smaller locales such as Pátzcuaro, Michoacán, however, lower economic strata are better represented.

The Federal District, which is almost entirely urban, presents a striking contrast to Michoacán. This is a dynamic, modern area in which live the nation's political, economic, and cultural leaders. The very size of the metropolis, approaching eight million in greater Mexico City, creates diversity and anonymity. Here, the socioeconomic composition of PAN membership differs drastically from Michoacán. This membership contains many businessmen and professionals but, according to reliable PAN sources, approximately half of the members come from student ranks and the working classes, who do most of the political work of the party. Even though there is no available hard data to support this assertion, I accept it for several reasons. The informants were in a position to know and have proven reliable on other information. The composition of the Federal District delegations to recent party conventions corroborates it. The capital's large student population, which is recruited nationally, and its extremely large working population made it highly likely that such a skew occurs within PAN's Federal District membership, which is small compared to the total capital population. In 1970, PAN picked up votes in two districts which have a greater than average working class population. Party internal training documents, not meant for public consumption and easily disputed by members, note that PAN is changing to a mass party. This change has necessitated special training and indoctrination sessions because members are now coming from a lower and less educated social strata. Although these documents do not say that this is occurring primarily in the Federal District, this is where it is most likely to occur. In general, Federal District *panistas* are more sophisticated, secular, and independent in attitude. They are attuned to the currents of the modern world and are constantly reminded of the contrasts between rich and poor countries by the steady stream of tourists through the city. Living in the national capital makes them more conscious politically than they would be if they resided in the provinces.

Unlike their copartisans in such places as Michoacán, the old Church-State conflict is largely meaningless.

The central problem for PAN recruiters is that belonging to PAN is deviant political behavior in Mexico. Most Mexicans are apolitical or nonparticipants.[21] Most PRI members affiliate because they belong to an organization, such as CTM or CNC, which automatically affiliates them. PAN members, on the other hand, have consciously chosen to join a party which has been labeled anti-Revolutionary, conservative, and reactionary and which has little immediate hope of gaining power at a significant level. For many Mexicans PAN membership borders on being non-Mexican. PAN leaders have recognized these problems and have spent considerable time arguing in favor of a two-party or multiparty system, trying to convince Mexicans that it is possible to be in an opposition party without being disloyal to Mexico or the Revolution. This has had moderate success, indicated by the increased numbers of PAN members, but the party has not been able to convince most Mexicans that it has no interest in reversing the Revolution. Consequently, PAN members tend to be alienated from the society, for only those persons sufficiently dissatisfied with Mexican conditions would affiliate with a party suffering such liabilities.[22]

Number

The quantity of PAN members is very difficult to determine for the party does not release membership figures. PAN leaders become evasive when questioned about the number of *panistas* there actually are. They assert that (1) the CEN does not know because membership figures are kept at the local level, (2) all persons who vote for PAN are party members in at least the adherent sense, (3) that PAN easily meets Federal Electoral Law requirements, and (4) that more people would join PAN if repression did not exist in Mexico. It is possible, of course, that the CEN does not know how many members the party has but it probably has a rough approximation. Voting figures probably represent the upper limit of membership. PAN's ability to meet Federal Electoral Law requirements has never been seriously questioned. The assertion about repression is gratuitous regardless of its validity.

Scattered information about the number of PAN members is available, however, and it indicates that the party has steadily grown in numbers since it was founded. Concrete data exist for the very earliest years of the party. An internal party memorandum from the files of a membership secretary showed that Acción Nacional had 2,535 male members in February 1940 and 4,226 in May 1941. In March 1941, there were 4,629 women in the party.[23] Membership increased from this point onwards. One indication of this has been attendance at national conventions and general assemblies. The number of delegates has commonly been over 2,000 and has reached 4,000.[24] It met the 1954 Federal Electoral Law membership requirement of 100,000 members easily.[25] During the 1960s the party was able to field federal deputy candidates in every district in the country. In 1970, the government recognized more than 1,942,000 votes for the PAN presidential candidate, or 14% of the total cast.[26] More precise figures are scarce. In Michoacán, in non-election years, PAN has approximately 3,000 members, centered in Morelia, Uruapan, and Zamora. In the Federal District, PAN has approximately 24,000.[27] There were 105 PAN members in Nogales, Sonora, out of a population of approximately 38,000 in 1969.[28] Between elections, the number of PAN activists peaks at 180,000 members.[29] PAN admits that it is a minority party and cannot approximate the size of PRI.

Geographical Distribution

The geographical distribution of PAN membership is clearer but also based upon impressions. PAN recruits the bulk of its membership from the Federal District, Jalisco, Mexico state, Michoacán, Baja California state, Chihuahua, and Guanajuato.[30] In addition it has had numerous members recently in Yucatán because of dissatisfaction there with PRI attempts, or lack of them, to improve economic conditions, and in Sonora because of resentment of the imposition of an unpopular governor. PAN membership in Nayarit, Campeche, Quintana Roo, Baja California territory, Tabasco, and Chiapas is negligible. Of these only Chiapas and Nayarit had regional committees in 1969. PAN members are most likely to be found in middle and large urban centers such as Mexico City, Guadalajara, Monterrey, Ciudad Juárez, Chihuahua city, Mérida, Tijuana, Hermosillo, Saltillo, Torreón, León, Guanajuato, San Luis Potosí, Querétaro, Morelia, Oaxaca, Puebla, Cuernavaca, and Veracruz—wherever there is an appreciable middle class.

This class and geographical basis of PAN membership is likely to continue and to benefit PAN. Appeals to workers and farmers have not been effective in recruiting from these groups and party leaders are in a quandary as to how to improve this recruitment in the face of the current political situation. They have little expectation that they will be able to make significant inroads into PRI's influence over these groups. The urbanization and modernization of Mexico will create more persons engaged in occupations from which PAN can recruit. Several observers, as well as some PAN leaders, believe that urbanization will increase PAN numbers and influence.[31] The increases in PAN membership since 1939 have probably come with the economic and social changes in Mexico since 1940, changes which have meant rapid industrialization, diversification of economic activity, and urbanization of the population, and, as Chapter IX shows, this is where PAN has received its greatest support. A dissenting view asserts that PRI has also been gaining rapidly in the urbanizing, wealthier areas and that opposition pictures cannot expect to gain from these trends.[32]

The characteristics of Acción Nacional membership make the party more influential than numbers suggest. It is a highly educated, politically conscious group which is less dependent upon the government than the average citizen. Its concentration in urban areas maximizes the party's exposure and masses party power in the locales where decisions are made. PAN membership is concentrated where PRI membership strength has traditionally been weakest. The government has been distributing benefits in these very areas in part to end this weakness. In addition, PRI, regardless of its official statements, is run by the same strata that runs PAN. The latter's membership recruitment strikes at PRI's heart. If PAN can significantly increase its middle class membership, it can increase its influence even without peasant-labor support.

<h2>LEADERSHIP</h2>

For the purpose of this study, leaders are defined as those persons able to influence or to make decisions within PAN, whether they hold statutory leadership positions, such as party president, or whether their personal prestige within the party endows them with influence, such as Manuel Gómez Morín. These leaders include, therefore, key statutory officers, primarily at the national and regional levels, and various other individuals who may not be holding a current office. District and municipal chiefs are excluded because they usually execute rather than make decisions. Committees and councils below the national level tend to follow the direction of the national organs and the regional chief. Although the National Council might appear to be a leadership organ, it has been excluded from analysis for two reasons: (1) it usually defers decision-making to the CEN or the president, and (2) when it does exert itself, a full meeting of the party is usually called. Biographical data on the CEN, founders, regional chiefs, and PAN federal deputies collectively represent the National Council throughout party history since the Council normally is composed of these groups. The first Council was analyzed in Chapter II.

A tentative typology of PAN leadership is largely impressionistic but sufficiently grounded in hard data to be suggestive. The following is suggested as an approximate rank order of major PAN leaders:

1. incumbent president
2. CEN
3. regional chiefs
4. federal deputy delegation
5. PAN presidential candidates
6. key party founders.

This list does not include persons who hold neither a position within the PAN hierarchy nor were party founders but who may play an important role in decision-making. If they exist, they are the hardest to identify and discuss. At best one is operating at the conjecture level. At a later point in the chapter, some tentative conjectures will be made. The founders' category is not so amorphous since the party not only identifies who falls within this category but also because it is possible to discern which founders play important roles.

Most of the data presented is biographical in nature[33] and is used to suggest patterns of recruitment, training, and mobility, as well as social class and ideological predelictions. Several methodological notes of caution must be sounded. Occupational or religious affiliation data should not be interpreted to mean that most Mexicans in these categories join or support PAN. The percentage who do is unknown. It is possible that most of the persons in these two classifications are PRI supporters or apolitical. In other words, the data suggests recruitment patterns for PAN but for no other Mexican institution. Its importance is its ability to suggest who leads this opposition party. The official anticlericalism of PRI combined with the high number of Catholic lay leaders in PAN does, however, strongly suggest that most politized lay Catholics would join PAN.

President

The incumbent party president is the most important individual in the leadership structure. He is visibly the party. His statements, whether authorized or not, are treated as official by the Mexican public. Moreover, he has broad powers granted to him both by statute and tradition.

The success of the party depends in large measure upon his personality. He leads the party and imparts his moods to it.

The biographical data presented in Table 5 indicates that PAN presidents have similar backgrounds. Gómez Morín differs from the others in being both a lawyer and a financier, having been born before the Revolution, and having served as president for a decade. All had income sources independent of the government, allowing them to be free agents, and lived in the capital at time of election. Ituarte Servín was the only president who did not practice a profession but operated his own business. Conchello Dávila, though a lawyer, earns his income from CONCAMIN and as a director of the National Advertisers' Association. He and Gómez Morín are the only two born outside of central Mexico. Involvement in Catholic lay organizations is one of their most consistent characteristics. Data on the involvement of Gómez Morín and Conchello Dávila in such organizations is not available, but it appears that neither has been a Catholic lay leader. Christlieb Ibarrola was a devout Catholic influenced by his religious beliefs. Whatever official ties he had with Catholic Action or similar organizations were not publicized but, because of his religious fervor, he should be included. Thus, most presidents since Gómez Morín have had extensive experience as members and leaders of Catholic lay organizations, providing them with thorough knowledge of Catholic doctrine. The peak of PAN's clerical tendencies came in 1962, however. Subsequent presidents have guided PAN carefully along secular lines, notwithstanding the obvious Catholic sources of party doctrine.

Even though the party literature has asserted that changes in leadership have resulted from the desire of younger men to assume control of party affairs,[34] the data on presidents does not support this generalization. Gómez Morín was the exceptional case. One finds that five of seven presidents were born within eight years of one another, that they entered the party at about the same time, and that they went through a similar apprenticeship program prior to being selected president. All served on the CEN as well as having served the party in some other official capacity. Three were federal deputies at the time of their election; one was PAN secretary-general; and one was PAN representative to the Federal Electoral Commission. González Hinojosa was unusual in assuming the presidency at the late age of fifty-seven, since most were in their early forties. Conchello Davila represents the sharpest break in the presidential selection process since he ended dominance by central Mexican natives and is a newcomer. Internal factors are useful in explaining presidential selection. The first president, Gómez Morín, was, of course, the key individual in forming the party. His departure from the presidency in 1949

TABLE 5

Acción Nacional Presidents, 1939–1972, Biographical Data

	Gómez Morín	Gutiérrez Lascuráin	Iturarte Servín	González Torres	Christlieb Ibarrola	González Hinojosa	Conchello Davila
Term	1939–49	1949–56	1956–59	1959–62	1962–68	1969–72	1972–
Birthplace	Chihua.	D.F.	D.F.	Mich.	D.F.	S.L.P.	N.L.
Year of birth	1897	1911	1914	1919	1919	1912	1923
Highest degree	Law	Eng.	Acct.	Law	Law	Law	Law
Occupation	Law	Eng.	Bus.	Law	Law	Law	Bus.
Catholic lay leader	n.a.	yes	yes	yes	yes	yes	n.a.
Highest PAN office before presidency	—	CEN, FD	CEN, FD	CEN, SG	CEN	CEN, FD	CEN, FD
Federal Deputy	no	1946–49	1955–58 1967–70	no	1964–68	1967–70	1970–73
Entrance into PAN	1939	1943	1939	1941	1941	1939	1955

KEY: Chihua. = Chihuahua
Mich. = Michoacán
D.F. = Distrito Federal
S.L.P. = San Luis Potosí
N.L. = Nuevo León

Eng. = Engineering
Acct. = Accounting
Bus. = Business

CEN = National Executive Committee
FD = Federal Deputy
SG = Secretary-General

merits attention, therefore, not his selection. Officially, the party says that he wished to turn direction over to younger men both to institutionalize party leadership and to assert PAN's position against personalism in government.[35] This has some validity since his successor was of a different generation. Another possibility must be acknowledged. By 1949, one of the basic goals of the party had been achieved—the turning of the Mexican government away from an antibusiness and anticlerical position. This having been accomplished, Gómez Morín stepped into the background where he would remain influential but would not have the daily burdens of operating a political party. Gutiérrez Lascuráin had had extensive experience in Catholic lay activity, making him acceptable to the most important single interest group with PAN. Private enterprise remained an important influence on the 1949 CEN and the González Luna presidential candidacy may represent the assertion and assurance of Catholic control of PAN. He was a lackluster president, lacking the ability to inspire activity. He was living in the shadow, and probably under the direction, of his predecessor. In short, he performed a caretaker role, to which some party members strenuously objected.[36]

The desire for dynamism in party activity, especially from militant Catholics, led to the selection of Ituarte Servín and then González Torres as PAN presidents. Ituarte Servín had spent much of his youth fighting government anticlericalism and had helped found important Catholic social institutions such as workers' and students' centers in the Federal District. Ituarte Servín selected his fellow Catholic militant, José González Torres, as his secretary-general. Of the two, the basic difference appears to have been the decisiveness of González Torres, a strong-willed, energetic, and committed man. When 1958 Federal electoral events went beyond Ituarte Servín's ability to control them, González Torres, first as secretary-general, then as president, assumed control. Both men gave fuller decision-making powers to party young men and embarked upon a program of militant political Catholicism, particularly towards some form of Christian Democracy.

The combination of intransigence in front of the government and the militant Catholic posture threatened to bring both internal defections and reprisals from the government; hence, it was necessary to select a president who would satisfy all party elements and the government. The result was the election of Adolfo Christlieb Ibarrola, the party's best politician. He not only saved the party from massive defections by those who disagreed with the militant Catholic posture, from cancellation of registration by the government, and from the withdrawal of financial support from private enterprise sources, but he also extended PAN's influence in Mexico by altering its ideology and tactics. His ability to accomplish these tasks emanated from respect for his intellectually, his deep commitment to Catholicism, his ability to contest the government without alienating it, and his strong personal will. He ran the party by reconciling its factions so that his proposals appeared to be the best available.

His elected successor, González Hinojosa, is a mild-mannered self-effacing party founder whose role appeared to be that of moderator while PAN tried to decide its future role in the Mexican political system. González Hinojosa had been a PAN state leader before migrating to the Federal District in the mid 1950s. He also had been active in Catholic lay organizations. He did not lead the party to the extent that his predecessors did, more closely representing Gutiérrez Lascuráin in temperament and leadership function. He implemented the Christlieb Ibarrola ideological trajectory but appeared to be guiding PAN back toward intransigence. He is more heavily dependent upon the CEN and other party organs than his predecessors, partly because he psychologically cannot force his will upon the party.

The meaning of the election of Conchello Dávila can only be suggested at this point. The González Hinojosa presidency had been uninspiring and the president had been unable to control the internal struggles which had been occurring since the Yucatán debacle. The newly elected president may well have been chosen because he could pacify these factions. He is popular within the party and was elected with 75 percent of the votes. He was strongly supported by González Morfín, leader of the Christian Socialist faction, but his close connections with private enterprise would mollify the conservative elements. Regionalistic antagonisms toward Mexico City control should abate now that this Nuevo León native has finally broken the central Mexican monopoly of the presidency.

CEN

Four CENs over a thirty-year period have been studied for occupational and religious organization affiliation. Table 6 shows their occupational distribution. Several methodological notes are necessary. The 1939 CEN was chosen because it was the first, reflecting some of the reasons for the creation of Acción Nacional. The 1969 CEN was used because it was the incumbent CEN when the bulk of the research was being done. This is the first CEN of González Hinojosa, but there was extensive carry-over from the CEN of Christlieb Ibarrola. The 1949 CEN was that of Gutiérrez Lascuráin. The 1959 CEN was that of González Torres. The selection of these four provides data on the first CENs

TABLE 6
CEN, 1939–1969 Occupational Data

Occupation	Number				Percentage of Each Committee				1939–1969 CEN Inclusive	
	1939	1949	1959	1969	1939	1949	1959	1969	No.	Percent
Lawyers	9	11	9	16	31.0	40.7	36.0	47.0	31	36.0
Bankers	7	5	3	—	24.2	18.5	12.0	—	10	11.6
Dentists	—	1	1	1	—	3.7	4.0	2.9	1	1.2
Physicians	2	1	—	—	6.9	3.7	—	—	3	3.5
Engineers	—	2	3	2	—	7.4	12.0	5.9	8	9.3
Journalists/ writers	4	1	1	1	13.8	3.7	4.0	2.9	7	8.1
Artists	—	1	1	1	—	3.7	4.0	2.9	2	2.3
Teachers	—	—	1	1	—	—	4.0	2.9	1	1.2
Rentiers	1	1	—	—	3.4	3.7	—	—	1	1.2
Architects	1	—	1	2	3.4	—	4.0	5.9	2	2.3
Cattlemen	—	1	1	—	—	—	4.0	—	1	1.2
Businessmen	4	2	2	3	13.8	7.4	8.0	8.8	9	10.5
Workers	1	1	—	1	3.4	3.7	—	2.9	2	2.3
Housewives	—	—	—	1	—	—	—	2.9	1	1.2
Economists	—	—	—	1	—	—	—	2.9	1	1.2
Unknown	—	1	2	4	—	3.7	8.0	11.8	5	5.8
TOTALS	29	27	25	34	99.8	99.9	100.0	99.6	86	98.9

Thirty of the eighty-six (34.9%), at least, can be identified as members of UNEC, Catholic Action, or some other Catholic lay organization.

of four of six PAN presidents as well as giving a ten-year spread between them, indicating the long-term trends within party leadership. The second methodological note concerns occupations. Occupations are difficult to discover and define; the data here presented probably has some error within it. The author has tried to reduce this to a minimum, and it is doubted that there is significant error. An attempt was made to show the principal occupation of the members. Hence, a lawyer who works for a bank is called a banker since banking is his primary source of income and probably his chief economic interest. All persons working for a bank, whether they are owners or clerks, are identified as bankers. More precision is obviously desirable but difficult to obtain without listing and explaining each occupation separately.

Occupational data on the CEN confirms the previous generalization that bankers and businessmen have become less important to PAN since 1939. Whereas 24.2% of the 1939 CEN were bankers, this figure has dropped to 12% in 1959 and to none in 1969. In 1959, the only member prominent as a banker was Gómez Morín. Of the other two, one was González Luna who was as much a lawyer as a banker and more motivated by his religious beliefs than by his economic interests, whereas the other was an employee. The percentage of businessmen was significantly higher in 1939 than in any other year. The businessmen of 1959 and 1969 were not owners of enterprises whereas most of the 1939 and 1949 members were.

Most CEN members have been recruited from the ranks of men in the liberal professions. Lawyers consistently have been the most important group of PAN leaders, as the CEN data indicates. If one includes lawyers, architects, physicians, dentists, engineers, teachers, economists, and journalists as professionals, the CEN has consistently been composed of over 55% professionals. Teachers have probably been more important recently than the figures suggest. Most of the unknowns in 1959 and 1969 are female members who are probably teachers.

Affiliation with Catholic lay organizations is equally important in categorizing the CEN. PAN leaders deny that their affiliation with Catholic lay organizations has any relationship with their politics, but I disagree. Because of the research difficulties presented by the Church-State conflict in Mexico and the desire of PAN leaders to minimize the importance of Catholic lay activity, my data on PAN leaders as active members of Catholic lay organizations are represented as the minimum. Such membership is undoubtedly higher. Of the 1939 CEN 41.4% were active in UNEC, Catholic Action, National Parents' Union, or some other Catholic lay group. In 1949, this group composed 33.3%; in 1959, 44%; and in 1969, 41.2%. Active Catholic laymen clearly have been important as a recruitment source for PAN leadership. Moreover, many of these Catholic laymen were public leaders of lay Catholicism. González Torres had been president of the ACJM, Catholic Action, and international president of *Pax Romana*. González Luna had been one of the principal Catholic Action leaders in Mexico since the 1920s. The single most important Catholic lay group in 1939 and 1949 as a source of PAN leadership was the relatively progressive UNEC. Nevertheless, it was impossible to find evidence that these leaders were Church agents. Further comments about PAN leadership and Catholicism will be made later in the chapter.

Regional Presidents

Data on regional presidents is harder to gather because they are less likely to be identified in the popular press, but available occupational data for the 1970 regional presidents conforms to that of the CEN. Biographical data on twenty-three of twenty-nine regional presidents in 1970–71 is available.[37] Table 7 shows the composition.

TABLE 7

Regional Presidents, Occupational Data

Occupation	Number	%
Lawyers	7	30.4
Engineers	4	17.4
Brokers	2	8.7
Businessmen	2	8.7
Teachers	2	8.7
Architects	1	4.3
Jewelers	1	4.3
Physicians	1	4.3
Employees	1	4.3
Housewives	1	4.3
Industrialists	1	4.3
TOTALS	23	99.7

Michoacán regional presidents are typical for all regional presidents. The founder of PAN in Michoacán and its regional president for seventeen years, Miguel Estrada Iturbide, deserves special attention. As a young man, he was one of the principal founders and leaders of UNEC. He obtained his law degree from the Free School of Law of Michoacán,

Members of his family have been Michoacán aristocrats for generations as signaled by his maternal name Iturbide. They are direct descendants of General Agustín de Iturbide who effected Mexican independence from Spain in 1821–22. This prestigious genealogy is a political liability, however, because General Iturbide, a conservative monarchist and clericalist, is one of the villains of Revolutionary historiography. Although socially prominent, Miguel Estrada Iturbide is not rich. He was a founding partner of General Hipotecaria, S.A., a Morelia mortgage bank with branches in Mexico City and Guadalajara; his income allows him to live well, not luxuriantly. All of his sons received university training, principally in law. Two received their university degrees from American Catholic institutions. The father is known as one of the best orators in Mexico. From our lengthy interview in the board room of General Hipotecaria, it was apparent that this reputation rests on his precise legal mind rather than his raspy voice. Ideologically, he is hard to categorize. Although he was an ardent fighter for Church causes as a youth, in his maturity he argues for the complete separation of Church and State as well as complete ideological tolerance. He was a guest observer to the International Christian Democratic Congress in Santiago, Chile, in 1962. When pressed, he told me that he would probably be a Christian Democrat if he were Chilean or a Venezuelan and a Kennedy Democrat if he were an American, but he stressed that it was impossible to know.[38]

Other Michoacán regional presidents are not as talented nor as prosperous as Estrada Iturbide. Each has been an intelligent, dedicated leader but each also recognizes Estrada Iturbide's brilliance. Dr. Rafael Morelos Valdés, a prominent Morelian physician, is a fortyish man who recently ran for governor. He is the largest single financial contributor to the party's regional budget. Carlos Guzmán Guerrero, a lawyer in his mid-thirties, is a handsome, quick-witted, and personable young man. He spends most of his time on his law practice in order to earn a moderate income. He indicated to me that his capitalistic orientation has been greatly altered by his interest in Marxism and Christian Democracy. In 1964, he was the guest of COPEI at the Christian Democratic convention in Caracas, Venezuela. Gabriel Pérez Gil González is the only one without a university degree, but he operates a successful insurance business and owns one of the most beautiful colonial houses in Morelia. The fiftyish ex-president enjoys a local reputation for being fair and honest in his business and political activities. Manuel Torres Serranía, now dead, was extremely personable and well liked within PAN. The current president, the fortyish J. Jesús Quiroz Pedraza, is the sixth president of PAN's Michoacán regional committee. Trained as an engineer, he is a house contractor. Because he has no children and a prosperous business, he has the time and money to devote to political activity, one of the primary reasons he was chosen. An affable man, Quiroz is an earnest but amateurish political leader. He entered PAN in Uruapan, Michoacán (where he was a friend of PRI members) when Dr. Morelos Valdés asked him to serve as a pollwatcher for PAN. Previously apolitical, the experience shocked him as he observed numerous irregularities and coercion. He became a *panista*. Working in PAN does not serve his economic interests. He does rent an old house to the party for its headquarters but he could obtain higher rents on the open market.[39]

Unlike other regional presidents, the Federal District regional chiefs are actually chosen by the national president after consulting Federal District leaders. This is done because the actions of this regional organization are often seen as official national policy and because this committee is dependent upon the national party for economic support. One consequence is that there have been many regional presidents in the Federal District. Their identification is difficult. The first regional president was Ernesto Robles León, now director of Bacardí rum in Mexico. He has not been active in PAN for years. Efraín González Morfín served as regional president for a few months in 1969 as preparation for his presidential nomination that year. González Hinojosa put Efraín into this office to strengthen his candidacy. José G. Minondo was selected a secretary-general, an office which automatically gave him the presidency when Efraín resigned to devote his time to the national presidential campaign. The forty-one-year-old Minondo has been a disciple of González Hinojosa for years. Both are from San Luis Potosí. When Minondo finished his law degree, he found a post in González Hinojosa's largely *potosino* law firm. Minondo is a bright, debonair, and energetic leader who speaks beautiful Castillian Spanish, learned from his Spanish mother. He told me that he entered PAN as a disciple of González Hinojosa and later became a *panista*. He is very modern in his outlook and believes that Mexico has to adopt something akin to the Christian Democratic "revolution in liberty" or Scandanavian socialism to solve its problems.[40]

The leadership of PAN organizations in states where the party has little influence is also chosen by the national president. Historically, this has meant that the national president has had their votes at his command. When PAN increases its influence to the point that the organizations can survive without national party help they become independent.

Federal Deputies

Occupational data in Table 8 on the 1970–73 PAN Federal Deputy delegation parallels the CEN data, but the former data provides additional and suggestive information.[41] Most of the Federal Deputies were born in central Mexico, received their professional degrees from the national university, practice a profession, and represent the Federal District. They entered PAN after finishing their university careers (age 25.6 years), and did not move into one of the leadership positions until middle age (44.5 years). Although age and geographical data is not available for the CEN, it is probable that the CEN members have followed a similar pattern.

Presidential Candidates

PAN presidential candidates do not differ from the other sectors of PAN leadership except that they have been closely linked with Catholic lay activity. Table 9 gives a synopsis of the basic biographical data. Alvarez, González Torres, and González Morfín were not party founders as many other PAN leaders have been. Presidential candidates are

TABLE 8

1970–1973 PAN Federal Deputies, Biographical Data

TOTAL — 20

Average Age, Years		Occupation	
At entering PAN	25.6	Law	40%
At election	44.5	Business	15%
		Medicine	10%
Place of Birth		Accounting	10%
Distrito Federal	20%	Employee	10%
Jalisco	20%	Teacher	5%
Michoacán	20%	Dentist	5%
Puebla	15%	Engineer	5%
Mexico	5%		
Veracruz	5%	Entities Represented	
Tamaulipas	5%	Fed. Dist.	65%
Yucatán	5%	Jalisco	15%
Unknown	5%	Mexico	10%
		Guanajuato	5%
Highest Degree		Yucatán	5%
Law	40%		
Accounting	15%	Federal Deputies Prior	
M.D.	10%	to 1970–73	40%
Engineering	10%		
Normal School	10%		
Dentistry	5%		
Unknown	5%		

SOURCE: Biographical data provided by Enrique Creel Luján.

TABLE 9

PAN Candidates to the Mexican Presidency, Biographical Data

	González Luna	Alvarez	González Torres	González Morfín
Year	1952	1958	1964	1970
Birthplace	Jalisco	Chihuahua	Michoacán	Jalisco
Year of birth	1898	1919	1919	1929
Highest degree	Law	Eng. (Master)	Law	Economics Law
Occupation	Law	Textile mfg.	Law	Economist
Catholic lay leader	Yes	Yes	Yes	Yes
Highest PAN office	CEN	CEN	President	D.F. President
Federal Deputy	No	No	No	1967–70
Entrance into PAN	1939	ca. 1953	1941	1959

KEY: Eng.   = Engineering
Master = Master's degree
Mfg.   = Manufacturing
CEN   = National Executive Committee
D.F.   = Distrito Federal

important as PAN leaders because of their public exposure. They are chosen for oratorical ability, devotion to the party cause, and willingness to contribute six to eight months to the campaign. In this respect, their recruitment differs from other leaders. The late entrance into PAN of González Morfín indicates that being a son of an important founder vitiates the necessity of long experience with the party. The date of the Alvarez entrance into the party is unknown. It has been asserted that he joined PAN after flirting with other political parties, including PRI. The veracity of the damning assertion is unknown although it is not unlikely that he entered PAN in the first half of the 1950s.

Founders

Biographical detail on party founders presented in Chapter II will not be repeated here; instead, other comments about the founders will be made. Less than half of the party founders continue taking an active role in PAN. Those who do are important because their prestige as founders carries some force with other party members. Several important founders are not visible to the general public, such as Miguel Estrada Iturbide, Manuel Ulloa Ortiz, Luis Calderón Vega, and Bernardo Elosúa, but they can influence decisions within the party. If there are covert PAN leaders, most are probably within this category. Characterizing them is extremely difficult. Most are educated, practicing Catholics who understand the doctrinal debates within their church. Some are important entrepreneurs, such as Elosúa, but others have middle-level incomes, such as Calderón Vega.

The common assertion that PAN is a party of the rich or of bankers is not supported by the evidence. It is clear that PAN leadership was heavily business-oriented in its first decade of existence, but middle income groups and occupations not only have been important in PAN from the beginning but have become increasingly so. Without comparative figures on the percentage of bankers and wealthy men who have supported PRI, overtly or covertly, since 1940, a true picture of support for various political persuasions in Mexico is unavailable. The assertion that PAN was a bankers' club was based upon two pieces of evidence: (1) some founders were important financiers, and (2) PAN has opposed some key Revolutionary provisions. Opponents of PAN, especially leftists, have automatically assumed that this combination meant that financiers represent PAN. Since 1939 the financiers have left PAN in order to support PRI or to become publicly apolitical to the point that almost none remain. PAN has concurrently become more revolutionary in its stance. Editorial cartoonists and leftist writers have recognized this change.[42] A recent *Tiempo* cover story on Aníbal de Iturbide, a former *panista* and prominent Mexican banker, gives details on the switch.[43] According to this story, Iturbide and other bankers left PAN because they became convinced that the Revolution was just, an implicit argument that the Revolution would protect bankers. It is probably the case today that PRI, not PAN, is the bankers' party, for only the PRI can and will protect banking interests.

Catholicism As a Factor

Interpreting the significance of the high number of Catholic activists in PAN's leadership, past or present, necessitates the use of extreme caution. Important qualifications must be made while generalizing. Although it is obvious that many PAN leaders are also Catholic lay leaders, this does not say that most, or the most important, Catholic lay leaders are in PAN or that the Church hierarchy supports PAN. Moreover, there is tension within PAN over clerical issues. Estrada Iturbide, for example, had to remind the party in a debate that PAN was not a clerical party and could not act as if it were.[44] Whenever the ardent clericalists, men interested primarily in fighting Church causes, try to take control of the party, other PAN leaders, both Catholic and secular, resist.[45] The clericalism of the Ituarte Servín-González Torres period resulted as much from the political ambitions of PAN's Youth Organization as it did from clerical fervor. Furthermore, it was a devout Catholic and Church supporter, Christlieb Ibarrola, who brought a halt to the clerically oriented politics of the Ituarte Servín-González Torres period. However, Church attempts to force PAN leaders to fight for clerical ends would fail, as did attempts by the Church to stop PAN's use of Article 3 as a political issue. PAN leaders assert that, while they recognize the Church's authority in the spiritual sphere, they do not in the temporal sphere.

The Catholic Church in Mexico is divided and lay Catholic leaders reflect this division. Ivan Vallier's typology is perhaps suggestive in this context.[46] Vallier defines four Catholic elites, including laymen as well as clergy. The traditional elite which allies the Church with the government and the upper classes is termed *politicians*. *Papists,* strong in Mexico, are militant, modern Catholics interested in re-Christianizing the world by building a Church that relies upon its own authority and its own resources. They are action-oriented and spread the ideas of the social encyclicals in functional interest groups. Catholic Action falls into this classification. They eschew traditional sources of political involvement. *Pastors* try to make the parish church relevant to the needs of the parishioners and to build strong, worship-centered congregations. *Pluralists* seek to develop, in conjunction with non-Catholics, programs and policies that will assist the institutionalization of social justice on all fronts. The Christian Democrats of Chile recruit significantly from the *pluralists*. *Papists,* according to Vallier, pave the way for the *pastors* and *pluralists* by making change respectable to Catholics. *Papists* and *pluralists* are rivals, with the *pluralists* calling the *papists* sacristans or "goon squads." Vallier suggests that the last three, the new elites, are emerging in most Latin American countries. The existence of strong ties between Church and State, a position favoring the *politicians,* encourages the development of *pluralists* as a reaction.

The dissection of PAN Catholic leaders along these lines is no more than suggestive, but perhaps helps to explain the tensions within the party and hindrances to PAN becoming a truly clerical party. Most *politicians* in Vallier's typology would not be in PAN but in PRI. Although Mexico is officially an anticlerical state, in practice relations between the two institutions have become quite warm, probably to the point that the two mutually support one another. This is the complaint of both leftists and PAN leaders. *Pastors* who engage in political activity are difficult to identify. PAN Catholic leadership appears to be divided primarily between *papists* and *pluralists*. Most of the UNEC group, the Youth Organization leaders in the Ituarte Servín-González Torres period, Christlieb Ibarrola, González Morfín, most young people currently in PAN, and important leaders such as Eugenio Ortiz Walls, Luis Calderón Vega, and Gerardo Medina Valdés are *pluralists*. They are willing to forget Article 3 in order to get on with the problem of achieving social justice in Mexico. The *papists* are not. Although committed to social justice because of the social encyclicals they are also committed to the rights and prerogatives of the Church. Within the Catholic leadership of PAN, therefore, a major source of factionalism is between these two groups. The question of the continuation of the Christlieb Ibarrola ideological stance is also the question of the continued leadership of the *pluralists*. González Hinojosa appears to be a *papist* who is willing to buy *pluralist* ideology but not sure to what extent he is willing to execute it. González Luna was a *papist* but he moved from that camp into the *pluralist* camp, making the new position respectable. PAN collaboration with the UNS was easy for the *papists,* but the *pluralist* leadership is very unhappy with the ties. The *pluralists* may have won the argument since dissatisfaction with UNS cooperation in the 1970 presidential campaign was widespread throughout PAN.

As this study repeatedly notes, too many PAN leaders over too long a time period have been actively engaged in Catholic lay activities to deny, as *panistas* do, that Catholicism has been the primary influence on party leadership. The very origins of the party, described in Chapter II, point out that the party was very much the product of the general Catholic reform movement of the twentieth century and specifically of the Mexican Church-State conflict of the 1920s and 1930s. The Catholic activists who formed PAN, however, and who have continued to enter the party have been politicized members of the reform wing of Mexican Catholicism. They are engaged in secular politics because their religious-social beliefs have given them a social conscience and made them desirous of reforming society along lines consistent with Catholic social doctrine. They cannot do this through Church organizations or PRI. They can do it through PAN as long as they do not allow the party to become identified with clerical ends. Their Catholicism, as far as it affects their political behavior, serves as a philosophical or theological framework and as a justification of their actions. It gives them a long-range, universal view which enables them to live with defeat and frustration in Mexican politics. Acción Nacional would not have been created and continued if it had not been for the Catholic reform impulse. The relationship between the party and the Church, as opposed to the leadership and Catholicism, will be discussed in Chapter IX.

These comments on the nature of the Catholic leadership of PAN are not meant to be definitive but suggestive. Further research is needed using the Vallier typology. It will be rather difficult to conduct since PAN leaders are extremely sensitive about connecting religion and politics.

Other important sources of factionalism among PAN leaders are religious-secular conflicts, regionalism, and the party's posture vis-à-vis the government. The conflict between the religiously oriented leadership and the secularly oriented leadership has already been mentioned. Some secular leaders resent and resist attempts by the religiously oriented to inject religious issues into politics or to use PAN to further the interests of the Catholic Church. This dichotomy is not definitive, however, for progressive seculars tend to ally with the *pluralists* and the less progressive or nonprogressive seculars ally with the *papists* on issues not involving religious questions.[47]

Regionalistic factionalism emanate from the extreme concentration of party leadership in the Federal District. Party presidents, most of the CEN, and most of the PAN federal deputies live in the Federal District. The importance of the Federal District is augmented by the strength of the Federal District regional organization. In order to reach the top leadership levels of PAN, one should move to the Federal District. When one adds Mexico, Michoacán, and Jalisco to the Federal District, one has the basic geographical grouping for control of PAN. Strong, important PAN leaders from Baja California, Chihuahua, Coahuila, and Yucatán resent this domination by the Federal District and these four entities. This resentment has flared in party meetings, but may have been reduced by the 1971 statutory changes.

The question of tactics vis-à-vis the government is another source of factionalism. The basic split has been over the dispute as to whether or not PAN should legitimize the Mexican political system by participating in elections. In addition, it is a question of which tactics will maximize PAN influence. This issue has been discussed in Chapter V. The evidence does not show a discernible pattern of tactical splits within the leadership except that national offices and residents of Mexico City usually favor participation.

PAN leadership recruitment and training has been suggested by the foregoing comments on the nature of the leadership. Most PAN leaders have been men with sources of income and occupations that allow them to engage in political activity. Recruitment has come from Catholic lay organizations, from the universities, and from personal contacts within occupational, religious, or family circles. Most PAN leaders have no special training, except that their occupations have already trained them for positions of leadership. Until 1962, PAN leaders were informally trained, along with the membership, by study conferences and party literature. Beginning in 1962, future leaders were trained in the Institute of Social and Political Studies. In 1971, Acción Nacional created a Center of Directors' Training to overcome two problems: most of its leaders have not been full-time professional politicians but part-time neophytes (even though some of these amateurs have been extremely effective) and membership recruitment increasingly has brought in workers and peasants.

PAN members who seek leadership positions are not so much recruited, therefore, as allowed to move into positions of leadership by working for the party. Young men from universities, for example, can join PAN, work in campaigns, and distribute literature and thus acquire leadership posts within a few years. The open debates at conventions allow people ample opportunity for the ambitious to gain public recognition of their talents. Older men who already have some public standing, as politicians, as prominent businessmen, or as government employees can move quickly into PAN leadership positions. PAN treasurer Enrique Creel Luján, joined PAN in 1958 and became treasurer in 1959. He was from a famous, important family in Mexico which had been extremely rich before the Revolution and his social prominence facilitated his entry into the leadership.[48] Gilberto Arvizu Suárez had been an important government official and PRI member prior to his defection during the events surrounding the 1967 Sonora gubernatorial race. The 1970–73 PAN Federal Deputies (Table 8) illustrate this easy entry into PAN leadership positions. Of the twenty, four joined PAN in the 1960s and six joined in the 1950s.

Leadership mobility is also illustrated by the CEN. Using the four CENs represented in Table 6, one finds remarkable personnel changes. Only one member, Rafael Preciado Hernández, served on all four committees. Three persons have served on three CENs. Twenty were on two. This lack of continuity is further indicated by figures on the pattern of repeaters. Of the thirty-four members of the 1969 CEN, twelve (35.5%) had been on the 1959 CEN, two (5.9%) on the 1949, and two (5.9%) on the 1939 committee. The 1959 CEN had five repeaters (20%) from the 1949 CEN out of its twenty-five members and only two (8%) from the 1939 CEN. The 1949 CEN had nine of its twenty-seven members (33.3%) repeating from the 1939 CEN. The tendency is for the repeaters to have served on the CEN ten years prior. Even so, the majority of comitteemen are relatively new to leadership positions. The 1969 CEN has the greatest spread of previous CEN members, indicating the desire of González Hinojosa to satisfy all elements within the party.

Acción Nacional leadership is composed of part-time politicians recruited from occupations which allow them to engage in political activity on a part-time basis. Although a knowledge of their religious beliefs is important in understanding them, it should be noted that they are not fighting for ecclesiastical privilege. Diversity in their religious commitment as well as their regionalistic sentiment are the two most important distinguishing characteristics. Leadership fluctuates partly because access to leadership positions is relatively easy.

CHAPTER IX

The Support System

The key to understanding PAN's support system is recognizing who might benefit from aiding a small, powerless opposition party which can influence decisions and the outcome of events but cannot control them, especially when such support also risks alienating a coalition which has ruled Mexico for over forty years and rewards its supporters. Benefits derived from supporting PAN are primarily psychological since the party has never controlled the decision-making machinery. In a few instances PAN has been able to bestow material benefits on its supporters but their frequency is so rare that they do not merit mention. On the other hand, the government can dispense favors to its friends and penalties to its enemies, for it makes the rules, levies the taxes, exercises the police power, and regulates income. Therefore, any group or individual wanting or needing governmental favors has to support the government and its political party, PRI.[1]

Observers who assert that PAN is the party of big business or the Church ignore Mexican reality. Almost all segments of Mexican business are dependent upon the government in some way, either for tariff protection, import quotas, taxation policy, labor laws, control of organized labor, subsidies, construction of the economic infrastructure, or for some other public action affecting business interests.[2] Self-interest, therefore, dictates that business should ingratiate itself with the government. Private enterprise–governmental cooperation also benefits politicians because wealthy capitalists can also bestow favors. Such a symbiotic relationship serves both groups. The Mexican Catholic Church is even more dependent upon the government since it unsuccessfully contested with the latter for control of Mexico. Anticlericalism is still a potent force and can be aroused from its dormant state when necessary. If the Church wishes the continued operation of illegal parochial schools, it must not antagonize the government. The Church can also aid the government. Even though the government legitimizes itself with the Revolutionary mystique, additional sanctification from ecclesiastical sources facilitates

162

peaceful rule. In both cases, then, supporting the government is advantageous while overt opposition is disadvantageous.

Other organized interest groups face a similar situation. The vast majority of labor unions, farmer organizations, teachers' unions, and bureaucrats' associations are automatically members of one of PRI's sector organizations. PRI's heterogeneous Popular Sector even includes lottery ticket sellers, cab drivers, small businessmen, and professionals. The PRI-staffed government controls such important items as wages, jobs, irrigation, and licenses. On another plane, citizen groups must convince PRI-controlled governments when they try to influence decisions.

Since most Mexicans are either members of one of these interest groups or unorganized and, consequently, no threat, the government coalition, including PRI, has potential control of almost every source of political party support. When necessary, it exercises this control but has not become a totalitarian state. Under such circumstances, PAN has been hard pressed to find adequate support for its activities.

Nevertheless, PAN has managed to build a support system (including Church and private enterprise support) but not from the sources usually identified by political commentators. Data on support of political parties are always difficult to obtain as parties are usually silent on such matters. During the more than two-year period that the present author has been cultivating PAN leaders, after having been introduced to them by mutual friends, he has obtained special access to PAN records and had numerous frank, confidential interviews with important party leaders. The data will be presented in the following categories: institutional support, financial support, and electoral support.

INSTITUTIONAL SUPPORT

Private Enterprise

At its inception PAN was quickly tagged as procapitalist because it opposed the "socialism" of the Cárdenas government and because many of its prominent founders were leading bankers or industrialists.[3] Both PAN and private enterprise saw the socioeconomic reforms of Cárdenas, especially the giving of management of the railway industry to workers, as a threat to economic progress. Both asserted that Communists and other Marxian socialists were influencing Mexico towards socialism.[4] They have also shared other common opinions: municipal autonomy; dislike of strong, centralized government; the necessity of governmental consultation of private enterprise in economic decision-making; opposition to Article 3; and opposition to statism. Both groups have made similar public statements on governmental economic policy.[5] Prior comments in this book have shown that many key *panistas* were also prominent Mexican capitalists. PAN aided this identification of itself as primarily a bulwark of capitalism by supporting Almazán in 1940. Leftists and other anticapitalists recognized that labeling PAN reactionary, conservative, and anti-Revolutionary would discredit it. As PAN moved to the Christian Democratic position, however, use of these labels declined.[6]

Such characterizations of PAN do not identify the party's private enterprise support. Most of this support has been indirect. Because PAN and private enterprise have adopted similar positions on some key issues, PAN has probably gained support from persons favorable to private enterprise. Since private enterprise's communication net is the more extensive of the two, the effect has been to disseminate ideas which PAN favors over a larger area than the party could possibly hope to cover. Moreover, the recipients of propaganda emanating from CONCANACO, CONCAMIN, COPARMEX, or CNIT, to mention the largest confederations of private enterprise, become more sympathetic to PAN and may contribute money as a consequence. None of these confederations or other large-scale enterprises contribute money to PAN. Similarly, the *Sembradores de Amistad* (a Monterrey-based businessmen's club which defected from Rotary International) and the Social Union of Mexican Businessmen (a paternalistically inclined Catholic businessmen's club; USEM) aid PAN when they assert that socially responsible capitalism is needed but they do not aid the party economically.

PAN's financial support from private enterprise has come from individuals. Most of this support has come from PAN leaders and their friends and has been meager.[7] Gómez Morín, for example, has been able to wheedle a few thousand dollars monthly from rich friends, but those friends give more to PRI. Monterrey industrialists contribute small amounts to PAN partly to aid compatriots who are PAN politicians, partly to encourage the spread of probusiness ideas, and partly to annoy the central government in Mexico City, so powerful and so distant. The bulk of private enterprise financial support comes from individuals engaged in small- and medium-sized businesses. They are attracted to PAN because the confederations are dominated by large-scale enterprises.

Support from important capitalists has dwindled since its early 1940s peak as PAN has supported positions distasteful to private enterprise. Laissez-faire capitalism has come under severe PAN attack as a retrogressive economic system which produces misery for the masses. Since 1939, PAN has argued for extensive social security coverage, strong unions, and national planning. PAN began advocating profit-sharing in 1950 before organized labor or PRI picked up the issue. Christlieb made

Acción Nacional's position on labor clear in speeches to businessmen's clubs—labor should not only participate in profits but should also participate in property ownership and management of enterprises. During the 1969 debate on the new Federal Labor Law, sponsored by PRI and opposed by private enterprise, PAN deputies condemned the measure for not being favorable enough to labor and attacked private enterprise for resisting even this inadequate measure.[8] There is a direct positive correlation between private enterprise support of PAN and the party's probusiness stances. Since 1945, the party has been able to survive without support from major capitalists.

Catholic Church Support

Numerous factors have supported the equally common assertion that PAN is a Catholic or clerical party. At times the suggestion is made that the party is a secular instrument of the hierarchy.[9] Previously mentioned factors include: recruitment of party leadership from Catholic lay associations; PAN's admittedly Catholic doctrine; common opposition to Article 3; PAN-UNS cooperation; PAN ties to the international Christian Democratic movement; the correlation between changes in PAN ideology and the issuance of social encyclicals;[10] and scattered instances of priestly aid in PAN electoral campaigns. Additional factors include: various *panistas* calling for the creation of a Christian social order in Mexico; the majority of PAN leadership having been educated in parochial schools; numerous United States–educated *panistas* having studied at Notre Dame, Fordham, Catholic, and Georgetown Universities; organized labor support having come almost exclusively from Catholic labor unions; *La Nación* printing Catholic news and the Catholic Action journalism school being named after its founder; the widespread anti-Mason sentiment within PAN; and the messianic zeal of *panistas* suggesting that they see themselves as modern-day crusaders.

Catholic *panistas* admit that these factors superficially suggest an intimate relationship between PAN and Catholicism, but they argue that the relationship is limited to just that: Catholics in a Catholic country drawing upon their cultural heritage as the primary source of their ideas. They claim that PRI has a larger Catholic membership and that the Church supports the government. In addition, they point out that many *panistas* are agnostics, atheists, Protestants, or Mormons. Further, they assert that they neither receive nor want ecclesiastical aid because such aid is improper. An internal PAN anecdote illustrates this position. When the Church hierarchy demanded of PAN that it drop its anti–Article 3 campaigns because the Church had reached a *modus vivendi* with the government, the continuance of which was threatened by PAN's action, party leaders reminded the hierarchy that it was not competent to speak on political matters and that they would not drop the campaigns unless the Church made it a matter of dogma.[11]

The anecdote probably best suggests the relationship between PAN and Catholicism. Most of PAN's founders and its subsequent leadership have been politicized Catholics, often working simultaneously as Catholic lay leaders. On matters of dogma they followed Church teachings but make political decisions without ecclesiastical direction. Since the Mexican Catholic Church is not monolithic they have been able to choose which trends in Catholic thought they wish to follow. Most Mexican Catholics support the government since the Church does. Right-wing Catholics joined or supported the UNS. Moderate and progressive militant Catholics have joined PAN. PAN represents, then, neither the Church nor a majority of Mexico's Catholics.

Indirectly, however, the Church aids PAN. Through Catholic Action and other lay associations, future PAN leaders have received leadership training, learned ideas, and established personal contacts. As is the case with private enterprise, the Church's extensive communication network aids PAN whenever the Church takes public stands similar to the party's, that is to say, on social doctrine.

Labor

Apart from the nascent Catholic labor movement, PAN has been unable to obtain support from organized labor. The support of the Santa Barbara (Chihuahua) Local #11 in 1956 was unusual and a result of temporary dissatisfaction with its usual PRI ties.[12] Most unions affiliate all their members with PRI and potential PAN supporters are discouraged. In Michoacán, where the labor movement is extremely weak, a few union members openly support PAN but most support PRI in the belief that only PRI can help them.[13] Unorganized workers have joined the party but in insignificant numbers. Beginning in 1970, however, PAN has been successfully recruiting workers in large numbers in urban areas such as the Federal District.

Organized Middle Classes

Few organized middle class groups engaged in politics affiliate with PAN; most are members of CNOP, the key organization of PRI's Popular Sector. In 1953, the Employees Club of Monterrey was created to support PAN.[14] Various members of the National Parents' Union and the Federation of Private Schools probably support PAN for its proparochial school stands. PAN receives, then, negligible institutional support and most of what it does receive is indirect and essentially verbal in nature. Even if PRI did not monopolize institutional support, PAN probably would reject institutional affiliations as inconsistent with its ideology.

FINANCES

National Budget

The party has managed to operate without extensive institutional support because its budgetary requirements are so small. As of November 30, 1939, the party had a balance of 2,174.29 pesos. Between then and April 24, 1940, it had collected 61,307.83 pesos more, spent 55,689.26, and had a balance of 7,792.80.[15] These figures represent a campaign year and part of the party's first year of formal existence. In 1953, the peso was devalued from twelve and one-half United States cents to eight cents. By December 1969 and January 1970, the operating budget had grown. In the first month, the party collected 57,777.30 pesos and spent 63,735.25; in January, 98,539.70 pesos entered the party while 71,027.49 left. These are representative figures for the nonelection year operating budget. On the average, then, PAN spends slightly more than 78,000 pesos monthly.[16] Campaign expenses are separate. Of the 2.6 million pesos spent in the 1964 federal campaign, 1,155,627.81 pesos were spent nationally.[17] For the 1970 federal campaign the party spent 2,099,353.28 pesos. Of the total, 86,146.70 pesos went for staff salaries; 152,828.00 for motor vehicles; 46,048.00 for furniture and equipment; 616,745.25 for trip expenses; 1,104,737.67 for propaganda; and 92,847.66 for vehicle maintenance, paper, postage, and telegrams.[18] Convention expenses are also modest.[19] For the November 1969 national nominating convention, the party spent 372,500 pesos. For the August 1971 ordinary and extraordinary general assembly, 225,510 pesos were budgeted, 122,010 for convention expenses proper and 103,500 for publications and other propaganda resulting from the convention.[20]

Income originates in many ways but contributions are the most important source. PAN leaders expend considerable amounts of time discussing who might aid the party financially and soliciting contributions. Gómez Morín guarantees 12,000 pesos monthly, part of which he contributes personally and part of which comes from his friends.[21] PAN federal deputies are required to contribute 1,000 pesos monthly if they live in the Federal District and 500 pesos if they live outside. When a deputy is also contributing time to the party, as in the case of the party president, he only contributes 500 pesos. For the 1970–73 federal deputy term, PAN will receive approximately 16,000 pesos monthly from this source. The balance comes from raffles, dues, sale of food at conventions, and bond sales.[22]

These budgetary figures suggest that PAN barely survives. Eight thousand pesos monthly are spent for rent on party headquarters. Salaries for the sixteen employees of national headquarters are unknown, but supporting five secretaries, three general employees, a general administrator, a doctrinal and organizational specialist (who earns approximately 5,000 pesos yearly), and six La Nación employees cuts into the budget deeply. Although PAN sells La Nación and other publications, part of the printing bill must be paid from general funds. In short, the national party is greatly hindered by the lack of adequate financial support.[23]

Regional Budgets

The national party also helps to support the Federal District regional organization which it dominates by giving it office space in national headquarters and paying its utility bills. The salary for the one full-time employee in these headquarters and the costs of maintaining part-time offices in each electoral district are borne by the regional organization itself.[24]

Available data on the budget of the Michoacán regional committee is representative for those states which have a permanent PAN apparatus. Table 10 shows the operating income for the Michoacán committee from July 13, 1967, through December 31, 1970. The arithmetical mean is 2,336.70 pesos, the range is 1,268.13 pesos to 4,314.00. The table includes the state election year of 1968 and the federal election year of 1970. The monies are expended for the office (800 pesos monthly), one secretary's salary, utilities, supplies, stamps, telegrams, and occasional payments to individuals for trips.[25] The bulk of the income comes from dues. Table 11 shows the distribution of dues income for January 1968. It is significant that the most common amount of dues is 10 pesos monthly, indicating that people of modest means are the backbone of PAN. The committee also raises money through a dispensary, in which it sells used clothing at a small profit; bond sales, bake sales, and raffles.[26] Much of the committee's weekly meeting is devoted to identifying potential contributors and deciding who should approach them.[27] Regional committees, then, if Michoacán is representative, face financial

TABLE 10

PAN Michoacán Regional Committee Operating Budget (in Pesos)
(July 13, 1967–December 31, 1970)

1967		1969	
13 July–10 August	2,357.70	January	2,450.70
10 August–14 September	3,354.35	February	2,104.65
14 September–14 October	3,578.35	March	1,626.05
14 October–14 November	3,247.35	April	1,487.00
14 November–18 December	2,334.35	May	1,584.00
18 December–17 January	4,314.00	June	1,499.30
		July	1,525.80
TOTAL	19,186.10	August	1,423.50
1968		September	1,437.25
		October	1,598.45
17 January–18 February	3,384.95	November	1,597.50
19 February–13 March	3,281.30	December	2,199.10
March (total)	3,939.00		
April	2,004.25	TOTAL	20,533.30
May	3,719.40	1970	
June	2,282.40	January	1,799.25
July	2,636.30	February	1,710.25
August	3,519.55	March	2,551.30
September	1,527.25	April	2,019.35
October	1,935.30	May	2,819.75
November	1,593.80	June	1,930.90
December	1,268.15	July	2,345.05
		August	3,354.00
TOTAL	31,091.65[a]	September	2,513.65
		October	1,703.10
		November	2,102.30
		December	1,313.30
		TOTAL	26,162.20[b]

Total (1967–70): 96,973.25
Average: 2,336.70
Range: 1,268.13–4,314.00

SOURCE: Treasury Account books of Michoacán Regional Committee.

[a] State election year

[b] National election year

difficulties equal to that of the national organization. Even though the latter supplies 90 percent of the printed propaganda, these committees are hard pressed to compete against the well-financed PRI machinery.

All PAN candidates must supply most of their campaign financing. This has three consequences: (1) it limits the number of people who can seek a PAN candidacy; (2) it temporarily, at least, impoverishes

TABLE 11

PAN Michoacán Regional Committee Monthly Dues (in Pesos)
(January 1968)

Amount	No. Contributing	Yield
200–300	2	550.00
100–199	1	100.00
50–99	4	200.00
25–49	15	390.00
10–24	48	590.83
1–9	39	175.65
TOTAL	109	2,006.48

Range: 1.00–300.00   Mean: 18.58   Mode: 10.00
SOURCE: PAN Michoacán regional committee treasury files.

the average candidate; and (3) it favors the selection of wealthy candidates. Most *panistas* can afford to run for office only once or once every several years thereby limiting their ability to build voter identification. It also forces PAN to use rich men as candidates even though their candidacies reinforce PAN's image as a rich man's party.[28]

The budgetary data, however, indicates that PAN is not a rich man's party, that it does not receive substantial or significant support from private enterprise, and that it desperately needs more money if it hopes to challenge PRI successfully.

ELECTORAL SUPPORT

Mexican voting statistics must be used with extreme caution, for their validity is dubious. Several factors prompt this statement. Mexicans themselves are cynical about the validity of the election statistics because Mexico has a long history of fraudulent elections and vote manipulation. The government not only does not admit defeat in a major election (presidential, senatorial, and gubernatorial) but also usually claims at least 90 percent of the vote for the official party; even the popular Revolutionary party probably has more opposition than this. Moreover, PRI members issue voter credentials, control the voting process, count the ballots, and, in Congress, qualify the results. Voter participation has been extremely high in large, rural states with difficult terrain such as Chiapas, while being much smaller in urban areas which have better communications and higher literacy rates. Foreign scholars have long suggested or asserted that the government manipulates the results to suit its needs. Recently, former Mexican president Emilio Portes Gil stated that this was the case.[29]

In light of the government's obvious strong popular support, such charges seem incredible. The government has successfully identified itself with a Revolution which has been modernizing and industrializing Mexico while delivering increased social benefits. Its party, PRI, is a large, disciplined, umbrella organization with extensive contacts with the population through its sector organization, its network of offices and officeholders, and its social welfare measures. PRI is identified with Mexicanism, reinforced by its legal monopolization of the use of the national colors. PRI has more money and talent than rival groups and only its politicians can possibly deliver on promises. It is difficult, therefore, to see any necessity for vote manipulation or other forms of electoral fraud since PRI is almost impossible to beat.

Skeptics agree that PRI wins the vast majority of elections but assert that PRI manipulates the vote to enhance its image of omnipotence with extremely high percentages in its favor, to guarantee public posts to party regulars and friends, to overturn elections which seem to threaten future PRI control, and to select which opposition members can hold public office. According to the first charge, the victorious PRI is not content with normal majorities so it adds in enough votes to create 80 to 99 percent majorities. The second charge claims that PRI candidates who actually lose are given seats by manipulating the vote counting in their favor, one reason PRI completely staffs the Senate. The third charge is more complicated. It argues that the opposition occasionally wins a governorship, control of a state, senatorial seats, or larger numbers of federal deputy seats. These successes, if they were allowed to be consummated, would encourage the growth of opposition because those groups would have patronage and success with which to build an electoral machine. PRI, therefore, overturns the election by whatever means necessary, demonstrating its invincibility and discouraging dissenters. The disputed elections in Sonora (1967), Baja California (1968), and Yucatán (1969) are cited as recent examples of this tactic. Finally, victories of most effective and/or popular opposition leaders are overturned in the counting process so as to place ineffective opposition members in office.

My tentative judgment is that PRI has probably committed each of these acts in various instances but that there should be no question that PRI is the majority political party nor that it probably wins 90 percent of the elections. Close to a majority of the races have not been contested until recent years. Even PAN admits that PRI wins almost every election.[30] I base my judgment not only upon my study of Mexican politics but also on frank, confidential conversations with high government officials. They agree with the vote manipulation charges and explain the policy as a necessity because: (1) the Mexican people still need "guided democracy," (2) Mexico needs political stability which only PRI can provide, and (3) PAN would be incapable of actually administering public affairs if it were allowed to take office.[31] If this is true, an interesting question for future research is: When does PRI feel sufficiently threatened to take the extreme action of overturning elections?

In this context, PAN's broader assertions that Mexican elections are fraudulent merit serious attention. PAN claims that, although it is not the majority party, it does win more federal deputy seats, some senate seats, some governorships, more state legislative seats, and more *municipios* than the government and PRI are willing to concede. It believes that some of these "victories" are stolen by the government and PRI. The party does not claim that it wins presidential races but that its candidate fares better than the official figures show. According to PAN sources, the official figures for PAN's share of the vote normally agree with PAN tabulations, but the government adds in votes for PRI. That is to say, that PAN's Efraín González Morfín actually received the almost two million votes credited to him in the 1970 election but that PRI's Echeverría did not receive the 11,948,412 votes shown in official figures. PAN believes the government added fictitious votes to the Echeverría total. It asserts that an authentic vote total would show 55–65% for Echeverría and 35–45% for González Morfín. It also believes that it won several senate seats in the 1970 election, one being in the Federal District where it is strongest. In private conversations, the most federal deputy seats that I ever heard party leaders claim that Acción Nacional actually won in a single election was fifty. PAN only disputes a few federal deputy seats in the Electoral College. At the state level, PAN claims that it has won such governorships of Baja California (1953), Sonora (1967), and Yucatán (1969) and some municipal elections such as Baja California (1968), Mexico (1969), and Nuevo León (1969).[32]

A close analysis of PAN assertions about electoral fraud reveals that the party actually makes two distinct arguments. One is general and is applied to all elections. The specific argument is applied in those elections where the party actually believes that its candidates won.

The general argument is that the Mexican political system is fraudulent, that fair elections are impossible under existing arrangements. Opposition parties are forced to compete against a party which has government backing, almost unlimited public and private resources, involuntary mass membership, exclusive use of the national colors for its propaganda and for ballots (important in a country with a high illiteracy rate), control of police powers and complete control of the electoral process. In addition, PRI, with the aid of the government, identifies itself as the only true "Mexican," Revolutionary, and progressive party. The government aids PRI also by its control of the media, for the government has a newsprint monopoly, subsidizes newspapers, subsidizes journalists, and controls radio and television licensing. When opposition groups are successful in spite of the system, the system allows the government to use coercion to enforce its will.[33]

On those occasions when the opposition threatens government control of Mexico by winning key posts, the government, through PRI and public power, manipulates the election. Included in that manipulation are the following techniques: illegal issuance of voting certificates; multiple voting; invalidation of authentic votes; robbery of ballot boxes; expulsion or neutralization of opposition pollwatchers; use of coercion to force votes for PRI; and juggling of vote returns.[34]

If these charges are true, scholars can at least still view the electoral statistics as indicating the amount of opposition the government is willing to admit. Other possible interpretations need further study. The recent suggestion of Professor Wilkie that it might be possible to determine true opposition strength through a times-series showing patterns of opposition is one possibility.[35] This approach has at least one serious problem. Even if one assumes that the electoral returns are perverted, it is still not possible to know how they are perverted without detailed studies of the conditions in the entities at the time of the election. In some cases PRI might claim only 70 percent victory because it is confident of its strength but at other times a 70 percent figure might mean that the opposition actually won. Manipulation of electoral statistics is probably not systematic but based upon local needs.

In the present work, the use of electoral statistics is based on the assumption that they at least represent what the government is willing to concede. If they are in error, they probably show too little support for PAN. Nonelectoral data is also used to derive conclusions as to their meaning.

National Voting

Two conclusions are obvious from time-series data showing PAN's share of national vote totals. Table 12 shows that PAN's share has increased slowly but steadily. One of two possibilities are suggested by this

TABLE 12

Federal Entities of Greatest PAN Opposition, 1952, 1958–1970*
(10% or More of the Vote)

Region* Entity	Presidential Elections				Federal Deputy Elections			
	1952	1958	1964	1970	1961	1964	1967	1970[a]
DISTRITO FEDERAL	12.1	20.1	25.1	30.4	20.9	29.4	27.1	29.8
NORTH								
Baja California (S)	8.9	39.3	21.4	25.6	26.3	25.4	22.1	25.7
Chihuahua	11.9	35.4	21.3	19.0	17.7	22.3	23.0	10.0
Coahuila	xxxx[b]	xxxx	xxxx	xxxx	xxxx	xxxx	xxxx	xxxx
Nuevo León	9.5	9.7	15.7	15.9	5.1	16.1	16.7	16.1
Sonora	2.3	2.7	1.0	6.5	1.0	1.7	20.8	6.9
Tamaulipas	xxxx	xxxx	xxxx	xxxx	xxxx	xxxx	xxxx	xxxx
WEST								
Aguascalientes	7.3	6.8	8.8	12.6	9.6	8.5	15.0	12.2
Colima	7.4	10.4	12.7	9.2	11.9	13.1	9.4	9.2
Durango	11.9	15.1	10.0	13.3	—[c]	9.8	11.4	12.1
Jalisco	22.9	11.0	13.0	17.2	8.1	13.4	14.5	17.2
Nayarit	xxxx	xxxx	xxxx	xxxx	xxxx	xxxx	xxxx	xxxx
Sinaloa	xxxx	xxxx	xxxx	xxxx	xxxx	xxxx	xxxx	xxxx
Baja California (T)	xxxx	xxxx	xxxx	xxxx	xxxx	xxxx	xxxx	xxxx
WEST CENTRAL								
Guanajuato	20.4	10.5	20.4	19.2	3.0	21.2	14.5	19.1
Mexico	2.4	1.1	8.3	15.3	—	7.6	11.4	15.5

Michoacán	13.3	16.4	14.2	11.3	13.1	14.0	12.8	22.4
Morelos	7.8	17.3	5.7	8.2	9.7	5.8	4.2	3.8
EAST CENTRAL								
Hidalgo	xxxx	xxxx	xxxx	xxxx	xxxx	xxxx	xxxx	xxxx
Puebla	14.1	9.0	n.a.	n.a.	14.5	6.3	4.8	n.a.
Querétaro	8.7	6.3	8.5	5.0	9.3	8.7	10.4	10.4
San Luis Potosí	11.0	6.0	n.a.	n.a.	10.0	8.4	5.7	n.a.
Tlaxcala	xxxx	xxxx	xxxx	xxxx	xxxx	xxxx	xxxx	xxxx
Zacatecas	8.7	8.3	13.9	4.0	9.0	20.5	8.3	9.6
GULF								
Campeche	3.9	0.6	3.5	8.7	1.9	4.0	12.2	6.0
Quintana Roo (T)	—	—	—	—	1.8	3.4	20.1	—
Tabasco	xxxx	xxxx	xxxx	xxxx	xxxx	xxxx	xxxx	xxxx
Veracruz	xxxx	xxxx	xxxx	xxxx	xxxx	xxxx	xxxx	xxxx
Yucatán	15.7	10.6	14.0	—	15.0	14.2	22.6	12.2
SOUTH								
Chiapas	xxxx	xxxx	xxxx	xxxx	xxxx	xxxx	xxxx	xxxx
Guerrero	xxxx	xxxx	xxxx	xxxx	xxxx	xxxx	xxxx	xxxx
Oaxaca	xxxx	xxxx	xxxx	xxxx	xxxx	xxxx	xxxx	xxxx
NATIONAL	14.1	12.4	11.5	7.6	14.0	11.0	9.3	7.8

[a] Approximate percentage derived by dividing actual PAN vote by gross entity vote in presidential election.

[b] xxxx = never obtained 10.0% of vote in any election.

[c] No candidate(s) or less than 0.5% of vote.

* Regions from Wilkie, *The Mexican Revolution.*

increase: if the electoral statistics are valid, the party is slowly growing in strength; if the statistics are fraudulent, the government is encouraging and supporting PAN, but at a level which will not threaten PRI ascendency until the distant future. Part of the explanation of this phenomena may be found in Table 13, showing the opposition's share of the total vote in presidential elections since 1917. Of the thirteen elections, PAN ran candidates in four. Only the opposition in the 1924, 1946, and 1952 elections have fared better than PAN's four candidates, according to these official statistics. The opposition vote in 1946 was split three ways, but the principal opposition candidate, Ezequiel Padilla, a PRI dissident, polled 18.1%. In 1952, Miguel Henríquez Guzmán, the principal opposition candidate and erstwhile PRI member, polled 15.8%, while PAN's Efraín González Luna polled 7.8% and PPS's Vicente Lombardo Toledano polled 2.0%.[36] Over the long run, then, PAN has fared better than any other electoral opposition. Of course, it is possible that the government has manipulated the results to encourage PAN as the preferred opposition, but this would be atypical behavior.

Regional Voting

Table 12 also shows those federal entities (federal district, state, or territory) arranged by region, in which PAN ever obtained 10 or more percent of the vote—the 1952 and 1958 presidential elections and both presidential and federal deputy elections since 1961. Ten percent was chosen as the cutoff point because the government usually claims it won better than 90 percent of the vote. PAN has never obtained the cutoff point in twelve of the thirty-two entities and has consistently obtained it in only three. Over the long range, however, PAN has increased the number of states in which it can give opposition at this level from eight to thirteen. Several other items merit comment. Baja California demographic and economic growth rates spurted after it became a state in 1953. The 1952 Jalisco percentage reflects the fact that González Luna was a Jaliscan native and prominent resident. The 1958 Quintana Roo figure is unexplainable at present unless, as a thinly populated area, slight shifts in the vote would drastically affect the percentages. PAN ran one of its least effective federal deputy campaigns in 1961, a fact reflected in these voting statistics.

PAN's ability to give opposition is directly related to regionalistic sentiment. That its most important and consistent support comes from the Federal District does not belie this generalization. As one travels away

TABLE 13

PAN Opposition and Mexican Presidential Elections since 1917
(in Percentages of Total Vote)

	1917	1920	1924	1928	1929	1934	1940	1946	1952	1958	1965	1970
Official Candidate Total	97.1	95.8	84.1	100.0	93.6	98.2	93.9	77.9	74.3	90.4	89.0	86.0
Opposition	2.9	4.2	15.9	00.0	6.4	1.8	6.1	22.1	25.7	9.6	11.0	14.0
PAN	—	—	—	—	—	—	—	—	7.8	9.6	11.0	14.0

SOURCE: James W. Wilkie, "Statistical Research in Recent Mexican History," *Latin American Research Review*, VI:2 (Summer 1971), 5; Howard Cline, *Mexico and the United States* (New York: Atheneum, 1965), 328.

from Mexico City, electoral support for PAN increases.[37] States on Mexico's periphery, such as Baja California, Yucatán, Chihuahua, Nuevo León, and Jalisco, consistently give large shares of their votes to PAN. Durango, although not peripheral, is also distant from the capital and usually gives more than 10 percent of the vote to PAN. Guanajuato and Michoacán, though closer to Mexico City, are states with strong regionalistic sentiments.[38] Regionalism, then, is one of the greatest sources of PAN electoral support.

Economic Factors

Support for PAN also fluctuates in direct proportion to the degree of industrialization, modernization, and wealth of the regions. The poorest region is the South followed by, in ascending order, East Central, West Central, Gulf, North, and the Federal District (Table 14). The tendency

TABLE 14

Regional Poverty in Mexico and Percentage of PAN Opposition
of 10 or More Percent Within Region

Region	Poverty Index		Presidential Elections			
	1950	1960	1952	1958	1964	1970
Distrito Fed.	8.8	8.8	100.0	100.0	100.0	100.0
North	26.2	21.3	16.7	33.3	50.0	50.0
West	37.7	32.0	28.6	43.9	43.9	43.9
Gulf	39.8	35.0	20.0	60.0	20.0	20.0
West Central	43.7	36.9	50.0	50.0	50.0	75.0
East Central	49.7	45.0	16.7	16.7	16.7	33.3
South	46.3	51.1	00.0	00.0	00.0	00.0
Nation	39.4	33.1	25.0	34.4	34.4	40.6

is that the wealthier the region is, the greater support it gives to PAN. This conclusion is supported by another study which sought to correlate the above-mentioned factors with voter participation. The author discovered not only a high positive correlation between low voter turnouts and the wealth and modernization in the federal entities, but also between these factors and electoral support of PAN. The party fared best in the ten richest states and worst in the ten poorest states.[39]

Urban Support

Within the states and regions, PAN's greatest electoral support is found in urban areas. PAN leaders argue that the party also has rural support and wants more, but assert that PRI controls the countryside by threats of economic reprisals against opposition supporters. Nevertheless, PAN is essentially an urban party. PAN claims that the size, wealth, anonymity, and pluralistic nature of the cities make them harder for the government to control. The pattern of urban versus rural support of PAN demonstrates the party's appeal in urban areas. The greatest area of PAN support is Mexico City. Since the city spills over into the neighboring states of Mexico and Puebla, the magnitude of this support is masked when one looks only at Federal District statistics. One reason for the increased PAN vote in Mexico state since 1967 and in Puebla in 1970 (Table 12) is that part of these votes came from the Mexico City megalopolis. In the 1970 federal deputy elections, PAN ran best in Mexico City and in districts bordering it.[40] Puebla City, the state capital, is also a large and industrializing city which gave a significant proportion of its vote to PAN. Most of the other states with large urban clusters— Baja California, Chihuahua, Nuevo León, Jalisco, Guanajuato, Michoacán, Morelos, and Yucatán—also gave higher vote percentages to PAN.

Class Support

Class-based support is more difficult to ascertain but it appears that the bulk of such support comes from the middle classes. Not only Mexican observers but also González Morfín assert that PAN's support is from the lower-middle and middle classes, which is directly related to PAN's urban support. This tendency is reinforced by the middle-class language of PAN appeals and the middle classes' greater freedom from political control. The party also has a broad spectrum of class support, however. In the 1967 and 1970 federal deputy elections in Mexico City, PAN's share of the vote remained relatively constant across the socially heterogeneous districts, indicating that, in Mexico City, at least, class does not determine PAN support (Table 15).[41] Party leaders claim that PAN began recruiting workers and young adults in large numbers in 1969–70 as a result of increased repression in Mexico and the personal attractiveness of González Morfín. Since PAN substantially improved its position in the first and second federal deputy districts of the capital, which have higher percentages of workers, this might verify this recruitment claim.

TABLE 15

Congressional Voting in Mexico, D.F., 1967, 1970
(in 1,000)

Electoral District	1967		1970	
	PRI	PAN	PRI	PAN
1	48	17	57	23
2	46	20	51	33
3	42	14	42	21
4	40	13	42	20
5	37	11	41	17
6	46	15	50	26
7	44	18	56	25
8	38	19	45	28
9	*	37	47	27
10	54	21	63	33
11	32	21	39	26
12	45	17	55	30
13	47	24	65	34
14	56	21	68	34
15	46	15	61	27
16	40	20	48	31
17	37	19	47	29
18	45	17	57	28
19	49	23	64	35
20	71	23	94	45
21	66	24	92	43
22	54	23	68	40
23	39	22	53	32
24	37	15	58	29

Female Support

Women are also attracted to PAN. Since its founding, the party has been more progressive toward women's rights than other political parties. It allowed them to speak in party councils and vote from the very beginning of the party; it supported female suffrage for federal elections before PRI; it had the first woman federal deputy; it has had female mayors and party officers; and it uses female candidates.[42] One possible explanation is that women are attracted by PAN's obvious religious connections. Another is that the party had had to augment its small numbers by actively recruiting women and allowing them to participate in decision-making. Still another explanation may be that women have less fear of losing their jobs by participating in opposition politics, and, if they are housewives, have more time to devote to political activities.

Protest Votes

PAN derives most of its electoral support from protest voting. Votes for PAN because of regionalism and independent attitudes fall into this category as do middle-class votes. One reason for middle-class votes for PAN is the belief that the government favors the rich and the poor.[43] Election figures (Table 12) support the contention that PAN receives protest votes. The extremely high Baja California PAN vote in 1958 reflected discontent which spilled over into the disputed 1959 gubernatorial election. The fantastic increase in the PAN vote in Sonora in 1967 was consistent with PAN's strong electoral campaign in state elections of that year and, perhaps, an indicator that PAN won. As explained in an earlier chapter, the disputed 1968 Baja California and 1969 Yucatán elections were occasions of mass disenchantment with PRI and the government. As the only true opposition party, PAN is a natural vehicle for such protests. Commonly, it is the only other party on the ballot in state and local elections.

Acción Nacional believes that these protest votes serve its purposes. The party must achieve state and local victories in order to build an organization capable of capturing control of the presidency. As the party participates in elections, it tries to indoctrinate the citizenry. Electoral success, even though protest voting, will aid this process as the party demonstrates its viability, or so *panistas* believe. In the short run, according to PAN, such protest votes force the government to make concessions to the population in order to avoid repetitions of high electoral support for the opposition and the necessity of engaging in vote fraud. PAN further believes that protest votes will increase in the future because the country is becoming more industrialized, urbanized, and sophisticated, and, consequently, wealthier and better educated. In addition, the party believes that the government is rapidly losing support because the Revolution has failed to solve Mexico's problems while claiming to have all the answers, that the population knows this, and that the government has had to increase repressive measures to maintain itself in power. PAN believes that it will benefit from this phenomenon.[44] The importance of these beliefs is that they encourage the party to continue by giving the members some sense of utility.

In summary, Acción Nacional is a poor, middle-class political party which has exploited discontent in order to become the most effective opposition party since 1911, if not in the entire history of Mexico. Contrary to many previously published studies, Acción Nacional is not the party of big business nor of the Church, but does receive indirect ideological support from them. The party's support system has been large and effective enough to allow it to increase its modest role as PRI's principal opposition within the context of party politics, but not large enough to allow PAN to take significant power in Mexico. The extent of PAN's electoral support is in doubt but official figures probably represent a minimum.

CHAPTER X

Perspectives

Acción Nacional is both a product of Mexican history and a response to the Catholic social reform impulse in Latin America.[1] As the former, its origins are found, first, in the Church-State conflict which has been a major issue in Mexican history for a century and a half, especially in its more recent phases and, second, in the Cárdenas phase of the Mexican Revolution. Its present status is that of being the major opposition party in an essentially one-party political system. As a Catholic-oriented party, Acción Nacional is a Christian Democratic party in all but name. PAN is another instance of socially concerned Catholics turning to politics as a means of solving social ills.

The purpose of this chapter is to put Acción Nacional into its proper perspective, first, in recent Mexican history and, second, in relationship to Latin American Christian Socialism. Although summary comments will be made, the purpose of the chapter is not to recapitulate the major points raised in the course of the study.

PAN AND THE MEXICAN REVOLUTION

The original and continuing goal of Acción Nacional was to become a force for the political reeducation of Mexico along Catholic social doctrine lines *so as to save the Revolution from producing either a socialist-Communist or a national bourgeois-liberal capitalist state,* both of which were inherently exploitive in the PAN view. This goal was more important than political power, which *panistas* did not expect to acquire until after the party had had time to carry through its educational efforts. Power remained an ultimate not an immediate goal, although the party quickly moved to contest governmental power through elections. Its destiny as a thorn in the side of the Revolutionary coalition was not the one it had wanted in 1939, nor the one that it still wants. Instead, it had been trying to create a political party composed of men who believed in its Christian Humanism, a number which would necessarily be small in the beginning but which, the party hoped, would rapidly increase. The party's task was to formulate and vigorously to defend postulates with universal validity and to apply them to Mexican reality.[2] The basic thrust of Acción Nacional ideas were moderate to progressive in 1939 and have become more progressive since then.

Acción Nacional was not created to reverse the Mexican Revolution nor the Cárdenas stage of the Revolution. Because the party was a coalition which included important men more conservative than the bulk of the membership, the *Principios de Doctrina* and the *Programa Mínimo de Acción Política* had intentionally been couched in vague terms. In pamphlets, studies, and speeches, however, *panistas* began to make their position clear. The words of González Luna are especially useful in this context because he was the party's principal ideologue until his death in the mid-1960s and because he was a leading capitalist in Guadalajara. In 1942, he attacked conservatives for their selfishness while attacking socialism for trying to use workers to produce authoritarian governments run by selfish elite groups. He argued for state intervention to avoid egotistical and antisocial domination of either type.[3] The state had the moral duty of providing social security and other welfare measures.[4] Workers had to have the means to obtain decent wages which would provide them not only with food, clothing, shelter, health care, recreation, and education but also savings. Ultimately, the wage system itself either had to be abolished or substantially modified. His suggestion was that this could be done through the use of cooperatives and worker participation in the capital, management, and profits of enterprises.[5] Social justice had to be instituted in Mexico immediately. One roadblock in 1943 was the directive or possessor classes of Mexico, who, in the aggregate, never had had a social conscience.[6]

Equally, the Revolution itself was a roadblock to social progress and justice. In answer to those who argued that Mexico could have had social reform without the Revolution, a favorite argument of conservatives, including PAN's Gómez Morín, González Luna argued that:

> To deny that the Revolution has been an active agent of social reform in Mexico is to deny the sun to the middle of the day. A dispute over the possibility of arriving at the same results that the Revolution has obtained in a third of century by using different (pacific and constitutional) roads would have the character of academic inutility.

At the same time, however, he asserted "that it took twenty-five years to promulgate the first Social Security Law is symptomatic of the reforming efficiency of the Revolution." The problem, in the Acción Nacional view, was that:

> The political system which has given its name—the Revolution—to one of the most agitated and obscure chapters of our history offers two outstanding features to objective observation: on the one hand, it has characterized itself, in emphatic and persistent form, as a movement of social reform, as a force of betterment of the material conditions of workers' lives, of peasant access to landed property, and of the subjection of labor relations to the norms of justice; on the other hand, it has been and continues to be a dirty factory of millionaires, an Eden for the most unchecked appetites for lucre that has ever been imposed upon Mexico, worse than one imposed on conquered territory.

These mutually exclusive traits of the Revolution made it counterproductive to the realization of its own goals. Acción Nacional believed in 1939 that the second tendency—the drive for pelf—was winning.[7]

Acción Nacional especially condemned the Cárdenas stage of the Revolution for being antirevolutionary. On the one hand, the party objected to its Marxian aspects as being counterproductive to the production of social justice because Marxism was a false doctrine which would produce a totalitarian state in which no one would be free. Those Mexicans who were using Marxism as a justification or a model for their actions would prevent social reform. On the other hand, those who were trying to use a liberal-capitalist model sought power and wealth, not the happiness of the population. Because many leftists hailed the Cárdenas step as the embodiment of the true Revolution, this made PAN appear to be conservative or even reactionary. González Luna, in 1943, however, saw Cárdenas's actions in a different light. In reality, he said, there was greatness neither in the conception nor the execution of the Cárdenas reforms. What Cárdenas had done was to destroy without creating better institutions. Using the torch or dynamite was easy; building was hard. PAN agreed with the goals invoked to justify the Cárdenas efforts. Further, it agreed that expropriations of the petroleum and railroad industries and the massive redistribution of land were necessary and desirable, but it objected to the techniques used to implement these reforms. Management of the two industries had been given to untrained workers, and, as a consequence, neither was able to satisfy the demands of the Mexican economy at a low cost. Peasants did not get land, liberty, prosperity, and a system of production but only access to politically controlled tiny plots which were incapable of supporting a family at a decent level.[8]

To PAN, this failure of the Revolution was the inevitable result of its pragmatic nature, for Mexican leadership did not understand the true nature of man and his relationship to society. Acción Nacional believed that authoritarian, paternalistic governments, regardless of their intentions, could not create a just society because only the people know what the common good is. Mexico has been suffering from the illusion that the Revolution was being fulfilled because the government has fostered a Revolutionary myth and punished those who question its validity. Opposition to authoritarian, centralized government has increased and the government increasingly has had to resort to institutionalized violence to maintain control. Such a government, in the PAN view, is illegitimate.

Acción Nacional ideology posits a revolution in liberty to create a modern pluralistic and humanistic society based upon the recognition and implementation of the inalienable rights of the human person and upon solidarity and communitarianism.

The party argues that no society can be just unless it is democratic because each person must have the means to defend his own interests. The rights traditionally associated with political liberalism are insufficient because they leave the person at the mercy of the wealthy. Each person, in the PAN view, must have: (1) a modicum of economic security, (2) the right to join strong, independent work associations, and (3) the right to participate in *all* decisions which affect him whether the decision is made in an economic, political, or avocational context. Each person and each institution must have the means with which to defend their interests. Thus, persons and institutions must have control over property in sufficient quantity for this purpose. Out of the interplay of these forces comes the just society. The emasculation of the power of any of these will automatically produce an unnatural and, consequently, unjust system.

This, then, has been PAN's criticism of the Mexican Revolution, not that its social reform goals should be combated but that the Revolution chose the wrong road to social reform. That poverty and misery continue to coexist with opulence sixty years after the Revolution began was predictable according to PAN. Even though the party initially feared the "socialism" of the Cárdenas stage, it recognized early in the 1940s that the Revolution was heading toward quite different ends. Because of its initial weakness and uncertainty, coupled with its early dependence upon entrepreneurs for financial support, Acción Nacional equivocated somewhat in its attacks on the Revolution. But, as the Revolution shifted rightward, PAN shifted leftward. The retirement of Gómez Morín as

Acción Nacional president freed the party's Catholic activists to attack the Revolution from the center and the moderate left. By 1972, what had originally been a center-right coalition had become a center-left coalition with a small but growing radical wing.

The principal PAN goal has been to obtain the positions of power which would allow it to remold society along the lines suggested in this study, but it has primarily been able to work for its secondary goal of educating Mexicans, especially decision-makers, in Acción Nacional ideology. From exhaustive examination of Acción Nacional sources and extensive interviewing of *panistas*, I believe that the party wants power. At the same time, there is also no doubt that *panistas* see themselves as political missionaries and derive psychological rewards from prostelyzing and martyrdom.

By exploiting voter discontent, Acción Nacional has been institutionalized as Mexico's major opposition party. Contrary to its hope of conquering power through its strategy of ideologically reorienting Mexico, PAN has served as a protest vehicle and gadfly to the Revolutionary coalition. The party has actively sought this latter role while devoting most of its energies to political education with the expectation that it would eventually rule Mexico, but neither intransigence nor dialogue vis-à-vis the government has enabled Acción Nacional to expand its influence beyond this marginal role.

In part, the composition of Acción Nacional explains this phenomenon. The party began as a small Catholic-oriented group of intellectuals, professionals, Catholic activists, and businessmen. Over the course of its history, the coalition changed. It lost most of its prominent private enterprise support but increased its middle- and lower-class membership. However, PAN has been able to acquire neither the necessary financial support nor a corps of professional politicians to increase its electoral victories substantially. Political patronage and administrative experience have eluded PAN's grasp. As a result, the party's leadership and propaganda have been too intellectualized and PAN has failed to articulate its ideology and program to the majority of the population. Acción Nacional history is one example of the inability of intellectuals to influence politics.

PAN has been able to make inroads among the urban middle classes, PRI's weakest point, however, because they are more receptive to intellectual appeals. Through the National Farmers' Confederation and various governmental agencies, PRI has almost complete control in rural areas. This is not surprising since much of this devotion to PRI and its predecessors came because only Revolutionary governments have tried to help *campesinos*. The Peasant Sector of PRI guarantees this extremely large segment of the population some voice in decision-making, a reward for peasants having fought to defend the Revolution in the 1920s. In cities, however, PRI control and influence are less sure. Even though almost all of organized labor, all federal bureaucrats, all public school teachers, and various other urban dwellers automatically belong to PRI, they do not constitute a majority of the party nor, in the anonymity of urban life, can they be disciplined as easily as *campesinos*. The rapidly increasing Mexican middle classes who staff the government and private enterprise are more sophisticated and independent than labor or peasants. The government has recognized this threat by beefing up the middle-class Popular Sector of PRI and concentrating social security and other benefits in the cities. Nevertheless, middle-class PAN has been strongest in the cities (Mexico City, Guadalajara, Tijuana, Mexicali, León in Guanajuato, for example), and its increased strength has come in urban areas. By 1970, PAN was presenting an even greater threat to PRI in the cities because large numbers of university and secondary students and lower-middle- and lower-class people were pouring into PAN. The majority of Mexico's population now lives in cities and urban areas which continue to grow faster than the rest of the country.

PAN's success cannot be measured by the same standards applied to political parties in Western Europe and the United States because the political systems are so divergent. Neither proportional representation nor reliable election statistics exist in Mexico. Mexican voting figures almost always show miniscule support of opposition groups regardless of the circumstances surrounding elections. As James W. Wilkie has recently noted, an opposition vote of more than 20 percent may mean that the opposition actually won. Since usually 3 to 5 percent of the vote is registered for the opposition, 10 percent of the vote becomes significant.

According to official electoral statistics, Acción Nacional has not only become the major opposition party but has been giving the greatest electoral opposition to the government since 1911 when the Revolution began in earnest. The *Partido Popular Socialista* and the *Partido Auténtico de la Revolución Mexicana* can only muster between 1 and 3 percent of the vote in recent federal elections. At the state and local level, PAN is almost the only opposition party. In such states as Baja California and Chihuahua, PAN has occasionally been able to obtain as much as 25 to 40 percent of the vote in official vote tallies. Some students of Mexican politics, the present author included, believe that PAN has actually won some gubernatorial and other elections but that the results were reversed to protect the PRI monopoly. Such was the case in Sonora (1967), Baja California (1968), and Yucatán (1969).

In a country which has seldom had political parties, opposition parties, or parties independent of the government, Acción Nacional's rise to the status of major opposition party while maintaining financial independence of official sources is significant. If one believes that political party competition is an indicator of modernity and sophistication, then PAN's role in Mexico assumes even greater significance. Regardless, PAN has done what no other Mexican political party has been able to do; it has survived over thirty years as an independent loyal opposition.

The irony of Acción Nacional history is that a Catholic-oriented party has had to compete against an anticlerical, secular government which uses the techniques of the Catholic Church to maintain itself in power. A suggestive analogy to explain the complex and sophisticated Mexican political system and PAN's role in it would proceed as follows. Mexican counterparts to Church experience are put into parentheses. The Catholic Church (Mexican government) claims to have a monopoly on the Truth (Revolutionary myth). Among the staff (PRI) of the institution are widely divergent ideological debates (the wings of PRI), but the institution maintains a united front through discipline (party discipline). Dissenters who accept discipline are isolated from real power (the similar fate of such men within PRI). Dissenters who refuse to accept discipline or were never part of the institution (PAN, UNS, Mexican Communist Party) are labeled heretics (Communists, fascists, counterrevolutionaries). Talented young men are constantly recruited into the institution and, if they demonstrate orthodoxy (adherence to the official line), demonstrate the proper zeal for expanding and maintaining the institution (political militancy), and cultivate influential friends (the political clique system of PRI), they can be promoted to the hierarchy. Institutional leadership (elected officials, especially those who fall under the no-reelection rule) is rotated, but the institution is stabilized by tradition (the Revolutionary tradition) and a competent bureaucracy committed to institutional goals (the massive governmental bureaucracies in Mexico). The institution promises a future heaven (social justice) for all true believers, engages in constant and elaborate rituals (sanctification of all public policies, events, and laws by calling them Revolutionary), and occasionally produces evidence to support its ideology (gradual extension of socioeconomic benefits). Both institutions have convinced the masses that they have the only true role to salvation. Both show the ability to make the adjustments necessary in the face of popular demand which the communications network (PRI sectors and organized business, protests, and election campaigns) discovers. Through the diversity of opinion within the institution and its internal discipline, the institution can shift its course of action while claiming to adhere to the orthodox line (both the liberal-left Cárdenas and the conservative-reactionary

Alemán were orthodox Revolutionaries). Unlike Martin Luther, PAN has been unable to find strong backers in its reformation attempts.

Acción Nacional is an unwilling tool of the Revolutionary coalition. Without questioning the validity of Mexican election statistics, it is obvious that PAN's opposition to official party candidates lends credence to PRI and governmental claims that Mexico is a democratic state in which the official party wins by gigantic margins because it is implementing the goals of a very popular revolution, a claim that is buttressed by the relative lack of overt repression against PAN. A real but ineffectual opposition party is necessary to maintain the semblance of democracy in Mexico. To serve the Revolutionary purposes best, such a party must be identified as being to the right of the Revolution, whether it is or not, or identified as foreign, or both. In the first case, the Revolutionary coalition can stand as the defender of the population against atavistic men who worship nineteenth-century ideas. Tying an opposition party to foreign interests means that Mexican xenophobia will limit the opposition's influence. Until the last decade PAN has been identified as both rightist and foreign-inspired, making it a perfect foil for the Revolutionary coalition because it serves as a legitimizer of the Revolutionary credentials of the ruling elite, regardless of actual governmental policy.

At another level, PAN is also a *palero* (tool) of the government in the former's role as a conduit of discontent. Although most dissent can be contained within the large and ideologically diverse PRI, it does occasionally break out of these confines as defections or electoral repudiation of PRI. PAN has absorbed some of the dissidents, although usually for short time periods, making this a minor function. More important, especially in recent years, has been the tendency of Mexicans to vote for PAN as a means of expressing discontent with PRI or the government because of regionalistic resentment, bossism, or lack of attention to a locale's needs and desires. This is the best explanation of the recent elections in Sonora (1967), Baja California (1968), and Yucatán (1969). These occurrences allow the ruling coalition to identify and repair weak links in the system of control before they threaten the system's continuance.

Competition from PAN candidates also serves as part of PRI's disciplinary system. Ex-PRI president Martínez Domínguez summarized this aspect of PAN's role in Mexican politics when he stated that PAN forces PRI to stay in trim.[9] PRI candidates and organizations have to maximize their efforts when they face strong PAN opposition. The existence of able PAN orators in the Chamber of Deputies has forced PRI to choose better deputy candidates so as not to be embarrassed. If PRI politicians offer too much resistance to party discipline, PRI can always punish them by recognizing PAN victories.

Acción Nacional has also performed the traditional role of third parties in the United States, that of gadfly. On the positive side, such issues as female suffrage, social security, profit-sharing, and extension of territorial limits were exploited by PAN before PRI coopted them. On the negative side, PAN's criticism of governmental policy has served as a check upon governmental action, a check which aids the government to rectify errors quickly. This had been an important function because PAN can engage in political heresy whereas PRI cannot.

As a tool of the Revolutionary coalition, Acción Nacional performs, then, an important function in the maintenance of the Mexican political system. One of its greatest effects upon Mexico had been to aid the regularization of the political system by offering competition in major electoral contests. PRI can assume that it will have opposition for these contests and that, if it fails to articulate voter demands properly, this opposition can exploit the discontent which results. In one sense, PAN is PRI's devil's advocate. As other political parties have disappeared in the last twenty years or generally supported PRI (as is the case with PPS and PARM), the importance of PAN's role has increased to the extent that, if PAN did not exist, PRI would have to invent it.

Awareness of this aspect of PAN's significance has led many observers to conclude erroneously that PAN is a "kept" opposition party. This assertion has been made in three ways that: (1) PAN receives governmental subsidies, (2) PAN leaders receive governmental subsidies or preferential treatment in their occupations, and (3) the government encourages PAN by giving it electoral posts which it cannot win on its own. Because PPS and PARM apparently do receive such subsidies, the conclusion is drawn that PAN must also receive them. These observers find it difficult to believe that a political party with PAN's poor track record could exist so long without such aid.

The evidence presented in this study belies these assertions. PAN's finances at the state and national levels are meager. At the state level, PAN's income comes from dues, donations, and sales of various kinds, in that order. At the national level, donations from party leaders and their friends provide the largest single source of income, followed by portions of the federal deputies' salaries and by sales. PAN's income is easily within the reach of the party membership and its friends. Income from federal deputy salaries increased PAN's income, thus making the party deputy system a subsidy of PAN, but the party had survived twenty-three years without it. PAN has been able to do as much as it has because it has tapped a reservoir of volunteer labor among its dedicated followers. Interestingly enough, the assertions that PAN is a kept party are never supported by evidence. The validity of the second assertion is more difficult to ascertain, but it appears equally erroneous. PAN's leaders have sufficient income from their occupations to allow them to earn decent incomes without positive governmental action toward them. They complain that their PAN activity actually cuts their income because of governmental retaliation or loss of business through fear of trafficking with the government's opposition. Any large-scale aid would be highly visible and commented upon. Moreover, PAN leaders tend to be alienated from the government. In light of these factors, it seems unlikely that PAN leaders accept governmental aid.

The assertion that the government gives PAN elected posts which it has not won has more validity, but not in the sense usually meant by PAN detractors. It is based on the assumption that PAN cannot win elections on its own. The section of this study concerned with PAN's electoral support shows that it can; that, if anything, the government curtails PAN victories rather than augments them. On the other hand, the party deputy system was apparently designed to guarantee federal deputy seats to opposition parties such as PAN. The party asserts, however, that it actually wins outright more seats than it is awarded through the party deputy system and that what the system really means is that the government can reward all its candidates while simulating democracy by guaranteeing some representation to the opposition. The operation of the system since its institution supports this contention. In PAN's case, recognition of its outright victories dropped rapidly until it hit the zero point in 1970. Privately, some party leaders agree that not all of PAN's public officeholders actually won their contests and that some were selected by the government. They believe, however, that it actually has won more than the government is willing to concede and that the government selects which *panistas* it prefers to have in office.

In a negative sense, the government does support PAN by allowing it to exist. Were PAN a serious threat to governmental hegemony, the government could take the step of canceling the party's registration as a legal party by interpreting PAN's qualifications unfavorably or by changing the Electoral Law slightly. Vote totals could be altered to deny all public offices. Even PAN's access to the media campaigns could be blocked. PAN has been able to exist only because it has been useful to the government. The destruction of PAN, however, would be dangerous for two reasons. For one, the government might provoke a strong reaction by admitting in such terms that opposition parties are myths. Second, many PAN leaders would probably reorganize as an underground movement and add their experience and contacts to already existing resistance movements. Although the government would eventually crush such a combination, the effort might well destroy the last remnants of governmental legitimacy.

The constant tactical debates within PAN, which are public in preelectoral conventions, support the contention that PAN is truly an independent party. *Panistas* realize that their electoral participation supports the system which they contest. They see no alternative, however, because their ideology commits them to participation because it argues that political participation is the moral duty of every citizen. Nonparticipation would catch them in a significant contradiction. Further, they believe that participation is the only legitimate means of obtaining power. They condemn violence as illegitimate and believe that revolution would bring greater evils than already exist. The party does not believe that electoral participation is meaningless, even if the system is fraudulent, because it forces the government to allow PAN to spread the propaganda which PAN hopes will eventually allow it to conquer power. Nevertheless, *panistas* are constantly seeking better ways to influence decision-making and to gain access to power, but with little hope of success. This frustration led a near-majority of *panistas* close to the step of disbanding the party and converting it into an underground resistance movement. The enthusiasm generated by the Efraín González Morfín campaign in 1970 temporarily, at least, saved the party from this fate.

PAN has been sustained for over thirty years not by governmental aid or encouragement but by the commitment of its Catholic leadership. PAN leaders, for the most part, believe that they are political missionaries who can eventually win over both the Mexican masses and the governmental to their ideology. They fervently believe their Catholic social doctrine ideology. My conversations with and observations of *panistas* over a two-year period would seem to validate this concept. At the same time, this fanaticism is tempered by political realism. They do not believe the task can be accomplished overnight. They also are politically ambitious. To many PAN leaders, public recognition and access to power are equally important with their ideological convictions, but it is the last which sustains them.

Inasmuch as the majority of PAN's leadership has been recruited from Catholic lay organizations and because the party posits Catholic social doctrine as its solution to Mexican ills, Acción Nacional's struggle with the government is a continuation of the Church-State conflict in Mexico. The Church no longer speaks on political questions. Institutional Catholic opinion on political issues emanates from two sources: the conservative National Sinarquist Union and the progressive Acción Nacional. Both picked up the load which the Church dropped in the 1930s in the face of strong anticlericalism. The *sinarquista* movement peaked in the mid-1940s, however, leaving Acción Nacional as the only strong political group which could be easily identified as Catholic in orientation. PAN and the Church deny any connection. This is true insofar as the assertion that the Church supports PAN, which it does not. PAN, however, is attacking a secular government because it is not Catholic and does not implement Catholic ideology. It is consciously trying to remake Mexico in a Catholic image. For this argument, whether the ideology is conservative or progressive is irrelevant. What has happened is that some committed Catholics, many of whom fought the State in the 1920s and 1930s, created a political party to continue the fight by carrying it into the political arena where the Church could not go. They made this decision without the Church's approval or support and operated independently of the Church, which had no need for such a group since it obtained special access to Mexican decision-makers. That the detente between Church and State was reached prior to the founding of PAN in 1939 is significant because it suggests that PAN's Catholic founders were repudiating the detente and arguing, instead, that the fight for Catholic social justice in Mexico should not be abandoned in favor of harmonious Church-State relations. PAN leaders, however, do not want a theocratic state nor a restoration of ecclesiastical privilege in Mexico. To that extent, they are anticlerical. They were responding not to the specific orders of the Mexican ecclesiastical hierarchy but to their consciences, which had been molded by the Catholic humanist writings of the twentieth century.

PAN and Latin American Christian Socialism

Acción Nacional would have existed even if the Mexican Revolution had never occurred, for it is another instance of Catholic social reformers turning to politics to solve social ills. Before the Revolution even began in 1910, some Mexican Catholics, through the Social Congresses and the forerunner to the ACJM, were trying to solve some of Mexico's problems. This modest and moderate reform effort was abruptly ended by the Revolution which diverted everyone's attention. Catholics such as PAN founder Manuel Herrera y Lasso created the National Catholic Party to gain power to implement the Church's social doctrine. Significantly, the periodical of both the National Catholic Party and Acción Nacional have been named *La Nación*. The National Catholic Party compromised itself by supporting the Huerta usurpation of power, but some Catholics continued to fight for Catholic social justice in Mexico. This movement became the Social Secretariat of the Church and then Catholic Action, from which Acción Nacional derives its name. Even the *cristero* rebellion was part of this trend in Mexican Catholicism, for as one author has recently observed, the *cristeros* based their political program on progressive Catholic doctrine. Many Acción Nacional founders were *cristeros,* either as combatants, or as partisans in Catholic lay organizations. The *cristeros* were split into conservative and progressive wings. Future *panistas* came from the progressive wing, particularly from UNEC which declared itself for Catholicism and Revolution. Created in 1926 under another name, UNEC was renamed in 1931 to continue the fight for the minds of young Mexicans in universities. UNEC members led the creation of the Iberoamerican Confederation of Catholic Students or Iberoamerican University Catholic Action, as it was also called. Participating with them in this organization were many future Christian Democratic leaders of Latin America, including Rafael Caldera of Venezuela and Eduardo Frei of Chile. In 1934, they were called to Rome to participate in the International Congress of Catholic Youth out of which the present Latin American Christian Democratic movement was born. A few years later, the UNEC group led the creation of Acción Nacional, bringing into the coalition many other Catholic Action militants. Since its founding in 1939, Acción Nacional has developed its ideology and programs in tandem with other Latin American Christian Democratic parties.

Many twentieth-century Catholics, especially in Latin countries, have been in a state of ferment trying to find a Catholic alternative to socialism on the one hand and capitalism on the other.[10] This quest for a socioeconomic system which meets the requirements of Catholic social justice led some Catholics into espousing fascism, whereas it led others into espousing some form of authoritarian corporatism, and still others into espousing democratic corporatism. The neo-Thomist school of Jacques Maritain and others greatly influenced large numbers of young Catholic intellectuals and professionals in the 1930s to argue for democratic corporatism. The papal encyclicals *Rerum Novarum* (1891) and *Qudragesimo Anno* (1931) served as official justifications for these positions, but the latter was especially important as a justification of corporatist thought.

To many Catholics, the 1930s offered few acceptable alternatives. Ultraconservative Catholics could look to Mussolini as the guide to the world's future whereas conservative and moderate Catholics saw Spain's *falangista* movement, the corporatism of Portugal's Salazar, or Brazil's New State as a solution. In the 1940s, some looked to Argentina's Juan

Perón for leadership. Such liberal capitalist (and Protestant) countries as the United States and Great Britain were in economic crisis and unappealing. On the other extreme was Soviet Russia which was aiding anticlericals directly or indirectly, or so many Catholics thought. Progressive Catholics sought a third way which would reconcile social justice with order and liberty. This movement created such parties as COPEI in Venezuela, the National Falange (later the Christian Democratic Party) in Chile, and Acción Nacional in Mexico.

The major difference among them is that Acción Nacional was created after a major social revolution was already established. This revolution had anticlericalism as one of its main themes and witnessed a violent Church-State conflict, forcing even progressive Catholics to worry about the very survival of their religion and thereby to assume a defensive or negative posture. Latin American Christian Democratic parties, save those of Bolivia and Cuba, have not faced a similar set of circumstances and Bolivia and Cuba have only in that social revolutions occurred in those countries. Contesting a successful Revolution which posits both social justice as its goal and anticlericalism has had three major effects upon PAN which has made it appear more different from its Christian Democratic counterparts than it really is. In the first place, the anticlericalism of the Revolution, combined with some Catholic support of conservative movements, has enabled the Mexican Revolutionary coalition to label Acción Nacional a clerical and conservative party which seeks the restoration of ecclesiastical privilege, thereby giving it a negative popular image. In the second place, because PAN has had to attack an existing revolution, Mexican politicians have been able to suggest that the party is not only clerical but counterrevolutionary, seeking to wipe out the gains of the Revolution. PAN disclaimers and actions to the contrary have been ignored. As pointed out in Chapter VI, its legislative proposals and writings have sought to enable the Revolution to achieve its goals in purely secular terms. In the third place, Revolutionary governments have so restricted PAN access to the citizenry that the party has been unable to develop the kinds of support, tactics, and institutions which have enabled Catholic reform parties in other countries to be mass-based, well-financed, positive alternatives to incumbent governments. PAN's Christian Socialism pales in the light of the socialist promises and capitalist accomplishments of the Mexican Revolution. A similar fate may be befalling Chilean Christian Democrats as they compete against the government of Marxist Salvador Allende.

Acción Nacional was founded for the same purposes as other Latin American Christian Democratic parties: to offer an alternative to liberal or laissez faire capitalism and socialism which would be democratic and consistent with progressive Catholic social justice doctrines. It favored social reform; it even favored the Mexican Revolution. What it did not favor was a Marxist or a liberal-capitalist social revolution because it did not believe that either could achieve the desired end. As Efraín González Luna expressed it in April 1940, in a preamble speech to the second national convention of Acción Nacional:

> If the Revolution were only that; if the Revolution were an intelligent legislation and an honest action for the redemption of the worker; if the Revolution were only its primitive agrarian program, the creation of a rural middle class through the access to rustic property by the greatest number of peasants liberated from peonage; if the Revolution were really the purity in principles and political proceedings, effective suffrage and no-reelection; if the Revolution were truly the economic independence of Mexico; if the Revolution were truly the consubstantiation with the national aspirations, the desire of greatness for the country, the force for liberation, for cleanness, for the elevation of Mexico in all its aspects, we would declare ourselves totally revolutionaries.
>
> But it is, gentlemen, that that concatenacion of political regimes, of Mexican public administrations that are covered under the name of the Revolution and that culminate with the political and administrative disaster that is the actual regime, is simply a system of sullying, of degrading, and of defrauding the aspirations and hopes of Mexico.[11]

Yet this speech represents Acción Nacional in its most conservative stage. From the mid-1940s to the present day, Acción Nacional has evolved towards a Christian Socialist or Democratic position. Party leaders moved from what was essentially welfare capitalism to a non-Marxist socialist position based upon the Christian humanistic ethic so aptly stated in recent social encyclicals.

Although the resemblance between Acción Nacional doctrine and that of members of the Christian Democratic International may be superficial, the similarities are too close to be dismissed lightly. Great differences also exist within the Christian Democratic International itself, differences which are often greater than those between PAN and any single Christian Democratic party. Operationally, of course, the differences become greater since each party must respond to the conditions peculiar to its own political system. To understand how all these parties relate to each other, if they do, more research is needed into their origins, particularly the reaction of educated lay Catholics to the secular (often

Marxist) threat of the 1920s and 1930s, into the origin and circulation
of ideas within the Latin American political Catholic world, and into the
interrelationships that seem to exist among them. Research into the relationship between the Society of Jesus and the development of Catholic
reform parties in Latin America might be particularly revealing. In the
course of the present research, the author saw scattered references to
Jesuits being involved in the creation of these reform parties either as
teachers of the lay founders or as founders themselves. They also seem
to serve as political advisers. Scholars know very little about Latin
American political Catholicism even though the Catholic Church historically has been one of the most important institutions of the area. Catholic political parties have had some success in influencing events, and
some Catholic leaders, lay and ecclesiastical, have excited many Latin
and North Americans with their pronouncements on the necessity of
social reform or revolution.

In the case of Acción Nacional, the party has been offering a Catholic
alternative to revolution in Mexico and throughout the world. During
most of its history, it has been offering this alternative to what most
Mexicans consider to be a continuing revolution and, as such, PAN has
been a postrevolutionary movement, unlike other Christian Socialist
movements. The successes of the Mexican Revolution have meant that
the appeal of PAN's reform ideology has been extremely limited and
have obscured the fact that PAN is essentially progressive. Although
PAN's increased importance in the Mexican political system has come
from its role as a protest vehicle, its use of a broad social reform ideology in recent years has made it more acceptable in this role.

Acción Nacional's experience in Mexico seems to demonstrate both
the limits of Latin American Christian Socialist movements and the re-
siliency of the Mexican Revolution. If they operate within the context of
their ideology, particularly by respecting private property and individual
rights, they cannot outbid secular socialists for mass support. If they
adopt the ideology of their competitors, they cease being Christian Socialists. Leaders of the Mexican Revolution have never faced this problem because they have never been tied to a rigid ideology. They can shift
directions abruptly yet stay within the broad context of the Revolution.
Because only they have power, they can modify their behavior to out-
flank the opposition. The inroads that PAN was making in the second
half of the 1960s because of growing popular discontent with the policies of Díaz Ordaz are apparently being reversed by the reforming zeal
of Echeverría. PAN was instrumental in forcing the reform effort to
occur but this is a meager return on its investment.

Nevertheless, Acción Nacional has had an important impact upon

Mexican politics. It has demonstrated that it is possible to have loyal opposition parties in a country which had never known them previously. It has helped to train Mexicans to use debate instead of violence to solve problems. It has acted as the conscience of the Revolution as well as the initiator of new ideas. Finally, PAN has offered greater electoral opposition than has ever been offered in Mexico before. Although the party has no real hopes of running the country, it has had a significant impact upon Mexico's political development. Moreover, and perhaps most important, PAN history offers the student of Mexico a different and deeper perspective on the Mexican political system.

NOTES TO CHAPTERS

Chapter I: THE HISTORICAL ENVIRONMENT

1. Acción Nacional (National Action) is the official name of the party and the one which members most commonly use. The party is also called Partido Acción Nacional or PAN. PAN and Acción Nacional will be used interchangeably in this study. The acronym PAN was created as a result of ballot requirements, not to suggest *pan*, the Spanish word for bread. Members of Acción Nacional are often called *panistas*.

2. Revolution with a capital "R" will always refer to the great upheaval which began in 1910–11. Mexicans assert that the Revolution has not ended; hence, they label all governments as Revolutionary. The term is used in the same sense in this study.

3. The historical sketch is based upon Frank R. Brandenburg, *The Making of Modern Mexico* (Englewood Cliffs, N.J.: Prentice-Hall, 1964); Howard F. Cline, *The United States and Mexico* (New York: Atheneum, 1965) and *Mexico, Revolution to Evolution, 1940–1960* (New York: Oxford University Press, 1963); Charles C. Cumberland, *Mexico: The Struggle for Modernity* (New York: Oxford University Press, 1968); J. W. F. Dulles, *Yesterday in Mexico* (Austin: University of Texas Press, 1961); and Daniel Cosío Villegas, ed., *Historia Moderna de México*, 7 vols. (Mexico: Editorial Hermes, 1965).

4. See Cline, *United States and Mexico*, p. 204 for one such comparison.

5. Cumberland, *Mexico*, pp. 276–85; James W. Wilkie, "The Meaning of the Cristero War Against the Mexican Revolution," *A Journal of Church and State*, VIII (1966), pp. 214–33. Technically, it was not an interdict and private masses were held, but the similarities between an interdict and the Mexican action are striking.

6. Ibid. The twentieth-century Church-State conflict will be discussed more fully in Chapter II.

7. The history of this party and its subsequent forms may be found in Cline, *United States and Mexico;* Brandenburg, *Modern Mexico;* Cumberland, *Mexico;* Dulles, *Yesterday in Mexico;* Robert E. Scott, *Mexican Government in Transition,* rev. ed. (Urbana: University of Illinois Press, 1964); L. Vincent Padgett, *The Mexican Political System* (Boston: Houghton-Mifflin, 1966); Kenneth F. Johnson, *Mexican Democracy: A Critical View* (Boston: Allyn and Bacon, 1971); Bertha Lerner Sigal, "Partido Revolucionario Institucional," in *México: realidad política de sus partidos* (Mexico: Instituto Mexicano de Estudios Políticos, A.C., 1970), ed. by Antonio Delhumeau A., pp. 43–96; Vicente Fuentes Díaz, *Los partidos políticos en México,* (2d ed.; Mexico: Editorial Altiplano, 1969); and Daniel

Moreno, *Los partidos políticos del México contemporáneo* (*1926–1970*) (Mexico: B. Costa-Amic, 1970).

8. The voting statistics are found in James W. Wilkie, "New Hypotheses for Statistical Research in Recent Mexican History," *Latin American Research Review*, VI:2 (summer 1971), p. 5. Dulles, *Yesterday in Mexico*, pp. 469–80 gives an account of the Vasconcelos campaign. Padgett, *Mexican Political System*, p. 33, suggests that the election was not that lopsided.

9. James W. Wilkie, *The Mexican Revolution: Federal Expenditure and Social Change Since 1910* (Berkeley and Los Angeles: University of California Press, 1967), pp. 282–83.

10. Brandenburg, *Modern Mexico*, pp. 7–18. This segment of the chapter relies heavily upon this brilliant synthesis.

11. Pablo González Casanova, *Democracy in Mexico* (New York: Oxford University Press, 1970), pp. 16–30.

12. Brandenburg, *Modern Mexico*, pp. 164–65; Johnson, *Mexican Democracy*, passim; Padgett, *Mexican Political System*, pp. 149–52; and Wilkie, *Mexican Revolution*, p. 279.

13. Cline, *Mexico, Revolution to Evolution*, pp. 193–94; Wilkie, *Mexican Revolution*, pp. 161–64.

14. Cline, *Mexico, Revolution to Evolution*, is the classic statement of this change in emphasis. Wilkie, *Mexican Revolution*, details the change through budgetary analysis. The debate as to whether the Revolution died in 1940 is found in Stanley R. Ross, ed., *Is the Mexican Revolution Dead?* (New York: Knopf, 1966).

15. Wilkie, *Mexican Revolution*, p. 282; Cline, *Mexico, Revolution to Evolution*, p. 34.

16. Brandenburg, *Modern Mexico*, pp. 131–40; Padgett, *Mexican Political System*, pp. 134–35; Scott, *Mexican Government*, pp. 143, 205–10; Lerner Sigal, "Partido Revolucionario Institucional," pp. 66–67, 83–85; Ronald H. McDonald, *Party Systems and Elections in Latin America* (Chicago: Markham, 1971), pp. 245–48.

17. Johnson, *Mexican Democracy*, passim; González Casanova, *Democracy in Mexico*, pp. 195–97; Scott, *Mexican Government*, p. 301.

18. Brandenburg, *Modern Mexico;* Cline, *United States and Mexico* and *Mexico, Revolution to Evolution;* Johnson, *Mexican Democracy;* Padgett, *Mexican Political System;* Antonio Delhumeau, et al., *México: realidad política de sus partidos;* González Casanova, *Democracy in Mexico;* Wilkie, *Mexican Revolution;* Scott, *Mexican Government;* and Martin C. Needler, "The Political Development of Mexico," *American Political Science Review*, LV (June 1962), pp. 308–12 are examples. Carolyn Needleman and Martin Needleman, "Who Rules Mexico? A Critique of Some Current Views of the Mexican Political Process," *Journal of Politics*, XXXI (1969), pp. 1011–34 is a valuable analysis indicating continuing disagreement among scholars.

19. This is a common opinion in Mexico. The most complete scholarly investigation of popular participation to date is Patricia McIntire Richmond, "Mexico: A Case Study of One-Party Politics," unpublished Ph.D. dissertation in sociology, University of California, Berkeley, 1965.

20. See Mexico City *News* for July 1966 and Johnson, *Mexican Democracy*, p. 35.

21. Emilio Portes Gil in an interview with Australian scholar David Potts in Mexico City, February 1970. I express my thanks to Professor Potts for relaying

this information. The meaning of electoral statistics will be discussed more fully in Chapter IX.

22. The best account of the Madrazo episode is Johnson, *Mexican Democracy*, pp. 45–47.

23. González Casanova, *Democracy in Mexico*, pp. 120–34.

Chapter II: ORIGINS OF ACCIÓN NACIONAL

1. Acción Nacional, *Efemérides* (Mexico: Acción Nacional, 1942), pp. 7–8; *Excélsior*, September 15, 1939; Luis Calderón Vega, *Memorias de Acción Nacional*, Vol. I (Morelia: Editorial Fimax, 1967), pp. 18–22, 28; Luis Calderón Vega, "Germén y germinación del PAN, las condiciones de su nacimiento," *La Nación*, XII (March 8, 1953), pp. 10–11; Efraín González Luna, introduction to Manuel Gómez Morín, *Diez Años de México* (Mexico: Editorial Jus, 1950), pp. x–xvi; Manuel Gómez Morín, "Informe a la Segunda Convención Nacional de Acción Nacional," *Diez Años*, pp. 57–69 and "Discurso Pronunciado en la Asamblea de Conmemoración del Segundo Aniversario de Acción Nacional," *Diez Años*, pp. 77–88.

2. The National Sinarchist Union founded in 1937 which espoused a fascist or near-fascist doctrine. Sinarquista means "without anarchy." Its history is traced in Mario Gill [pseud. Carlos M. Velasco Gill], *Sinarquismo: su orígen, su esencia, su misión* (Mexico: Ediciones Club del Libro "Mexico," 1941); Nathan Whetten, *Rural Mexico* (Chicago: University of Chicago Press, 1948), pp. 485–522; Harold E. Davis, "The Enigma of Sinarquism," *Mexican Life*, XIX (June 1943), pp. 13–15, 51–55; Fuentes Díaz, *Los partidos políticos*, pp. 321–45; Raymond V. Michaels, "Sinarquismo, a Survey of its History, Ideology, Organization, and Programs," unpublished M.A. thesis in international relations, Mexico City College, 1961; and Albert L. Michaels, "Fascism and Sinarquism; Popular Sovereignty Against the Mexican Revolution," *A Journal of Church and State*, VIII (1966), pp. 234–50 and "El nacionalismo conservador mexicano desde la revolución hasta 1940," *Historia Mexicana*, XVI (October–December 1966), pp. 213–38.

3. Manuel Gómez Morín, "Informe a la Asamblea Constituyente de Acción Nacional," *Diez Años*, pp. 7–8; Calderón Vega, *Memorias*, pp. 18–22 and "Germén," pp. 10–11.

4. Robert E. Quirk, "The Mexican Revolution and the Catholic Church, 1910–1929, An Ideological Study," unpublished Ph.D. dissertation in history, Harvard University, 1950, pp. 28–32; Alicia Olivera Sedano, *Aspectos del Conflicto Religioso de 1926 a 1929: Sus Antecedentes y consecuencias* (Mexico: Instituto Nacional de Antropología E Historia, 1966), pp. 29–34; and Andres Barquín y Ruiz, *Bernardo Bergöend, S.J.* (Mexico: Editorial Jus, 1968). Bergöend was a principal vehicle for the importation of European ideas.

5. Quirk, "Mexican Revolution," pp. 28–32, 48–53; Robert E. Quirk, "Religion and the Mexican Social Revolution," *Religion, Revolution, and Reform: New Forces for Change in Latin America* (New York: Praeger, 1964), edited by William V. D'Antonio and Frederick B. Pike, pp. 67–68; Olivera Sedano, *Aspectos*, pp. 29–42.

6. Quirk, "Mexican Revolution," pp. 51–52 and "Religion," p. 69; Barquín y Ruiz, *Bergöend*, passim; Antonio Rius Facius, "Trascendencia nacional de la A.C.J.M.," *Excélsior*, August 11, 1958 and *La juventud mejicana y la revolución*

204 MEXICO'S ACCION NACIONAL

mejicana (Mexico: Editorial Jus, 1963), pp. 43 ff.; Joseph Ledit, S.J., *Rise of the Downtrodden* (New York: Society of St. Paul, 1959), p. 24.

7. Ledit, *Rise*, p. 24.

8. Quirk, "Mexican Revolution," pp. 62–66.

9. Quirk, "Mexican Revolution," pp. 141–47; Cumberland, *Mexico*, pp. 126–27.

10. Ledit, *Rise*, p. 64; Quirk, "Mexican Revolution," p. 66.

11. Ledit, *Rise*, pp. 113–14; Michaels, "El nacionalismo conservador," pp. 218–20; Quirk, "Mexican Revolution," pp. 165 ff.; Olivera Sedano, *Aspectos*, pp. 85–90.

12. Michael Williams, *The Catholic Church in Action* (New York: Kennedy & Sons, 1958), pp. 310–31; Raymond F. Cour, C.S.C., "Catholic Action and Politics in the Writings of Pope Pius XI," unpublished Ph.D. dissertation, Notre Dame University, 1953, passim. Williams terms Catholic Action "the participation of the laity in the apostolic work of the Church" (p. 310) and "the Catholic life lived out" (p. 331). Catholic Action's putative purpose is to teach Catholic principles to the laity to supplement the work of priests, but Father Cour admits that Catholic Action is used because the Church often cannot enter politics (p. 121).

13. Ledit, *Rise*, pp. 52, 81–82; Quirk, "Mexican Revolution," pp. 30–31, 163–65; Williams, *Catholic Church*, pp. 320–21; John J. Kennedy, *Catholicism, Nationalism, and Democracy in Argentina* (Notre Dame, Indiana: University of Notre Dame Press, 1958), pp. 143–44, 180–86; Stanley G. Payne, *Falange: A History of Spanish Fascism* (Stanford: Stanford University Press, 1961), p. 22; Carlos E. Castañeda, "Social Developments and Movements in Latin America," *Church and Society*, Joseph N. Moody, ed. (New York: Arts, Inc., 1953), pp. 766–67; Pius XI, *On the Religious Situation in Mexico* (Washington, D.C.: National Catholic Welfare Conference, 1937), pp. 12–19; Edward R. Gotshall, Jr., "Catholicism and Catholic Action in Mexico, 1929–1941: A Church's Response to a Revolutionary Society and the Politics of the Modern Age," unpublished Ph.D. dissertation in history, University of Pittsburgh, 1970.

14. The most comprehensive work on the Church-State conflict (1926–29) is Olivera Sedano, *Aspectos*. See also James W. Wilkie, "The Meaning of the Cristero Religious War Against the Mexican Revolution," *A Journal of Church and State*, VIII (1966) pp. 214–33; Quirk, "Mexican Revolution," pp. 259–61.

15. Quirk, "Mexican Revolution," pp. 262, 266 ff.; Olivera Sedano, *Aspectos*, p. 249; Ledit, *Rise*, p. 25; Hugh G. Campbell, "The Radical Right in Mexico, 1929–1949," unpublished Ph.D. dissertation, UCLA, 1968, pp. 31–32.

16. Quirk, "Mexican Revolution," pp. 262, 266; Olivera Sedano, *Aspectos*, pp. 126 ff.; Ledit, *Rise*, pp. 32–35.

17. Antonio Rius Facius, *Mexico Cristero* (Mexico, 1960), pp. 153–55 as cited in Campbell, "The Radical Right," p. 38.

18. Ledit, *Rise*, pp. 24–36; Campbell, "The Radical Right," p. 40.

19. Luis Calderón Vega, *Cuba 88: Memorias de la UNEC* (Morelia: Editorial Fimax, 1963), pp. 8–10 ff.; Ledit, *Rise*, pp. 68–69. Calderón Vega was a leading participant in CNECM, the forerunner of UNEC.

20. Quirk, "Mexican Revolution," pp. 286–87.

21. Quirk, "Mexican Revolution," pp. 287–91.

22. Quirk, "Mexican Revolution," pp. 282–84.

23. Ledit, *Rise*, p. 49; Campbell, "The Radical Right," pp. 54–55.

24. Dulles, *Yesterday in Mexico*, pp. 469–73.

25. Dulles, *Yesterday in Mexico*, pp. 473–80; Manuel Gómez Morín as quoted

in James W. Wilkie and Edna Monzón de Wilkie, *México Visto en el Siglo XX* (Mexico: Instituto Mexicano de Investigaciones Económicos, 1969), pp. 157, 196, 226; interview with Gómez Morín, December 4, 1969, in Mexico City; "Los fundadores del partido," *La Nación*, XVIII (September 27, 1959), pp. 9–11.

26. Calderón Vega, *Cuba 88*, pp. 23–25; interviews with Calderón Vega, September–March 1969–70 and July–August 1971, in Mexico City and Morelia; interview with Dr. Edmundo Meouchi, UNEC participant, February 24, 1970, in Mexico City; interview with Miguel Estrada Iturbide, an UNEC founder, August 1971, in Morelia; Ledit, *Rise*, p. 69. In 1936 Venezuelan university students formed the National Students' Union (UNE), a forerunner of the Christian Democratic party there, for the same purposes; see José Elías Rivera Oviedo, "History and Ideology of the Christian Democratic Movement in Venezuela," unpublished M.A. thesis, University of Notre Dame, 1970, pp. 7–27.

27. Calderón Vega, *Cuba 88*, p. 26; Calderón Vega interviews cited above; Isabel Robelino, "Quince años del movimiento católico iberoamericano," *La Nación*, VI (December 21, 1946), pp. 19, 23. Calderón Vega was president of the Confederation in 1944.

28. Interview with Calderón Vega.

29. Ledit, *Rise*, p. 69; interviews with Calderón Vega.

30. Ledit, *Rise*, p. 69; Joe C. Ashby, *Organized Labor and the Mexican Revolution under Lazaro Cardenas* (Chapel Hill: University of North Carolina Press, 1967), pp. 43–46.

31. Calderón Vega, *Cuba 88*, pp. 136–41.

32. Calderón Vega, *Cuba 88*, p. 72.

33. Ledit, *Rise*, p. 72.

34. Calderón Vega, *Cuba 88*, p. 51.

35. Calderón Vega, *Cuba 88*, pp. 136–41; Ledit, *Rise*, p. 72.

36. Calderón Vega, *Cuba 88*, pp. 136–41; Ledit, *Rise*, p. 72; interviews with Calderón Vega, July–August 1971.

37. The *conejos* were from a Catholic secret society about which little is known; see Ledit, *Rise*, pp. 72–73 and Calderón Vega, *Cuba 88*, pp. 141–53. They were antisemitic and reactionary. The *conejos* came from such prestigious schools as the Escuela Frances-Morelos in Mexico City; interviews with Calderón Vega, July–August 1971.

38. Interviews with Calderón Vega, Dr. Meouchi, and Estrada Iturbide; Ledit, *Rise*, p. 72.

39. Cumberland, *Mexico*, pp. 282–84, 288, who calls this anticlerical phase persecution.

40. Campbell, "The Radical Right," pp. 89–92; Ledit, *Rise*, p. 103; interview with Calderón Vega, July–August 1971. Calderón Vega was a member of the Base.

41. Leopoldo Lara y Torres [First Bishop of Tacambaro], *Documentos para la Historia de la Persecución Religiosa en México* (Mexico: Editorial Jus, 1954), p. 1006.

42. Ledit, *Rise*, pp. 101–3; Campbell, "The Radical Right," pp. 92–94.

43. Ledit, *Rise*, pp. 103–4; Campbell, "The Radical Right," pp. 112–18; interviews with Calderón Vega, July–August 1971; Fuentes Díaz, *Los partidos políticos*, pp. 327–28. It is significant that Ledit is a Jesuit and that Antonio Santacruz helped him translate the English language edition of the above work because the Base was sponsored by the Jesuits and Santacruz was the Base's head.

44. This is the opinion of Campbell, "The Radical Right," pp. 107–8, but see the comments below on the Base and a possible coup.

45. Ledit, *Rise,* pp. 103–4.

46. Campbell, "The Radical Right," p. 118.

47. Fuentes Díaz, *Los partidos políticos,* pp. 293–94.

48. Interviews with Estrada Iturbide, July–August 1971; Manuel Ulloa Ortiz, October–December 1969.

49. Fuentes Díaz, *Los partidos políticos,* p. 308; Vicente Fernández Bravo, *Política y administración* (Mexico: B. Costa-Amic, 1965), pp. 98, 106; Alejandro Carillo, *Genealogía política del sinarquismo y de Acción Nacional* (Mexico, 1944), pp. 4, 10; Betty Kirk, *Covering the Mexican Front* (Norman: University of Oklahoma Press, 1942), pp. 31–34; and Allan Chase, *Falange: The Axis Secret Army in the Americas* (New York: Putnam, 1943), pp. 150–66. According to Calderón Vega, Dr. Meouchi, and Ernesto Ayala Echávarri, interviews with author, *panistas* were interested in Italian fascism but more interested in the corporatism of Antonio Salazar of Portugal. Dr. Meouchi wrote his doctoral dissertation on Salazar because of this interest.

50. Calderón Vega interviews, July–August 1971. Calderón Vega left the Base in 1936 or 1937 because of these activities.

51. At the time of this writing, the only scholarly examinations of UNS are Whetten, *Rural Mexico,* and Michaels, "Fascism and Sinarquism," cited above. Comments in this book are based primarily upon these two studies.

52. Whetten, *Rural Mexico,* pp. 485–522.

53. Cumberland, *Mexico,* pp. 288–89; Lyle C. Brown, "Mexican Church-State Relations, 1933–1940," *A Journal of Church and State,* IV (1964), pp. 202–22.

54. Brown, "Church-State Relations," pp. 202–22; Michaels, "El nacionalismo conservador," p. 223; Castañeda, "Social Developments," pp. 758–60; Frederick C. Turner, "The Compatibility of Church and State in Mexico," *Journal of Inter-American Studies and World Affairs,* 9:4 (1967), pp. 591–602.

55. Ibid.

56. The best account of the 1936 to 1940 crises is Albert L. Michaels, "The Crisis of Cardenismo," *Journal of Latin American Studies,* II:1 (May 1970), pp. 51–79.

57. Michaels, "Crisis," pp. 51–79; interviews with Calderón Vega, Ayala Echávarri, Gómez Morín, and Dr. Meouchi.

58. See the excellent Michaels article cited above. This section draws heavily upon this work and a synthesis obtained from reading numerous sources of the period and interviewing participants.

59. Cline, *United States and Mexico,* pp. 262–63.

60. Ibid.

61. Gill, *Sinarquismo,* p. 61.

62. *Excélsior,* February 1, 1939, and *Excélsior,* March 3, 1939. Luis Calderón Vega, "En momentos de confusión ideológica y de efímeros brotes electorales," *La Nación,* XXI (March 15, 1953), pp. 14–15 denies that Acción Nacional and the Front had any connection. The present author has seen a letter in the files of Clicerio Cardoso Eguiluz, first PAN membership secretary, from one of the "signers" denying that he signed the advertisement and stating that he had no knowledge of the existence of such a group. Future Mexican President Adolfo López Mateos was also one of the supposed signers.

Chapter III: THE FOUNDING DECADE, 1939–1949

1. Miguel Castro Ruiz, "Gómez Morín: El Hombre, El Universitario, El Político," *La Nación,* X (September 10, 1951), pp. 12–13; Wilkie and Wilkie, *México Visto,* pp. 196, 226; Fuentes Díaz, *Los partidos políticos,* pp. 294–300; interview with Gómez Morín, December 4, 1969, in Mexico City.

2. His eligibility was impugned when he ran for a federal deputy seat in Chihuahua in 1946; see Calderón Vega, *Memorias,* pp. 195–99; Gilberto M. Moreno, "Política: Opinión," *La Nación,* V (August 31, 1946), pp. 4–9; and Ramón Víctor Santoyo, "El Caso Gómez Morín," *Hechos y Hombres del Parlamento* (Mexico, 1947), pp. 117–48. Santoyo was the leader of the fight to prevent Gómez Morín from being seated in the Chamber. The father was Spanish, but Gómez Morín argued that the Constitution of 1857 applied to him, which put him in the same category as a Mexican with Mexican parents (the 1917 Constitution's requirement), and that the 1917 Constitution recognized these earlier provisions. The details of the argument are in *Excélsior,* August 30, 1946 and *La Nación,* V (September 7, 1946).

3. Manuel Gómez Morín, *1915* (Mexico: Editorial CVLTVRA, 1927).

4. Interviews with Ayala Echávarri, Dr. Meouchi, Calderón Vega, and Estrada Iturbide.

5. Calderón Vega, *Memorias,* p. 18; Gómez Morín in Wilkie and Wilkie, *México Visto,* p. 157; "Los fundadores del partido," *La Nación,* XVIII (September 27, 1959), pp. 9–11; interview with Gómez Morín, December 4, 1969, in Mexico City.

6. Calderón Vega, *Memorias,* pp. 27–34; Acción Nacional, *Efemérides* (Mexico: Acción Nacional, 1942), pp. 3–4; Calderón Vega, "1929 y 1939, años decisivos en la ciudadanía mexicana," *La Nación,* IX (April 3, 1950), pp. 12–13, 22; Calderón Vega, "Biografía," *La Nación,* XII (April 12, 1953), pp. 10–11; and Fuentes Díaz, *Los partidos políticos,* p. 304.

7. Calderón Vega, "Germén," pp. 10–11 and "En momentos de confusión," pp. 14–15; interviews with Calderón Vega, Dr. Meouchi, and Estrada Iturbide; Castañeda, "Social Developments," p. 763 says that Gómez Morín was a Catholic leader and that the party's purpose was to influence public opinion with Catholic social teaching. See also Jaime González Graf and Alicia Ramírez Lugo, "Partido Acción Nacional," *México: realidad política de sus partidos,* p. 164.

8. Calderón Vega, *Memorias,* pp. 18–22, 28; Calderón Vega, "Germén," pp. 10–11; González Luna, introduction to *Diez Años,* pp. x–xvi; Gómez Morín, "Informe a la Segunda Convención Nacional de Acción Nacional," *Diez Años,* pp. 57–69; and Gómez Morín, "Discurso Pronunciado en la Asamblea de Conmemoración del Segundo Aniversario de Acción Nacional," *Diez Años,* pp. 77–84.

9. Calderón Vega, "Germén," pp. 10–11; "En momentos de confusión," pp. 14–15; and "1929 y 1939," pp. 12–13, 22; numerous interviews with PAN founders.

10. Efraín González Luna, *La Reforma Social* (Mexico, 1946); interviews with Calderón Vega, Dr. Meouchi, Cardoso Eguiluz, and Manuel González Hinojosa. Further comments on this departure will be made in subsequent pages.

11. The biographical data in this book was obtained from many different sources: biographical dictionaries, periodicals, biographies, *La Nación,* and interviews. The most useful books were Francisco Naranjo, *Diccionario biográfico revolucionario* (Mexico: Imprenta Editorial Cosmos, 1935); José López Escalera, *Diccionario biográfico y de historia de México* (Mexico: Editorial del Magisterio, 1964); *Diccionario Porrua* (Mexico: Libreria de Porrua Hnos., 1964); José Bravo Ugarte,

Efraín González Luna, Abogado, Humanista, Político, Católico; Homenaje a un gran amigo (Mexico: Ediciones de Acción Nacional, 1968); and Rius Facius, *La juventud catolica.*

That important public men joined Acción Nacional raises the question of what happened to pre-Cárdenas Revolutionaries; that is to say, what happened to public figures in this period when their *caudillo* was no longer in power. Such a study would be suggestive of leadership mobility within the Revolution, to mention only the most obvious topic.

12. Ledit, *Rise,* pp. 164–70. Ledit describes the paternalism of Bernardo Elosúa, a PAN founder in Monterrey. Confidential sources within PAN and within private enterprise stress this as a motive.

13. Bravo Ugarte, *González Luna,* p. 40 states that González Luna and Maritain were friends. According to numerous PAN sources, including Calderón Vega and Estrada Iturbide, many PAN founders were disciples of Maritain.

14. Interviews with Gómez Morín and Estrada Iturbide; Calderón Vega, *Memorias,* p. 30. The *Principios de Doctrina* were published in Mexico City in 1939 and in 1941 and are reprinted in Calderón Vega, *Memorias,* pp. 235–44.

15. Interview with Gómez Morín, December 4, 1969, in Mexico City.

16. Bravo Ugarte, *González Luna,* p. 48.

17. Calderón Vega, "Germén," pp. 10–11.

18. Gómez Morín, "Informe a la Asamblea," *Diez Años,* pp. 10–17.

19. Calderón Vega, *Memorias,* pp. 32–34; Gómez Morín as quoted in *México Visto,* p. 177.

20. González Luna, introduction to *Diez Años,* p. 34.

21. Interview with Cardoso Eguiluz, February 25, 1970. Calderón Vega, "Biografía," pp. 14–15 says Gómez Morín wanted a candidate. This was not the sense of his speech at the convention; see Gómez Morín, "Informe a la Asamblea," *Diez Años,* pp. 10–17.

22. *Efemérides,* pp. 7–8; Calderón Vega, *Memorias,* pp. 30–33.

23. Calderón Vega, *Memorias,* pp. 32–34.

24. Gómez Morín as quoted in *México Visto,* p. 177; Calderón Vega, *Memorias,* pp. 33–34.

25. See Campbell, "Radical Right," pp. 285–86 which agrees with my interviews of PAN founders.

26. Juan Andrew Almazán, "Memorias," *El Universal,* August 2, 1958, pp. 4–5, 20.

27. Almazán's program is well stated in John E. Kelley, "Who is Juan Almazán and What is His Program?" *America,* LXIII (September 7, 1940), pp. 594–95 and "Almazán Has a Program of Security in Mexico," *America,* LXIII (September 21, 1940), pp. 654–55. The membership decline is hinted in Calderón Vega, "Biografía," *La Nación,* XII (May 10, 1953), p. 14, but interviews with founders indicated that the loss was substantial.

28. Much of the early financial support of PAN was meant to support the Almazán candidacy; few of these supporters anticipated or cared about Acción Nacional's survival of the election.

29. Gómez Morín, "Informe a la Asamblea," *Diez Años,* pp. 7–8 and "Informe a la Tercera Convención Nacional de Acción Nacional," *Diez Años,* pp. 117–20.

30. *Efemérides,* pp. 8, 11–14; Calderón Vega, *Memorias,* pp. 39–46, 76.

31. Calderón Vega, *Memorias,* pp. 47–48. The *Programa Mínimo de Acción*

Política was printed by PAN in Mexico City in 1940 and later years. It can be found in Calderón Vega, *Memorias*, pp. 245–64.

32. The first interregional convention met in Tampico in January, 1940 and the second in Guadalajara early that same year with the *municipio* as the theme; *Efemérides*, pp. 8, 11–14; Calderón Vega, *Memorias*, pp. 39–46, 76. Representative of the papers produced by such meetings are: Roberto Cossío y Cosío and Pedro Zuloaga, *Estudio Sobre el Problema Agrario* (Mexico, 1944); Luis de Garay, *La Anarquía Económica* (Mexico, 1944); and Daniel Kuri Breña and Manuel Ulloa Ortiz, *Esquema de un Programa Municipal* (Mexico, 1942).

33. Examples of this cooperation may be found in *La Nación*, I (November 22, 1941), pp. 3–4 and III (July 8, 1944), pp. 5–6; *Efemérides*, pp. 8, 14, 18; and Calderón Vega, *Memorias*, p. 49.

34. Acción Nacional, *Representación Política: Reforma del Sistema Electoral* (Mexico, 1941), passim.

35. The anti–Article 3 campaigns have already been noted; for the municipal campaigns, see Calderón Vega, *Memorias*, pp. 156–57.

36. Gómez Morín, "Informe a la Asamblea," *Diez Años*, pp. 11–19; Gómez Morín, "Informe a la Nación," *Diez Años*, pp. 34–36.

37. Fernández Bravo, *Política y administración*, pp. 98, 106; Carillo, *Genealogía*, pp. 4, 10; Kirk, *Mexican Front*, pp. 310–14; Chase, *Falange*, pp. 150–66. Kirk and Chase have numerous significant facts, events, and relationships wrong. Fuentes Díaz, *Los partidos políticos*, pp. 308–9 says that Acción Nacional was not pro-Nazi. Fuentes Díaz has always been an enemy of Acción Nacional.

38. In "Informe a la Nación," *Diez Años*, pp. 24–26 Gómez Morín calls the government communizoid and "popular-frontist." This is a slight distinction. In "Discourso pronunciado en la Asamblea de Conmemoración del Segundo Aniversario de Acción Nacional el 18 de Septiembre de 1941," *Diez Años*, pp. 78–80, Gómez Morín saw Marxist materialism as the threat. Other examples are scattered throughout PAN literature of the period.

39. Efraín González Luna, "Una guerra ideológica: causes, pretextos, desmenes —los casos de España, Portugal y Argentina . . . 'una guerra antimaquiavéllica que terminen con la apoteosis del maquiavellismo;' " *La Nación*, V (November 3, 1945), pp. 6–7; and "Opinión," *La Nación*, III (May 20, 1944), pp. 23–25; interviews with Dr. Meouchi, Calderón Vega, Ayala Echávarri, and Creel Luján.

40. Gómez Morín as quoted in Arturo Sotomayor, "La guerra Europea," *Hoy*, September 23, 1939, p. 34; interviews with Calderón Vega, Dr. Meouchi, and Ayala Echávarri; Acción Nacional, *Programa Mínimo*.

41. Efraín González Luna, "Bases para una política realista," *Humanismo Político* (Mexico: Editorial Jus, 1955), p. 66.

42. See note 37 above.

43. Efraín González Luna, *Visión del México Futuro* (Mexico, 1943), passim, an address to the Third National Convention of Acción Nacional.

44. Calderón Vega, *Memorias*, pp. 80–81; Bernardo Claracal, "La Guerra," *Boletín de Acción Nacional* (June 1, 1940), pp. 6–7; Efraín González Luna, "En la Voragine," *La Nación*, I (December 1, 1941), p. 8; González Luna, "Sobre la política de guerra," *La Nación*, I (June 13, 1942), pp. 11–12; "El Chamizal," *La Nación*, III (August 19, 1944), pp. 4–5; Gumersindo Galván, Jr., "El sonedo caso del Chamizal," *La Nación*, I (December 6, 1941), pp. 7–8; José N. Chávez González, "penetración," *La Nación*, III (August 26, 1944), p. 7; *La Nación*, I (October 18, 1941), pp. 12–13; See *Humanismo Político*, pp. 309–67 for

an excellent series of articles on PAN's international position written by González Luna.

45. *La Nación*, I (December 20, 1941), p. 4; Calderón Vega, *Memorias*, pp. 77–78; *Excélsior*, June 2–3, 1942.

46. Gómez Morín as quoted in Sotomayor, "La guerra Europea," p. 34; Gómez Morín, "Informe a la Segunda Convención Nacional de Acción Nacional, rendido el 20 de Abril de 1940," *Diez Años*, pp. 45–47 is a 1940 reaffirmation of that position.

47. "La lección de las naciones menores," *La Nación*, I (November 8, 1941), p. 9.

48. Calderón Vega, *Memorias*, pp. 77–78.

49. Gómez Morín, "Informe a la Tercera Convención," pp. 128–29; Editorial, "El enrolamiento de nuestros nacionales en el extranjero, decretado por la Secretería de Relaciones es un acto contrario a los principios de derecho y los propios acuerdos panamericanos," *La Nación*, II (November 7, 1942), pp. 4–5; Gómez Morín as quoted in Sotomayor, "La guerra Europea," p. 34; Sansep, "Miles de braceros mexicanos abandonados en los Estados Unidos por las autoridades del trabajo," *La Nación*, V (December 22, 1945), p. 12. Though written after the war, this last article is representative of the tone and arguments used. PAN support for the war may be found in González Luna, *Servicio Militar: Una Nueva Conciencia* (Mexico, 1943) and Editorial, "El patriotismo tiene derechos," *La Nación*, II (October 31, 1942), pp. 3–4.

50. Calderón Vega, *Memorias*, pp. 70–71.

51. Gómez Morín as quoted in *México Visto*, p. 181; Calderón Vega, *Memorias*, p. 59. It is not uncommon in Mexico for the government to appoint leftist or rightist leaders to high office to isolate them.

52. Calderón Vega, *Memorias*, pp. 87–93; *La Nación*, III (May 15, 1943), pp. 4–5, 14–19; *Tiempo*, May 14, 1943, pp. 7–8; *Excélsior*, May 10, 1943.

53. Gómez Morín as quoted in *México Visto*, p. 185. Manuel Castillo, "Acción Nacional y las elecciones de diputados," *La Nación*, II (March 27, 1943), p. 7 observed that PAN would have difficulty finding candidates. The list of candidates, the platform, a manifesto to the nation, and a call to the citizenry to participate in the election can be found in Acción Nacional, *La Campaña Electoral de 1943* (Mexico, 1943). The pamphlet incorrectly lists Aquiles Elorduy as a candidate. Appeals made during the election are found in the pamphlet and in the following Acción Nacional publications: *Aprovechamiento de Recursos Naturales, Salarios y Costo de la Vida*, and *Seguridad Social*. Vote figures are in Calderón Vega, *Memorias*, pp. 93–94; Acción Nacional, *El Fraude Electoral* (Mexico, 1943); and *Tiempo*, July 16, 1943, p. 16.

54. *El Fraude Electoral;* "Declaraciones del 8 de julio," *La Campaña Electoral de 1943*, pp. 15–19; and Calderón Vega, "Biografía," *La Nación*, XII (June 7, 1953), p. 14.

55. "Declaraciones del 8 de julio," pp. 15–19; Gómez Morín, *Quinto Aniversario; Informe a la Asamblea General Ordinaria* (Mexico, 1944).

56. That capitalists began leaving the party in large numbers came from interviews with Calderón Vega, Dr. Meouchi, Cardoso Eguiluz, and González Hinojosa; José Alvarado, "Despertar Político en Puerta, *Siempre!*, January 18, 1956, pp. 20–21. The *La Reforma Social* (Mexico, ca. 1946) pamphlet of González Luna was one indication that the Catholics were assuming control of the party.

57. Cline, *United States and Mexico*, p. 310.

58. "La IV Convención de Acción Nacional," *La Nación*, V (February 8, 1946), pp. 3–6; Calderón Vega, *Memorias*, pp. 143, 154–55. The anti-Padilla attitude, reflected in the expression "Mr." Padilla can be seen in non-PAN sources: Hernando Laborde, "Donde y Como hació la candidatura de Padilla," *Todo*, June 27, 1946, p. 18 and Gerardo de Isolbi, "Alemanismo y Padillismo," *Hoy*, July 7, 1945, pp. 22–23.

59. Calderón Vega, *Memorias*, pp. 166–68.

60. Acción Nacional, *IV Convención Nacional, Dictamen de la Comisión Política* (Mexico, 1946); Calderón Vega, *Memorias*, p. 166.

61. "La IV Convención," pp. 3–6; Calderón Vega, *Memorias*, pp. 168–72. The third vote does not total 168 as do the others. The sources offer no explanation. One possibility is that delegates departed rather than vote for Cabrera.

62. "La IV Convención," pp. 3–6; Calderón Vega, *Memorias*, pp. 173–79. Examples of these nominations were those from Guerrero, Jalisco, and Michoacán. Cline, *Mexico*, p. 169; Scott, *Mexican Government*, p. 182; Padgett, *Mexican Political System*, p. 68 incorrectly assert that Padilla was the PAN candidate.

63. The complete list of candidates and their district can be found in Calderón Vega, *Memorias*, pp. 265–69. Biographical data on eight candidates can be found in Fernando Hernández Ochoa, "Política," *La Nación*, V (October 5, 1946), pp. 15–18. Information on the non-PAN candidates came from Calderón Vega, *Memorias*, pp. 265–69; *La Nación*, V (June 1, 1946), pp. 5–6; and interviews with PAN leaders. Prominent sympathizers who ran under the PAN label were Alfonso Junco, public accountant of the Compañía Industrial Veracruzana of Monterrey and famous Catholic writer, and Gilberto Valenzuela, Minister of Government under Alvaro Obregón.

64. Donald J. Mabry, "Acción Nacional: The Institutionalization of an Opposition Party," unpublished Ph.D. dissertation in history, Syracuse University, 1970, p. 116.

65. Gilberto M. Moreno, "Política: Opinión," *La Nación*, V (August 31, 1946), pp. 4–9; Calderón Vega, *Memorias*, pp. 195–99. Acción Nacional argues that the government selects which of its candidates will have deputy seats. This is not a gift, in their view, because they believe that they win more than the government recognizes. Gómez Morín as quoted in *México Visto*, p. 186 says that Acción Nacional won 23 or 24 seats in 1946.

66. Cline, *United States and Mexico*, p. 311.

67. Calderón Vega, *Memorias*, pp. 166–67.

68. See, for example, the J. R. Domínguez articles "3,627 millones en papelitos de inflación no han sido capaces de crear una industria nueva," *La Nación*, V (June 8, 1946), pp. 21, 27; "Un año despues de terminara el periodo de guerra, nuestra economía sigue igual," *La Nación*, V (May 4, 1946), pp. 8–9, 22; "El informe del Banco de México reconoce el fracaso del sistema de controles aplicado con tanta profusión de 'distribuidores' y 'reguladores.' . . ." *La Nación*, V (May 11, 1946), pp. 10–11, 25; and "Marina, ferrocarriles, y correos cooperan eficazmente para bloquear a Mexico y aisarlo del mundo," *La Nación*, V (March 2, 1946), pp. 10–11; and Fernando Hernández Ochoa, "Elecciones internas en el partido oficial; votos de ancianos y niños a cambio de bolsas de viveres," *La Nación*, V (May 4, 1946), pp. 4–5, 25.

69. Acción Nacional, *Reforma el Art. 115 para otorgar el voto municipal a la mujer, devolver sus bienes y derechos y garantizar su libertad a los Municipios,*

December 23, 1946; "La discusión del voto a la mujer en la Camara de Diputados," *La Nación*, VI (January 4, 1947), pp. 8–9.

70. Acción Nacional, *Organización de la Ciudadanía* (Mexico, 1948).

71. Acción Nacional, *Contra la corrupción electoral* (Mexico, 1947); Acción Nacional, *Intervención de la Suprema Corte de Justicia para garantía de los derechos personales y ciudadanos* (Mexico, 1947).

72. Acción Nacional, *Reforma al Art. 115*. The text of the municipal reform portion is reprinted in Calderón Vega, *Memorias*, pp. 226–28.

73. *Contra la corrupción electoral*.

74. Acción Nacional, *La Crisis Económica* (Mexico, 1948); Acción Nacional, *Urgencia de Asegurar y Aumentar el Renimiento de las Siembras* (Mexico, 1948); "La Gran Esperanza de la Seguridad Social," in Manuel Gómez Morín, *Seguridad Social* (Mexico: Ediciones de Acción Nacional, 1966), pp. 67–76.

75. "La Gran Esperanza."

76. Acción Nacional, *Necesario Control de las Empresas en que participe el Estado* (Mexico, 1948).

77. Acción Nacional, *Falsificación de un Mercado de Valores* (Mexico, 1948); *La Moneda y el Crédito Instrumentos Básicos de la Economía* (Mexico, 1948); and *La Crisis Económica*, p. 306.

78. Acción Nacional, *Necesidad de Rehabilitar los Ferrocarriles Nacionales; Reforma de la Ley que Creo la Administración de los Ferrocarriles* (Mexico, 1948), and *La Crisis Económica*.

79. Acción Nacional, *Reformas a la Ley Federal del Trabajo contra los abusos de lideres y con otras garantías para los obreros* (October 20, 1948); *La Crisis Económica*, p. 14. *Tiempo*, February 20, 1948, p. 7, remarked that Acción Nacional was moving toward more workerism, following the lead given by Pope Leo XIII.

80. Gumersindo Galván, Jr., "Ferrocarriles: los industriales . . ." *La Nación*, III (July 29, 1944), pp. 10–11.

81. *Tiempo*, July 4, 1947, pp. 5–6, and July 11, 1947, p. 3; James A. Magner, "Mexico on the Move," *The Commonweal*, October 31, 1947, p. 64. PAN members told me that Elorduy left because he had an independent nature and did not like being part of an organization. He apparently joined PRI later, however.

82. *La Nación*, VII (May 29, 1948), pp. 6–7 and VII (December 27, 1947), pp. 4–5, 23.

83. For an example of PAN ideology on Article 3 at this time, see Manuel Ulloa Ortiz, "La tres reducciones del Articulo 3 constitutional sobre la educación," *La Nación*, VII (November 22, 1947), pp. 8–9. This was the first of a series of articles that ran for three more issues.

84. On González Torres, see "El que recibe: José González Torres," *La Nación*, XVIII (March 29, 1959), p. 19.

85. Calderón Vega, *Memorias*, p. 207. Caldera attended the annual PAN Christmas supper in December 1946 and had been visiting Gómez Morín and other *panistas*.

86. Alejandro Aviles, "Hispanoamerica. . . ." *La Nación*, VI (August 17, 1946), pp. 12–13 and "Iberoamerica: La verdadera situación en Venezuela. . . ." *La Nación*, VIII (February 14, 1949), p. 19. Aviles visited the Venezuelan Christian Democratic Party (COPEI); the articles reprint sections of articles in support of PAN from their journal *COPEI*.

87. "El Orden Social Cristiano: Un Nuevo Fascismo," *Tiempo*, July 4, 1947,

p. 8. This was reportage of a conference held by José Rogelio Alvarez of the Mexican National Liberal Party. Apparently, PAN ideology, according to this version, was fascist because it was Catholic.

88. *La Nación*, VIII (March 7, 1949) and *Excélsior*, February 27–28, 1949.

89. Ibid.

90. Frank Brandenburg, "Mexico: An Experiment in One-Party Democracy," unpublished dissertation in political science, University of Pennsylvania, 1955, pp. 346–47, and confidential PAN sources.

91. Manuel Gómez Morín, "Informe a la VIII Convención Nacional de Acción Nacional," *Diez Años*, pp. 277–83.

92. *Excélsior*, July 5, 1949.

93. Hinojosa represented Nuevo León capitalists according to a high PAN official and an important official in private enterprise who is not a *panista*. Hinojosa has continued to represent these interests in PAN.

94. Mario Huacuja, "Ha pasado ya el tiempo de las rebeliones armadas: G. Morín," *Novedades*, May 25, 1951.

95. Gómez Morín, "Informe a la VIII Convención," p. 287.

96. "Triunfan los regidores de AN en Acámbaro a pesar del Gobierno local," *La Nación*, VII (January 3, 1948), p. 17; "Municipio," *La Nación*, VI (January 25, 1947), p. 7; "Acción Nacional rompe el monopolio político en el Estado de Michoacán. . . ." *La Nación*, VI (June 28, 1947), pp. 5–7; and "Triunfo en Oaxaca: Credencial para candidato independiente en Huajuapan," *La Nación*, VI (August 16, 1947), p. 10.

97. Gómez Morín, "Informe a la VIII Convención," pp. 293–96.

98. Ibid., p. 287.

99. Manuel Gómez Morín to first national convention of Acción Nacional as quoted in Luis Calderón Vega, "Maestro Gómez Morín," *La Nación*, XXVIII (September 15, 1969), p. 3.

Chapter IV: CATHOLIC MILITANCY, 1949–1962

1. Gilberto Moreno, "Cuatro jefes y cuatro etapas," *La Nación*, XVIII (September 27, 1959), p. 13; *Excélsior*, September 18, 1949. Biographical data on Ituarte Servín and González Torres, to be discussed below, is based on "El que Entrega: Alfonso Ituarte Servín," *La Nación*, XVIII (March 29, 1959), p. 18; "Esto Sí Es El Mero Mero," *Siempre!*, October 24, 1956, p. 6; "El que recibe: José González Torres," *La Nación*, XVIII (March 29, 1959), p. 19; and interview material and personal observation. The *Siempre!* article asserts that Ituarte Servín was a *sinarquista*.

2. This assessment is based upon interviews with many *panistas* as well as with many members of Mexican private enterprise. It is corroborated by Table 6 in Chapter VIII. Enrique Navarro Palacios, "De Nuestros Lectores," *Mañana*, July 19, 1958, p. 6, asserted years later that the government and private enterprise, of which PAN had only represented a "ten-thousandth part," had reached a rapprochement.

3. *Excélsior*, November 19, 1951; "IX Convención: El PAN lucha por la creación del complemento familiar del salario," *La Nación*, X (October 20, 1950), pp. 12–14, 21; "El problema del Trabajo; Su Plantamientos: 1. Deficiencias, Errores y Abusos, 2. Soluciones," *La Nación*, XIII (November 8, 1953), pp. 8–9.

4. Miguel Castro Ruiz, "La Iglesia abrió los caminos de la justicia social en

México . . . sus exigencias, desde antes de la Revolución, superan al Art. 123,"
La Nación, X (December 18, 1950), pp. 14–15; "Doctrina: Normas de Justicia
Social," *La Nación,* X (March 19, 1951), p. 6, which is reportage on the social
views of Pius XII; "La Asamblea de la UCM acuerda directivas políticas y sociales," *La Nación,* XII (October 19, 1952), p. 11; Manuel Ulloa Ortiz, "La Co-
educación es contraria a la Naturaleza del Hombre," *La Nación,* XII (April 26,
1953), p. 3; "El Dilema: Justicia Social o Comunismo," *La Nación,* XII (July 5,
1953), p. 7, which is reportage of a speech by José González Torres, vice-president
of Catholic Action and an Acción Nacional leader; Alejandro Aviles, "Encuesta,"
La Nación, XIII (June 20, 1954), p. 16, an interview with González Torres speaking as a Church lay leader; Luis de Bolonia, "Educación: el Estado monopolista
de la enseñanza," *La Nación,* XIV (November 21, 1954), pp. 12–13; and Gerardo
Medina V., "Justicia Social: Normas para el trabajador, en la ciudad y en el
campo," *La Nación,* XV (February 19, 1956), pp. 10–11, 18, which contains the
most important points of Catholic social doctrine as interpreted by the Interameri-
can Confederation of Catholic Social Action.

   5. *Excélsior,* October 13, 1950, for cooperation between the party and the
Catholic lay group. An example of the anti–Article 3 campaign is found in *La
Nación,* (October 16, 1950), pp. 3–4, 24. The Jesuit article is José A. Romero,
"El Articulo III y la libertad ciudadana," *Mañana,* October 21, 1950, pp. 14–15.
Castañeda, "Social Developments," p. 765, has the account of the diocesan con-
vention.

   6. *La Nación,* XI (January 14, 1952), p. 3; *La Nación,* XI (April 28, 1952),
p. 5; (May 12, 1952), pp. 6–10; and "Así pelea el pueblo de Jalisco; inconenible
decisión de victoria . . . ," *La Nación,* XII (November 23, 1952), pp. 16–17.
For Baja California, see *La Nación,* XI (April 5, 1953), p. 8. For aid to Padilla,
see *La Nación,* XII (December 28, 1952), p. 2. For the 1955 federal deputy elections, see "El sinarquismo define su actitud," *La Nación,* XIV (April 17, 1955),
p. 3; and "El sinarquismo dará la batalla," *La Nación,* XIV (April 24, 1955), pp.
5–6. The terms of the agreement found in *La Nación,* XV (June 10, 1956), p. 2.
See also "Asamblea sinarquista," *La Nación,* XIII (September 26, 1954), p. 6 for
an example of González Torres as a *panista* giving a major address at an UNS
rally.

   7. "La Décima Convención del PAN designa candidato a la Presidencia y
señala caminos inmediatos y prácticos de salvación colectiva," *La Nación,* XI
(November 26, 1951), pp. 8–11; *Excélsior,* November 21, 1951.

   8. "El Consejo del Partido delibera con vistas a la campaña presidencial," *La
Nación,* X (October 1, 1951), pp. 9–11.

   9. Acción Nacional, *Plataforma que Sostendrá el PAN en la campaña electoral
. . . en 1952 . . .* (Mexico, 1951); Editorial, "Los Diez Puntos del PAN,"
Excélsior, November 21, 1951, p. 6.

   10. "La Acción Católica Mexicana señala a los católicos sus normas políticas,"
La Nación, XI (March 10, 1952), p. 8; *Excélsior,* April 25, 1952; *La Nación,* XI
(June 16, 1952), p. 23; "El Frente Nacional de Trabajadores apoya a Efraín
González Luna," *La Nación,* XI (March 3, 1952), pp. 15–16.

   11. *La Nación,* XI (September 15, 1952), pp. 8–9 has biographical data on the
PAN deputies. Ramón Garcilita Partida had contributed to the founding of the
Social Secretariat; Felipe Gómez Mont was active in the UCM; and Francisco
González Chávez had helped found the Church's Michoacán Workers' Social Union.

12. James W. Wilkie, "Statistical Indicators of the Impact of National Revolution on the Catholic Church in Mexico, 1910–1967," *A Journal of Church and State,* VIII (winter 1970), pp. 89–90; Turner, "The Compatibility of Church and State in Mexico," *Journal of Inter-American Studies,* IX (1967), pp. 591–602.

13. *La Nación,* XI (April 5, 1953), p. 8.

14. "El sinarquismo dará la batalla," *La Nación,* XIV (April 24, 1955), pp. 5–6.

15. Data on the 1955 federal deputy victors are found in *La Nación,* XIV (July 10, 1955), pp. 16–19; *La Nación,* XIV (August 21, 1955), pp. 3, 5; "Tres nuevas victorias de Acción Nacional," *La Nación,* XIV (August 21, 1955), p. 5; and *Tiempo,* July 11, 1955, p. 4. Biographical data on Alvarez are located in *Plataforma de Acción Nacional* (Mexico, 1957), pp. 31–32. That he has a degree from MIT is not well known; the information came from a PAN leader.

16. "El XV Consejo acuerda importantes tareas concretas para los panistas," *La Nación,* XII (February 15, 1953), pp. 9–12.

17. *La Nación,* XIII (October 17, 1954); Alejandro Aviles, "XIII Consejo de Acción Nacional," *La Nación,* XVI (October 21, 1956), pp. 8–16.

18. "La organización juvenil del PAN," *La Nación,* XVI (November 25, 1956), pp. 16–17; *Excélsior,* November 19, 1956.

19. "Que se rompa con Rusia," *La Nación,* XVI (November 25, 1956), pp. 4–5; "manifestación," *La Nación,* XVI (November 25, 1956), p. 5; "Mensaje del Sector Juvenil de Acción Nacional en el D.F.," *La Nación,* XVI (April 21, 1957), pp. 2, 15; "A La Juventud de México," *La Nación,* XVIII (December 21, 1958), p. 16.

20. "Coahuila, la Constitución y el rescate," *La Nación,* XVI (June 16, 1957), pp. 4–5; *La Nación,* XVI (July 7, 1957), pp. 12–13; and "Coahuila: el pueblo se organiza para la lucha . . . ," *La Nación,* XVI (July 21, 1957), pp. 11–13.

21. "Acuerdos de los Jefes Regionales," *La Nación,* XVI (May 12, 1957), pp. 14–16.

22. *La Nación,* XVI (September 22, 1957), p. 1; "Convención del PAN en el DF," *La Nación,* XVI (September 22, 1957), pp. 20–25; *La Nación,* XVI (October 6, 1957), p. 1; "En Querétaro: Ejemplar limpieza," *La Nación,* XVII (November 17, 1957), p. 17; CEN, "Sobre la Participación en la Campaña," *La Nación,* XVII (November 10, 1957), p. 36; Luis Tercero Gallardo, "XIII Convención del PAN," *La Nación,* XVII (December 1, 1957), pp. 10–23.

23. The best account of this convention is Tercero Gallardo, "XIII Convención." *Excélsior,* November 24, 25, 1957, gives less complete coverage. See also "El PAN Ya Tiene Candidato," *Siempre!,* December 4, 1957, p. 6. The reasons for the Rodríguez withdrawal were suggested by a political column in *Excélsior,* October 29, 1969, and confirmed by my interviews with PAN leaders.

24. *Plataforma Política de Acción Nacional* (1957); *La Nación,* XVII (December 1, 1957), pp. 3–4; "Entrevista: la verdad de Mexico," *La Nación,* XVII (May 25, 1958), pp. 4–8.

25. Emilio Portes Gil, *La crisis política de la revolución y la próxima eleccion presidencial* (Mexico: Ediciones Botas, 1957), pp. 92–93.

26. Manuel Gómez Morín in a letter to me, January 19, 1970, stated that the youth were reckless. Scott, *Mexican Government,* pp. 239–40, gives some of the details of the incidents which took place. The Gómez Morín letter was the source of the data on the imprisonment and flight. The assassination is recounted in "Sobre los sucesos de Chihuahua," *La Nación,* XVII (June 22, 1958), p. 2. An

example of one appeal by *panistas* to party members to abstain from violence is Luis H. Alvarez, "Sin Odios, Ni Rencores, Ni Venganza," *La Nación,* XVII (June 29, 1958), p. 2.

27. Cline, *Mexico,* p. 166; *La Nación,* XVIII (July 20, 1958), p. 9; Philip B. Taylor, Jr., "The Mexican Elections of 1958: Affirmation of Authoritarianism?" *Western Political Quarterly,* XIII (September 1960), p. 722; "Confirmación posterior; Acción Nacional reitera . . . ," *La Nación,* XVII (July 13, 1958), pp. 5–6; and "El PAN retira a su Comisionado de la DFE . . . texto integro del importante documento," *La Nación,* XVII (June 1, 1958), pp. 10–11.

28. The data on the Council meeting come from "Consejo: 'La lucha apenas se ha inciado.'—LHA," *La Nación,* XVII (July 20, 1958), pp. 13–17; and interviews and correspondence with Calderón Vega, Gómez Morín, Ayala Echávarri, Estrada Iturbide, Rafael Preciado Hernández, and Ortiz Walls.

29. "Consejo," pp. 16–17; "Definición Política de acción immediata," *La Nación,* XVII (July 20, 1958), pp. 27–31.

30. "Definición," pp. 30–32; "A La Nación," *La Nación,* XVII (July 20, 1958), pp. 2–3.

31. *La Nación,* XVII (August 10, 1958), p. 2; José R. Colín, " 'La lucha apenas comencienza,' " *La Nación,* XVII (August 17, 1958), p. 9; *La Nación,* XVII (September 14, 1958), p. 7; Scott, *Mexican Government,* pp. 167–68; and Taylor, "The Mexican Elections of 1958," pp. 722–44. Colín was a leading leftist intellectual.

32. "Que no se hable de 'campaña pasada,' " *La Nación,* XVII (August 17, 1958), pp. 17–22; "Díctamen de la Comisión Política," *La Nación,* XVII (August 17, 1958), pp. 14–16.

33. *La Nación,* XVII (August 31, 1958), pp. 4–8; *La Nación,* XVII (October 19, 1958), pp. 4–6.

34. "Eso Que Llaman Política," *Siempre!,* July 23, 1958, p. 6; Taylor, "The Mexican Elections of 1958," p. 742; *Excélsior,* July 19 and 21, 1958, p. 7.

35. José González Torres, "Al Pueblo Mexicano," *La Nación,* XVIII (June 14, 1959), pp. 2–3; A. Valencia González, "Ituarte Servín fija las Metas del PAN," *Siempre!,* April 8, 1959, p. 34.

36. *Excélsior,* March 21–23, 1959; *El Universal,* March 21–23, 1959; and *Novedades,* March 21–23, 1959, cover all these meetings. The youth meeting is given special attention in "Reunión Juvenil: Organización agresiva y movil," *La Nación,* XVIII (March 29, 1959), pp. 20–21. The Council session is reported in "Sesión del Consejo: Nuevo Comité Ejecutivo," *La Nación,* XVIII (March 29, 1959), pp. 10–11. The Assembly coverage is in "III Asamblea Extraordinaria: Reforma de los Estatutos," *La Nación,* XVIII (March 29, 1959), pp. 8–9. Gerardo Medina, "XIV Convención: Creo en Acción Nacional," *La Nación,* XVIII (March 29, 1959), pp. 12–17, contains the essential points and description of the events. Other related attitudes are found in Rafael Preciado Hernández, "Actividades en el Campo Político," in Acción Nacional, *XIV Convención Nacional* (Mexico, 1959), pp. 21–30; and Manuel González Hinojosa, "Actividades en el Campo Económico, Social y Cívico," *XIV Convención,* pp. 5–20. This section is based on these sources.

37. Scott, *Mexican Government,* p. 185, has misunderstood the changes, having interpreted them as an increase in presidential power.

38. *El Universal,* March 23, 1959.

39. Gerardo Medina, "XIV Convención," pp. 12–17; *Excélsior,* March 23, 1959;

El Universal, March 23, 1959; and interviews with Fernando Estrada Sámano and Calderón Vega. *Excélsior* used the term direct action, but PAN adopted a position of immediate action, protests, and demonstrations, and of long-term action (its continuous effort at citizen education). The *Excélsior* article appears to be why Professor Scott, an able scholar, was misled into stating that PAN had adopted a position toward violence; see his *Mexican Government,* pp. 184–85. He and Padgett, *Mexican Political System,* p. 70, apparently following Scott's lead, interpreted the convention debate as a fight between a González Luna–Gómez Mont-Youth sector faction versus a faction led by Gómez Morín in which the former won. This was not the case. González Luna and Gómez Morín were on the same side, as they usually were, and Gómez Mont was on the other side. It was not a question of "old guard" versus "new guard" because most of the youth group supported party leadership and because regional animosities played an important role.

40. Scott, *Mexican Government,* p. 185.

41. The fullest account of this election is Carlos Ortega G., *Democracia Dirigida . . . Con Ametralladoras: Baja California: 1958–1960* (El Paso, Texas: n.p., 1961). Ortega has written articles in *La Nación* but has been an independent leftist, not a *panista.* This work is well documented and includes photographs of events and newspaper stories. Ortega, as an antigovernment writer, must be used carefully, but his account is in agreement with other nonofficial sources. See Johnson, *Mexican Democracy,* pp. 134–36, for the best description in English. Mexico City newspapers and *La Nación* followed events in Baja California beginning in January 1959. Maldonado's version is found in his *Baja California: Comentarios Políticos,* 3d ed. (Mexico: B. Costa-Amic, 1960). Acción Nacional's version of the election is *El Caso de Baja California* (Mexico, 1959) and *Mas Sobre el Caso de Baja California* (Mexico, 1959).

42. Details of PAN's campaigns are found in *La Nación* beginning in January 1959; and in Acción Nacional, *El Caso.*

43. *Ultimas Noticias,* June 16, 1956; Acción Nacional, *El Caso,* pp. 1–32; Acción Nacional, *Mas Sobre El Caso de Baja California* (Mexico, December 1959), pp. 1–40; Johnson, *Mexican Democracy,* pp. 134–35.

44. Acción Nacional, *El Caso,* pp. 4–7; Acción Nacional, *Mas Sobre,* pp. 38–40; *La Nación,* XVIII (October 11, 1959), pp. 2, 18.

45. Victor Ocampo, *El Universal,* September 2, 1959; for the newspaper coverage, see Ortega G., *Democracia Dirigida,* which also presents a well-documented case; *Excélsior,* October 8, 1959; Alejandro Aviles, "Desaparación de Poderes; Nueva Elecciones!" *La Nación,* XVIII (October 11, 1959), pp. 2, 18. Kenneth F. Johnson, "Urbanization and political change in Mexico," Ph.D. dissertation, UCLA, 1964, pp. 103–7 asserts that PAN would have won in an honest election. "De Veras se va a aplicar la Ley de Responsibilidades?" *La Nación,* XIX (January 10, 1969), pp. 2–3, contains the news of the arrest.

46. "A la opinión pública," *La Nación,* XVIII (April 5, 1959), p. 2; Carlos Alvear Acevedo, "El Laicismo, ataque hipocrítica a la fé," *La Nación,* XIX (November 1, 1959), pp. 2–3; "El totalitarismo en los libros," *La Nación,* XIX (February 21, 1960), pp. 16–17; Adolfo Christlieb Ibarrola, *Monopolio Educativo o Unidad Nacional* (Mexico: Editorial Jus, 1962), passim, PAN's comprehensive statement on education involving the textbook program.

47. Manuel Rodríguez Lapuente, "Campaña de la Juventud," *La Nación,* XX (April 9, 1961), p. 3; "Manifesto a la Nación Mexicana," *La Nación,* XX (April 30, 1961), p. 2; Efraín González Morfín, "Imperialismo 'Anti-imperialista,'" *La*

Nación, XX (May 14, 1961), p. 3. *La Nación* began a series in May using the communism–social justice dichotomy.

48. See Mexico City press, July 3–7, 1961, for charges of fraud. *La Nación*, XX (August 27, 1961), pp. 8–11, and *La Nación*, XX (September 3, 1961), pp. 11–16, contain data on the party's new deputies.

49. See note 27 in Chapter II.

50. The origins of PAN have been discussed in Chapter II. Similar data on COPEI is found in Rivera Oviedo, "History and Ideology of the Christian Democratic Movement in Venezuela," unpublished M.A. thesis, University of Notre Dame, 1970, pp. 7–36; and Franklin Tugwell, "The Christian Democrats of Venezuela," *Journal of Inter-American Studies*, VII (April, 1965), pp. 245–69. For Chile, see Ernst Halperin, *Nationalism and Communism in Chile* (Cambridge: MIT Press, 1965), pp. 179–93. Interesting for comparative purposes is Mario Einsudi and Francois Goguel, *Christian Democracy in Italy and France* (South Bend, Ind.: Notre Dame Press, 1952).

51. Luis Calderón Vega, "Un mexicano ha visto una elección democrática!" *La Nación*, III (April 29, 1944), pp. 10–11; Calderón Vega, *Memorias*, p. 207, for the 1946 Caldera visit; Alejandro Aviles, "Hispanoamerica. . . ." *La Nación*, V (August 17, 1946), pp. 12–13; "Iberoamerica, *La Nación* V (August 24, 1946), pp. 12–13; "Iberoamerica: la verdadera situación de Venezuela: un golpe militar contra los comunistas," *La Nación*, VIII (February 14, 1959), p. 19; *La Nación*, XIX (January 31, 1960), p. 18; and *La Nación*, XIX (May 22, 1960), p. 17, for example of mutual support; the relations between the two are noted in Gerardo Medina, "Este es el camino de la salvación popular," *La Nación*, XXII (November 25, 1962), pp. 12–17. Data concerning the friendship between Caldera and PAN leaders and the sending of PAN observers to the Christian Democratic meetings came from interviews with many PAN leaders, including Miguel Estrada Iturbide, who attended the 1962 Santiago meeting, Enrique Creel Luján, and Manuel González Hinojosa, both of whom attended the Caracas conference.

52. To date, the best history of COPEI is the sympathetic Rivera Oviedo, "History and Ideology." Rivera Oviedo says that the Venezuelan student group which organized what became COPEI was the Unión Nacional de Estudiantes (UNE), a group extremely similar to Mexico's Unión Nacional de Estudiantes Católicos (UNEC) which founded PAN. It would be difficult for the two to have paralleled each other any more closely than they did. The historical sections of Tugwell, "Christian Democrats," pp. 245–69, as well as John D. Martz, *Accion Democratica* (Princeton, N.J.: Princeton University Press, 1966), pp. 66–67, corroborate Rivera Oviedo's interpretation.

53. José González Torres, "Que es la Democracia Cristiana," *La Nación*, XIX (December 6, 1959), p. 10; Rafael Caldera, "The Christian Democratic Idea," *America*, April 7, 1962, pp. 12–15; Eduardo Frei, "The Aims of Christian Democracy," *The Commonweal*, October 9, 1964, pp. 63–66; Partido Demócrata Cristiano (Chile), *El A.B.C. de la Democracia Cristiana* (Santiago, Chile, 1969) and PDC, Departamento Nacional de Periodistas del P.D.C., *La D.C. en marcha*, 4th ed. (Santiago, Chile: Editores de Sol de Septiembre, 1966); James Petras, *Chilean Christian Democracy: Politics and Social Forces* (Berkeley, Calif.: Institute of International Studies, 1967), pp. 12–39; Edward J. Williams, *Latin American Christian Democratic Parties* (Knoxville: University of Tennessee Press, 1967), pp. 36–65, 94–160.

54. "La organización juvenil del PAN," *La Nación*, XVI (November 25, 1956),

pp. 16–17; "Mensaje del Sector Juvenil de Acción Nacional en el D.F.," *La Nación,* XVI (April 21, 1957), pp. 2, 15; "A La Juventud de México," *La Nación,* XVIII (December 21, 1958), p. 16; "Discurso de Gutiérrez Vega: 'Ni Izquierda Ni Derecha: Democracia Cristiana!' " *La Nación,* XVIII (December 21, 1958), p. 17; "Discurso de Preciado Hernández: Para Servir al Pueblo Conquistaremos el Poder," *La Nación,* XVIII (December 21, 1958), p. 16; "Orígen y sentido de la Democracia," *La Nación,* XIX (January 27, 1960), p. 21; Rafael Preciado Hernández, "Doctrina Social Católica vs Clericalismo," *La Nación,* XX (October 1, 1961), p. 2; and *La Nación,* XXI (March 18, 1962), p. 16.

55. "Comentarios a la visita de López Mateos," *La Nación,* XIX (February 14, 1960), pp. 20–21, reprinted comments made by Caldera and other Copeyanos in their party organ, *COPEI.* Similar comments are found in "Caldera y la visita del Presidente," *La Nación,* XIX (February 21, 1960), p. 12; and "Entrevista a Alejandro Aviles," *La Nación,* XIX (May 22, 1960), p. 17. Aviles was visiting COPEI in Venezuela. The 1962 statements of Caldera are found in "Mensaje de Rafael Caldera a la Convención de Acción Nacional," *La Nación,* XXII (December 2, 1962), p. 21, which contains his entire speech to the convention; and *La Nación* (December 9, 1962), p. 31. The words of encouragement are found in *La Nación,* XIX (January 31, 1960), p. 18. The information that the German and Italian Christian Democratic parties were offering money came from interviews with Calderón Vega, Francisco Cabrera, Fernando Estrada Sámano, Salvador Morales Múñoz, and Carlos Guzmán Guerrero.

56. Acción Nacional, *Plataforma política de Acción Nacional; aprobada en la XV Convención* (Mexico, 1961); "Cuando lo Propuso El Pan No Era Bueno," *La Nación,* XXIII (November 25, 1962), pp. 2–3; response to questionnaire sent to regional party chiefs, January–February, 1970; interviews with numerous party leaders; Adolfo Christlieb Ibarrola, *Transformación de los Empresarios* (Mexico Editorial Jus, 1962), pp. 1–3; Manuel Rodríguez Lapuente, "La participación en las utilidades," *La Nación,* XXI (July 22, 1962), p. 2; Adolfo Christlieb Ibarrola, *Comentario sobre el Proyecto de Reformas de Articulo 123 de la Constitución,* reprint of a speech delivered to the *Club Sembradores de Amistad* (Sowers of Friendship Club), February 28, 1962.

57. Mexico City press, July 3–7, 1961; *La Nación,* XX (August 27, 1961), pp. 8–11; and *La Nación,* XX (September 3, 1961), pp. 11–16, contain electoral results and data on the new PAN deputies.

Chapter V: THE LIMITS OF INFLUENCE, 1962–1972

1. *La Nación,* XXVIII (December 15, 1969), pp. 5, 7; interviews with PAN leaders.

2. The term esoteric democracy was borrowed from Johnson, *Mexican Democracy.* That Christlieb was a Christian Democrat was learned from numerous *panistas.*

3. The identification of these tendencies in Acción Nacional is based on numerous interviews, conversations, and observations of *panistas* during the course of this research. It was only toward the end of the research that some *panistas* became willing to discuss these matters openly; by July and August 1971, they knew that I had talked with all four groups, and so each group made an effort to tell its views. The most valuable interviews were with Luis Calderón Vega, Eugenio Ortiz Walls, Fernando Estrada Sámano, Enrique Creel Luján, Miguel Estrada

Iturbide, federal deputy Ernesto Velasco Lafarga, and the Mejía Guerrero brothers in Morelia, Michoacán. "Capitalist" in this sense means the welfare capitalism of moderate and liberal Democrats in the United States. "Socialist" means evolutionary socialism on the Scandanavian and British models.

4. This information was supplied by many *panistas*, who must remain anonymous, and by my reading party literature and observing party leaders in action.

5. Newspaper coverage can be found in the Mexico City press for the first two weeks of April. Christlieb Ibarrola's reply to them can be found in *La Nación*, XXII (April 15, 1963), p. 18. The departure of the two youth leaders was also a result of their believing that they had not been properly rewarded for their party activity. See also Gómez Morín as quoted in Wilkie and Wilkie, *México Visto*, p. 211. Aviles, in a letter to *La Nación*, denied that he was resigning the party; see *La Nación*, XXII (May 1, 1963), p. 6.

6. As quoted in "De Política," *Mañana*, April 13, 1963, p. 23; and "La Derecha: Candidato del PAN," *Política*, December 1, 1963, pp. 16–17. Shortly after leaving PAN, Gutiérrez Vega was appointed cultural attaché in Italy, which suggested that the government had encouraged his departure; see *Excélsior*, July 16, 1963. The Mexican Christian Democratic movement never grew.

7. Adolfo Christlieb Ibarrola, "Que es Acción Nacional," *La Nación*, XXII (May 1, 1963), pp. 12–15, reprinted from an interview in *Mañana;* Christlieb Ibarrola, "Religión y Política," *Temas Políticas* (Mexico: Ediciones de Acción Nacional, 1963), pp. 29–50, reprinted from interviews in *Excélsior;* and Christlieb Ibarrola, "El Cristiano y la Política," *Solidaridad Participación* (Mexico: Ediciones de Acción Nacional, 1969), pp. 27–32.

8. The denial is in "Que es Acción Nacional"; the affirmation is in "Religión y Política," p. 40. Vicente Lombardo Toledano, "Las 5 Reformas de la Revolución Mexicana," *Siempre!*, May 7, 1964, p. 33; and José Natividad Rosales, "El Balance de una campaña; México de su Nuevo Destino," *Siempre!*, July 8, 1964, p. 51, saw PAN as a Christian Democratic party.

9. Acción Nacional, *Plataforma política y social, 1964–1970* (Mexico, 1963).

10. Christlieb Ibarrola, "Derecho al Trabajo y Libertad Política," *La Oposición* (Mexico: Ediciones de Acción Nacional, 1965), pp. 51–52. This book is a collection of articles and speeches given by the author during the 1964 campaign. Christlieb Ibarrola, "Partidos, Grupos y Acción Política," *Temas Políticas* (Mexico: Ediciones de Acción Nacional, 1963), p. 76. Christlieb Ibarrola, "Por que Luchamos En Acción Nacional," *La Oposición*, p. 67; Gerardo Medina, "La Vivienda," *La Nación*, XXIII (April 5, 1964), pp. 8–11; José González Torres, "De la Ignorancia y Su Natural Remedio, La Educación," supplement to *La Nación*, XXIII (April 26, 1964); Acción Nacional, *10 Razones Por Que Votar* (Mexico, 1964); Efraín González Morfín, "Cuestiones Social," *Cuestiones Políticas y Sociales* (Mexico: Ediciones de Acción Nacional, 1965), pp. 5–19.

11. Acción Nacional, *Principios de Doctrina—su proyección en 1965* (Mexico, 1965).

12. Acción Nacional, *Plataforma Política y Social, 1967–70* (Mexico, 1967).

13. Francisco Martínez de la Vega, "Oposición legalista en vez de Rebeldía Delirante," *Siempre!*, March 1, 1967, pp. 28–29, gave a contemporary leftist assessment, stating that PAN was no longer counterrevolutionary and, at times, spoke "inspired of a most accentuated radicalism." The similarity of PRI and PAN principles and programs can be seen in "Principios y Programa de los partidos políticos nacionales," *Pensamiento Político*, I (August 1969), pp. 501–30,

which also includes PPS and PARM documents. Comparison between PAN and these Catholic ideas is found in Antonio Delhumeau A., et al., *México: realidad política*, pp. 212–33. The official statement of the dialogue policy is Adolfo Christlieb Ibarrola, *Libertad Frente al Poder, agilidad y verdad ante el Pueblo*, supplement to *La Nación*, XXVII (April 1, 1968).

14. Examples are "Acción Nacional enjuicia el primer informe del Presidente Díaz Ordaz," supplement to *La Nación*, XXIV (September 1, 1965) and *La oposición democrática enjuicia el segundo informe del Presidente Díaz Ordaz* (Mexico, 1966); Supplement to *La Nación*, XXVII (April 1, 1968), p. 11.

15. The text is found in "Declaraciones del Partido Acción Nacional . . . ," *La Nación*, XXVIII (July 19, 1964), p. 233.

16. Since 1963, Congressional deputy seats are won two ways: election by a majority of votes (these deputies are called *diputados de mayoría*, majority deputies) and by receiving a very high number of votes (these deputies are called *diputados de partido*, party deputies). According to the terms of the law which created the party deputy system, national political parties are given five seats in the Chamber of Deputies if they win 2.5 percent of the national vote. For every additional 0.5 percent of the vote, they receive an additional seat, up to a maximum of twenty seats. If a party wins twenty seats by a majority of votes, it is not entitled to party deputies. If a party wins five seats by majority votes, then its maximum number of party deputies becomes fifteen. PAN's vote totals were high enough before the law was passed to guarantee twenty seats to it. The law was designed to give minority parties, such as PAN, more voice in the Chamber without reducing the number of PRI deputies.

17. Interviews with Calderón Vega, Creel Luján, Francisco Cabrera, Miguel and Fernando Estrada Sámano; Fuentes Díaz, *Los partidos políticos*, p. 31. Fuentes Díaz was a PRI senator from Guerrero for the 1970–76 term.

18. "Un gran victoria parlamentaria del Partido Acción Nacional," *La Nación*, XXIII (January 1, 1964), pp. 17–21.

19. Javier Blanco Sánchez, "Protección al capital nacional bancario," *La Nación*, XXV (January 1, 1966), p. 19; the party position on foreign investments is detailed in Adolfo Christlieb Ibarrola, *Inversiones Extranjeras En México* (Mexico, 1965); Christlieb Ibarrola, "Comentario Sobre el Proyecto."

20. Adolfo Christlieb Ibarrola, *Informe al Consejo 5 de Febrero de 1966* (Mexico, 1966), pp. 3–6. See also Chapter VI of the present study.

21. Johnson, *Mexican Democracy*, p. 126.

22. "El PAN Gana A Pulso Con Votos 20 Curules; El PPS y El PARM Sin Votos Reciben 14 Regaladas," *La Nación*, XXIII (September 6, 1964), pp. 9–18. The breakdown of votes for Acción Nacional by states as well as the percentage figures for both elections are found in "Cifras Comparativas de las Votaciones Para Diputados Federales Del PAN," *La Nación*, XXVI (July 15, 1967), p. 1. These figures agree with Federal Election Commission data reported in Mexico City newspapers.

23. This event was reported in the Mexico City press, April 18–22, 1967. This was a district, however, which traditionally sent a *panista* to the Chamber of Deputies. Federico Estrada Valera, PAN district chief, left the party shortly after; Mexico City *News*, April 20–21, 1967; *Tiempo*, April 24, 1967, pp. 9–10; " 'Cisma' y 'crisis' en el PAN," *La Nación*, XXVI (May 1, 1967), p. 8. He had been a dissident for a number of years and his departure had no significant effect.

24. "Plena ratificación de la confianza," *La Nación*, XXV (February 15, 1966),

pp. 12–15; and Gustavo Mora, "La Oposición se Desmorona," *Novedades,* January 5, 1966, pp. 1, 8. Felipe Gómez Mont, one of those who was reported dissatisfied with the leadership, denied any conflict between himself and the party president in *La Nación,* XXV (January 15, 1966), p. 5, and in *Novedades,* January 7, 1966.

25. "XIX Convención Nacional—Debate sobre la Plataforma . . . Testimonio de la Democracia," *La Nación,* XXVI (March 1, 1967), pp. 11–13. The report of the political commission is found in "Dictamen de la Comisión Política . . . ," *La Nación,* XXVI (March 1, 1967), pp. 4–5; *Excélsior,* February 13, 1967.

26. For 1964, see "El PAN Gana a Pulso con votos 20 curules; el PPS y el PARM sin votos reciben 14 regaladas," *La Nación,* XXIII (September 6, 1964), pp. 9–18; "El díctamen del colegio electoral sobre diputados del partido," *La Nación,* XXIII (October 1, 1964), pp. 23–26. The Mexican Foreign Relations Minister, interviewed in Portugal, was quoted in *Excélsior* (September 1, 1964) as saying that the PPS had scarcely more than 1 percent of the vote. For 1967, see Mexico City *News,* July 24 and August 31, 1967; Juan Manuel Gómez Morín, "Diputados De (Y Sin) Partido: ante la mala fe de un 'pobre e ignorante mexicano,'" *La Nación,* XXVI (October 1, 1967), pp. 24–25.

27. These events can be followed in the Mexico City press. The Mexico City *News,* June 6, 1967, has an interesting analysis of the causes of this conflict. The announcement of PAN's entry into the squabble is in the *News,* May 26, 1967, and *La Nación,* XXVI (June 1, 1967), pp. 2–5. The best account of the election, upon which this study draws, is Johnson, *Mexican Democracy,* pp. 133–34. See also Mabry, "Acción Nacional," pp. 256–59.

28. "Sonora para la Democracia," *La Nación,* XXVI (June 1, 1967), pp. 2–3, gives the biographical details.

29. Gilberto Moreno, "A quien pretende que enganara el Gobierno?" *La Nación,* XXVI (July 15, 1967), pp. 8–13. There is, of course, no way to know who really won. Government officials have told me that PAN won. That is also the sense of Johnson, *Mexican Democracy,* pp. 133–34. Ronald H. McDonald, *Party Systems and Elections in Latin America* (Chicago: Markham, 1971), pp. 258–95, believes PAN won.

30. The Baja California regional committee had published a book of studies it had made on the state, *Seis Estudios sobre Baja California* (Mexico: Ediciones de Acción Nacional, 1964). The degree of organization information came from Luis Calderón Vega and various Baja California delegates to the November 1969 national convention.

31. Johnson, *Mexican Democracy,* p. 136.

32. Manuel Gutiérrez Aguilar, *La Derrota Del Régimen* (Hermosillo, Sonora: Imprenta Regional, 1971) is a pro-PAN but essentially accurate account of the events. Johnson, *Mexican Democracy,* pp. 134–40 is excellent.

33. *Excélsior,* June 1–2, 1968. A June 2, 1968, article reported that bankers, industrialists, Chambers of Commerce, and Chambers of Industries of Transformation spoke directly or indirectly for PRI.

34. *Tiempo,* June 10, 1968, pp. 27–28; *Excélsior,* June 4–7, 1968; Johnson, *Mexican Democracy,* pp. 139–40; and Gutiérrez Aguilar, *La Derrota,* pp. 62 ff. *Excélsior,* June 7, 1968 has two full-page advertisements by the Acción Nacional municipal committees in Mexicali and Tijuana. The official PAN statement on the events surrounding the election is Adolfo Christlieb Ibarrola, *Baja California*

Avanzada de la Democracia (Mexico, 1968). The electoral figures cited therein vary considerably from official figures.

35. Manuel Becerra Acosta, Jr., "Desayuno," *Excélsior*, June 9, 1968, pp. 1, 16, 18; Editorial, "Democracia en B.C.," *Excélsior*, June 4, 1968.

36. Johnson, *Mexican Democracy*, pp. 139–40; Guillermo Jordan, "Antonia Democrática en Baja California: El Poder de la Minoría," *Ultimas Noticias*, August 6, 1971. That a non-PAN columnist asserted in a Mexico City daily that PAN won is an almost unprecedented act. The legislative manipulations can be followed in Christlieb Ibarrola, *Baja California*, pp. 17–18.

37. *Tiempo*, September 23, 1968, pp. 14–15; Christlieb Ibarrola, *Baja California* is the appeal to the Supreme Court. See also *Excélsior*, June 20, 1968.

38. Johnson, "The Saliency of Alienation: Mire + Muro + Sph = Tlatelolco," *Mexican Democracy*, pp. 148–64. This is the most penetrating analysis of the events. My comments are also based upon media accounts, interviews, and Roberto Blanco Moheno, *Tlatelolco: Historia de una infamia*, 4th ed. (Mexico: Editorial Diana, 1969). See Mexico City *News* and *Excélsior*, August 30–31, 1968, for PAN's support of the students, and *Tiempo*, October 7, 1968, pp. 12–14, for its condemnation of the Tlatelolco incident.

39. *Tiempo*, September 23, 1968, p. 16; Mexico City *News*, November 26, 1968.

40. *La Prensa*, September 23, 1969; Fuentes Díaz, *Los partidos políticos*, pp. 313–14; "La Elección de González Hinojosa . . . ," *La Nación*, XXVIII (February 15, 1969), pp. 8–9.

41. "La Elección de González Hinojosa," p. 28.

42. This section of the study is based on José Antonio Arce Caballero, "Polvorín Yucateco," *gente*, November 1, 1969, pp. 20–22; Abraham López Lara, "Una Nueva Era?:Elecciones en Yucatán," *Excélsior*, November 17, 1969, pp. 6, 8–9; Roberto Blanco Moheno, "Hay Dos Castas en Yucatán Ahora," *Siempre!*, November 12, 1969, p. 30; Mario Menéndez Rodríguez, "Correa Rachó Habla a *Por Que?*" *Por Que?*, November 6, 1969, pp. 2–23; "La Votación Legal Favoreció a Correa Rachó," *Por Que?*, extraordinary issue (December 1969), pp. 28–29; Alejandro Sánchez Ch., "Yucatán: La muerte de una Esperanza," *gente*, December 16, 1969, pp. 11–14; the Mexico City and Mérida press from August through December 1969; Johnson, *Mexican Democracy*, pp. 140–42; interviews with *panistas* and with government officials (who must remain anonymous). The magazine *gente* is a conservative, non-PAN publication, whereas *Por Que?* is an independent Marxist-left publication; both agree on this issue.

43. Robert Bezdek, an American political scientist who was in Yucatán at the time studying the election, attended rallies of both parties. He is currently preparing a study of this election, that of Sonora (1967), and Baja California (1968) which promises to shed additional light on Mexican opposition politics. I wish to thank Professor Bezdek for his aid.

44. Arce Caballero, "Polvorín Yucateco," pp. 12–14.

45. *Excélsior*, November 21, 1969.

46. *Excélsior*, November 23, 1969.

47. Alejandro Sánchez Ch., "Yucatán: La muerte de una Esperanza," pp. 11–14. The foreign reporters were from Reuters, UPI, Visión, Journal de Brazil, France Presse, and AP. They are quoted in *El Universal Gráfico*, November 24, 1969. See also Juan de Onís, *New York Times*, November 24, 1969.

48. *Excélsior*, November 24–26, 1969; *Ultimas Noticias*, November 24, 1969; *El Heraldo de México*, November 25, 1969; and *Novedades*, November 25, 1969,

49. *Excélsior* and *El Universal,* November 10, 1969; *La Nación,* XXVIII (November 15, 1969), pp. 7–15, 31.

50. The convention and the vote were reported in the Mexico City press and *La Nación. La Nación* is the best source since its coverage is more complete. Enrique Creel Luján provided the data on the CEN vote split. The regionalism problem was evident from the speeches and from conversation with delegates.

51. One of these was Aníbal de Iturbide, one of Mexico's leading bankers and a founder of PAN; see "La Revolución y el Banquero," *Tiempo,* LVI (March 16, 1970), pp. 23–25.

52. The major campaign speeches were reprinted in their entirety in fifteen pamphlets. All were authored by Efraín González Morfín and published by Acción Nacional in Mexico City in 1970. They are: *Juventud; Individualismo, Colectivismo, Solidarismo; Educación y Magisterio; Congruencia de Vida Privada y Pública; Cambio Democrático de Estructuras; Democracia O Violencia; Trabajo; Planeación y Desarrollo; Sociedades Intermedias; Colonialismo Interno; Orden Internacional y La Farsa Electoral; Libertad de Conciencia; Propiedad Pública y Privada; Igualdad y Derechos Humanos* and *Metas de la Protesta Juvenil;* and *Complementación Agrícola—Industrial.* Syntheses of these speeches were published in 1970 by PAN as *Campaña 1970,* nos. 14 and 15 of Ediciones de Acción Nacional.

53. These data come from two sources. I was frequently in PAN national offices from September 1969 to April 1970, and again in July and August 1971, during which time numerous students and workers were coming into these offices to join the party. In July and August 1971, I had long interviews with José G. Minondo, Federal District regional president, and Eugenio Ortiz Walls, *oficial mayor* of PAN. They and other *panistas* were making such assertions about the changes in party membership. On this question, I believe they are trustworthy. In addition, Luis Calderón Vega, in the internal training document "Seminario de Orientación Social y Política: Sus Propósitos," p. 1, asserted that the party was changing to a mass party composed in its majority by the humble and middle classes.

54. The vote figures were released by the Federal Election Commission and by PRI to Mexico City dailies; see *El Día,* July 18, 1970. The statement that González Morfín carried the deputy candidates with him is based on my judgment that PAN had been having difficulties in finding enough candidates, indicated in part by the fact that the party did not run a full slate.

55. "Mas Fuertes Por Mas Unidos, Vamos a Ser Mas Eficaces," *La Nación,* XXX (February 15, 1971), pp. 21–24.

56. These documents were for internal circulation only. I obtained them from Luis Calderón Vega. Because they were written only for intraparty use, they provide an invaluable insight into PAN's thinking in 1971. All were mimeographed by PAN in its national offices. Luis Calderón Vega directed their preparation. They are: Luis Calderón Vega, "Seminario de Orientación Social y Política:sus Propósitos," 3 pp.; PAN, "Cuaderno de Trabajo," 16 pp.; Luis Calderón Vega, "Tema 1: La Nación y el Bien Común," 14 pp.; Efraín González Morfín, "Doctrina de Acción Nacional," 17 pp.; J. Blas Briseño, "Tema III: Partidos Políticos, Notas Históricas de Acción Nacional," 15 pp.; Luis Calderón Vega, "Tema IV: Doctrina y Posiciones del P.A.N.," 18 pp.

57. The proposed reforms are in Acción Nacional, "Proyecto de Reformas a Los Estatutos de Acción Nacional," mimeographed, 17 pp. Partial coverage of the

reforms adopted in the August meeting is found in Luis Alberto García Orosa, "Reforma de estatutos: no solución, sino aprovechamiento de experencias," *La Nación*, XXX (September 1, 1971), pp. 2–6.

58. Mexico City newspapers began coverage of the events on June 11, 1971. The National Broadcasting Company of the United States also showed film clips of the events of June 10. Acción Nacional's version is found in "10 de Junio de 1971: Jornada de Sangre y Cieno," *la batalla 71*, no. 17, passim.

59. *Excélsior*, June 11, 1971.

60. *Excélsior*, June 16, 1971. The resignations had the appearance of actually being dismissals, or at least that was the common interpretation in Mexico at the time.

61. Manuel González Hinojosa, "El Informe de González Hinojosa," supplement to *La Nación*, XXX (September 1, 1971), pp. vii–viii.

62. Ernesto Julio Teissier, "Columna de Media Semana," *Novedades*, August 4, 1971, p. 23; Jordan, "Antonia Democratica,"; Editorial, "Abstención: Voto de Censura," *Excélsior*, August 7, 1971.

63. "Del Análisis de la Situación: Hacer historicamente posibles nuestros ideales de servir a México," *La Nación*, XXX (September 1, 1971), pp. 14–16; *PAN, Asambleas Generales 7ᴬ Ordinarias—5ᴬ Extraordinaria—Documentos* (Mexico, 1971), pp. 25–57. The following discussion is based on these two documents.

64. González Hinojosa, "Informe," p. viii, is the statement by the president of the party. The "Del Analisis" article (p. 16) also makes the same judgment. My comments are also based on having observed and interviewed *panistas* for two years. The changes which this chapter relates were very apparent, and I had the opportunity to conduct long and penetrating interviews with *panistas* of all levels. The Yucatán experience in 1969 and the June 10 conflict of 1971 had drastically altered their perceptions of Mexican politics. Party leaders were working to avoid the adoption of violence as a tactic while finding a more satisfactory means of changing Mexico.

Chapter VI: DOCTRINE, PROGRAM, APPEALS

1. González Graf and Ramírez Lugo, "Partido Acción Nacional," *México: realidad política de sus partidos*, pp. 212–33, have a chart comparing PAN ideology to these sources (except Maritain). PAN's ideological statements are too numerous to cite here. The bibliographical essay at the end of this study discusses them and Catholic social doctrines. Citations will be used only for specific purposes.

2. Luis Calderón Vega, introduction to *Humanismo político*, p. 9; Efraín González Luna, "La Dignidad del Trabajo," *Humanismo político*, p. 257, refers to PAN ideology as Christian Humanism. Williams, *Latin American Christian Democratic Parties*, p. 52. Maritain calls his philosophy true humanism.

3. For the PAN view, see Efraín González Luna, *El Hombre y el Estado* (Mexico: Acción Nacional, 1940) and Calderón Vega, *Memorias*, p. 42. For the Latin American Christian Democrats' identical view, see Williams, *Latin American Christian Democratic Parties*, pp. 52 ff. Efraín González Luna, "Propósitos y Condiciones de la Reforma Social," *Humanismo político*, pp. 272–73, also defines PAN's attitude.

4. González Graf and Ramírez Lugo, "Partido Acción Nacional," pp. 192–93, make this assessment. *Panistas* have consistently made this argument as well, especially in tactical debates. See Efraín González Luna, "Técnica de Salvación,"

Humanismo político, pp. 15–25, a speech he gave during the tactical debate of the first national convention in 1939.

5. Acción Nacional's view of international affairs to 1955 is summarized best in "Panamericanismo e Hispandidad," the fifth section of *Humanismo político,* pp. 309–79, a collection of speeches and articles by González Luna; see also Efraín González Luna, "Una guerra ideológica; causes, pretextos, desmenes—los casos de España, Portugal y Argentina . . . 'una guerra antimaquivéllica que terminen con la apoteosis del maquiavellismo,' " *La Nación,* V (November 3, 1945), pp. 6–7; and "Opinión," *La Nación,* III (May 20, 1944), pp. 23–25. References to the special relations between Mexico and Hispanic nations can be found in the *Principios de Doctrina* (Mexico: PAN, 1939) and *Programa Mínimo de Acción Política* (Mexico: PAN, 1940).

6. See Chapter III, note 37.

7. "Un Panamericanismo en Busca de Nombre," *Humanismo político,* pp. 319–25, originally published in *La Nación,* I (December 6, 1941); "La America de Mestizaje," *Humanismo político,* pp. 331–36, originally published in *La Nación,* I (November 22, 1942); "La Nación en el Choque de los Imperios," *Humanismo político,* pp. 343–58, originally published in *Boletín de Acción Nacional,* (March 17, 1941), in which he said: "Not even do we need to subscribe to transplantations of the victorious political regime in Spain that serves hispanidad but cannot be identified with it" (p. 356); and "Retorno a lo Nuestro," *Humanismo político,* pp. 359–67, originally published in *La Nación,* I (December 27, 1941). See also Gumersindo Galván, Jr., "Los partidos políticos y la emergencia nacional," *La Nación,* I (December 20, 1941), p. 7. Part of my judgment is based on interviews with Luis Calderón Vega, Ernesto Ayala Echavárri, and Dr. Edmundo Meouchi. Dr. Meouchi was a fascist sympathizer at the time.

8. See, for example, Efraín González Luna, "Isabel la Católica," *Humanismo político,* pp. 309–18.

9. Acción Nacional, *Cambio Democrático de las Estructuras,* p. v.

10. Turner, *Catholicism and Political Development,* pp. 11–19, 139–93; and Williams, *Latin American Christian Democratic Parties,* pp. 240–58, indicate the goals of the left wing of the Christian Democratic movement.

11. González Graf and Ramírez Lugo, "Partido Acción Nacional," p. 173.

12. González Graf and Ramírez Lugo, "Partido Acción Nacional," pp. 226–33.

13. For example, see Gómez Morín, "Informe a la Asamblea Constituyente de Acción Nacional," pp. 4–8; Gómez Morín, "Informe rendido en Chilpancingo," pp. 163, 173–74; Efraín González Luna, introduction to *Diez Años,* pp. xii–xiii; and "Espigas Políticas: Doctrina," *Hoy* (September 16, 1939), p. 10. González Graf and Ramírez Lugo, "Partido Acción Nacional," pp. 202–3 also recognized this.

14. The classic statement is Efraín González Luna, "Mecánica de Opción y Opción Moral," *Humanismo político,* pp. 38–49, but it abounds in PAN literature.

15. González Graf and Ramírez Lugo, "Partido Acción Nacional," p. 173. Even a cursory glance at these platforms confirms this.

16. See the *Programa Mínimo de Acción Política,* pp. 9–11, which was reprinted through 1949 without change, and the campaign platforms since 1952. These will not be individually cited; the pertinent bibliographical information is located in the bibliographic essay. PAN studies and recommendations on rural problems are Acción Nacional, *Pequeña Propriedad* (Mexico: PAN, 1943), 16 pp.; Roberto Cossío y Cosío and Pedro Zuloaga, *Estudio Sobre el Problema*

Agrario (Mexico: PAN, ca. 1943), 32 pp.; and Manuel Ulloa Ortiz, *Problemas del Campo Mexicano (Aspecto Económico)* (Mexico: PAN, 1960), 36 pp.

17. *Reforma del Art. 27 constitucional para proteger a los ejidatarios y pequeños proprietarios,* legislative proposal presented to Chamber of Deputies, October 17, 1946.

18. Acción Nacional, *La Crísis Económica* (Mexico: PAN, 1948), pp. 6–12, 16, contains the legislative bills; Acción Nacional, *Urgencia de Asegurar el Renimiento de las Siembras* (Mexico: PAN, 1948); and "La Gran Esperanza de la Seguridad Social," in Manuel Gómez Morín, *Seguridad Social* (Mexico: Ediciones de Acción Nacional, 1966), pp. 67–76.

19. *Ley que crea la Comisión Nacional de Planeación del Campo,* bill introduced into the Chamber of Deputies, October 20, 1947. PAN's interest in planning, as shown by this bill, clearly demonstrates that they did not believe in laissez-faire economic theory.

20. *Ley de Organización del Patrimonio Familiar.*

21. *Reforma al Art. 115 para otorgar el voto municipal a la mujer, devoter sus bienes y derechos y garantizar su libertad a los Municipios,* introduced in the Chamber of Deputies, December 23, 1946, was the attempt to implement the party's municipal program. Municipal government has been a primary PAN concern since 1939 and the party has produced a substantial body of literature on the subject. Besides the *Principios de Doctrina* (1939), *Principios de Doctrina—su proyección en 1965, Cambio Democrático de las Estructuras, Programa Mínimo de Acción Política,* and the platforms (1943–70), the most important documents are Acción Nacional, *La ciudad: necesidad del municipio libre* (Mexico, 1942), and *Esquema de un programa municipal* (Guadalajara, 1942); Manuel Gómez Morín, *Importancia Vital del Municipio* (Mexico, 1947); and Efraín González Luna, *Naturaleza y funciones del municipio* (Guadalajara, 1940), and *Ruina y esperanza del municipio mexicano* (Mexico, 1942).

22. Acción Nacional, *Plataforma política y social, 1967–1970* (Mexico: PAN, 1967).

23. Acción Nacional, *Plataforma política y social, 1970–1976* (Mexico: PAN, 1969).

24. *Iniciativa de reformas a la base primera de la fracción VI del artículo 73 de la Constitución Política de los Estados Unidos Mexicanos* (Mexico: PAN, 1965), and *Iniciativa de reformas a la ley orgánica del Distrito Federal* (Mexico: PAN, 1965).

25. See the *Programa Mínimo* and PAN's platforms since 1952 for the general educational program. Acción Nacional, *Libertad de Enseñanza: Reforma Constitucional* (Mexico: PAN, 1941), contains PAN's proposed reforms to Article 3. José González Torres, *De la ignorancia y su natural remedio, la educación* (Mexico: PAN, 1964), and Christlieb Ibarrola, *Monopolio Educativo O Unidad Nacional* (Mexico: Editorial Jus, 1962), are the best statements of PAN's educational position in the 1960s.

26. *Iniciativa de Ley de Educación Rural para promoverla y ampliarla,* introduced October 31, 1963.

27. *Iniciativa de Ley para crear la Comisión Nacional de Crédito Escolar,* November 5, 1968.

28. *Proposición presentada para que se aumenten los sueldos a los maestros de Primaria en el Distrito Federal,* December 3, 1968.

29. *Reformas a la Ley Federal del Trabajo contra los abusos de los líderes y*

con otras garantías para los obreros, October 20, 1948; see also Acción Nacional, *La Crísis Económica,* p. 14. *Tiempo,* February 20, 1948, p. 7, remarked that PAN was moving toward more workerism, following the lead given by Leo XIII.

30. *Ley de Garantías del Trabajador y del Sindicato,* October 30, 1951, and *Reformas a la Ley Federal del Trabajo para garantizar la democracia sindical y la libertad política de los trabajadores,* December 30, 1966.

31. *Reforma a la Ley Federal del Trabajo* (1948); *Ley de Garantías* (1951); and *Reformas a la Ley Federal del Trabajo* (1966).

32. "La Gran Esperanza de la Seguridad Social," pp. 67–76, and *La Crísis Económica,* pp. 14–16.

33. *Reformas a la Ley de Pensiones, en beneficio de los burocratas del Estado,* December 10, 1956.

34. *Inicitativa de Ley que crea un organismo público denominado Servicio Nacional de Empleo,* October 8, 1968.

35. *Initiativa de ley que reforma el Art. 21 constitucional con el fin de que las multas administrativas no excedan del importe de un día y medio de salario, cuando los infractores sean ejidatarios, comuneros, minifundistas, trabajadores no asalariados, mujeres y menores de 18 años que dependan economicamente de otra persona,* November 12, 1968. Passed December 17, 1968.

36. See the Mexico City dailies' coverage for fall 1969. PAN specifically attacked COPARMEX, the Mexican Employers' Association, for resisting the bill, as well as organized labor's leadership for settling for less than labor needed. Since this was gratuitous, it may have represented demagoguery on PAN's part. From interviews with *panistas,* however, this author believes the party was sincere.

37. *Reformas a la Ley de Imprenta para frenar la pornografía,* November 30, 1965. This proposal reflected PAN's Catholic heritage. One should remember that Mexicans are less tolerant of nudity in printed matter than are Americans and many Europeans; this proposal would have prevented the publication of seminude or nude photographs, for example.

38. *Reformas al Código Penal para proteger del abandono de persona a la conyuge y a los hijos y para sancionar a litigantes sin escrupulos,* December 22, 1966.

39. *Iniciativa para establecer, en el Código Civil del Distrito Federal, la institución jurídica conocida como "separación personal" y proteger con ello la institución familiar,* October 23, 1969. PAN's Catholic concern for avoiding divorce can also be seen in *Iniciativa de decreto para suprimir la causal de divorcio prevista en el artículo 267, fracción IX del Código Civil para el Distrito y Territorios,* December 26, 1969.

40. *Ley sobre Complemento Familiar del Salario: sistema de compensaciones en función del número de personas que dependen del trabajador.* December 30, 1966.

41. *Iniciativa de reformas al Art. 54 de la Ley del Seguro Social, tendiente a prorrogar el derecho de beneficiarios del Seguro a los hijos del asegurado; hasta los 21 años cumplidos, cuando sean estudiantes.* December 29, 1967.

42. Besides the *Programa Mínimo* and the platforms, see *Necesidad de Rehabilitar los Ferrocarriles Nacionales; Reforma de la Ley que Creo la Administración de los Ferrocarriles* (Mexico, 1948); *La Crisis Económica,* passim; *Falsificación de un Mercado de Valores* (Mexico, 1948); *La Moneda y el Crédito Instrumentos Básicos de la Economía* (Mexico, 1948); and Adolfo Christlieb Ibarrola, *Inver-*

siones Extranjeras en México (Mexico: PAN, 1965). PAN's earliest documents are significantly more conservative on economic statism.

43. *Aprovechamiento de recursos naturales* (Mexico: PAN, 1943) is an early demand for multisectorial planning after making an inventory of national resources. *La Crisis Económica* contains planning proposals for agriculture and railroads. See also *Programa Mínimo* and *Principios de Doctrina* (1939). Efraín González Morfín, *Planeación y Desarrollo* (Mexico: PAN, 1970), a campaign speech is the most recent statement of the party's position.

44. According to Robert J. Shafer, of the Syracuse University history department, whose study of organized business in Mexico is in press.

45. *Reformas a los artículos 73 y 74 para responsabilizar a las empresas descentralizadas o de participación estatal, exigiendo rendición de cuentas,* October 1953, and *Iniciativa de reformas a la Ley para el control, por parte del Gobierno Federal, de los organismos descentralizados y de empresas de participación estatal,* December 4, 1968.

46. *Moción suspensiva del dictamen sobre la iniciativa presidencial que crea el 1% de impuesto para educación, que viene a gravar a los asalariados,* December 15, 1962. This action put Acción Nacional in the unenviable position of appearing to oppose public education.

47. *Iniciativa para crear el Fondo de Fomento Económico Regional,* December 15, 1968.

48. Christlieb Ibarrola, *Inversiones Extranjeras,* passim.

49. *Iniciativa de reformas a la Ley General de Bienes Nacionales para proteger las riquezas del subsuelo y, en particular, las llamadas petrolíferas en las zonas fronterizas y en la plataforma continental,* October 14, 1969.

50. *Reformas al Art. 107 para hacer la justicia mas pronta y expedita y evitar el sobreseimiento de ciertos amparos,* October 15, 1953.

51. *Reformas al la Ley de Amparo para proteger mas eficazmente la libertad personal,* December 6, 1966, and *Iniciativa de Ley para adicionar la Ley de Amparo, dando facultades a las partes, en juicio de amparo, para presentar proyectos de sentencia y para que los Ministros puedan hacer suyos cualesquiera de esos proyectos, con lo que se daría mayor rapidez a los juicios y se desahogaría el tremendo retraso que existe en la Corte,* October 10, 1968.

52. *Reformas el Código de Procedimientos Penales para garantizar la libertad de los inculpados,* December 27, 1966.

53. *Petición para que la Camara solicite la intervención de la Suprema Corte de Justicia en la investigación de los hechos occurridos con motivo de las elecciones locales en Baja California,* November 10, 1968.

54. Two examples are *Mas Sobre el Caso de Baja California* (Mexico: PAN, 1959); and *A La Opinión Pública: Chihuahua y La Suprema Corte* (Mexico: PAN, 1956).

55. *Intervención de la Suprema Corte de Justicia para garantía de los derechos personales y ciudadanos* (Mexico: PAN, 1947).

56. *Reformas al Código Penal para incluir y distinguir varias figuras delictivas de genocidio,* October 19, 1965.

57. *Iniciativa para reformas los artículos 27, 42, y 48 de la Constitución política de los Estados Unidos Mexicanos para incluir expresamente el Golfo de California dentro del territorio nacional, bajo el dominio de la Federación, suscrita por los CC. Diputados a XLVI Legislatura, miembros del Partido Acción Nacional,* No-

vember 19, 1965, and *Iniciativa para reformar el articulo 17 de la Ley de Bienes Nacionales,* November 27, 1966.

58. "Cuando lo Propuso el PAN no era Bueno," *La Nación,* XXIII (November 25, 1962), pp. 2–3.

59. This is the PAN view of the Mexican political system found in political platforms and such works as González Luna, *Humanismo político;* Gómez Morín, *Diez Años;* and, recently, Adolfo Christlieb Ibarrola, *Partido y gobierno* (Mexico: PAN, 1966). PAN wants a democratic state along the lines of those in the United States, Europe, and various Latin American countries instead of what it considers to be the myth of democracy in Mexico. Most of the published nonpartisan scholarly commentary on the Mexican political system agrees with this aspect of the PAN analysis; see Brandenburg, *Modern Mexico,* pp. 141–65; Scott, *Mexican Government,* pp. 294–318; Padgett, *Mexican Political System,* passim; Johnson, *Mexican Democracy,* passim; and James W. Wilkie, *The Mexican Revolution: Federal Expenditure and Social Change Since 1910* (Berkeley and Los Angeles: University of California Press, 1967), among others.

60. *Reforma al Art. 115 para otogar de voto municipal a la mujer, devolver sus bienes y derechos y garantizar su libertad a los Municipios,* December 23, 1946; "La discusión del voto a la mujer en la Cámara de Diputados," *La Nación,* VI (January 4, 1947), pp. 8–9.

61. Presented as part of PAN's proposed reforms to the Federal Electoral Law, October 12, 1948. For its inclusion in the 1949 campaign platform, see *La Nación,* VIII (March 7, 1949), and *Excélsior,* February 27–28, 1949. Women were granted the right to vote in federal elections in the 1952–53 congressional session.

62. *Excélsior, El Universal,* and Mexico City *News,* fall 1969.

63. The 1947 proposals are found in Acción Nacional, *Contra la corrupción electoral* (Mexico: PAN, 1947) and *Ley del Registro Nacional de Electores,* October 3, 1947; the 1948 proposal was *Reformas constitucionales para crear el Tribunal de Elecciones,* November 12, 1948; *Reformas para crear el Registro Permanente de Electores y establecer el sistema de diputados de partido en los Congresos Locales, y de Senadores de Partido, y renovación y utilización del Senado,* December 7, 1966, contains the 1966 proposal. The 1968 proposal is found in *Iniciativa de reformas a la Ley Federal Electoral,* December 20, 1968.

64. *Reformas a la Ley Electoral para prohibir la utilización de los colores de la Bandera como distinctivos de partido,* October 29, 1957.

65. *Excélsior,* December 27, 1957.

66. See Chapter V for a discussion of the party deputy system. Manuel González Hinojosa, quoted in "El jefe del Partido aclara a 'Excélsior,'" *La Nación,* XXIX (August 1, 1970), pp. 16–18, made this assertion, one which I heard many times from *panistas.*

67. *Reformas para crear el Registro Permanente de Electores y establecer el sistema de diputados de partido en los Congresos Locales . . . ,* December 7, 1966. Christlieb Ibarrola began arguing for this extension of the party deputy system during the 1964 federal election campaign; see his "Por Que luchamos en Acción Nacional," *La oposición* (Mexico: Ediciones de Acción Nacional, 1965), p. 67. The proposal was also included in the 1967 and 1970 platforms.

68. *Excélsior,* November 4–5, 1947; Acción Nacional, *La función esencial de aprobar los gastos públicos* (Mexico: PAN, 1947); *Excélsior,* December 31, 1968; *Excélsior,* December 13, 1967; and *Iniciativa de reforma a los artículos 1, 85, 94,*

y 179 del reglamento para el gobierno interior del Congreso General de los Estados Unidos Mexicanos (Mexico: PAN, 1965); *Iniciativa para crear una Comisión que restaure y proteja el archivo del Congreso de la Unión,* December 30, 1966; and *Inicitiativa de reformas al Art. 18, contra el proyecto del Ejecutivo, para evitar que se reduzca mas la soberanía de los Estados,* October 13, 1964.

69. Examples are Brandenburg, *Modern Mexico,* pp. 127–29; Scott, *Mexican Government,* pp. 182–86; Padgett, *Mexican Political System,* pp. 67–73; Fuentes Díaz, *Los partidos políticos,* pp. 293–320.

70. Based on interviews with such *panistas* as Gómez Morín, González Hinojosa, Calderón Vega, Ortiz Walls, Creel Luján, and González Morfin. That the party needs to occupy positions of power to be seen as a real alternative is self-evident, of course.

Chapter VII: STRUCTURE: DESCRIPTION AND OPERATION

1. See Cline, *The United States and Mexico,* pp. 326–27; William P. Tucker, *The Mexican Government Today* (Minneapolis: University of Minnesota Press, 1957), pp. 65–67; and Padgett, *Mexican Political System,* pp. 79–80.

2. Padgett, *Mexican Political System,* pp. 79–80.

3. Mexico, Comisión Federal Electoral, Secretaría de Gobernación, *Ley Electoral Federal* (Mexico: Talleres Gráficos de la Nación, 1951), and *Ley Electoral Federal* (Mexico, 1964). The 1951 edition of the law is identical to the 1945 edition.

4. Acción Nacional has made few statutory changes. The original statutes were Acción Nacional, *Estatutos* (Mexico, 1939). The 1951 edition of the 1949 *Estatutos* represented not substantive changes but slight alterations to meet the 1945 Federal Electoral Law. The *Reglamentos* (Mexico: PAN, 1943) governed membership and intraparty regulations, particularly between the national level and lower levels; in 1959, they were incorporated, intact, into the *Estatutos Generales* (Mexico: PAN, 1959), the first real change in the statutes. In 1962, the statutes were changed again; see *Reformas a los artículos 35, 36, 38, 40, y 46 de los Estatutos Generales de Acción Nacional aprobadas en la Asamblea General extraordinaria celebrada en la ciudad de México el dia 20 de noviembre de 1962* (Mexico, 1962). Most of the proposed 1971 reforms found in *Proyectos de Reformas* were passed.

5. Until 1971, the CEN had as many votes as the largest regional organization. The 1971 change was designed to reduce the power of the CEN.

6. Attempts in the August 1971 assembly to raise this percentage to 90 percent failed.

7. This is the opinion of the *panistas* whom I interviewed and is obvious from observing the operation of the party.

8. See Chapter VIII for a discussion of the adherent status. It is significant that PAN allowed nonmembers to sit on such an important decision-making body. Each of the CEN commissions merits some consideration for its own sake; the commissions do most of the work of the CEN. In 1970–71, the propaganda and treasury commissions contained seven members each, the political and organization commissions six, the studies commission five, and the national and press commission two.

The political commission makes studies and recommendations on strategy and tactics. Its primary task is to recommend participation in elections. Probably, it also does studies of the effectiveness of PAN appeals and campaigns and suggests means by which the public can be reached and votes aggregated as well as means by which decisions outside the power of the party can be influenced. The organization commission works with the problems of organizing and training members and potential members. Youth and female representatives are usually included on this commission. The commission also examines the problems of extending PAN organization throughout the country, especially into areas where its influence is little felt. Moreover, the commission works with membership recruitment and aids local and regional party levels with their problems.

The propaganda commission concerns itself with the problems of distributing propaganda rather than that of creating it. For example, it decides which speeches of party leaders merit reprinting in cheap form for general distribution.

Propaganda creation, ideological delineation, and programmatic statements originate in the studies commission. Most of its members are party intellectuals. The commission studies the propaganda of other parties, studies the writings of politicians both domestic and foreign, and consults with membership to determine the best ideology and programs for the party. The training documents for members and leaders are prepared by this commission.

The treasury commission collects monies, prepares the budget, elicits contributions, collects some dues from lower party organizations and runs party finances in general. The party treasurer is customarily commission president.

The nation and press commission is an occasional vehicle for party statements to the press. Usually the editor of *La Nación,* the party organ, is on the commission.

The secretary-general is a coordinator within the CEN. He oversees the operation of the commissions of the CEN, acts as its secretary and as the secretary of the National Council, General Assembly, and the National Convention. In case of death, resignation, or disability of the president he becomes the temporary party president.

The adjunct secretary and the treasurer are creations from the broad powers given by the Statutes. The adjunct secretary (*oficial mayor*) is the office manager at national headquarters. He is a full-time salaried employee. The treasurer is selected to oversee the financial operations and to be responsible for party finances. His duties are typical of any treasurer except that he also serves as a fund-raiser.

9. Acción Nacional, *Efermérides,* pp. 8–13; Carlos Septién García, "Que es *La Nación* y como se ha hecho desde su fundición," *La Nación,* VII (October 4, 1948), pp. 2, 30. Septién García was founder of *La Nación.*

10. The duties of the secretary-general and the commissions are specified in some detail. The secretary-general is an adjunct to the regional chief, coordinating intraregional and extraregional relations with lower levels. The secretary of studies procures and analyzes data of general interest; prepares the courses, conferences, and publication projects; prepares programs and studies for party conventions; and helps to train PAN organizers and propagandists. The secretary of propaganda selects the themes and texts of propaganda with the aid of the studies secretary; aids in training organizers and propagandists; supervises propagandists; distributes propaganda; acts as press secretary; and communicates reports to the national press and party. The organization secretary recruits and disciplines members; arranges meetings; supervises municipal committees; and establishes municipal committees when the regional committee cannot. The treasury secretary not only prepares the budgets for the regional organs but also audits municipal committee budgets, giving them financial aid when needed. This functionary collects members'

dues, distributing some of the proceeds to the municipal committees and some to the CEN.

11. Interviews with José G. Minondo, Federal District regional president; Ernesto Velasco LaFarga, federal deputy and immediate past president of the 17th district committee of the Federal District organization; Eugenio Ortiz Wall, *oficial mayor* of PAN; Luis Calderón Vega; and the following Michoacán *panistas:* Miguel Estrada Iturbide, Michoacán founder; Carlos Guzmán Guerrero, past president of Michoacán regional committee and regional committeeman; José Antonio Estrada Sámano, regional committeeman; Juan José Mejía Guerrero, regional secretary-general; Luis Mejía Guerrero, regional youth leader; and Esperanza Ruiz Vigil, regional office secretary, July and August 1971.

12. Adolfo Christlieb Ibarrola, "Informe del Presidente del Partido Acción Nacional," *La Nación,* XXIV (June 1, 1965), pp. 17–23; *Excelsiór,* May 15, 1965. Interviews confirm that this extension has not been significantly altered.

13. Interviews with Calderón Vega, Creel Luján, González Hinojosa, and delegates to the November 1969 national convention.

14. Interviews with Minondo and Velasco LaFarga, July and August 1971.

15. Based on the number of regional delegations to the national conventions.

16. Interviews cited in note 12, and a letter sent to me by González Hinojosa, February 17, 1970.

17. Based on interviews cited in note 12, and a questionnaire sent to regional leaders January–March 1970. PRI's organization, on the other hand, is this extensive. The extension of PAN's organization is a clear indication that it is a small, minority party which can only contest PRI's strength in selected places.

18. Interviews with Calderón Vega; Dr. Meouchi (who wrote his doctoral dissertation on Salazar); Ayala Echávarri; Estrada Iturbide; and Clicerio Cardoso Eguiluz. Scattered articles in the first years of *La Nación* indicated this concern.

19. Memorandum in personal files of Clicerio Cardoso Eguiluz, first membership secretary.

20. Gómez Morín, "Informe a la Asamblea Constituyente," pp. 6 ff., is an early example of PAN's desire to end class conflict.

21. Interviews with Sra. María Carmen Hinojosa de Calderón Vega, regional committeewoman; Calderón Vega; the Mejía Guerrero brothers; and Esperanza Ruiz Vigil.

22. Interview with Calderón Vega.

23. *La Nación,* XXX (February 1, 1971), p. 28.

24. *Efemérides,* pp. 8, 11–14; and Calderón Vega, *Memorias,* pp. 39–46, contain news of the 1940 Tampico and Guadalajara interregional conventions.

25. Representative of the studies produced are Roberto Cossío y Cosío and Pedro Zuloaga, *Estudio Sobre el Problema Agrario* (Mexico, 1944); Luis de Garay, *La Anarquía Económica* (Mexico, 1944); Acción Nacional, *Pequeña Propriedad* (Mexico, 1943); and Daniel Kuri Breña and Manuel Ulloa Ortiz, *Esquema de un Programa Municipal* (Mexico, 1942).

26. *Excélsior,* September 22, 1969.

27. Adolfo Christlieb Ibarrola, *Presencia Viva de la Juventud* (Mexico, 1966), speech delivered at the annual PAN Christmas supper, December 14, 1966.

28. "En marcha el Instituto de Estudios Sociales y Políticos," *La Nación,* XXIII (November 1, 1964), p. 13. This organization no longer functions, having been replaced by seminars.

Chapter VIII: MEMBERSHIP AND LEADERSHIP

1. Comments on statutory requirements are based on *Estatutos* (1939) and *Reglamentos* (1943) unless otherwise noted.

2. *Estatutos* (1939) and *Reglamentos* (1943).

3. Interviews with Cardoso Eguiluz, Ayala Echávarri, Ortiz Walls, and Calderón Vega.

4. Stanley G. Payne, *Falange: A History of Spanish Fascism* (Stanford, Calif.: Stanford University Press, 1961), p. 81.

5. Martz, *Accion Democratica*, p. 216.

6. *Tiempo*, July 4, 1947, pp. 5–6; *Tiempo*, July 11, 1947, p. 3; James A. Magner, "Mexico on the Move," *The Commonweal*, October 31, 1947, p. 64.

7. *La Nación*, XVIII (November 30, 1958), p. 8.

8. Interviews with Cardoso Eguiluz and Calderón Vega.

9. Calderón Vega, *Memorias*, pp. 27–34; *Efermérides*, pp. 3–4; "1929 y 1939, años decisivos en la ciudadanía mexicana," *La Nación*, IX (April 3, 1950), pp. 12–13, 22; Luis Calderón Vega, "Biografía," *La Nación*, XII (April 12, 1953), pp. 10–11; Fuentes Díaz, *Los partidos políticos*, p. 304.

10. Calderón Vega, *Cuba 88*, passim; and Ledit, *Rise of the Downtrodden*, p. 72, provide information on UNEC members joining Acción Nacional. From interviews with *panistas* and the reading of PAN literature, it was obvious that Acción Nacional still recruits from these sources. One PAN federal deputy candidate in 1970 was director of Catholic Action; see *La Nación*, XXIX (June 14, 1970), p. 11.

11. Untitled membership application. The completed applications are stored in filing cases in the Michoacán regional headquarters. I saw no such files in national or Federal District headquarters.

12. See Chapter III.

13. Fuentes Díaz, *Los partidos políticos*, p. 304.

14. Calderón Vega, *Memorias*, p. 24, stresses that most of the founders were young men. Interviews with PAN leaders also stressed this point. From all the evidence that I have seen, the PAN figures appear to be the more accurate. The prominent private entrepreneurs mentioned in Chapter III were exceptions, not the rule.

15. *El Universal*, November 25, 1941.

16. Anthony Ugalde, "Conflict and Consensus in a Mexican City: A Study in Political Integration," unpublished Ph.D. dissertation, Stanford University, 1968, pp. 313–15; William D'Antonio and William Form, *Influentials in Two Border Cities* (Notre Dame, Ind.: University of Notre Dame Press, 1965), pp. 37–38.

17. Ugalde, "Conflict and Consensus," Table 35, p. 315.

18. Interviews with the Mejía Guerrero brothers, Guzmán Guerrero, Estrada Iturbide, José Antonio Estrada Sámano, all of PAN, and Raquel Núñez González, Michoacán labor leader and PRI member.

19. Fuentes Díaz, *Los partidos políticos*, p. 304; Froylan M. López Narvaez, "Los Dos Caras: Gana el Mejor," *Excélsior*, October 15, 1969, and "Convención del PAN . . . ," *Excélsior*, November 7, 1969; and Mauricio González de la Garza, "efraín, efraín, ra, ra, ra, ra," *Ovaciones*, July 8, 1970. González de la Garza asserts that PAN is supported by many Mexicans and that he was in error when he thought that PAN was a willing tool of the government.

20. As quoted in the Mexico City *News*, January 12, 1970,

21. Pablo González Casanova, *Democracy in Mexico*, pp. 71–103, discusses political marginality.

22. Kenneth F. Johnson, "Ideological Correlates of Right-Wing Political Alienation in Mexico," *American Political Science Review*, LIX (September 1965), pp. 656–64. This is also based on my personal knowledge of *panistas*.

23. "Acción Nacional—1939," memorandum from personal files of Cardoso Eguiluz.

24. Judging from the convention attendance reported in *La Nación, Excélsior,* and *El Universal.*

25. "Registro de Acción Nacional," *La Nación*, XIII (July 4, 1954), p. 3.

26. *El Día*, July 18, 1970. This is the highest vote figure ever recognized for PAN.

27. The Michoacán figure is based on interviews with Michoacán *panistas*. An exact figure was hard to acquire since the interviewees did not want to give an exact opinion. Some asserted that the 3,000 figure was for Morelia alone. My use of the figure is for consistently active members. During elections the figure would rise. The Federal District figure is based on interviews with Velasco Lafarga and José G. Minondo. It, too, is only an approximation. If anything, it is probably too low.

28. Alberto Genda, Nogales municipal committee president, letter to José González Torres, November 12, 1969. The letter was in national headquarters files. It was the only one of its type that I saw.

29. Eugenio Ortiz Walls interview. This figure is for continuously active members and is approximate.

30. Manuel González Hinojosa letter to me, February 17, 1970.

31. López Narvaez, "Las Dos Caras;" "Convención del PAN;" and "Lapidan al PAN: Los Meritos," *Excélsior*, October 15, 1969; José Luis Reyna, "Desarrollo Económico, Distribución del Poder y Participación Política; el Caso Mexicano," *El Día*, July 17, 1968, p. 4; and Johnson, *Mexican Democracy*, p. 145, and "Urbanization and Political Change," pp. 99 ff. *Panistas,* whom I interviewed, made this assertion. See also Chapter IX.

32. Barry Ames, "Bases of Support for Mexico's Dominant Party," *American Political Science Review*, LXIV (March 1970), pp. 153–67. One should also see Johnson, *Mexican Democracy*, p. 84, which gives a convincing rebuttal to Ames. Ames uses voting data (which is suspect) to assert that PRI is not losing support in urban areas, while also using other evidence to assert that PRI distributes most benefits to highly urbanized areas, a clear indication of PRI weakness there. In the 1970 federal elections, PRI showed concern that PAN did so well in the Federal District; see *Excélsior*, July 11, 1970.

33. The biographical data presented in this and other chapters were drawn from many sources, among which were: interviews with Luis Calderón Vega, Enrique Creel Luján, Dr. Edmundo Meouchi, Clicerio Cardoso Eguiluz, Ernesto Ayala Echávarri, and Fernando Estrada Sámano; Francisco Naranjo, *Diccionario biográfico revolucionario* (Mexico: Imprenta Editorial Cosmos, 1935); José López de Escalera, *Diccionario Biográfico y de Historia de México* (Mexico: Editorial del Magisterio, 1964); *Diccionario Porrua* (Mexico: Libreria de Porrua Hns., 1964); José Bravo Ugarte, *Efraín González Luna, Abogado, Humanista, Político, Católico; Homenaje a un gran amigo* (Mexico: Ediciones de Acción Nacional, 1968); Antonio Ruiz Facius, *La juventud católica y la revolución mejicana, 1910–*

1925 (Mexico: Editorial Jus, 1963); and various periodical sources. *La Nación,* in particular, is an excellent source.

34. Manuel Gómez Morín, "Informe a la VIII Convención," *Diez Años,* pp. 293–96; and "Sesión del Consejo: Nuevo Comité Ejecutivo," *La Nación,* XVIII (March 29, 1959), pp. 10–11, are two examples.

35. Interviews with Manuel Gómez Morín and Luis Calderón Vega.

36. See Chapter IV.

37. This data was gathered from scattered issues of *La Nación.*

38. Interviews with Estrada Iturbide and his sons, Miguel Estrada Sámano and Fernando Estrada Sámano; with Calderón Vega; and various other *panistas.*

39. Interviews with Guzmán Guerrero, the Mejía Guerrero brothers, Calderón Vega, and Esperanza Ruiz Vigil.

40. Interviews with Velasco LaFarga and José G. Minondo.

41. These data were prepared by Enrique Creel Luján at my request. I would like to thank Arq. Creel Luján for his generosity.

42. Scott, *Mexican Government,* p. 233, describes the *Hoy,* February 22, 1958, cartoon with Luis H. Alvarez in traditional revolutionary garb and Adolfo López Mateos in clerical garb with the caption, "Do you know me, do you know me, masked one?" See the political cartoons of *Siempre!* in 1969–70. A. López Aparicio, "El panorama político en Mexico," *Latinoamerica,* IV (April 1, 1952), pp. 187–88; "Maderistas en el PAN," *Siempre!,* September 26, 1953, p. 5; Francisco Martínez de la Vega, "Paladines de la Oposición Inofensiva: El P.A.N. y el P.P.S.," *Siempre!,* September 26, 1953, pp. 14–15, 74; Emilio Portes Gil, *La Crisis Política,* p. 92; "El PAN Mete Reversa," *Siempre!,* September 19, 1953, p. 5; Enrique Navarro Palacios, "De Nuestros Lectores," *Mañana,* July 19, 1958, p. 6; Francisco Martínez de la Vega, "Oposición legalista en vez de Rebeldía Delirante," *Siempre!,* March 1, 1967, pp. 28–29; and Fuentes Díaz, *Los partidos políticos,* pp. 311 ff. Not all leftists agree that PAN has changed, but it is significant that some do.

43. "La Revolución y el Banquero," *Tiempo,* LVI (March 16, 1970), pp. 23–25. Inasmuch as *Tiempo* is printed in a government printing shop and is edited by Luis Martín Guzmán, a leading PRI politician (1970–76 Senator from the Federal District), it is a semiofficial source. It is especially interesting, therefore, that this article admits that bankers were supporting PRI.

44. In the 1946 national convention, as quoted in Calderón Vega, *Memorias,* pp. 166–67. José Antonio Pérez Rivero had argued that abolition of Article 130 should be adopted as a platform plank. Estrada Iturbide replied that Acción Nacional was a post-Revolutionary party, not a party of another epoch or of a religious community. Estrada Iturbide won.

45. Based on confidential interviews with *panistas.* This was a problem during the González Torres presidency. In 1971, there was no committee for the 17th district of the Federal District because a Catholic Action group had taken over the committee and the regional committee had intervened, according to my interview with José G. Minondo.

46. Ivan Vallier, "Religious Elites: Differentiations and Developments in Roman Catholicism," in *Elites in Latin America* (New York: Oxford University Press, 1967), Seymour Martin Lipset and Aldo Solari, eds., pp. 190–232. See also his *Catholicism, Social Control and Modernization in Latin America* (Englewood Cliffs, N.J.: Prentice-Hall, 1970).

47. Interviews with confidential PAN sources which included all four groups.

48. He is the grandson of Enrique Creel who was Porfirio Díaz's ambassador to the United States and Cabinet Minister in 1909. Grandfather Creel was the nephew and son-in-law of Luis Terrazas. The two of them owned land in Chihuahua, slightly smaller than Costa Rica, or Maryland, Delaware, Rhode Island, and Connecticut combined; in addition, they controlled the banks, railroads, and industry of the state. See Michael C. Myer, *Mexican Rebel, Pascual Orozco and the Mexican Revolution, 1910–1915* (Lincoln: University of Nebraska Press, 1967). The grandson is a successful architect and part of the Mexican upper class. Hugo B. Margain, former ambassador to the United States and Minister of Finance and Public Credit in the Echeverría cabinet, is his brother-in-law.

Chapter IX: THE SUPPORT SYSTEM

1. Analysis of governmental power can be found in Scott, *Mexican Government,* pp. 109–14; Brandenburg, *Modern Mexico,* pp. 341–47; and Padgett, *Mexican Political System,* pp. 136–62, among others. These sources note that this power is concentrated in the hands of the Mexican presidency.

2. In addition to the studies cited above, see Robert J. Shafer, *Mexico: Mutual Adjustment Planning* (Syracuse, N.Y.: Syracuse University Press, 1966), pp. 4–24; and Raymond Vernon, *The Dilemma of Mexico's Development* (Cambridge, Mass.: Harvard University Press, 1963), passim.

3. Chase, *Falange,* pp. 150–66; Kirk, *Covering the Mexican Front,* pp. 310–14; Carillo, *Genealogía política del sinarquismo y de Acción Nacional,* pp. 4, 10; and Fernández Bravo, *Política y administración,* pp. 98, 106. Francisco Martínez de la Vega, a leftist, asserts that PAN was originally fascistic in impulse, but now has progressive banners at times; see his "Oposición," *Siempre!,* November 26, 1969, pp. 26–27. PAN was, of course, fearful of the socialistic tendencies of the Cárdenas regime, as explained in Chapters II and III, and did contain some leading bankers and industrialists among its founders. PAN preferred capitalism in 1939–45 if it were the alternative to socialism, but the party was arguing for a compromise between the two.

4. PAN's comments are found in Gómez Morín, *Diez Años.* Private enterprise statements are indicated by CONCANACO's call for a pluralist society; see *Carta Semanal,* February 2, 1938, pp. 11–12.

5. "La Iniciativa Privada y la Intervención Estatal," *Comercio Mexicano,* June–July 1958, pp. 7–12; *Carta Semanal,* August 15, 1942, on free *municipios;* Gumersindo Galván, Jr., "Ferrocarriles: los industriales . . . ," *La Nación,* III (July 29, 1944), pp. 10–11, quotes CONCAMIN as favoring a railroad plan similar to the one presented by PAN in 1948; and Ernesto Ayala Echávarri, then president of CONCANACO, as quoted in Alejandro Aviles, "Encuesta: habla el Secretario de Economía . . . la CONCANACO contra la intervensionismo," *La Nación,* XIII (May 30, 1954), pp. 8–9, 16, are a few of the many examples.

6. See note 42, Chapter VIII.

7. Interviews with confidential PAN sources; examination of national treasurer's report to National Executive Committee for 1969–70; examination of Michoacán regional committee records. See below. The number of contributors of 1,000 or more pesos is small. Some of these contributors apparently contribute much more than this to PRI. In short, from the treasury accounts I have seen and from sources whom I consider reliable, my conclusion is that the bulk of PAN revenues do not emanate from wealthy individuals but are raised by average party mem-

bers. See González de la Garza, "efraín, efraín, ra, ra, ra, ra," for an example of a PAN critic who realized in 1970 that PAN members raise money themselves for their campaign.

8. *Excélsior*, November 4, 1969. Specifically, PAN attacked COPARMEX.

9. Carillo, *Genealogía política del sinarquismo y de Acción Nacional*, pp. 4, 10; Fernández Bravo, *Política y administración*, pp. 98, 106; Gill, *Sinarquismo*, pp. 485–522; and Fuentes Díaz, *Los partidos políticos*, pp. 293–94, are the most easily accessible comments of this type. Others are scattered throughout periodical literature. *Panistas* have been attacked in the Chamber of Deputies on the same grounds. See Gustavo Mora, "Politics," Mexico City *News*, January 15, 1968, who quotes a PPS attack on PAN, comparing the party to the UNS. Jim Budd, Mexico City *News*, June 24, 1968, notes that PAN was thought of as the political arm of the Catholic Church.

10. See Chapter VI. Turner, *Political Catholicism*, p. 215, rightly comments that the use of papal encyclicals is often a means of justification rather than predominant influence, that all Catholics can read into these encyclicals the justifications for any Catholic position.

11. I heard it from many *panistas*. Its veracity is not as important as the fact that so many *panistas* believe it. They do not see themselves as tools of the hierarchy, nor do they want to be tools.

12. Luis Tercero Gallardo, "Campaña: La Sección 11 del Sindicato de Mineros conquista su libertad," *La Nación*, XV (June 17, 1956), pp. 10–11, 13.

13. Interview with Raquel Núñez González, secretary-general of COR in Michoacán. Sra. Núñez González asserted that her union members face no obstacle if they want to join PAN.

14. *La Nación*, XII (April 5, 1953), p. 8. A requirement of membership was adherence to PAN principles.

15. *Boletín de Acción Nacional*, I (June 1, 1940), p. 8.

16. Based on examination of the national treasurer's report to the National Executive Committee for 1969–70. These figures were chosen as representative of PAN finances. I thank Enrique Creel Luján, PAN treasurer, for access to his treasury files.

17. Adolfo Christlieb Ibarrola, "Informe del Presidente del Partido Acción Nacional," *La Nación*, XXIV (June 1, 1965), pp. 17–23; *Excélsior*, May 15, 1965.

18. *La Nación*, XXX (November 1, 1970), p. 2. PAN had planned to spend 3.72 million pesos for the campaign, 2.75 million of which would be financed by the issuance of 321,000 bonds, according to a proposed campaign budget in the files of Creel Luján which I saw in March 1970. That the party could not raise this amount indicates its financial difficulties.

19. From file folder labeled Finanzas: VII Asamblea General Ordinaria, V Asamblea General Extraordinaria, México, D.F., 1971. The file included various anticipated expense items for the upcoming convention. The cited information was obviously a reference point in trying to determine the cost of the convention.

20. Finanzas: VII Asamblea General Ordinaria, V Asamblea General Extraordinaria, México, D.F., 1971. The postconvention expenses included publication of new statutes and of pamphlets containing the position papers adopted by the meeting.

21. Treasurer's report cited above. Creel Luján and Ortiz Walls explained the sources of the Gómez Morín contribution.

22. Interviews with Creel Luján and Gerardo Medina Valdés, PAN federal

deputy for 1967–70. During both periods of my field work in Mexico, I was besieged by *panistas* trying to sell me bonds and raffle tickets. The raffle prizes were Ford and Volkswagon automobiles.

23. Interviews with Creel Luján, Ortiz Walls, and Calderón Vega.

24. Interviews with José G. Minondo, Velasco Lafarga, and Ortiz Walls.

25. Michoacán regional committee treasury account books.

26. Interviews with María Carmen Hinojosa de Calderón Vega, the Mejía Guerrero brothers, Estrada Iturbide, Esperanza Ruiz Vigil, and Guzmán Guerrero.

27. Michoacán regional committee minutes book for 1970.

28. Interviews with Creel Luján, Calderón Vega, and the Mejía Guerrero brothers. See Johnson, *Mexican Democracy,* p. 64, for a similar comment.

29. Taylor, "The Mexican Elections of 1958,"; Scott, *Mexican Government,* p. 209; Brandenburg, *Modern Mexico,* p. 342; Padgett, *Mexican Political System,* pp. 79–80; Wilkie, *The Mexican Revolution,* p. 95; Johnson, *Mexican Democracy,* passim; and Wilkie, "Statistical Research in Recent Mexican History," pp. 3–4. For the Portes Gil statement, see note 21, Chapter I.

30. Although PAN does charge fraud in every election, it does not claim that it won a majority of the votes. One test of the meaning of these charges in federal deputy elections is the number of races the party contests in the Electoral College. Thus far, the number has been less than a majority. Moreover, PAN leaders implicitly admit that PRI wins almost every election in that PAN has not contested a majority of elections in Mexico since 1939. Privately, PAN leaders are candid that the party is only a minority party.

31. For what should be obvious reasons, these sources cannot be identified. They are people in a position to know and they are reliable.

32. Interviews with Creel Luján, Velasco Lafarga, Calderón Vega, and Estrada Iturbide; Wilkie, "Statistical Research in Recent Mexican History," pp. 6–7.

33. William Tuohy and David Ronfeldt, "Political Control and the Recruitment of Middle-level Elites in Mexico; an Example from Agrarian Politics," *Western Political Quarterly,* XXII (June 1969), p. 367, give data on control of the media.

34. An example of such charges is in Johnson, *Mexican Democracy,* pp. 131–32. Other examples are found in Christlieb Ibarrola, *Baja California;* Acción Nacional, *El Caso de Baja California* and *Mas Sobre; gente,* December 16, 1969; pp. 11–14; *El Universal Gráfico,* November 24, 1969; and *Por Que?,* extraordinary edition, December 1969. These practices, once common in Mexico, have declined substantially over the last thirty years. If they do occur, it is on rare occasions.

35. Wilkie, "Statistical Research in Recent Mexican History," pp. 3–7; James W. Wilkie, "New Approaches in Contemporary Mexican Historical Research," unpublished paper delivered at the Third Meeting of Historians of Mexico and the United States, Oaxtepec, Morelos, Mexico, November 4, 1969 (revised November 12, 1969), pp. 1–4. I wish to thank Professor Wilkie for his generosity in making this paper available to me.

36. Cline, *United States and Mexico,* p. 331.

37. See Table 12.

38. The best discussions to date of Mexican regionalism are Harry Bernstein, "Regionalism in the National History of Mexico," in Howard Cline, ed., *Latin American History,* I (Austin: University of Texas Press, 1967), pp. 389–94 and in his *Modern and Contemporary Latin America* (Philadelphia: Lippincott, 1952).

39. Reyna, "Desarrollo Económico," passim.

40. *Excélsior* and *Novedades,* July 1970 (various issues).

41. This approach appeared in Ronald H. McDonald, *Party Systems and Elections in Latin America* (Chicago: Markham Press, 1971), pp. 254–58, from which I obtained the idea and the 1967 figures. The 1970 figures are those released by the Federal Election Commission to Mexico City dailies in July 1970.

42. Johnson, *Mexican Democracy,* pp. 143–44, asserts that Acción Nacional uses female candidates because women are attracted to PAN because of its clericalism. My opinion differs, however. Although it is clear that some women are attracted to PAN because of its clerical image, it is probably true that more are attracted to PRI because of its *machismo* (masculine) image—its ability to conquer all by any means necessary. Nevertheless, PRI does not use female candidates to the extent that PAN does. Women do join PAN because of its clericalism but also because the party has always been progressive with regard to women's rights. In addition, PAN's membership weakness means that it has to accept whatever aid it can get. In short, it is easier for women to run for office as PAN candidates than as PRI candidates.

43. Padgett, *Mexican Political System,* pp. 123–35.

44. Interviews with González Hinojosa, Estrada Iturbide, Creel Luján, Ortiz Walls, Miguel Estrada Sámano, and Guzmán Guerrero.

Chapter X: PERSPECTIVES

1. See Turner, *Catholicism and Political Development,* for the best analysis of the Latin American Catholic social reform impulse. Williams, *Latin American Christian Democratic Parties;* Frederick B. Pike, ed., *Freedom and Reform in Latin America* (Notre Dame, Ind.: University of Notre Dame Press, 1967); William V. D'Antonio and Frederick B. Pike, ed., *Religion, Revolution, and Reform: New Forces for Social Change in Latin America* (New York: Praeger, 1964); Francine de Plessix Gray, *Divine Disobedience: Profiles in Catholic Radicalism* (New York: Vintage Books, 1969); John Gerassi, ed., *Revolutionary Priest: The Complete Writings and Messages of Camilo Torres* (New York: Vintage Books, 1971); Ivan Vallier, *Catholicism, Social Control, and Modernization in Latin America* (Englewood Cliffs, N.J.: Prentice-Hall, 1970); and John J. Considine, *Social Revolution in the New Latin America: A Catholic Appraisal* (Notre Dame, Ind.: Fides Press, 1965) are representative of useful works on the subject.

2. Efraín González Luna, "Ausencia y Presencia de un Partido Nacional," *Humanismo político,* pp. 240–41, reprinted from *La Nación,* I (March 21, 1942).

3. "Un Problema Abandonado," *Humanismo político,* pp. 265–69, reprinted from *La Nación,* I (January 15, 1942).

4. "La Dignidad del Trabajo," *Humanismo político,* pp. 254–55, reprint of a speech given in Guadalajara, Jalisco, September, 1940; "Propósitos y Condiciones de la Reforma Social," *Humanismo Político,* p. 279, reprinted from a speech given in Mexico City, September 1944; and "Un Problema Abandonado," p. 270.

5. "La Dignidad del Trabajo," pp. 251–55.

6. "Una Responsibilidad que no se Prescribe," *Humanismo político,* p. 287, articles reprinted from *La Nación,* I (February 20 and March 13, 1943).

7. "Una Responsibilidad que no Prescribe," pp. 284–91.

8. "Una Responsibilidad que no Prescribe," pp. 291–94.

9. As quoted in Jim Budd, "The Mexican Scene," Mexico City *News,* June 24, 1968. He went on to say that PRI deserves to be trounced now and again, that

PAN offers voters a chance to protest but little more, and that this is just the kind of competition that PRI needs and wants.

10. Williams, *Latin American Christian Democratic Parties,* pp. 41 ff.; Turner, *Catholicism and Political Development,* pp. 232–54.

11. "El Suicido del Régimen," *Humanismo político,* pp. 183–84.

BIBLIOGRAPHICAL ESSAY

Acción Nacional sources alone provided more than 60,000 pages of the documents upon which this study is based. These documents included statutes, programs of action, platforms, handbills, pamphlets, PAN periodicals, legislative proposals, speeches, internal working documents, books, and PAN letters. The bulk of these documents can be found in the headquarters of the National Executive Committee in Mexico City where I used them. The United States Embassy in Mexico City also has a small collection. A more extensive collection, but one which does not approach PAN's own file, is the material I have been assembling since initiating this study. *La Nación,* the principal PAN periodical, can be consulted in its offices in national headquarters in Mexico City but also in the Hemeroteca Nacional. The Hemeroteca Nacional also contains the *Voz Nacional,* the *Boletín de Acción Nacional,* and other Mexican periodicals. The variety and quantity of Acción Nacional sources consulted are too numerous to bear listing here. My "Acción Nacional: The Institutionalization of an Opposition Party," unpublished Ph.D. dissertation (Syracuse University, 1970) contains an annotated list of PAN documents published through March 1970. The footnotes in the present study should serve as a guide to the major sources utilized.

The remainder of this essay is categorized by the type of sources used. The major categories are: statutes and regulations; principles, platforms, and political action program; handbills and pamphlets; articles, books, letters and speeches; interviews; correspondence; party files; PAN periodicals; non-PAN sources; and studies. Because much of the material can be categorized in various ways, this is not a clear-cut distinction.

I. Statutes and Regulations

The Statutes under which PAN operated were printed periodically for distribution to members and other interested persons. New printings usually indicate that prior supplies were depleted, not that the statutes were changed. The original *Estatutos* were printed in 1939 and remained in force until 1949 when they were modified slightly in accordance with the requirements of the Federal Election Law of that year. I consulted a 1951 edition of the *Estatutos* after having compared it to the 1949 version. The first major change in the

243

Estatutos came in 1959 and the *Estatutos Generales* of that year incorporated those changes. In 1962, more changes were made in the statutes which can be found in the *Reformas a los artículos 35, 36, 38, 40, y 46 de los Estatutos Generales de Acción Nacional aprobadas en la Asamblea General extraordinaria celebrada en la ciudad de México el día 20 de noviembre de 1962*—or in the 1968 edition of the Statutes. The *Proyecto de reformas a los estatutos de Acción Nacional* gives the proposed 1971 reforms; the most important debates on them are noted in *La Nación*, XXX (September 1, 1971), and the final version is *Estatutos* (1971). In addition to statutes, Acción Nacional also issued regulations for the internal operation of the party. The *Reglamentos* were printed at various dates, but I used the 1943 edition. They were also bound with the 1949 *Estatutos*. All printings were by Acción Nacional in Mexico City and can be found either in the party's national headquarters or in my files.

II. Principles, Platforms, and Political Action Program

Because the party mixes ideological and programmatic statements in its publications, one has to consult various sources for basic PAN doctrine. The *Programa Mínimo de Acción Política* (1940) was reprinted several times until it was superseded by campaign platforms in 1952. It and the 1939 *Principios de Doctrina* are appendices of Luis Calderón Vega, *Memorias del PAN*, Vol. I. The *Principios* were reprinted various times. The *Principios de Doctrina— su proyección en 1965* (1965) represented the first official doctrinal change since 1939, although PAN doctrine had been evolving since the earlier date. The *Cambio Democrático de las Estructuras* (1969), published both as a supplement to *La Nación* and as a number on the Ediciones de Acción Nacional series, represented both doctrinal changes and a campaign platform. These four documents are rather vague in character since the party both wanted to please as many people as possible and was in the process of giving closer definition to its ideas. Consequently, the campaign platforms, which were published in 1951, 1955, 1957, 1961, 1963, 1967, and 1969 under slightly varying titles, gave more definition to PAN ideas. They, too, do not present precise programmatic statements on every issue of concern to PAN. The party platforms of the 1960s are more precise than their predecessors.

III. Handbills and Pamphlets

From the beginning of its history Acción Nacional produced numerous handbills and pamphlets, varying in length from one to fifty-four pages, as the party made appeals for membership and votes, defined its ideology and programs, and criticized governmental actions, providing one of the most valuable sources available in that they greatly supplement the *Principios, Programa,* and *Plataformas.* The approximately 1,800 pages almost completely exhausted this category. All were printed in Mexico City by PAN unless otherwise noted and are available in national party headquarters. Some are also in my personal collection. Only the ones I found most useful are cited here. I have categorized them by subject.

For general ideological statements, there is an abundance of pamphlet literature. Acción Nacional, *XIV Convención Nacional* (1959) is extremely valuable for leadership attitudes in the 1958–59 intraparty crisis. The party's *A los jefes de grupo de Acción Nacional* (1939) is basically a set of instructions to lower-level leaders but points out the directions the party was to pursue. *Visión del México Futuro* (1943) is an early statement of the party's desire for a democratic Mexico. Christlieb Ibarrola was a major source of ideology. His *Dialogo y testimonio* (1965) was a reprint of a speech to the annual PAN Christmas dinner in which he defended his dialogue policy with the government. In his *Discurso pronunciado por el Diputado Licenciado Adolfo Christlieb Ibarrola, Presidente del Partido Acción Nacional, en la Sesión Solemne Celebrada Por la Cámara de Diputados el día primero de diciembre de 1966 para conmemorar la Institución del Congreso Constituyente de 1916–1917 en Querétaro* he praised the current Mexican constitution and attacked the government for not obeying it. His *Informe al Consejo, 5 de febrero de 1966* was useful for his signaling of the party's ideological direction as well as for its report on party activities. In *Partidos grupos y acción política* (1963) Christlieb explained the party's views on the proper role of political parties and political activity in any political system but especially in Mexico's. Manuel Gómez Morín, *Diez Años de México* (1950) is fundamental to the study of PAN history in the 1940s as an anthology of the reports rendered by PAN's first president. Much of PAN's early attitudes toward the Revolution, Cárdenas, communism, and democracy can be found here. Some of the speeches anthologized here were produced earlier as pamphlets, but are more accessible in this form. Efraín González Luna's introduction is also useful as an introduction to PAN. Efraín González Luna's *Humanismo político* (1955) is even more important for Acción Nacional ideology because the author was the party's principal ideologist until his death and because its coverage extends beyond the author's 1952 presidential campaign. Most of the material in this anthology was published earlier as pamphlets. The introduction to the volume by Luis Calderón Vega and his footnotes to the articles are also valuable. González Luna also wrote *La Reforma Social* (1943), which emphasized the necessity of social reform and attacked capitalists for defending laissez faire.

Whereas *Diez Años* and *Humanismo político* contain pamphlets published through 1953, recent ideological statements in this form can be found in the 1970 campaign speeches of Efraín González Morfín. These covered a broad range of topics and are cited in the text. *Asambleas Generales: 7a Ordinaria–5a Extraordinaria-Documentos* (Ediciones de Acción Nacional, 1971) contains the presidential report to the August 1971 national assembly, the proposed statutory reforms, the *Problemática Nacional* document, and a study of Mexico's employment problem compared to other Latin American countries.

Some of his campaign speeches, including most from these pamphlets, were anthologized in the *Campaña 1970* series, which currently totals three volumes and was published as numbers thirteen, fourteen, and fifteen of the Ediciones de Acción Nacional series.

On politics, the party has published its most extensive collection of pamphlets and handbills. Two of its judgments of Mexican President Gustavo Díaz Ordaz's state of the union addresses are *Acción Nacional enjuicia el primer informe del Presidente Díaz Ordaz* (1965) and *La oposición democrática comenta el II informe presidencial de Díaz Ordaz* (1966). Similar commentary may be found in the editions of *La Nación* following the annual presidential address.

The 1943 federal deputy election was treated in *La campaña electoral de 1943,* a preelection statement of the reason's for PAN's participation, the party platform, a list of candidates, and an appeal for votes, and in *El Fraude Electoral,* a postelection condemnation and detailing of the fraud that PAN believed had been perpetrated. Similar in nature were *El caso de Baja California* (1959) and *Mas sobre el caso de Baja California* (1959); *Intervención de la Supreme Corte de Justicia para garantía de los derechos personales y ciudadanos* (1947), and *A la Opinión: Chihuahua y la Suprema Corte* (1956); Ciudadanos Morelenses Simpatizantes del PAN, *Carta Abierta Al Presidente de la República* (1970); and Adolfo Christlieb Ibarrola, *Defensa ante el colegio electoral* (1964).

The basic complaints that Acción Nacional has had with the Mexican political and electoral system have been catalogued in numerous publications. *Representación Política: Reforma del Sistema Electoral* (1941) is a twenty-four-page pamphlet criticizing the political system and making recommendations for its improvements. Some of these recommendations were adopted by subsequent federal electoral laws. *Contra la corrupción electoral* (1947); *Organización de la ciudadanía* (1948); and *La reforma política: una exigencia ciudadana que no puede ser burlada* (1948) are important as indicators that PAN was not completely satisfied with the 1945–46 reforms of the Federal Electoral Law and because they contain PAN legislative bills on the subject. *IV Convención Nacional: Dictamen de la Comisión Política* (1946) is a reprint of a convention committee report which favored participation in the 1946 federal elections even after predicting fraud. *Patria y política* (1960), although short, is an excellent PAN statement that politics is the best way to change Mexico. Individual Acción Nacional authors have also attacked the political system. Gonzalo Chapela y B., *Acción Nacional y el Problema Político Actual* (1945); Adolfo Christlieb Ibarrola, *Balance de Campaña* (1964); Efraín González Luna, *Dos paradojas e una experiencia* (n.d.), *Política vieja y Nueva Política* (n.d.), *A la Nación* (1951), *La normalidad política internacional* (1962), and *Primado del Orden Político* (Mexico: Editorial "Signo," 1958); and Rafael Preciado Hernández, *Gobierno Democrático o Gobierno Autoritario?* (1942), *La Servidumbre del Espíritu: Cultura y Libertad* (n.d.), and *Sin autenticidad en la representación política, no habría democracia en Mexico* (1962).

More positive in their approach are two recent statements of Acción Nacional's role in the system. *Metas de Acción Nacional* (1964) was a campaign document for the federal elections of that year, whereas *Liberated Frente al Poder, Agilidad y Verdad Ante el Pueblo* (1968) was a reaffirmation of PAN's desire to be an alternative to the government in a troubled year.

Since Acción Nacional comments on the nature and function of the Mexican *municipio* have changed little since 1939, except to show concern for the problems of crowding and megalopolis, the pamphlets of the 1940s can be used for the fundamental PAN view; see Efraín González Luna, *Naturaleza y funciones del Municipio* (Guadalajara, 1940) and *Ruina y esperanza del municipio mexicano* (1942); Acción Nacional, *La ciudad: Necesidad del municipio libre* (1942) and *Esquema de un programa municipal* (Guadalajara, 1942); and Manuel Gómez Morín, *Importancia Vital del Municipio* (1947).

Acción Nacional began to call for multisectoral national planning to solve Mexican economic problems early in party history. Its *Aprovechamiento de recursos naturales* (1943) stated that these problems could not be solved without planning. *La Crisis económica de México* (1948), which contains many of the party's proposed economic legislation for the 1946–49 Chamber of Deputies session, also contains proplanning statements. Similarly, *El problema ferrocarrilero* (1940) and *Necesidad de rehabilitar los ferrocarriles nacionales* (1948) are planning statements, as well as criticisms and proposed reforms of existing conditions. Luis de Garay, later a CONCANACO employee, attacked governmental economic policy along these lines in his *La anarquía económica* (1943).

PAN's concerns for the problems of labor took several different forms. The problem of wages and the cost of living were treated extensively by the third national convention in 1943. The convention report was published as *Salarios y Costa de Vida* (1943). Social security proposals appeared in pamphlet form as *La gran esperanza de la seguridad social* (1948) and *Seguridad Social* (1960), as well as in pamphlets reprinted in *Humanismo político* and Manuel Gómez Morín, ed., *Seguridad Social* (Ediciones de Acción Nacional, 1966). The importance of labor in economic life was treated by González Luna in *Dignidad del Trabajo*. Adolfo Christlieb Ibarrola, *Comentarios sobre el proyecto de reformas al artículo 123 de la Constitución* (1962); *Sindicatos, política, y clausula de exclusión* (n.d.); and *Transformación de los empresarios* (1962) are recent statements demanding the incorporation of workers into the capital, management, and profits of enterprise, and the creation of free, independent unions.

Three lengthy pamphlets discuss the agrarian problem. *Pequeña Propriedad* (1943) and Roberto Cossío y Cosío and Pedro Zuloaga, *Estudio Sobre el Problema Agrario* (ca. 1943) show PAN's preference for family farms. Manuel Ulloa Ortiz, *Problemas del Campo Mexicano (Aspecto Económico)* (1960) is a valuable technical criticism of Mexican agricultural policy.

Although Acción Nacional has been closely identified with the Roman Catholic Church because of its obviously Catholic ideology and although secular education has been a major source of tension between Church and State, the party has published few handbills and pamphlets on this question. The three most important (these represent almost all in this category) are: *Libertad de Enseñanza: Reforma Constitucional* (1941); Adolfo Christlieb Ibarrola, *Monopolio Educativo o Unidad Nacional* (Mexico: Editorial Jus, 1962); and José González Torres, *De la ignorancia y su natural remedio, la educación* (1964).

IV. ARTICLES, BOOKS, LETTERS, SPEECHES

This category is indispensable to the study of PAN, for the party had produced numerous books to explain its positions. Luis Calderón Vega, *Memorias del PAN*, Vol. I (1967) is essential for the 1939–46 period because he, as the party historian, has synthesized and quoted extensively from other party documents. As a founder of the party and one of its stalwarts, he has an insight into PAN operations which outsiders cannot always obtain. In addition, he utilizes numerous photographs in PAN history which are unavailable elsewhere as well as reprinting the 1939 *Principios*, the 1940 *Programa Mínimo*, and a list of the 1946 federal deputy and senatorial candidates. He has planned to issue a second volume but has been unable to do so. In 1970, however, he did publish *Reportaje Sobre el P.A.N.: 30 años de lucha*, which is a short but valuable survey of party history. His *Cuba 88: Memorias de la UNEC* is the only history of that interesting and important Catholic student organization which served as the primary source of PAN founders. In addition, he included documents from the founding convention of CIDEC. His *Política y Espíritu (Compromisos y Fugas de Cristiano)* (Morelia, 1965) is an important essay on the duty of Christians to engage in politics on the side of social reform while blocking the Church from political participation.

Additional historical material is found in Acción Nacional, *Efermérides* (1942) and *Las históricas jornadas de 1939* (1943), both of which are primarily listings of dates and events, although the latter contains some of the 1939 national convention debate. Bernardo J. Gastelum's *La Revolución Mexicana: Interpretación de un Espíritu* (Mexico: Editorial Porrua, 1966) is not strictly a PAN book, but the author is an Acción Nacional intellectual who influences party leaders.

The party's *Acción Nacional* (1939) is an early definition of the party which gave a broad outline of its intentions. Its *Municipio de Graza García, N.L.: primer año de trabajo* (Monterrey, 1964) praises the party's mayor for his work in that small suburb. *Seis estudios sobre Baja California* (1964), one of the Ediciones de Acción Nacional series, was written by the party's state committee there and is the only study of its kind. The party's Youth Organization published *La penetración comunista en México* (1960) which reflected the post-Castro hysteria and which argued for Catholic social justice as the only salvation of Mexico.

René Capistrán Garza, "Los católicos y política," *Vida Contemporánea,* VI (September 25, 1943), pp. 521–39 is an attack on Catholics who supported Huerta and Díaz. Capistrán Garza was an important *cristero* leader who joined PAN in 1939 but left it subsequently.

Adolfo Christlieb Ibarrola became a major PAN writer after he assumed the party presidency in 1962. His *Baja California Avanzada de la Democracia* (1968) is indispensable for the 1968 Baja California election. *Cronicas de la no reelección* (Ediciones de Acción Nacional, 1965) is both an apologia for a PAN legislative proposal and a more general discussion of the problems of the idea of no-reelection in the Mexican political system. *Idearios políticos* (1964); *La oposición* (Ediciones de Acción Nacional, 1965); *Partido y gobierno* (1966); *Política y civismo* (1962); *Solidaridad y Participación* (Ediciones de Acción Nacional, 1969); and *Temas políticos* (Ediciones de Acción Nacional, 1963) are all important for PAN history in the 1960s. *Solidaridad y Participación* is especially interesting because it is a collection of speeches delivered to a Guatemalan university where the author could not expect political gain and because he outlines his own Christian Democratic position.

Manuel Gómez Morín has written surprisingly few books as a PAN leader. His *1915* (Mexico: Editorial CVLTVRA, 1927) is a short work which argues that his generation was going to transform Mexico into a modern state. His *España fiel: Conferencia con XIV dibujos de Maroto* (Mexico: Editorial Cultura, 1928) is a homage to Spanish culture. More important is his *El crédito agricola en México* (Madrid Talleres Esposa Calpe, S.A., 1928), which gives his early views of the subject while he was tied to the Calles government. His *Diez Años de México* has already been indicated, as has his *Segurdad Social.* James W. Wilkie and Edna Monzón de Wilkie interviewed Gómez Morín at length and the transcripts of these interviews are printed in their *México Visto en el Siglo XX* (Mexico: Instituto Mexicano de Investigaciones Economicas, 1969). These interviews are important for Gómez Morín's views in retrospect.

Efraín González Luna's *Humanismo político* has already been mentioned as one of the most important sources of his ideas. His *El Fetiche de la Estabilidad Política* (Guadalajara: Centro Jalisciense de Productividad, A.C., 1965) is an anthology of his writings centering on his agrument that political stability without democracy and justice should be condemned. His views on Mexican agriculture during his 1952 presidential campaign are found in "El pensamiento agrario de los cuatro candidatos a la presidencia para el sexenio 1952–1958," *Problemas Agrícolos e Industrialies de México,* IV (October–December 1952), pp. 351–420. He was also joint author of *La democracia en México* (Mexico: Editorial Jus, 1962) with four other *panistas.*

His son, Efraín González Morfín, has been more prolific as an author of books. His *Justicia y Reforma Social* (Ediciones de Acción Nacional, 1967) is fundamental for Acción Nacional reform ideology of the period and for his use of social encyclicals to justify that ideology. *El puño y la mano tendida* (Ediciones de Acción Nacional, 1965) is an anticommunist statement which is rationally developed and which presents Catholic social justice as the alternative. González Morfín was also co-author of *Cuestiones políticas y sociales* (Ediciones de Acción Nacional, 1965) and *Tres esquemas* (Ediciones de Acción Nacional, 1969).

Two works by Jesús Guisa y Azevedo are especially useful because the author was a founder of PAN who left the party and has since become an outspoken enemy. His *La civitas mexicana y nosotros los católicos* (Mexico: Editorial Polis 1953) is a Catholic interpretation of the post-Revolutionary period. His *Acción Nacional es un equivoco* (Mexico: Editorial Polis, 1966), a bitter attack on Acción Nacional for moving leftward, asserts that PAN has not remained true to Catholicism. The author now denies that he was a *panista* even though he was a member of the first national council. It is interesting, therefore, as a Catholic criticism of PAN.

Manuel Gutiérrez Aguilar, *La Derrota del Régimen* (Hermosillo: Imprenta Regional, 1971) is an attack on the government for the 1968 Baja California election and is especially useful in that it reprints documents. The author may not be a *panista,* but I included him here because of his viewpoint and because I bought a copy of the book at a PAN convention.

Rafael Preciado Hernández, one of the principal founders and stalwarts, has reprinted some of his speeches in the Chamber of Deputies as *Discursos Parlamentarios* (1969) and *Tribuna Parlamentaria: 1968* (Mexico: Editorial Jus, 1969). In the latter, he gives his views of the 1968 Baja California election and the student revolt.

V. INTERVIEWS

Interviews formed an indispensable part of the data for this study, but they are not so easily listed. Information was sought that was both interpretative and descriptive. The interviews were both formal and informal, structured and nonstructured. The interviewing took place during two intervals. The first was from September 1969 through March 1970, principally in Mexico City. The second was from late July through late August 1971 in Mexico City and Morelia, Michoacán. Many of these interviews were multiple, especially with Luis Calderón Vega, Fernando Estrada Sámano, and Ernesto Ayala Echávarri. In 1971, Enrique Creel Luján and Eugenio Ortiz Walls were especially helpful. The number of PAN leaders, PAN members, and other Mexicans whom I interviewed or with whom I talked (over 100) is too numerous to allow me to list them all here. Many are cited in the text or are listed in my dissertation. Some cannot be listed because they were promised anonymity. Among the interviewees were two PAN presidents, numerous founders, some federal deputies, regional organization officers, average members, government officials, union members, politicians, and storekeepers.

VI. CORRESPONDENCE

Letters were sent to all thirty regional PAN chiefs in the first three months of 1970 and to prominent members of PAN. This was done with the cooperation of Manuel Gómez Morín and Luis Calderón Vega. Each letter differed somewhat from the others. The results were meager for the most part, but I was able to get a cross-section of data on occupations and perceptions of regional leaders. The letters from Manuel Gómez Morín, Manuel González Hinojosa, and Enrique Creel Luján were valuable. I am especially indebted to Creel Luján for compiling and forwarding data to me while I was out of Mexico.

VII. PARTY FILES

Acción Nacional does not allow outsiders to utilize its files, and I was able to get only limited access to them through the cooperation of some *panistas* who trusted my discretion. Many leaders would be upset if they knew who gave me such access, so I cannot identify them. The condition of the files, however, was such that it was more fruitful to utilize selected private files of prominent *panistas*. The national party does not have the money to pay trained employees and has had to rely heavily upon volunteer help. Consequently, the files are incomplete and unsystematic. The Michoacán regional committee files were in similar condition but, because they were smaller, I was able to make better use of them.

The most valuable documents examined from the national files were the legislative proposals and the internal training documents, copies of which were given to me by Luis Calderón Vega. They are: Acción Nacional, *Seminario de Orientación Social y Política: Cuadernos de Trabajo* (mimeographed, 1971), 17 pp.; Blas Briseño, *Partidos Políticos: Notas Históricas de Acción Nacional* (mimeographed, 1971), 15 pp.; Luis Calderón Vega, *Seminario de Orientación Social y Política: Sus Propósitos* (mimeographed, July 1971), 3 pp., *Doctrina y Posiciones del P.A.N.* (1971), 18 pp., and *La Nación y El Bien Común* (1971), 14 pp.; and Efraín González Morfín, *Doctrina de Acción Nacional* (1971), 17 pp. Calderón Vega directed the study and training program. The legislative proposals, under varying titles, some mimeographed, some reprints from the *Diario de Debates,* were scattered throughout the files. Some were also reprinted in party pamphlets and *La Nación.* All can also be found in Mexico, Cámara de Diputados, *Diario de Debates* for the date of the proposal.

The private files of Clicero Cardoso Eguiluz on organization and membership were especially important for the founding years of the party, whereas the private files of Enrique Creel Luján on finances for the December 1968–January 1970 period were useful for the later period.

The Michoacán files yielded the minutes books for the regional committee for 1971; the treasury expense books for 1968–71; and assorted correspondence and membership data.

VIII. PAN Periodicals

La Nación (1941–71) proved to be the single most valuable source because it gave extensive and usually accurate coverage of Acción Nacional activities and was the primary means of intraparty communication. Because *panistas* must rely upon it for news and because participants in the events can easily challenge its veracity, *La Nación* has trustworthy accounts of party conventions, assemblies, debates, and votes, to which it gives extensive coverage. Moreover, it prints many of the major party documents—platforms, principles of doctrine, presidential and committee reports, position papers, and speeches—as part of its regular coverage or as bound supplements. Convention debates are not usually printed in their entirety but in synopsis. Judging from the debates I have heard in conventions when compared to later *La Nación* treatment, this process captures the heart of the arguments. In comparing *La Nación* coverage of conventions and assemblies to that of the major Mexico City dailies, the significant difference is that the former gives a more complete account. *La Nación* is also valuable for its articles on specific issues, on elections in which it is interested, and on Mexican and world events. The magazine began in late 1941 as a weekly but became bimonthly in 1965. I read more than 40,000 pages in this source. Copies of it are located in its offices in Mexico City or in the Hemeroteca Nacional.

Several other PAN publications are worth comment even though they are not as useful as *La Nación*. *Voz Nacional* (1939–40) was not strictly a PAN magazine although it was edited by Bernardo Ponce, then a *panista*, and written largely by future *panistas*. Its editorial line was consistent with that which PAN was taking at the time, but it is not essential for the study of the party. The *Boletín de Acción Nacional* (1939–42) is more important. It began as the organ of the Federal District regional committee but quickly became the mouthpiece of the national executive committee. Its primary value to the researcher is as a source of the PAN pamphlets which it reprinted. I did not cite it extensively because I had already seen the pamphlets. In 1970, the party published a small newspaper for the federal election campaign called *Batalla '70*. Although I have a few copies, I was unable to find a collection of them. The party continued this newspaper into the following year as *Batalla '71*. I have also seen a few copies of the national executive committee's *boletín*, which was published in mimeographed form beginning in the spring of 1971.

Acción Nacional currently has newspapers in several important cities. These papers declared themselves to be independent but are clearly PAN papers either because of editorship or content. These are the Ciudad Juárez *Tribuna*, Guanajuato (city) *Debate*, Tijuana *Centinela!* and Monterrey *Oigame!*. After consulting several issues of each, I concluded that they were not particularly useful for this study.

IX. Non-PAN Periodicals

The Mexico City daily newspapers *Excélsior, Novedades,* and *El Universal;* the popular magazines *Tiempo, Hoy,* and *Todo;* and the political magazines *Siempre!* and *Política* were surveyed for a thirty-one-year period or for their entire history. Key dates, derived from events in PAN history such as elections, conventions, rumored splits, and introduction of major legislative programs, were used to select the issues to consult. That which was missed by this survey was probably minimal. Stanley R. Ross, ed., *Fuentes de la Historia Contemporánea de México: Periódicos y Revistas,* 2 vols. (Mexico: El Colegio de Mexico, 1965–67) was also useful in locating articles in these sources.

Excélsior proved to be the most useful of the non-PAN periodicals, having the most frequent, objective, and comprehensive coverage of PAN and the Mexican political scene. I used not only its news columns but also its featured articles and its editorials. The Mexico City *News* had coverage not provided by the Spanish language press. *Tiempo,* a weekly magazine modeled after *Time* magazine in the United States, should be considered a semiofficial source on political matters. Its publisher, Martín Luis Guzmán, is a leading PRI politician (as well as an eminent writer) and was a senator from the Federal District from 1970 to 1976. The magazine is printed in a government printing shop, the Talleres Gráficos de la Nación. *Tiempo* is a good source for governmental views of PAN, however.

In addition to these periodicals, consulted for long runs, I also examined scattered editions of the following newspapers: *El Día, La Prensa, Diario de Yucatán, El Heraldo de Yucatán, Ultimas Noticias, Universal Gráfico,* and *Cosmos al Servicio de la Juventud.* Scattered issues of the following were also consulted: *Abside, Carta Semanal, gente, Mañana, Por Qué?,* and *Revista de America. Por Qué?* was especially useful as an independent Marxist, antigovernment magazine.

X. Non-PAN Sources

In addition to those noted above in the interviews and periodical sections, I also consulted other non-PAN sources. There is a dearth of non-PAN sources. Much of what exists is not only polemical but repetitive. Catholic sources in particular were consulted as I attempted to tie down PAN's ideology and position within contemporary Catholicism. The works cited here are not comprehensive but provide a guide to reading in this area.

Useful for the history of the contemporary Church-State conflict in Mexico, particularly its *cristero* phase are Francisco Banegas Galván, *El porque del Partido Católico Nacional* (Mexico: Editorial Jus, 1960), a reprint of a 1915 work; Andres Barquín y Ruiz, *Bernardo Bergöend S.J.* (Mexico: Editorial Jus, 1968), a biography by a Catholic of the founder of the ACJM; Hugo Latorre Cabal, *La revolución de la Iglesia latinoamericana* (Mexico: Editorial Joaquin Mortiz, 1969), an explanation of the current reform movement in Latin American Catholicism by a priest; Luis Rivera del Val, *Entre Los Patas de los Caballos* (*Diario de un cristero*), 3d ed. (Mexico: Editorial Jus, 1961); Camilo Torres, *Revolutionary Priest: The Complete Writings and Messages of Camilo Torres*, John Gerassi, ed. (New York, 1971); "El PAN y la Acción Católica Mexicana," *CIDOC Informa*, I (4): 15–16 (June 1964); "La actitud de la iglesia de México frente a las elecciones," *CIDOC Informa* (4): 12–15 (June 1964); Antonio Rius Facius, *La juventud católica y la revolución mejicana, 1910–1925* (Mexico: Editorial Jus, 1963); Emilio Portes Gil, *The Conflict of the Civil Power and the Clergy* (Mexico, 1935); and Leopoldo Lara y Torres, *Documentos para la historia de la persecución religiosa en México* (Mexico, 1954).

José Bravo Ugarte, a Jesuit historian, wrote the only biography of a PAN leader; *Efraín González Luna, Abogado, Humanista, Político, Católico: Homenaje a un gran amigo* (Mexico: Ediciones de Acción Nacional, 1968).

Chilean and Venezuelan Christian Democrats, the most successful in Latin America, have offered basic explanations of the movement. Venezuela's Rafael Caldera explained the movement in "The Christian Democratic Idea," *America*, CVII (April 7, 1962), pp. 12–15, while Eduardo Frei explained it in "The Aims of Christian Democracy," *The Commonweal*, LXXI (October 9, 1964), pp. 63–66 and "Paternalism, Pluralism, and Christian Democratic Movements in Latin America," in *Religion, Revolution, and Reform: New Forces for Change in Latin America* (New York: Praeger, 1964), pp. 25–40, William V. D'Antonio and Frederick B. Pike, eds. I also consulted the Chilean Christian Democratic Party's *El A.B.C. de la Democracia Cristiana* (Santiago, Chile: PDC, n.d.) and *La D.C. en marcha: Declaración de Principios y el A.B.C. de la Democracia Cristiana*, 4th ed. (Santiago, Chile: Editores Sol de Septiembre, 1966).

The most important works of Jacques Maritain for this study were: *Man and the State* (Chicago, 1951), *The Person and the Common Good* (N.Y., 1947), *Scholasticism and Politics* (N.Y., 1940), and *True Humanism* (N.Y., 1938).

Divergent views of the 1959 Baja California election can be found in Braulio Maldonado, *Baja California: Comentarios Políticos*, 3d ed. (Mexico: B. Costa-Amic, 1960); and Carlos Ortega G., *Democracia Dirigida . . . Con Ametralladoras: Baja California: 1958–1960* (El Paso, Texas, 1961). Maldonado was the outgoing governor during the disputed election, while Ortega was an independent newspaperman who attacked the corruption of the Maldonado regime.

XI. STUDIES

The existing studies of PAN are superseded by the present work. The earliest study of PAN to my knowledge was George Lemus, "Partido Acción Nacional: A Mexican Opposition Party," unpublished M.A. thesis in Spanish (University of Texas, 1956). Lemus is a nephew of PAN founder Gustavo

Molina Font, and his work is highly uncritical and descriptive. Patrick J. McCaffrey, "Acción Nacional on the Mexican Political Scene," unpublished M.A. thesis in political science (Mexico City College, 1961), was hardly worth the effort. James F. Creagan, "Minority Political Parties in Mexico: Their Role in a One-Party Dominant System," unpublished Ph.D. dissertation (University of Virginia, 1965), is better, but it is essentially a study of PAN and PPS in the 1964 elections. William Robert Lux, "Acción Nacional: Mexico's Opposition Party," unpublished Ph.D. dissertation in Latin American Studies (University of Southern California, 1967), is descriptive, naive, totally hostile to the Revolution, and filled with citational errors and improper use of evidence. Lux does conclude that PAN is actually a Christian Democratic party but never presented evidence to support this thesis. My own "Acción Nacional: The Institutionalization of an Opposition Party," unpublished Ph.D. dissertation in history (Syracuse University, 1970), contains much data not within this study, but the current work is more extensive and more analytical. Jaime González Graf and Alicia Ramírez Lugo, "Partido Acción Nacional," in *México; realidad político de sus partidos* (Mexico: Instituto Mexicano de Estudios Políticos, A.C. 1970), Antonio Delhumeau A., ed., is valuable primarily for its content analysis of PAN's platforms and doctrinal statements and its comparison of these with Catholic documents.

Studies of Catholicism in contemporary Mexico are more extensive. Included in this category are studies of the Church-State conflict, the *cristero* rebellion, and the *sinarquista* movement. General coverage of the Church-State conflict was provided by Wilfred H. Callcott, *Church and State in Mexico, 1822–1857* (Durham, N.C.: Duke University Press, 1926); and *Liberalism in Mexico, 1857–1929* (Stanford, Calif.: Stanford University Press, 1931). The best study of the *cristero* rebellion based on archival sources is Alicia Olivera Sedano, *Aspectos del Conflicto Religioso de 1926 a 1929: sus antecedentes y consecuencias* (Mexico: Instituto Nacional de Antropologia e Historia, 1966). The best English language study is James W. Wilkie, "The Meaning of the Cristero Religious War Against the Mexican Revolution," *A Journal of Church and State*, VIII (1966), pp. 214–33. Mexican anticlericalism in the Revolutionary period was studied by contemporaries in Bishop Francis Clement Kelley, *The Book of the Red and the Yellow: Being a Story of Blood and a Yellow Streak* (Chicago, 1915) and *Blood-Drenched Altars: Mexican Study and Comment* (Milwaukee, 1935); Earl K. Jones, "Church and State in Mexico," *Foreign Policy Reports*, II:9 (1935); and Chester Lloyd Jones, "Roots of the Mexican Church Conflict," *Foreign Affairs*, 14:1 (1935). Three unpublished doctoral dissertations cover the Church-State conflict, in varying fashion, from 1919 to 1949. The best of these is Robert E. Quirk, "The Mexican Revolution and the Catholic Church: 1919–1929" (Harvard, 1950). Edward R. Gotshall, Jr., "Catholicism and Catholic Action in Mexico, 1929–1941: A Church's Response to a Revolutionary Society and the Politics of the Modern Age" (University of Pittsburgh, 1970) is too descriptive and legalistic but valuable for the period.

Hugh G. Campbell, "The Radical Right in Mexico, 1929–1949" (UCLA, 1968) covers both the *sinarquista* and secular rightist movements. He notes that PAN was not radical right according to his definition. Joseph Ledit, *Rise of the Downtrodden* (N.Y.: Society of St. Paul, 1959) is especially valuable because it was written by a Jesuit active in Mexico with the aid of the head of the Base, Antonio Santacruz.

Lyle C. Brown, "Mexican Church-State Relations, 1933–1940," *A Journal of Church and State*, VI (1964), pp. 202–22; Albert L. Michaels, "El nacionalismo conservador mexicano desde la revolución hasta 1940," *Historia Mexicana*, XVI (October–December 1966), pp. 213–38; Fanchon Royer, "Mexico's New Deal," *Catholic World*, (April 1952), pp. 30–36; Frederick C. Turner, "The Compatibility of Church and State in Mexico," *Journal of Inter-American Studies*, 9:4 (1967), pp. 591–602; and James W. Wilkie, "Statistical Indicators of th: Impact of the National Revolution on the Catholic Church in Mexico, 1910–1967," *A Journal of Church and State*, (winter 1970), pp. 89–106 are useful for recent analysis of the conflict and lack of it.

Sinarquismo is included within the Mexican Catholicism category because its ancestry and concerns were so obviously clerical. No thorough study of the movement exists at the time of this writing. One has to turn to the Campbell study cited above, to Albert L. Michaels, "Fascism and Sinarquismo: Popular Nationalism against the Mexican Revolution," *A Journal of Church and State*, VIII (1966), pp. 234–50; and Nathan Whetten, *Rural Mexico* (Chicago, 1948). Harold E. Davis, "The Enigma of Sinarquism," *Mexican Life*, XIX (June 1943), pp. 13–15, 51–55 and Margaret Shedd, "Thunder on the Right in Mexico," *Harpers*, (April 1945), pp. 414–25 are also useful. Raymond V. Michael, "Sinarquismo: A Survey of Its History, Ideology, Organization, and Programs," unpublished M.A. thesis (Mexico City College, 1961), asserts that *sinarquismo* was promoted by *callistas* to attack Cardenas. Hysterical and/or polemical in approach are Alejandro Carrillo, *Genealogía política del sinarquismo y de Acción Nacional* (Mexico, 1944); Allen Chase, *Falange: The Axis Secret Army in the Americas* (New York, 1943); Mario Gill (Carlos M. Velasco Gil), *Sinarquismo, su origén, su esencia, su misión*, 2d. ed. (Mexico: Club del Libro, 1944); "La Iglesia en América Latina: Trayectoría del Clero Político Mexicano Hacía las elecciones de 1958," *Problemas de Latino America*, III (February 1956); and Betty Kirk, *Covering the Mexican Front* (Norman: University of Oklahoma Press, 1942) on Acción Nacional and *sinarquismo*.

Studies of the Latin American Christian Democratic movement are almost nonexistent. Edward J. Williams, *Latin American Christian Democratic Parties* (Knoxville, 1967) is the only one of its kind. It should be supplemented by reading Frederick C. Turner, *Catholicism and Political Development in Latin America* (Chapel Hill, 1971) which has better analysis of Catholic sociopolitical thought. The Chilean party is examined in James Petras, *Chilean Christian Democracy: Politics and Social Forces* (Berkeley: Institute of International Studies, 1969): Ernst Halperin, *Nationalism and Communism in Chile* (Cambridge, 1965); Giles Wayland-Smith "The Christian Democratic Party in Chile: A Study of Political Organization and Activity with Primary Emphasis on the Local Level," unpublished Ph.D. dissertation (Syracuse University, 1968) or his *The Christian Democratic Party in Chile* (Cuernavaca, Mexico: CIDOC, 1969). The Venezuelan party received analysis in J. Elías Rivera Oviedo, "History and Ideology of the Christian Democratic Movement in Venezuela," unpublished M.A. thesis (University of Notre Dame, 1970) and Franklin Tugwell, "The Christian Democrats of Venezuela," *Journal of Inter-American Studies*, VII (April 1965), pp. 245–69. John J. Kennedy, *Catholicism, Nationalism, and Democracy in Argentina* (Notre Dame, 1958) places Catholic politics into perspective in that country. John D. Martz, *Acción Democratica* (Princeton, 1966) provides data on COPEI as well as the subject of the book. Insights into Latin American Christian Democracy can also be gained from reading Michael P. Fogarty, *Christian Democracy in Western Europe* (Notre Dame, 1957); Mario Einsudi and Francois Goguel, *Christian Democracy in Italy and France* (Notre Dame, 1952); and Stanley G. Payne, *Falange: A History of Spanish Fascism* (Stanford, 1961).

The literature on contemporary Latin American Catholicism is multiplying rapidly. My own reading has been more extensive than the list below suggests, but I have selected those works which proved most useful. J. Lloyd Mecham, *Church and State in Latin America, A History of Politico-Ecclesiastical Relations*, rev. ed. (Chapel Hill, 1966) is still the basic survey of Church-State relations. Frederick B. Pike, ed., *The Conflict Between Church and State in Latin America* (New York: Knopf, 1964) is an excellent anthology of views of the conflict. Carlos E. Castañeda, "Social Developments and Movements in Latin America," *Church and Society* (New York: Arts, Inc. 1953), edited by Joseph N. Moody, is useful for Catholic reform movements twenty years ago and for PAN's involvement with the Mexican Church. Melvin J. Williams, *Catholic Social Thought* (New York, 1950) is valuable for Catholic Action. James F. Colaianni, *The Catholic Left; The Crisis of Radicalism Within the Church* (Philadelphia, 1968); John J. Considine, ed., *Social Revolution in the New Latin America* (Notre Dame: Fides, 1965) and *The Church in the New Latin America* (Notre Dame: Fides, 1964); William V. D'Antonio and Frederick B. Pike, eds., *Religion, Revolution, and Reform,* cited above; Francine du Plessix Gray, *Divine Disobedience: Profiles of Catholic Radicalism* (New York, 1971), useful for Mexican Catholic progressives; Frederick B. Pike, ed., *Freedom and Reform in Latin America* (Notre Dame, 1967); Thomas G. Sanders, "The Church in Latin America," *Foreign Affairs*, 48:2 (January 1970), pp. 285–99; Ivan Vallier, *Catholicism, Social Control, and Modernization in Latin America* (Englewood Cliffs, 1970) and "Religious Elites: Differentiations and Developments in Roman Catholicism," *Elites in Latin America* (New York, 1967), edited by Seymour M. Lipset and Aldo Solari, pp. 190–232; and Turner, *Catholicism and Political Development in Latin America* give both breadth and depth of coverage. Henry A. Landsberger, ed., *The Church and Social Change in Latin America* (Notre Dame, 1970) contains papers by leading observers and participants while Francois Houtart and Emile Pin, *The Church and the Latin American Revolution*, trans. Gilbert Barth (New York, 1965) offers a European view of the Latin American Church. Raymond F. Cour, "Catholic Action and Politics in the Writings of Pope Pius XI," unpublished Ph.D. dissertation (University of Notre Dame, 1953), is a priest's interpretation of Catholic Action which is still valuable although dated and simplistic.

The existing literature on contemporary Mexican political parties is woefully inadequate. Eugene Maur Braderman, "A Study of Political Parties and Politics in Mexico Since 1890," unpublished Ph.D. dissertation (University of Illinois, 1938), offers a good sketch of the early period. Antonio Delhumeau A., ed., *México: realidad política de sus partidos* (Mexico: Instituto Mexicano de Estudios Politicos, A.C., 1970) uses content analysis of the major documents of the four legally recognized political parties. Vicente Fuentes Díaz, *Los partidos políticos en Mexico*, 2d ed. (Mexico: Editorial Altiplano, 1969) remains the best description of contemporary parties even though it is a pro-PRI account. Daniel Moreno, *Los partidos políticos del México contemporáneo (1926–1970)* (Mexico: B. Costa-Amic, 1970) has scanty analysis but does reprint documents. Such works as Felipe Celorio Celorio, *Los partidos políticos y el sufragio en México, Inglaterra, y Estados Unidos* (Mexico, 1949); Antonio Roa Hernández, *La doctrina de los partidos políticos y el Partido Revolucionario Institucional* (Mexico, 1961); and Hector Solis Quiroga, *Los partidos políticos en México* (Mexico: Editorial Orion, 1961) are of dubious value. Ronald H. McDonald, *Party Systems and Elections in Latin America* (Chicago, 1971) contains useful analysis of Mexican political parties.

The literature on the Mexican political system is more abundant and useful. Disagreement as to who wields power in Mexico is one of the substantive issues in the system's historiography. The existence of confusion is well argued in Carolyn Needleman and Martin Needleman, "Who Rules Mexico? A Critique of Some Current Views of the Mexican Political Process," *Journal of Politics*, XXXI (1969), pp. 1011–34.

A major split exists between those who believe that the system is democratic and social-reform oriented and those who disagree. In the former camp, either explicitly or implicitly, are: Gabriel Almond and Sidney Verba, *The Civic Culture* (Princeton, 1963); Lawrence R. Alschuler, "Political Participation and Urbanization in Mexico," unpublished Ph.D. dissertation (Northwestern University, 1967); Barry Ames, "Bases of Support for Mexico's Dominant Party," *American Political Science Review (APSR)*, LXIV (March 1970), pp. 153–67; Frank R. Brandenburg, "Mexico: An Experiment in One-Party Democracy," unpublished Ph.D. dissertation (Pennsylvania, 1955); Howard F. Cline, "Mexico: A Maturing Democracy," *Current History*, XXIV (March 1953), pp. 136–42, *Mexico: Revolution to Evolution: 1940–1960* (New York, 1963), and *The United States and Mexico*, rev. ed. (New York, 1965); Wayne A. Cornelious, Jr., "Urbanization as an Agent in Latin American Political Stability: The Case of Mexico," *APSR*, LXVI (September 1969); Martin C. Needler, "Changing the Guard in Mexico," *Current History*, XLVIII (January 1965), pp. 26–31, 52, "Mexico: Revolution as a Way of Life," *Political Systems of Latin America* (Princeton, 1964), and "The Political Development of Mexico," *APSR*, LV (June 1961), pp. 308–12, and *Politics and Society in Mexico* (Albuquerque, 1971); L. Vincent Padgett, *The Mexican Political System* (Boston, 1966), "Mexico's One-Party System: A Re-evaluation," *APSR*, LI (December 1957), pp. 995–1008, and "Popular Participation in the Mexican 'One-Party' System," unpublished Ph.D. dissertation (Northwestern, 1955); Luis Reyna, "Desarrollo Económico, Distribución del Poder y Participación Política; el Caso Mexicano," *El Día*, June 16, 17, 1968; Robert E. Scott, *Mexican Government in Transition*, rev. ed. (Urbana, 1965); and William P. Tucker, *The Mexican Government Today* (Minneapolis, 1957).

The dissenters range from scepticism to cynicism, sharing these views with a majority of Mexicans. Roger D. Hansen, *The Politics of Mexican Development* (Baltimore: Johns Hopkins University Press, 1971) appeared too late for me to cite it in the present work. His analysis of the entire Mexican political scene does not differ substantially with that presented here; where he does, he is more "tough-minded" toward the Mexican government. He effectively destroys any idea of functional democracy in Mexico. His work should be required reading for all those who hope to understand the complexities of the Mexican political system.

Robert F. Adie, "Agrarianism in the Mexican Political System," unpublished Ph.D. dissertation (Texas, 1970), examines the use of the agrarian reform myth as part of the system of control whereas Peter Calvert, "The Mexican Revolution: Theory or Fact?" *Journal of Latin American Studies*, I (May 1969), pp. 51–68 examines the entire Revolutionary myth. Frank R. Brandenburg is more cynical in his *Making of Modern Mexico* (Englewood Cliffs, 1964). J. D. Cochrane, "Mexico's New Científicos: The Díaz Ordaz Cabinet," *Inter-American Economic Affairs*, XXI (1968), pp. 61–72 compares the 1964–70 government to that of Porfírio Díaz. Pablo González Casanova, *Democracy in Mexico* (New York, 1970) implicitly suggests that the Revolution is not what it claims to be. Kenneth F. Johnson, *Mexican Democracy: A Critical View* (Boston, 1971) attacks the government's repressive side by utilizing protest sources. Johnson's work is provocative and not to be dismissed lightly. He substantially alters his earlier, "Ideological Correlates of Right-Wing Political Alienation in Mexico," *APSR*, LIX (September 1965), pp. 656–64. McDonald, cited above, warns his readers not to assume that the system operates as its leaders assert. Ward W. Horton, "The Mexican Political 'Establishment' in Operation," *The Carribean: Mexico Today*, edited by Curtis A. Wilgus (Gainesville, 1940); and Harry B. Murkland, "Toward More Democracy in Mexico?" *Foreign Policy Bulletin*, XXXI (June 15, 1952), pp. 1–2 point out that only PRI is allowed to win important elections. Patricia McI. Richmond, "Mexico: A Case Study of One-Party Politics," unpublished Ph.D. dissertation (Berkeley, 1965), concludes that popular participation in PRI is a bad joke. Merrill Rippy, "Who's Revolutionary in Mexico?" *Nation*, July 19, 1952, pp. 52–53 asserts that PRI is not revolutionary nor is PAN counterrevolutionary. Evelyn P. Stevens, "Legality and Extra-Legality in Mexico," *Journal of Inter-American Studies and World Affairs,* XII (January 1970), pp. 62–75 concludes that the government kept the crime of "social dissolution" because it feared the opposition. Philip B. Taylor, Jr., "The Mexican Elections of 1958: Affirmation of Authoritarianism?" *Western Political Quarterly,* XIII (September 1960), pp. 722–44 answered in the affirmative. William Tuohy and David Ronfeldt, "Political Control and the Recruitment of Middle-Level Elites in Mexico: an Example from Agrarian Politics," *Western Political Quarterly,* XXII (June 1969), pp. 365–75 discussed governmental control of the CNC and of the press. James W. Wilkie, *The Mexican Revolution: Federal Expenditure and Social Change Since 1910* (Berkeley, 1967) flatly warns his readers not to believe election statistics. John Womack, Jr., "The Spoils of the Mexican Revolution," *Foreign Affairs,* XLVIII (July 1970), pp. 677–87 sees present-day Mexico as a betrayal of *zapatista* ideals.

Although it is not possible to list all the studies on Mexico that I consulted, several additional investigations are important enough to warrant the space. On Mexican regionalism, the comments of Harry Bernstein, *Modern and Contemporary Latin America* (Philadelphia, 1952), chapters four and five, and "Regionalism in the National History of Mexico," *Latin American History,* Vol. I (Austin, 1967), pp. 389–94, edited by Howard F. Cline, are especially valuable. A later addition to this literature is Paul W. Drake, "Mexican Regionalism Reconsidered," *Journal of Inter-American Studies and World Affairs,* XII (July 1970), pp. 401–15. Ralph Eisenberg, "The Mexican Presidential Election of 1952," unpublished M.A. thesis (University of Illinois, 1953), is one of a kind. Albert L. Michaels, "Mexican Politics and Nationalism from Calles to Cárdenas," unpublished Ph.D. dissertation (Pennsylvania, 1966) and "The Crisis of Cardenismo," *Journal of Latin American Studies,* II (May 1970), pp. 51–79 as well as Lyle C. Brown, "General Lazaro Cárdenas and Mexican Presidential Politics, 1933–1940: A Study in the Acquisition and Manipulation of Political Power," unpublished Ph.D. dissertation (Texas, 1964) are indispensable for the 1930s. William D'Antonio and William Form, *Influentials in Two Border Cities* (Notre Dame, 1965) and Anthony Ugalde, "Conflict and Consensus in a Mexican City: A Study of Political Integration," unpublished Ph.D. dissertation (Stanford, 1968), were valuable for local politics. Emilio Portes Gil, *La crisis política y la próxima elección presidencial* (Mexico: Ediciones Botas, 1957), written by an ex-Mexican President, is one of the few inside sources available.

The complexity of the Mexican political system and the controversy surrounding its nature cannot be understood until scholars devote more effort to the subject. In particular, examination of specific elections, analysis of voting statistics in conjunction with detailed study of the electoral districts, thorough and penetrating analysis of the decision-making process within the government and PRI are a few of the subjects demanding investigation. Although much ink has been used much more needs to be done.

INDEX

Abascal, Salvador, 26

Acción Nacional (PAN): and *Acción Católica* (Catholic Action), 37; appeals of, 44, 57, 111–12; and Article 3, 39, 47, 74, 106–7; and *Asociación Católica de la Juventud Mexicana*, 17–18; and Base, 26; and *campo,* 45–46, 101, 105, 184–85; and capitalists, 34, 35–36, 38, 47, 51–52, 162–65, 208n–28, 213n93; and Christian Democracy, 47, 65–70, 66, 68, 74–75, 99, 183, 194–98, 205n26, 218n52; and Catholic Church, 27, 39, 47, 52, 54, 165–66, 183, 184, 193–94, 195–98; and *Confederación Nacional de Estudiantes Católicos,* 21; and COPEI, 47, 65–66, 205n26, 218n52; conventions of, 16, 39, 41–42, 43, 129; decision-making in, 129–30; doctrine, 40, 44, 64, 91–93, 99–103, 186, 195–98, 230n59; elections, 37–39, 41–43, 47–48, 53–54, 55–57, 63–64, 76–80, 82–84, 89, 91, 173–78, 188–89, 190, 192–93, 210n53, 239n30; factions, 51–52, 55, 58, 61–62, 72–73, 77, 85–87, 89, 131, 159; federal deputies, 43–44, 47–48, 59, 125, 127, 153–54, 211n65; female suffrage, 44, 47, 109–10, 126; and foreign powers, 39–41 *passim,* 195–96; founders, 34–37; and government, 1, 39–42, 60, 104, 183–94, 197, 198–99; organizational steps, 16, 32–34, 36–37, 206n62; Institute of Social and Political Studies, 128; interregional conventions, 127–28; leadership, 130, 143–61; and labor, 46–47, 58–59, 67, 75, 107, 166, 184–85; membership, 16, 26, 34–37, 38, 67, 72–73, 124–25, 130–43, 240n42; and municipio, 39, 44–45, 75, 100, 101, 105–6, 111, 119, 127; National Council, 34–37, 114–15, 116, 117, 127; National Executive Committee (CEN), 34–36, 114–19 *passim,* 121, 126, 127, 129–30, 146–51, 231n8; president, 114, 117–18, 129–30; party deputy system, 76, 77, 221n16; and planning, 45–46, 74, 108; platforms, 47, 53, 57, 67, 74–75, 88, 103, 106, 128, 131; and profit-sharing, 52, 66–67; programs, 44–49, 76, 103–11; and proportional representation, 60, 109–10; and social security, 45–46, 75, 184; statutes, 61, 89, 119, 129, 132–34; accrued organizations, 125–29; dissolution of, 119; bureaucracy, 125, 129; structure, 89, 113–28; district organizations, 122–24; and student movements, 80–81, 89–90; support, 56, 166–81, 187–89, 191–93; and Supreme Court, 44–45, 47; tactical debates, 37–38, 42, 55, 57–63, 77, 86–87, 130–31, 193; tactics, 38–39, 43, 55, 57–59, 71, 71–72, 75–76, 84–85, 187–89, 190–93, 216n39; and *Unión Nacional de Estudiantes Católicos,* 24, 195; and *Unión Nacional Sinarquista,* 26–27, 39, 43–44, 47, 52–53, 76, 88, 165; Women's Organization, 61, 126; Youth Organization, 55–56, 61, 66, 125–28

Action Française, 37

Alemán, President Miguel (1946–52), 12, 42, 45, 52

Alessio Robles, Miguel, 35

261

Almazán, Juan Andreu, 31, 37–38
Alvarez, Luis H.: biography, 55; presidential candidate, 56–57
Amezcua, Juan B., 35
Anticlericalism: and Liberals, 2; under Calles, 6; and Constitution of 1917, 6; and cristero rebellion, 6; of the 1930s, 24–29, 31
Aragón, Agustín, 34
Article 3: provisions, 6; opposed by Church, 27; opposed by PAN, 39, 47; amended under Avila Camacho, 41; and PAN decision-making, 129
Article 130, 6. See also Anticlericalism; Article 3
Asociación Católica de la Juventud Mexicana (ACJM): organized, 17; purposes, 17; and Catholic Association of French Youth, 17; and PAN, 17–18; and cristero rebellion, 20; and Confederación Nacional de Estudiantes Católicos, 21; and Catholic Action, 22; and UNEC, 24; Gutiérrez Lascuráin as member, 50; Ituarte Servín as member, 51
Avila Camacho, President Manuel (1940–46): 8; national unity government, 12; selection of, 30; candidate, 31; and PAN, 40–41

Baja California elections: 1953, 53–54; 1959, 63–64; 1968, 77–80; 1971, 89, 91
Banco de Mexico, 33
Bankers: and PAN, 35–36. See also Capitalists; Private enterprise
Base: history, 25–27; purpose, 26; and UNS, 26–27; and anticlericalism, 26; and PAN, 26; and Opus Dei, 27; and Jesuits, 205n43
Bolshevik Revolution, 28
Bonilla, Manuel, 34

Cabrera, Luis, 43
Caldera, Rafael: visits PAN, 47; supports PAN, 65; speaks to PAN convention, 67, 70. See also COPEI
Calderón Vega, Luis, 21, 26–27
Calles, President Plutarco (1924–28): overthrows Carranza, 5–6; and anti-

clericalism, 6, 20–22; and cristero rebellion, 6; creates PNR, 7; exiled, 7; and CROM, 8; and Gómez Morín, 33
Cambio Democrático de las Estructuras, 103
Campaign appeals, 44, 57, 111–12. See also Elections; Tactics
Campo: PAN legislation, 45–46; and PAN doctrine, 101, 105; and PAN on, 184–85
Campos, Mauricio, 34
Capitalists: joint PAN, 34; leave PAN, 38, 51–52; support PRI, 87; and PAN doctrine, 101; and PAN membership, 135–39 passim; and PAN, 35–36, 47, 162–65, 208n28, 213n93; and CEN, 149, 150. See also CONCAMIN; CONCANACO; Private enterprise; Sowers of Friendship; Unión Social de Empresarios Mexicanos
Cárdenas, President Lázaro (1934–40): political biography, 7; presidency, 7–9, 27–28; opposition to, 29–31; and labor, 8; and peasants, 8; and railroads, 8; and petroleum expropriation, 8; and ejidos, 8; and PRM, 8; and Italian fascism, 8; and Marxism, 8; and organized business, 8–9; and Church, 8–9; and 1952 elections, 12; and collectivization, 28; and Spanish Loyalists, 28; as seen by PAN, 185–86
Carranza, President Venustiano (1914–20), 5–6
Casasús, Joaquín, 36
Castro, Fidel, 12
Catholic Action: defined, 19, 204n12; and Rerum Novarum, 19; in Spain, 19; in United States, 19; organized in Mexico, 19–22; incorporates ACJM, 22; and Legion, 25; and PAN, 34, 134; and Ituarte Servín, 51
Catholic Association of French Youth, 17
Catholic Church (Roman): supports Conservatives, 1; attacked by Liberals, 2; and education, 2, 6, 9, 27; and Porfirio Díaz, 4; and Calles, 6;

and *cristero* rebellion, 6, 17–21 *passim;* and Cárdenas, 9, 27–28; and petroleum expropriation, 9; and social reform, 16–19; Social Secretariat, 18, 20; Women's Social Union, 18; Federation of Trade Unions, 18; Confederation of Catholic Associations of Mexico, 18; and Madero, 18; and Huerta, 18; lay associations, 17–19; and *Liga,* 20; and students, 21; and Legion, 25; and PAN, 27, 52, 54, 103, 110–12, 156–59, 165–66, 183, 184, 193–98; and Base, 27; and UNS, 27; and Marxism, 27, 28; and liberal capitalism, 28–29

Catholic National Federation of Labor, 18

Catholic progressives, 29

Catholic Social Congresses (Mexico): programs, 17; and PAN doctrine, 102

Catholic social thought, 28, 29, 44, 195, 196, 197

Catholic Women, 20–21

Catholic Workers' Unions, 18, 21

Catholics, and fascism, 29

Cervi, Emilio, 35

Chapela y B., Gonzalo, 48

Chávez, Ezequiel A., 34

Chávez Camacho, Armando, 21

Chávez González, Francisco, 55

Chihuahua elections: 1956, 55; 1959, 63

Christian Democracy: and González Torres, 51; and Chávez González, 55; and PAN Youth Organization, 66, 127; of Latin America, 68, 99, 103; and PAN, 72, 74–75, 99, 111–12, 147, 148, 183, 194–98

Christian Democrats, 73–74

Christian Socialism. *See* Christian Democracy

Christlieb Ibarrola, Adolfo: 1958 tactical debate, 58; attacks capitalists, 67; supports labor, 67; elected PAN president, 70; tactical changes of, 71, 75–76; biography, 71–72; expels Christian Democrats, 73–74; on religion and politics, 74; death, 81; contrasted with González Hinojosa, 82; and doctrine, 103; and Institute of Social and Political Studies, 128; and leadership, 145–48; and CEN, 148; mentioned, 71

Church-State conflict, 6, 16, 19–22. *See also* Anticlericalism; Base; Church; *Cristero* rebellion; Legion; *Liga*

Científicos, 3

Coahuila, 55–56

Comité Ejecutivo Nacional (CEN): analyzed, 34–36, 148–51; and structure, 114–19 *passim;* and regional committees, 121; and Women's Organization, 126; and federal deputies, 127; and president, 129–30; and leadership, 148–51; and capitalists, 149–50; and Catholicism, 150–51; commissions of, 231n8

CONCAMIN (National Confederation of Mexican Chambers of Industry), 947. *See also* Private enterprise

CONCANACO (National Chamber of Chambers of Commerce). *See* Private enterprise

Conchello Dávila, José Angel: elected PAN president, 93; biography, 93; and leadership, 145–46, 148

Confederación Iberoamericana de Estudiantes Católicos (CIDEC), 23–24, 65

Confederación Nacional Campesina (CNC), 8

Confederación Nacional de Estudiantes Católicos de México (CNECM), 21, 23

Confederación Regional de Obreros Mexicanos (CROM), 8

Confederación de Trabajadores Mexicanos (CTM), 28

Confederation of Catholic Associations of Mexico, 18

Conservatives, 1, 2, 3

Constitution of 1857, 2, 3, 5, 18

Constitution of 1917, 5, 6, 10, 18

Conventions (PAN): 1939, 16; 1940, 39; 1943, 41–42; 1946, 42–43; 1949, 47–48; 1950, 52; 1951, 53; 1953, 52; 1958, 56; 1959, 60–63; 1961, 64–65;

Conventions (PAN) (*cont.*)
1962, 67, 70; 1969, 85, 86; 1970, 86–87; 1971, 89, 91–93, 129; and structure, 114–15
COPEI (Venezuelan Christian Democratic Party), 47, 65–66, 205n26, 218n52. *See also* Christian Democracy
Correa Rachó, Víctor Manuel, 83–84
Cossío y Cosío, Roberto, 36
Creel Luján, Enrique, 237n48
Cristero rebellion, 6, 20–21; aid of González Luna, 36; and PAN, 134

Decision-making (PAN); and Statutes, 129; and president, 129; and regional organizations, 129–30; in 1971 convention, 129; and membership, 130–31; and 1970 crisis, 130; and tactical debates, 130–31
Díaz Ordaz, President Gustavo (1964–70): and political reform, 14; and PAN, 76, 84–85; and students, 81
Díaz, Pascual, archbishop, 22
Diaz, President Porfirio (1876–80, 1884–1911): 1, 3, 4–5, 16. *See also* *Porfiriato*
District organizations, 122–24 *passim*
Doctrine (PAN): and *Hispanidad*, 40, 102–3; and Pan-Americanism, 40; and Catholic social thought, 44, 99, 102, 103, 195, 196, 197; anticlericalism in, 44; secularism in, 44; and *Movimento Nacional de Liberación*, 64; and official textbooks, 64; discussed, 91–93, 99–103, 186, 197–98, 230n59; and papal encyclicals, 99, 103; and Jacques Maritain, 99; and person, 99–101; and family, 100, 101; and *municipio*, 100, 101; and labor, 101, 102; and fascism, 101, 102; and Marxism, 101; and *campo*, 101; and social security, 101; and capitalism, 101; and politics, 102; in 1965, 102; and women, 102; and *ejidos*, 102; and Franco, 102–3; and González Luna, 102–3; in 1969, 103; and Latin American Christian Democracy, 103; and Latin American Bishops' General Conference, 103;

and Mexican Church, 103; composition of, 103
Durango, 14

Echeverría Alvarez, President Luis (1970–76): and Baja California, 79; and students, 81, 90–91; election of, 87; activities, 94–95
Education: and Church, 2; and PAN, 106
Ejidos, 8, 28, 102, 105
Elections: Baja California, 53–54, 63–64; 77–80, 89, 91
—national: and PAN, 173–78, 188–90, 192–93; 1911, 18; 1929, 7, 22–23, 33; 1940, 16, 30–31, 37–38, 129; 1943, 41–42, 210n53; 1946, 42–44, 47; 1949, 47–48; 1952, 53–54; 1955, 54–55; 1958, 56–58, 60; 1961, 64–65; 1964, 76; 1967, 76–77; 1970, 85–88 *passim*, 128, 130
Electoral system: and PAN, 170–73
Elorduy, Aquiles, 35, 43, 44, 47, 212n81
Elosúa, Bernardo, 36
Escandón, Manuel F., 35
Estrada Iturbide, Miguel, 21, 26, 35
Ezquivel Obregón, Toribio, 34

Facha Gutiérrez, Eduardo, 48
Factions (PAN), 51–52, 55, 61–62, 73, 77, 85–87, 89, 131, 159
Falcons. See Student movements
Family, 100–101, 107–8
Fascism: and PAN doctrine, 101–2, 195–96; and UNS, 27
Federal deputies, 43–44, 47–48, 57, 59, 125, 127, 153–54, 211n65
Federal electoral laws: and PAN structure, 113–14
Federation of Trade Unions, 18
Female suffrage, 44, 47, 109–10, 126
Foreign influence, 2–5 *passim*
Franco, Francisco (Spain): supported by UNS, 27; and Mexican Catholics, 29; and PAN doctrine, 102–3
Frei, Eduardo, 65

Gama, Valentín, 34
García, Trinidad, 34

García Naranjo, Nemesio, 34
Garay, Luis de, 21, 23
Gastélum, Bernardo, 34, 35
González Flores, Anacleto, 21, 54
González Hinojosa, Manuel: biography, 81–82; contrasted with Christlieb, 82; and leadership, 145–46, 148; and CEN, 148; mentioned, 71
González Luna, Efraín: biography, 36; and Principios de Doctrina, 36; opposes electoral participation, 37, 41; suggested as 1946 candidate, 43; presidential candidate, 52–54; supported by UNS, 53–54; tactical debates, 58, 61–62; and PAN doctrine, 102–3; view of Mexican Revolution, 184–85, 197
González Morfín, Efraín: Christian Socialist, 73; presidential candidate, 86–88; biography, 88–89; and PAN doctrine, 91–92, 103; and leadership, 148
González Torres, José: Catholic lay leader, 47; biography, 51; Christian Democrat, 51, 61, 66; PAN president, 61; damages PAN, 70; leadership, 146–47; and CEN, 148
Gómez Mont, Felipe, 58
Gómez Morín, Manuel: and Vasconcelos, 23, 33; suggests opposition party, 23; organizes PAN, 32–34; biography, 32–33; and Lombardo Toledano, 32; in Obregón government, 33; advises Calles, 33; and Banco de Mexico, 33; university rector, 33; banker, 33; influenced by Salazar, 33; and PAN goals, 38; views 1949 election, 48; resignation, 48; assesses PAN, 48–49; secular politician, 50, 73; contrasted with Gutiérrez Lascuráin, 50; tactical debates, 58, 61–62; and membership, 134; presidency assessed, 48–50, 145–47; and Youth Organization, 127; nationality impugned, 207n2
Guadalupe Silva, Jacinto, 54
Guiza y Acevedo, Jesús, 34
Gutiérrez Lascuráin, Juan: federal deputy, 44; president, 48; biography, 50; contrasted with Gómez Morín, 50; and clericalism, 50; resignation, 55;

and leadership, 146–47; and CEN, 148
Gutiérrez Vega, Hugo, 58, 126

Henríquez Guzmán, Miguel, 43
Hernández Díaz, Jesús, 21, 127
Hinojosa, Juan José, 48
Hinojosa, Luis, 21
Hispanidad: PAN opposes, 40; and PAN doctrine, 102–3
Huerta, President Victoriano (1913–14), 5

Ibero-American Congress of University Catholic Action, 24. See also Confederación Iberoamericana de Estudiantes Católicos
Institute of Social and Political Studies, 125, 128
Interregional conventions, 125–30 passim
Islas García, Luis, 21
Italian fascism, 8, 29
Ituarte Servín, Alfonso: president, 50; biography, 50–51; federal deputy, 51; elected, 55; leadership of, 145–47

Jesuits: and CNECM, 21; and Base, 205n43
Juárez, President Benito (1855–72), 1, 2, 3

Knights of Columbus, 20
Kuri Breña, Daniel, 21

Labor: supports Calles, 6; supports Obregón, 6; supports Cárdenas, 8, 30; opposes students, 14; PAN support of, 67, 75, 101, 107, 166; PAN view of, 184–85
La Laguna, 8, 28, 30
Land program of Cárdenas, 28
Latin American Bishops' General Conference, 103
Leadership: and decision-making, 130; discussed, 143–61; defined, 143–44; and president, 144–48; and Gómez Morín, 145, 146, 147; and Conchello Dávila, 145–46, 148; and Christlieb Ibarrola, 145–48 passim; and González Hinojosa, 145–48 passim; and

Leadership (*cont.*)
Gutiérrez Lascuráin, 146, 147; and González Torres, 146, 147; and Christian Democracy, 147, 148; and González Morfín, 148; and CEN, 148–51; and Catholicism, 150–53, 156–59; and regional presidents, 151–53; and federal deputies, 153–54; and presidential candidates, 154–55; and founders, 155–56; factionalism within, 159; and tactics, 159; recruitment and training of, 159–60
Legion, 25
Ley Juárez, 2
Ley Lerdo, 2
Liberal-Conservative struggle, 2
Liberalism, 2
Liberals, 1–5
Liga Nacional Defensora de la Libertad Religiosa: organized, 20; activities, 20; member organizations, 20–21; intransigence of, 22; and Legion, 25; Ituarte Servín as member, 51
Limón, Ignacio Maurer, 81
Lombardo Toledano, Vicente: supports Cárdenas, 8; organizes CTM, 8, 28; and UNEC, 24; and university struggle, 24; rivalry with Gómez Morín, 32;
López, Mateos, President Adolfo (1958–64), 57
Loret de Mola, Carlos, 83–84

Madero, President Francisco I (1911–13): revolt against Díaz, 1; and Huerta, 5; program of, 5; overthrow, 5; and Church, 18
Madero, Raúl, 56
Madrazo, Carlos, 14
Maldonado, Braulio, 63–64
Maritain, Jacques, 26, 27, 99
Martínez Domínguez, Alfonso, 190
Marxism: and Cárdenas, 8; and PAN doctrine, 101
Maximilian of Hapsburg, 2, 3
Mejía Guerrero, Juan José, 121
Membership: founders, 16; from Base, 26; initial, 34–37; Catholic, 34; declines in 1940, 38; vertical organization of, 124–25; and corporate

thought, 125; and decision-making, 130–31; and statutes, 132–34; and General Assembly, 132; types of, 133; organization of, 134; and UNEC, 134; and Catholic lay associations, 134, and *cristeros,* 134; and Gómez Morín, 134; and Catholic Action, 134; recruitment of, 134–35; socioeconomic characteristics of, 135–41; and capitalists, 135–39 *passim;* number, 141–42; geographical distribution of, 143; and women, 240n42; mentioned, 67, 72, 73
Méndez Medina, Father, 18
Mexican Employers' Confederation (COPARMEX), 9. *See also* Private enterprise
Mexican Nationalist Party, 76
Mexican Revolution: opposed by UNS, 27; and PAN, 183–94, 198–99; González Luna views, 184–85, 197
Minimum Program of Political Action, 39, 44, 104, 128, 184
Mora y del Río, José, archbishop, 19, 20
Morrow, Dwight, 22
Movimiento Nacional de Liberación, 64
Múgica, Francisco, 31
Municipal elections: and PAN, 39, 48, 77, 83
Municipio: PAN bills on, 44–45; and PAN, 39, 75; in PAN doctrine, 100, 101; in PAN programs, 105–6; in 1970 platform, 106; and PAN appeals, 111; number of, 119; and PAN interregional conventions, 127
Mutual Workmen's Society, 17

Napoleon III, 2–3
National Catholic Party, 18
National Confederation of Chambers of Commerce (CONCANACO). *See* Private enterprise
National Council, 34–37, 114–17 *passim,* 127
National Defense League of Religious Liberty. *See Liga Nacional Defensora de la Libertad Religiosa*
National Executive Committee. *See Comité Ejecutivo Nacional*

National Front of Professionals and Intellectuals, 31
National Front of Workers, 54
National Parents' Union: and education, 18; and *Liga,* 20; and PAN, 39
National Preparatory School, 21
Novoa, Carlos, 35

Obregón, President Alvaro (1920–24): 5, 6, 7, 22; and Gómez Morín, 33
Ocaranza, Fernando, 34
Official textbooks, 64, 106–7
Olympic Games (1968), 12
Orthodox Catholic Apostolic Church, 20
Ortiz Rubio, President Pascual (1930–32), 7

Padilla, Ezequiel, 42, 43
Padilla, Juan Ignacio, 53
Pan-Americanism, 40. *See also Hispanidad*
Papal encyclicals, 99, 103. *See also* Catholic social thought; Church; *Quadragessimo Anno; Rerum Novarum*
Parochial schools, 21. *See also* Anticlericalism; Education
Partido Auténtico de la Revolución Mexicana (PARM), 77
Partido Nacional Revolucionario (PRN), 7, 8
Partido Popular Socialista (PPS), 77
Partido de la Revolución Mexicana (PRM), 8, 28
Partido Revolucionario Institucional (PRI): renamed, 13; role in political system, 13; factions, 13; and Carlos Madrazo, 14; and Ezequiel Padilla, 42; support of, 44, 105, 139, 141, 143, 157, 163, 165, 166, 187–88, 236n43, 240n42; and female suffrage, 45; and regionalism, 55, 78–79, 83, 142, 190; and 1958 election, 57; nominates López Mateos, 59; persecutes PAN, 61; and Braulio Maldonado, 63; and 1959 elections, 64; and profit-sharing, 67; denounced by PAN, 74; and Christlieb, 76, 81; dissidents join PAN, 78, 124; manipulates elections, 78, 79–80, 84, 91, 171–73; and 1969 Yucatán election, 83; and private enterprise, 87; and Echeverría, 87; and Jesús Reyes Heroles, 95; identified with Mexicanism, 110, 171; advantages of, 171; compared with Church, 189
Partido Revolucionario de Unificación Nacional (PRUN), 31
Party deputy system: 76, 77, 110; defined, 221n16
Pérez Sandí, Jesús, 23
Petróleos Mexicanos (PEMEX), 8
Petroleum dispute, 6, 8, 30
Planning, 45–46, 74, 105, 108
Platforms (PAN): 1949, 47; 1952, 53; 1958, 57; 1961, 67, 74–75; 1964, 74–75; 1967, 74–75; 1970, 103, 106; 1971, 88; and Christian Democracy, 74; discussed, 128; importance of debates on, 131
Popular Force. *See Unión Nacional Sinarquista*
Popular Union, 21
Porfiriato, 1–5 passim. *See also* Porfirio Díaz
Portes Gil, President Emilio (1928–30): election of 1929, 7; on electoral fraud, 14; on PAN, 57
Positivism, 3
Preciado Hernández, Rafael, 36, 43
President (PAN): 114, 117–18; and decision-making, 129–30; powers of, 129–30. *See also* Leadership
Principios de Doctrina, 36, 128, 184. *See also* Doctrine
Private enterprise, 9, 110–11. *See also* Capitalists; CONCAMIN; CONCANACO
Profit-sharing, 52, 66, 67
Pro-Liberty of Teaching Association, 51
Proportional representation, 60, 109–10, 221n16

Quadragessimo Anno, 25, 29. *See also* Catholic social thought; Papal encyclicals
Quiroz Pedraza, J. Jesús, 121

Railroads, 4, 8, 46
Ramírez Munguía, Miguel, 44
Ramírez Zetina, Carlos, 21
Reforma, La, 2
Regional organizations: 119–23; regional committee, 119–22; regional council, 119–20; regional president, 119, 122, 151–53; extent of, 124; and decision-making, 129–30; secretary-general, 232n10; commissions of, 232n10
Reiffesen credit, 18
Rerum Novarum, 17, 29, 36. *See also* Catholic social thought; Papal encyclicals
Revolutionary Committee of National Reconstruction, 31
Revolutionary Creed, 9–12, 14
Robles León, Ernesto, 36
Rodríguez, President Abelardo (1932–34), 7
Rodríguez, Antonio L., 36, 44, 73
Rosas Magallón, Salvador, 58, 63, 86

Salazar, Antonio (Portugal), 29, 33
Septién García, Carlos, 21
Seven Sages of Greece, 32
Social Secretariat, 18, 20. *See also* Church
Social security, 46, 75, 101, 184
Social Union of Mexican Empresarios (USEM), 67
Socialist education: 25, 27–28, 31. *See also* Anticlericalism; Article 3; Article 130; Constitution of 1917; Education; Parochial schools
Sonora Dynasty, 6, 8
Sonora election, 77, 78–79, 124
Sowers of Friendship, 67
Spanish Loyalists, 28
State legislative elections, 48. *See also* Elections
Statutes, 61, 89, 119, 129, 132–34
Structure: National Council, 34–37, 114–17, 127; National Executive Committee (CEN), 34–36, 114–19, 121, 126, 127, 129–30, 148–51, 231n8; 1971 changes, 89; and federal election laws, 113–14; described, 113–23; and statutes, 114; General Assembly, 114–15, 132; national level, 114–19; national conventions, 114, 115; voting procedure, 114–15; General Board of Vigilance, 114, 116; periodicals, 118–19; amendments and dissolution, 119; regional presidents, 119, 122, 151–53; regional committees, 119–22; regional councils, 119–20; regional organizations, 119–23, 124, 129–30, 232n10; district organizations, 122, 123–24; municipal committees, 122–23; operation of, 123–31; rejection of corporativism, 125; federal deputies in, 125, 127; interregional conventions, 125, 129–30; Institute of Social and Political Studies, 125, 128; accrued organizations, 125–29; special election teams, 125, 128; Women's Organization, 125–26; bureaucracy, 125, 129; Youth Organization, 125, 126, 127
Student movements, 14, 16, 80–81, 89–91, 109
Suárez Arvizu, Gilberto, 78

Tactical debates. *See* Acción Nacional
Tactics. *See* Acción Nacional
Toral Moreno, Jesús, 23

Ulloa Ortiz, Manuel, 21, 23, 51
Unión Nacional de Estudiantes Católicos: organized, 23; described, 23–24; and CIDEC, 23–24; and Latin American Student Congress (Rome), 24; and university struggle, 24; and National Students' Confederation, 24; and social reform, 24; and PAN, 24, 26, 34, 65, 134, 195; and Base, 26; and UNS, 26
Unión Nacional Sinarquista (UNS): and Catholics, 16, 29; and Base, 26–27; and fascism, 26, 27; organized, 27; and Church, 27; and *Hispanidad,* 27; and PAN, 26, 39, 43–44, 47, 52–53, 56, 76, 88, 131, 165, 189, 193, 194; defined, 203n2
Union of Workers of Our Lady of Guadalupe, 17

Vargas, Getulio (Brazil), 29
Vasconcelos, José, 7, 23

Véjar Vásquez, Octavio, 43

Venezuelan Christian Democratic Party. *See* COPEI

Women and PAN, 102, 240n*42*

Women's Mutual Workmen's Society, 17

Yucatán; collectivization of, 8, 28; 1930s economic crisis, 30; 1969 election, 77, 82–84